THE DIARY OF
SAMUEL PEPYS

THE DIARY
OF
SAMUEL PEPYS

A new and complete
transcription edited by

ROBERT LATHAM
AND
WILLIAM MATTHEWS

CONTRIBUTING EDITORS
WILLIAM A. ARMSTRONG · MACDONALD EMSLIE
Sir OLIVER MILLAR · T. F. REDDAWAY

VOLUME III *1662*

HarperCollins*Publishers*

University of California Press
Berkeley and Los Angeles

Published in the UK by
HarperCollins*Publishers*
77–85 Fulham Palace Road
Hammersmith, London W6 8JB
www.**fire**and**water**.com

UK paperback edition 1995
Reissued 2000

Published in the USA by
University of California Press
Berkeley and Los Angeles, California

First US paperback edition 2000

1 3 5 7 9 8 6 4 2

First published by Bell & Hyman Limited 1971

ISBN 0 00 499023 4 (UK)
ISBN 0 520 22581 3 (USA)

Printed and bound in Great Britain by
Clays Ltd, St Ives plc

CONTENTS

LIST OF ILLUSTRATIONS

READER'S GUIDE

This section is meant for quick reference. More detailed information about the editorial methods used in this edition will be found in the Introduction and in the section 'Methods of the Commentary' in vol. I, and also in the statement preceding the Select Glossary at the end of each text volume.

I. THE TEXT

The fact that the MS. is mostly in shorthand makes exact reproduction (e.g. of spelling, capitalisation and punctuation) impossible.

Spelling is in modern British style, except for those longhand words which Pepys spelt differently, and words for which the shorthand indicates a variant pronunciation which is also shown by Pepys's longhand elsewhere. These latter are given in spellings which reflect Pepys's pronunciations.

Pepys's capitalisation is indicated only in his longhand.

Punctuation is almost all editorial, except for certain full-stops, colons, dashes and parentheses. Punctuation is almost non-existent in the original since the marks could be confused with shorthand.

Italics are all editorial, but (in e.g. headings to entries) often follow indications given in the MS. (by e.g. the use of larger writing).

The **paragraphing** is that of the MS.

Abbreviations of surnames, titles, place names and ordinary words are expanded.

Single **hyphens** are editorial, and represent Pepys's habit of disjoining the elements of compound words (e.g. Wh. hall/White-hall). Double hyphens represent Pepys's hyphens.

Single **angle-brackets** mark additions made by Pepys in the body of the MS.; double angle-brackets those made in the margins.

Light **asterisks** are editorial (see below, Section II); heavy asterisks are Pepys's own.

Pepys's **alterations** are indicated by the word 'replacing' ('repl.') in the textual footnotes.

II. THE COMMENTARY

1. **Footnotes** deal mainly with events and transactions. They also

identify MSS, books, plays, music and quotations, but give only occasional and minimal information about persons and places, words and phrases. The initials which follow certain notes indicate the work of the contributing editors. Light asterisks in the text direct the reader to the Select Glossary for the definition of words whose meanings have changed since the time of the diary.

2. The **Select List of Persons** is printed unchanged in each text volume. It covers the whole diary and identifies the principal persons, together with those who are described in the MS. by titles or in other ways that make for obscurity.

3. The **Select Glossary** is printed at the end of each text volume. It gives definitions of certain recurrent English words and phrases, and identifications of certain recurrent places.

4. The **Companion** (vol. X) is a collection of reference material. It contains maps, genealogical tables, and a Large Glossary, but consists mainly of articles, printed for ease of reference in a single alphabetical series. These give information about matters which are dealt with briefly or not at all in the footnotes and the Select Glossary: i.e. persons, places, words and phrases, food, drink, clothes etc. They also treat systematically the principal subjects with which the diary is concerned: Pepys's work, interests, health etc. References to the *Companion* are given only rarely in the footnotes.

III. DATES

In Pepys's time two reckonings of the calendar year were in use in Western Europe. Most countries had adopted the New Style – the revised calendar of Gregory XIII (1582); Britain until 1752 retained the Old Style – the ancient Roman, or Julian, calendar, which meant that its dates were ten days behind those of the rest of Western Europe in the seventeenth century. 1 January in England was therefore 11 January by the New Style abroad. On the single occasion during the period of the diary when Pepys was abroad (in Holland in May 1660) he continued to use the Old Style, thus avoiding a break in the run of his dates. In the editorial material of the present work dates relating to countries which had adopted the new reckoning are given in both styles (e.g. '1/11 January') in order to prevent confusion.

It will be noticed that the shortest and longest days of the year occur in the diary ten days earlier than in the modern calendar. So, too, does Lord Mayor's Day in London – on 29 October instead of 9 November.

For most legal purposes (from medieval times until 1752) the new year in England was held to begin on Lady Day, 25 March. But in accordance with the general custom, Pepys took it to begin on 1 January, as in the Julian calendar. He gives to all dates within the overlapping period between 1 January and 24 March a year-date which comprehends both styles – e.g. 'January 1 $16\frac{59}{60}$.' In the present commentary a single year-date, that of the New Style, has been used: e.g. '1 January 1660'.

THE DIARY
1662

JANUARY. $\frac{1661}{62}$.

1. Waking this morning out of my sleep on a sudden, I did with my elbow hit my wife a great blow over her face and nose, which waked her with pain – at which I was sorry. And to sleep again.

Up, and went forth with Sir Wm. Pen by coach toward Westminster; and in my way, seeing that *The Spanish Curate*[1] was acted today, I light and let him go alone; and I home again and sent to young Mr. Pen and his sister to go anon with my wife and I to the Theatre.[2]

That done, Mr. W. Pen came to me and he and I walked out, and to the Stacioners[3] and looked over some pictures and maps for my house. And so home again to dinner. And by and by came the two young Pens, and after we had eat a barrel of oysters, we went by coach to the play and there saw it well acted, and a good play it is. Only, Diego the Sexton did overdo his part too much.

From thence home, and they sat with us till late at night at Cards, very merry. But the jest was, Mr. Pen had left his sword in the Coach; and so my boy and he run out after the Coach, and by very great chance did at the Exchange meet with the Coach and got[a] his sword again.

So to bed.

2. An invitation sent us before we were upp from my Lady Sandwiches, to come and dine with her. So at the office all the morning; and at noon thither to dinner. Where there was a good and great dinner – and the company, Mr. Wm. Mountagu and his lady (but she seemed so far from the beauty that I expected

a MS. 'god'

---

1. A comedy by Fletcher and Massinger; see above, ii. 54, n. 4. (A).
2. The TR, Vere St. (A).
3. John Cade's in Cornhill. This is an early reference to Pepys's purchase of prints for the decoration of his house, and among the earliest known references to the increasing use of prints for this purpose. (OM).

I

her from my Lady's talk to be, that it put me into an ill humour all the day to find my expectacion so lost), Mr. Rumball and Townsend and their wifes. After dinner home by water and so to the office till night. And then I went forth by appointment to meet with Mr. Grant,[1] who promised to meet me at the Coffee-house to bring me acquainted with Cooper,[2] the great Limner in little – but they deceived me; and so I went home and there sat at my lute and singing till almost twelve at night; and so to bed.

Sir Rch. Fanshaw is come suddenly from Portugall, but nobody knows what his business is.[3]

3. Lay long in bed. And so up and abroad to several places about petty businesses. Among other, to Tom's, who I find great hopes of that he will do well, which I am glad of and am not now so hasty to get a wife for him as I was before. So to dinner to my Lord Crew's, with him and his Lady. And after dinner to Faithornes and there bought some pictures of him; and while I was there, comes by the Kings lifeguard, he being gone to Lincolns Inne this afternoon to see the Revells there; there being according to an old Custome, a Prince and all his nobles, and other matters of sport and charge.[4]

So home and up to my chamber – to look over papers and other things, my mind being much troubled for these four or

1. John Graunt, the pioneer social statistician. For his interest in art, see below, iv. 106.

2. Samuel Cooper. In 1668 he painted Mrs Pepys's portrait: below, ix. 138 & n. 2. (OM).

3. He had been sent as ambassador to Portugal in 1661 to exchange ratifications of the marriage treaty and to see that the Portuguese fulfilled their obligations under it. On 3/13 January the Venetian resident reported 'Sir Fanscio's' unexpected arrival on 31 December: 'The reason . . . is not known. It is supposed that it may be because all the things promised by Portugal . . . are not going well' (*CSPVen. 1661–4*, p. 95). He appears to have come by order of

Queen Catherine, and because her departure had been delayed: HMC, *Heathcote*, p. 123.

4. Evelyn (who attended) refers (1 January) to the occasion as a 'solemn foolerie of the *Prince de la Grange* . . . beginning with a grand Masque and a formal Pleading, before the mock-princes (Grandees), Nobles & knights of the *Sunn*: He had his L. Chancelor, Chamberlaine, Treasurer, & other royal officers gloriously clad & attended, which ended in a magnificent Banquet . . .'. See also *Merc. Pub.*, 26 December 1661, pp. 802+; *Records of Lincoln's Inn: Black Books*, iii. 440–3. Cf. E. Chamberlayne, *Angl. Not.* (1671), pp. 427+.

five days because of my present great expense, and will be so till I cast up and see how my estate stands. And that I am loath to do, for fear I have spent too much – and delay it, the rather that I may pay for my pictures and my wife's and the book that I am buying for Paul's Schoole[1] before I do cast up my accompts.

4. At home most of the morning, hanging up pictures and seeing how my pewter Sconces that I have bought will become my stayres and entry. And then with my wife by water to Westminster; whither she to her father's, and I to Westminster-hall and there walked a turn or two with Mr. Chetwin (who had a dog challenged of him by another man that said it was his, but Mr. Chetwin called the dog, and the dog at last would fallow him and not his old master, and so Chetwin got the dog) and W. Symons. And thence to my wife, who met me at my Lord's lodgings; and she and I and old East to Wilkinson's to dinner, where we had some base rost beefe and a mutton-pie and a mince-pie, but none of them pleased me. After dinner, by coach my wife and I home, and I to the office and there till late; and then I and my wife to Sir W. Pens to cards and supper, and were merry. And much correspondence there hath been between our two families all this Christmas. So home and to bed.

5. *Lords day.* Left my wife in bed not well, having her *moys.* And I to church; and so home to dinner and dined alone upon some marrow bones. And had a fine piece of roast beef, but being alone I eat none. So after dinner comes in my Brother Tom, and he tells me how he hath seen the father and mother of the girle which my Cosen Joyces would have him to have for a wife;[2] and they are much for it. But we are in a great Quandary what to do therein – 200*l* being but a little money; and I hope, if he continues as he begins, he may look for one with more.

To church; and before sermon there was a long psalm and half another sung out while the Sexton gathered what the church would give him for this last year[3] (I gave him 3*s*, and

1. See above, ii. 239 & n. 3.
2. See above, ii. 242.

3. It was usual to choose a long psalm when these New Year collections were made: cf. above, ii. 6.

have the last week given the Clerke 2s, which I set down that I may know what to do the next year, if it please the Lord that I live so long); but the jest was, the Clerke begins the 25 psalm, which hath a proper tune to it,[1] and then the 116, which cannot be sung with that tune, which seemed very ridiculous.

After church to Sir W. Battens (where on purpose I have not been this fortnight, and I am resolved to keep myself more reserved, to avoyd the contempt. which otherwise I must fall into); and so home and sat and talked and supped with my wife; and so up to prayers and to bed – having writ a letter this night to Sir J. Mennes in the Downes for his opinion in the business of striking of flaggs.[2]

6.[a] *Twelfe day.* This morning I sent my lute to the painter's; and there I stayed with him all the morning, to see him paint the neck of my lute in my picture[3] – which I was not much pleased with after it was done. Thence to dinner to Sir Wm. Pens (it being a solemn feast-day with him, his wedding day; and we have, besides a good chine of beef and other good cheer, eighteen mince-pies in a dish, the number of the years that he hath been married);[4] where Sir W. Batten and his Lady and daughter was, and Collonell Treswell and Major Holmes, who I perceive would fain get to be free and friends with my wife; but I shall prevent it, and she herself hath also a defyance* against him.[5] After dinner they set in to drinking, so that I could stay no longer but went away home; and Captain Cock, who was quite drunk, comes after me and there sat awhile, and so away. And anon I went again after[b] the company was gone, and sat and played at Cards with Sir W. Penn and his children; and so after supper, home. And there I hear that my man Gul:[6] was

a repl. '7'   *b* repl. 'and'

---

1. Cf. M. Frost, *Engl. and Scott. psalm and hymn tunes, c. 1543–1677,* nos 43–5, 128–9. (E).

2. See below, p. 6 & n. 4.

3. Savill's portrait: see above, ii. 218, n. 4. The lute may have been the theorbo mentioned above, at ii. 193, 201, 203. (OM).

4. He had married Margaret van der Schuren, widow, in 1643 at St Martin's, Ludgate. A certificate of 1652 in HMC, *Portland,* ii. 84, gives the date as 6 June – presumably a mistranscription.

5. Pepys earlier refers to the 'old business which he [Holmes] attempted upon my wife': above, ii. 237.

6. *Gulielmus* (William) Hewer.

gone to bed; and upon enquiry I hear that he did vomit before
he went to bed, and complained his head aked.   And thereupon,
though he was asleep, I sent for him out of his bed; and he rose
and came up to me, and I appeared very angry and did tax him
with being drunk; and he told [me] that he had been with Mr.
Southerne and Homewood[1] at the Dolphin and drank a Quart
of sack, but that his head did ake before he went out.   But I do
believe that he hath drunk too much; and so I did threaten him
to bid his Uncle[2] dispose of him some other way.   And sent
him down to bed and do resolve to continue to be angry with
him.   So I to bed to my wife and told her what hath passed.

7.   Long in bed.   And then rose and went along with Sir
W. Penn on foot to Stepny to Mrs. Chappells (who hath the
pretty boy to her son)[3] and there met my wife and Sir W. Pens
children all, and Mrs. Poole and her boy, and there dined and
were very merry; and home again by Coach and so to the office
in the afternoon; and at night to Sir Wm.*a* Pens and there supped
and played at Cards with them and were merry, the children
being to go all away to schoole again tomorrow.   Thence home
and to bed.

8.   I rose and went to Westminster-hall, and there walked
up and down upon several businesses; and among others, I met
with Sir W. Pen, who told me that he had this morning heard
Sir G. Carteret extreme angry against my man Will; that he
was every other day with the Comissioners of Parliament at
Westminster and that his uncle was a rogue and that he did tell
his uncle everything that passes at the office.[4]   And Sir Wm.
(though he loves the lad) did advise me to part with him –
which did with this surprize mightily trouble me, though I was
already angry with him.   And so to the Wardrobe by water, and
all the way did examine Will about the business, but did not
tell him upon what Scoare.   But I find the poor lad doth suspect

a MS. l.h. 'Wms.'

---

1. Clerks in the Navy Office.
2. Robert Blackborne, who had
obtained for him the post with Pepys.
3. ? the Protector's page: cf.
above, i. 176.

4. Blackborne was unpopular with
royalists such as Carteret because of his
service as Secretary to the Admiralty
Committee under the Protectorate.

something. To dinner with my Lady, and after dinner talked long with her; and so home and to Sir Wm. Battens and sat and talked with him; and so home, troubled in mind; and so up to my study and read the two treatys before Mr. Seldens *Mare Clausum*;[1] and so to bed. ⟨This night came about 100*l* from Brampton by the Carrier to me in Holsters from my father, which made me laugh.⟩*a*

---

9. At the office all the morning, private with Sir G. Carteret (who I expected something from about yesterday's business, but he said nothing), Sir Wms. Batten and Penn, about drawing up an answer to several demands of my Lord Treasurers, and late at it till 2 a-clock.[2] Then to dinner and my wife to Sir W. Pens; and so to the office again and sat till late; and so home – where I find Mr. Armiger below, talking with my wife; but being offended with him for his leaving of my brother Tom, I showed him no countenance, but did take notice of it to him plainly; and I perceive he was troubled at it, but I am glad I told him of it.[3] Then (when he was gone) up to write several letters by the post. And so to set my papers and things in order, and to bed. This morning we agreed upon some things to answer to the Duke about the practice of striking of the flags[4] – which will now put me upon finishing my resolution of writing something upon that subject.

a addition crowded into end of line

---

1. The 'treatys' (treatises) were two appendixes added by the translator (after, not before, the text) in the 1652 edition: *Additional evidences . . . relating to the reigns of K. James and K. Charls;* and *Dominium Maris . . . expressing the title, which the Venetians pretend unto the sole dominion, and absolute sovereigntie of the Adriatick Sea.* Cf. above, ii. 223 & nn. 1, 3.

2. The Lord Treasurer's request (sent to the Admiral on 4 January and forwarded by him on the 6th) was for information about stores, and for details of accounts for the period 24 June 1660–1 January 1662: *CTB*, i. 346–7. The Navy Board's reply (16 January) is full and detailed: ib., i. 349–52; PRO, Adm. 2/1745, f. 65*r*; copy (in Hayter's hand) in PL 2265, no. 15.

3. Armiger again had lodgings at Tom's by 14 June 1663.

4. See Navy Board to Duke of York, 21 January. Copies in PL 2877, pp. 151–4 BL, Add. 9311, ff. 79*v*–80*r*. For the flag issue, see above, ii. 223, n. 1.

10. To White-hall and there spoke with Sir Paul Neale[1] about a Mathematicall request of my Lord's to him; which I did deliver to him, and he promised to imploy somebody to answer it – something about observation of the Moone and stars; but what, I did not mind. Here I met Mr. Moore, who tells me that an Injuncion is granted in Chancery against T. Trice,[a] at which I was very glad, being before in some trouble for it.[2] With him to Westminster-hall, where I walked till noon talking[b] with one or other; and so to the Wardrobe to dinner. Where, tired with Mr. Pickerings company, I returned to Westminster by appointment to meet my wife at Mrs. Hunts to gossip with her; which we did alone and were very merry, and did give her a cup and spoon for my wife's god-child. And so home by Coach and I late reading in my Chamber; and then to bed, my wife being angry that I keep the house so late up.

11. My brother Tom came to me; and he and I to Mr. Turner the Drapers and paid 15*l* to him for cloth owing to him by my father for our Mourning for my Uncle.[3] And so to his house and there invited all the Honiwoods[4] to dinner on Monday next. So to the Exchange; and there all the news is of the French and Duch joyning against us; but I do not think it yet true.[5] So home to dinner and in the afternoon to the office; and so to Sir Wm. Battens, where in discourse I heard the Custome of the Eleccion of the Dukes of Genoa, who for two years are every day attended in the greatest state and[c] 4 or 500 men always waiting upon him as a king. And when the two years are out and another is chose, a messenger is sent to him, who stands at the bottom of the stairs, and he at the top, and says, *Vostra*

a MS. 'Trices'   *b* repl. 'takl'-   *c* preceded by symbol rendered illegible

1. A courtier, and an active F.R.S., particularly interested in astronomy.
2. This concerned the dispute over Robert Pepys's estate: see above, ii. 215 & n. 1. The injunction had the effect of stopping Trice's action at common law and bringing it into Chancery, where it slumbered for 18 months: see below, iv. 221 & n. 1.
3. The mourning was for Robert Pepys of Brampton (d. July 1661). William Turner the draper (Sheriff of London and knight, 1662; Lord Mayor, 1668–9) was a relative of Pepys by marriage.
4. The brothers who lodged at Tom's.
5. They were negotiating a treaty of commerce and mutual defence which was concluded on 17/27 April.

Illustrissima Serenidad sta finita et puede andar en casa[1] – "Your
serenity is now ended; and now you may be going home;" and
so claps on his hat and the old Duke (having by custome sent his
goods home before) walks away, it may be but with one man at
his heels, and the new one brought immediately in his room,
in the greatest state in the world.[2] Another account was told
us, how in the Dukedome of Regusa in the Adriatique (a State that
is little, but more ancient they say then Venice, and is called the
mother of Venice and the Turkes lie round about it) – that they
change all the officers of their guard, for fear of conspiracy,
every 24 houres, so that nobody knows who shall be Captain of
the guard tonight; but two men come to a man, and lay hold
of him as a prisoner and carry him to the place; and there he
hath the keys of the garrison given him, and he presently issues
his orders for that night's Watch; and so always, from night to
night.[3] Sir Wm. Rider told the first of his own knowledge;
and both he and Sir Wm. Batten confirm the last.

Hence home and to read; and so to bed, but very late again.

12. *Lords=day*. To church, where a stranger made a very
good sermon. At noon, Sir W. Pen and my good fr[iend]
Deane Fuller by appointment, and my wife's brother by chance,
dined with me very merry and handsomely. After dinner,
the Deane, my wife and I by (Sir Wm. Pens) coach, lent us, he
to White-hall and my wife and I to visit Mrs. Pierce and thence
Mrs. Turner, who continues very ill still, and The is also fallen
sick – which doth trouble me for the poor mother. So home
and to read, I being troubled to hear my wife rate, though not
without cause, at her mayd Nell, who is a lazy slut.

So to prayers and to bed.

13. All the morning at home, and Mr. Berchenshaw (whom
I have not seen a great while, came to see me), who stayed with
me a great while talking of Musique; and I am resolved to begin

1. Pepys uses a mixture of Spanish
and Italian.
2. For the Doge's functions (almost
entirely ceremonial), see E. Vincens,
Hist. de Gênes (1842), iii. 99+; J. T.
Bent, *Genoa*, p. 12.

3. Cf. L. Villari, *Republic of Ragusa*,
pp. 86–7. Venice was in fact the
older city.

to learne of him to compose and to begin tomorrow, he giving of me so great hopes that I shall soon do it.[1]

Before 12 a-clock comes by appointment Mr. Peter and the Deane and Collonell Honiwood, brothers,[2] to dine with me. But so soon that I was troubled at it. But however, I entertained them with talk and oysters till one a-clock; and then we sat down to dinner, not staying for my uncle and aunt Wight, at which I was troubled. But they came by and by, and so we dined very merry; at least I seemed so, but the dinner [did] not please me, and less the Deane and Collonell, whom I find to be pitiful sorry gentlemen, though good-natured. But Mr. Peter above them both – who after dinner did show us the experiment (which I have heard talk of) of the Chymicall glasses, which break all to dust by breaking off the little small end – which is a great mystery to me.[3] They being gone, my aunt Wight and my wife and I to Cards, she teaching of us two to play at Gleeke,[4] which is a pretty game but I have not my head so free as to be troubled with it. By and by comes my Uncle Wight back again, and so to supper and talk and then again to Cards, where my wife and I beat them two games and they us one; and so good-night and to bed.

14. All the morning at home – Mr. Berchenshaw, by appointment yesterday, coming to*[a]* me, and begun composition of Musique. And he being gone, I to settle my papers and things in my chamber; and so after dinner, in the afternoon to the office and thence to my chamber about several businesses of the

a symbol smudged

---

1. John Birchensha was a violist and music theorist, and had invented 'a mathematical way of composure very extraordinary': Evelyn, 3 August 1664. Pepys's course of lessons lasted until 27 February and cost £5. The diary's references to Pepys's music in this period generally relate to these lessons. (E).

2. I.e. Peter, Michael and Henry Honywood: see above, p. 7 & n. 4. Michael was Dean of Lincoln.

3. These were often known as 'Prince Rupert's drops' and were made from glass which broke into pieces when the small end was snapped off. The experiment was demonstrated before the 'Royal Society' on 6 March 1661: Birch, i. 17-18; Evelyn, s.d. Peter Honywood was not a fellow of the Royal Society.

4. A card game for three.

office and my own; and then to supper and to bed. This day
my brave vellum covers[1] to keep pictures in came in, which
pleases me very much.

15. This morning Mr. Berchenshaw came again; and after
he had examined me and taught me something in my work,
he and I went to breakfast in my chamber, upon a Coller of
brawne. And after we had eaten, he asked me whether we have
not committed a fault in eating today, telling me that it is a fast-
day, ordered by the parliament to pray for more seasonable
weather[2] – it having hitherto been some summer weather, that
it is, both as to warmth and every other thing, just as if it were
the middle of May or June, which doth threaten a plague (as all
men think) to fallow; for so it was almost the last winter, and
the whole year after hath been*a* a very sickly time, to this day.[3]
I did not stir out of my house all day, but con'd my Musique; and
at night, after supper to bed.

16. Towards Cheapeside; and in Pauls churchyard saw the
Funerall of my Lord Cornwallis, late Steward of the King's
house (a bold profane-talking man), go by.[4] And thence I to
the painter's and there paid him 6*l* for the two pictures and 36*s*
for the two frames. From thence home; and Mr. Holliard and
my brother Tom dined with me, and he did give me good
advice about my health. In the afternoon at the office; and at
night to Sir W. Batten and there saw him and Captain Cock
and Stokes play at Cards, and afterwards supped with them.
Stokes told us that notwithstanding the country of Gambo is

a repl. 'a'

---

1. These do not appear to have
survived. (OM).

2. The order for a fast came
originally from the King (proclamation, 8 January: Steele, no. 3349), and
parliament's arrangements (for its own
proceedings) had been made in consequence: e.g. *CJ*, viii. 343. It was
natural for anyone who had lived
through the Puritan Revolution to
attribute fasts to parliamentary
orders.

3. See above, ii. 131 & n. 4, 155 &
n. 3, 168.

4. He was Treasurer of the Household, and had died suddenly of
apoplexy. This entry settles the
doubt in GEC (iii. 453) about the date
of his death. According to Lloyd's
Characters (qu. ib., loc. cit.) he was 'a
man of so cheerful a spirit that no
sorrow came next his heart, and of so
resolved a mind, that no fear came into
his thoughts'.

so unhealthy, yet the people of that place live very long, so as the present King*ᵃ* there is 150 years old, which they count by Raynes because every year it rains continually four months together. He also told us that the kings there have above 100 wifes apiece, and offered him the choice of any of his wifes to lie with, and so he did Captain Holmes*ᵇ*.¹ So home and to bed.

17. To Westminster with Mr. Moore; and there, after several walks up and down to hear news, I met with Mr. Lany the Frenchman, who told me that he had a letter from France last night that tells him that my Lord Hinchingbrooke is dead,² and that he did die yesterday was sennit – which doth surprize [me] exceedingly (though we know that he hath been sick these two months), as*ᶜ* I hardly ever was in my life. But being fearful that my Lady should come to hear it too suddenly, he and I went up to my Lord Crews and there I dined with him, and after dinner we told him, and the whole family is much disturbed by it. So we consulted what to do to tell my Lady of it; and at last we thought of my going first to Mr. George Mountagu's to hear whether he hath any news of it; which I did, and there find all his house in great heavinesse for the death of his son Mr. George Mountagu, who did go with our young gentlemen into France, and that they hear nothing at all of our young Lord; so, believing that thence comes the mistake, I returned to my Lord Crew (in my way in the Piazza seeing a house on fire and all the streets*ᵈ* full of people to quench it) and told them of it; which they are much glad of, and conclude, and so I hope, that my Lord is well; and so I went to my Lady Sandwich and told her all; and after much talk I parted thence

a word smudged   *b* repl. 'Stok'-   *c* MS. 'so'
d l.h. repl. s.h. 'people'

---

1. Cf. the description of a visit to one of these kings in Gambia by a slave-trader, Capt. Phillips, in 1694: A. and J. Churchill, *Voyages* (1732), vi. 214+. He estimated his royal host to be c. 60, but says that these tribes kept no account of time (other travellers report them as reckoning in lunar months). Phillips's party got into severe trouble by merely peeping into the royal wives' quarters.
2. Sandwich's eldest son had been in Paris with his brother since August 1661, in the charge of a tutor. The report was false. He suffered all his life from ill-health, but did not die until 1688.

with my wife (who had been there all the day) and so home and to my musique, and then to bed.

18. This morning I went to Dr. Williams; and there he told me how T. Trice hath spoke to him about getting me to meet, that our difference might be made up between us by ourselfs – which I am glad of, and have appointed Monday next to be the day. Thence to the Wardrobe; and there hearing it would be late before they went to dinner, I went and spent some time in Pauls Churchyard among some books; and then returned thither and there dined with my Lady and Sir H. Wright and his Lady, all glad of yesterday's mistake. And after dinner to the office, and then home and wrote letters by the post to my father; and by and by comes Mr. Moore to give me an account how Mr. Mountagu was gone away of a sudden with the fleet, in such haste that he hath left behind some servants and many things of consequence; and among others, my Lord's commission for Embassador.[1] Whereupon, he and I took coach and to White-hall to my Lord's lodgings to have spoke with Mr. Ralph Mountagu his brother (and here we stayed talking with Sarah and the old man[2]); but by and by, hearing that he was in Covent Garden, we went thither and at my Lady Harvy's, his sister's, I spoke with him and he tells me that the Comission is not left behind;[3] and so I went thence by the same Coach (setting down Mr. Moore) home; and after having wrote a letter to my Lord at 12 a-clock at night by the post, I went to bed.

19. *Lords=day.* To church in the morning, where Mr. Mills preached upon Christ's being offered up for our sins. And there, proveing the æquity with what Justice God could lay our sins upon his Son, he did make such a sermon (among other things, pleading from God's universall Soverainty over all his Creatures, the power he hath of commanding what he would of

1. Edward Mountagu (Sandwich's cousin) had sailed on the 15th with the fleet carrying the new Governor and garrison of Tangier who were to take over the protection of the place from Sandwich's fleet. Routh, p. 12; Sandwich, p. 117.

2. East the porter.

3. It was delivered to Sandwich, with his instructions, on 1 March: Sandwich, p. 123.

his Son, by the same rule as that he might have made us all and the whole world from the beginning to have been in hell, arguing from the power the potter hath over his clay), that I could have wished he had let it alone. And speaking again, that God the Father is now so satisfyd by our Security for our debt that we might say at the last day, as many of us as have interest in Christ's death – Lord, we owe thee nothing – our debt is paid – we are not beholden to thee for anything, for thy debt is paid thee to the full – which methinks were very bold words.

Home to dinner; and then my wife and I on foot to see Mrs. Turner, who continues still sick; and thence into the old Bayly by appointment, to speak with Mrs. Norbury who lies at, it falls out, next door to my uncle Fenners; but (as God would have it, we having no desire to be seen by his people, he having lately married a midwife that is old and ugly and that hath already brought home to him a daughter and three children)[1] we were let in at a back doore. And here she offered me the refusall of some lands of her at Brampton, if I had a mind to buy – which I answered her I was not at present provided to do.[2] She took occasion to talk of her Sister Wights making much of the Wights; who for name sake only my uncle doth show great kindenesse to, and I fear may do us that are nearer to him a great deal of wrong, if he should die without children – which I am sorry for.[3] Thence to my uncle Wights and there we supped and were merry – though my uncle hath lately lost 2 or 300 at sea, and I am troubled to heare that the Turkes do take more and more of our ships in the Straights, and that our Merchants here in London do daily break, and are still likely to do so.[4]

1. Thomas Fenner's first wife (sister of Pepys's mother) had died in August 1661.

2. Cf. above, ii. 124.

3. George Norbury and William Wight had married sisters. The latter (half-brother of Pepys's father) was a merchant of London whose only son had died. In 1664 he proposed to Elizabeth Pepys that they should together have a child whom he would make his heir: below, v. 145–6. He died intestate in 1672 leaving £4000, of which, after litigation with his widow, Pepys's father was awarded one-third of a moiety: Whitear, pp. 161–5.

4. Twenty-two ships had been taken, 11 of them English: *CSPVen. 1661–4*, p. 94 (13 January). On 27 January the Venetian resident reported the capture of two further English ships and the unsuccessful chase of a third: ib., p. 100. This despite the presence of a Dutch and an English fleet in the W. Mediterranean.

So home and I put in at Sir W. Batten's, where Major Holmes was; and in our discourse and drinking, I did begin Sir J. Mennes's health – which he Swore*a* he would not pledge, and called him knave and coward (upon that business of Holmes's with the Swedish shipp lately),[1] which we all, and I perticularly, did desire him*b* to forbear, he being of our fraternity; which he took in great dudgeon, and I was vexed to hear him persist in calling him so, though I believe it to be true; but however, he is to blame and I am troubled at it.[2] So home and to prayers, and to bed.

20. This morning Sir Wm. Batten and Penn and [I] did begin the examining the Treasurers accounts – the first that ever he hath passed in the office. Which is very long – and we were all at it till noon. Then to dinner, he providing a fine dinner for us; and we eate it at Sir Wm. Batten's, where we were very merry, there being at table the Treasurer and we three – Mr. Wayth, Fenn, Smith, Turner, and Mr. Morrice the Wine Cooper (who this day did divide the two butts, which we four did send for, of Sherry from Cales, and mine was put into a hogshead and the vessell filled up with four gallons of Malago wine; but what it will stand us in I know not, but it is the first great Quantity of wine that I ever bought).[3] And after dinner to the office all the afternoon, till late at night. And then home, where my aunt and uncle Wight and Mrs. Anne Wight came to play at Cards (at gleeke, which she taught me and my wife the last week); and so to supper and then to Cards, and so good-night. Then I to my practice of Musique and then at 12 a-clock to bed.

This day the workmen begin to make me a sellar door out of the back yard – which will much please me.

21. To the finishing of the Treasurers accounts this morning; and then to dinner again, and were merry as yesterday. And

a l.h. repl. s.h. 'sord'   *b* l.h. repl. s.h. 'to'

---

1. See above, ii. 212 & n. 3.
2. On 7 December 1661 Pepys in his loyalty to Sandwich had been 'glad to hear' this reflection on Mennes.
3. It was usual to buy wine by the

cask; the habit of maturing it in bottles did not come in until the early 18th century with the introduction of cork stoppers: cf. below, iv. 18 & n. 2. A hogshead usually held c. 50 gallons.

so home; and then to the office till night, and then home to write letters and to practise my composition of Musique, and then to bed. We have heard nothing yet how far the fleet hath got toward Portugall. But the wind being changed again, we fear they are stopped and may be beat back again to the coast of Ireland.

22. After Musique practice, to Whitehall and thence to Westminster, in my way calling at Mr. George Mountagu's to condole him the loss of his son – who was a fine gentleman, and no doubt it is a great discomfort to our two young gentlemen, his companions in France. After this discourse, he told me, among other news, the great Jealousys that are now in the Parliament-house – the Lord Chancellor, it seems, taking occasion from this late plot[1] to raise fears in the people, did project the raising of an army forthwith, besides the constant Militia, thinking to make the Duke of Yorke Generall thereof. But the House did in very open tearmes say they were grown too wise to be fooled again into another army; and said they have found how the man that hath the command of an army is not beholden to anybody to make him King.[2] There are factions (private ones at Court) about Madam Palmer; but what it is about I know not. But it is something about the King's favour to her, now that the Queene is coming.

He told me too, what sport the King and Court do make at Mr. Edw. Mountagu's leaving his things behind him.[3] But the Chancellor (taking it a little more seriously) did openly say to my Lord Chamberlaine that had it been such a gallant as my Lord Mandevill, his son,[4] it might have been taken as a frolique.

---

1. The Yarranton Plot: see above, ii. 225 & n. 1.
2. Mountagu was M.P. for Dover and is here reporting a debate on the militia bill held on this day: *CJ*, viii. 349. It had been proposed in committee to raise a new army under the Duke: *CSPVen. 1661-4*, pp. 91, 106. A similar rumour that the Duke was to be made general is reported below, at 6 December 1665. Clarendon's enemies (quite unjustly) accused him of attempting to introduce a sort of militarism into government – a charge revived at his impeachment in 1667, and made colourable by his relationship to the Duke, his son-in-law.
3. See above, p. 12.
4. Viscount Mandeville, eldest son of the 2nd Earl of Manchester (Lord Chamberlain).

But for him, that would be thought a grave Coxcombe, it was very strange.

Thence to the Hall, where I heard the House hath ordered all the King's murderers that remain to be executed but Fleetwood and Downes.[1]

So to the Wardrobe and there I dined, meeting my wife there, who went after dinner with my Lady to see Mr. George Mountagu's Lady, and I to have a meeting by appointment with Tho. Trice and Dr. Williams, in order to a treating about the difference between us. But I find there is no hopes of ending it but by law; and so after a pint[a] or two of wine we parted.

So to the Wardrobe for my wife again; and so home, and after writing and[b] doing some things, to bed.

23. All the morning with Mr. Berchenshaw and after him Mr. Moore, in discourse of business; and at noon by Coach by invitacion to my Uncle Fenners,[2] where I find his new wife, a pitiful, old, ugly, illbread woman in a hatt, a midwife. Here were many of his and as many of her relations, sorry mean people. And after choosing our gloves, we all went over to the Three Crane taverne, and (though the best room of the house) in such a narrow dogghole we were crammed (and I believe we were near 40) that it made me loathe my company and victuals; and a sorry poor dinner it was too.

After dinner I took aside the two Joyces and took occasion to thank them for their kind thoughts for a wife for Tom; but that considering the possibility there is of my having no child, and what then I shall be able to leave him, I do think he may expect in that respect a wife with more money, and so desired them to think no more of it. Now the jest was, Anthony mistakes and thinks that I did all this while encourage him (from my thoughts of favour to Tom) to pursue the mach, till Will Joyce told him that he was mistaken. But how he takes it, I

a MS s.h. 'point'   *b* repl. ? 'letters'

---

1. By a vote of 21 January; Charles Fleetwood was reprieved because he had taken no part in the King's trial, and John Downes because he had acted under duress: *CJ*, viii. 349.
2. It being his birthday.

know not; but I endeavoured to tell it him in the most respectful way that I could.

This done, with my wife by Coach to my aunt Wights, where I left her and I to the office; and that being done, to her again and sat playing at cards after supper, till 12 at night; and so by moonshine home and to bed.

24. This morning came my Cosen T. Pepys the Executor to speak with me; and I had much talk with him, both about matters of money which my Lord Sandwich hath of his and I am bond for[1] – as also of my uncle Thomas, who I hear by him doth stand upon very high terms.[2]

Thence to my painter's, and there I saw our pictures in the frames, which please me well. Thence to the Wardrobe, where very merry with my Lady; and after dinner I sent for the pictures thither, and mine is well liked but she is much offended with my wife's; and I am of her opinion, that it doth much wrong her – but I will have it altered. So home, in my way calling at Popes-head alley and there bought me a pair of scissors and a brasse Square.[a] So home and to my study and to bed.

25. At home and the office all the morning. Walking in the garden to give[b] the gardener directions what to do this year (for I entend to have the garden handsome),[3] Sir Wm. Pen came to me and did break a business to me about removing his Son from Oxford to Cambrige to some private College.[4] I proposed Magdalen, but cannot name a Tutor at present. But I shall think and write about it.

Thence with him to the Trinity-house to dinner, where

a l.h. repl. l.h. 'Quadrant'   *b* repl. 'the'

---

1. The loan was for £1000 and caused Pepys some anxiety until it was paid off on 31 January 1666 from Sandwich's prize-money.

2. In claiming his annuity from the estate of Robert Pepys: see above, ii. 135 & n. 2.

3. Henry Wise, gardener, later submitted a bill (8 May 1662) for £3 15s. for work on the Navy Office garden: PRO, Adm. 20/2, p. 28.

Possibly he is the gardener here referred to. The famous Henry Wise, gardener to William III and Anne, may have been his son.

4. Sc. to a small college. William Penn (later the Quaker leader) had been sent down from Christ Church, Oxford, for nonconformity in the previous October: above, ii. 206 & n. 3. Nothing came of the proposal.

Sir Richard Brown (one of the clerks of the Council, and who is much concerned against Sir N. Crisp's project of making a great sasse in the King's Lands about Deptford, to be a wett dock to hold 200 sail of ships – but the ground, it seems, was long since given by the King to Sir Richd.) was;[1] and after the Trinity-house men had done their business, the maister, Sir Wm. Rider, came to bid us welcome; and so to dinner – where good cheer and discourse, but I eat a little too much beef, which made me sick; and so after dinner we went to the office, and there in the garden I went in the darke and vomited, whereby I did much ease my stomach. Thence to supper with my wife to Sir Wm. Pens – his daughter being come home today, not being very well.[2] And so while we were at supper, comes Mr. Moore with letters from[a] my Lord Sandwich, speaking of his lying still at Tanger, looking for the fleet – which we hope is now in a good way thither.

So home to write letters by the post tonight; and then again to Sir W. Penn to cards, where very merry; and so home and to bed.

26. *Lords=day*. To church in the morning and then home to dinner alone with my wife; and so both to church in the afternoon and home again; and so to read and talk with my wife, and to supper and bed.

It having been a very fine clear frosty day – God send us more of them, for the warm weather all this winter makes us fear a sick summer.[3]

But thanks be to God, since my leaving drinking of wine, I do find myself much better and to mind my business better and to spend less money, and less time lost in idle company.

a l.h. repl. s.h. 'of'

1. The Duke of York and Ormond had viewed the site on 16 January: Evelyn. Pepys later had a hand in securing the rejection of the proposal at the instance of a committee appointed by Trinity House and the Navy Board: below, pp. 30, 32–3; *EHR*, 44/573. For Browne's interest in the land, see Evelyn ii. 537 n.; iii.

59 n. Crisp had propounded the scheme to Evelyn in 1655: Evelyn, 31 October.

2. Margaret Penn was at school at Clerkenwell.

3. Cf. the contemporary proverb: 'A green winter makes a fat church-yard.'

27. This morning, both Sir Wms. and I by barge to Deptford yard to give order in businesses there; and called on several ships also to give orders. And so to Woolwich and there dined at Mr. Falconer's, of victuals we carried ourselfs – and one Mr. Dekins, the father of my Morena, of whom we have lately bought some hemp. That being done, we went home again.

This morning, going to take water upon Tower hill, we met with three Sleddes standing there to carry my Lord Monson and Sir H. Mildmay and another to the gallowes and back again, with ropes about their neck. Which is to be repeated every*a* year – this being the day of their sentenceing the King.[1]

28. This morning (after my musique practice with Mr. Berchensha) with my wife to the paynters, where we stayed very late to have her picture[2] mended; which at last is come to be very like her, and I think well done. But the paynter, though a very honest man, I find to be very silly as to matter of skill in shadowes – for we were long in discourse, till I was almost angry to hear him talk so simply. So home to dinner and then to the office, and so home for all night.

29. To Westminster, and at the parliament doore spoke with Mr. Coventry about business. And so to the Wardrobe to dinner and thence to several places; and so home, where I find Mrs. Pen and Mrs. Rooth and Smith – who played at Cards with my wife, and I did give them a barrel of oysters and had a pullet to supper for them; and when it was ready to come to table, the foolish girl[3] had not the manners to stay and sup with me, but went away; which did vex me cruelly. So I saw her home, and then to supper; and so to musique practice and to bed.

a MS. s.h. 'over'

---

1. Viscount Monson, Sir Henry Mildmay, and Robert Wallop had been members of the regicide tribunal, but had not attended its later meetings and did not sign the death-warrant. At their trial in July 1661 their lives had been spared, but they had suffered degradation from all titles and offices, forfeiture of estates and life imprisonment, as well as the punishment here described.

2. The portrait by Savill: see above, ii. 218 & n. 4. (OM).

3. Margaret Penn.

30. *Fast day for the murthering of the late King.* I went to church, and Mr. Mills made a good sermon upon Davids words, ("Who can lay his hands upon the Lord's annoynted and be guiltlesse");[1] so home and to dinner, and imployed all the afternoon in my chamber, setting things and papers to rights; which pleased me very well, and I think I shall begin to take pleasure in being at home and minding my business. I pray God I may, for I finde a great need thereof. At night to supper and to bed.

31. All the morning (after Musique practice) in my Sellar, ordering some alteracions therein, being much pleased with my new doore into the backyard. So to dinner; and all the afternoon within, thinking upon business. I did by night set many things in order, which pleased me well and puts me upon a resolution of keeping within doors and minding my business and the business of the office – which I pray God I may put in practice.

At night, to bed.

1. A loose recollection of 1 Sam., xxvi. 9: 'Who can stretch forth his hand . . .?'. For the service, see above, ii. 26, n. 1.

FEBRUARY.

1. This morning within till^a 11 a-clock; and then with Comissioner Pett to the office; and he stayed there writing while I and Sir W. Penn walked in the garden, talking about his business of removing his Son to Cambrige. And to that end I entend to write tonight to Dr. Fairebrother[1] to give me an account of Mr. Burton of Magdalen.

Thence with Mr. Pett to the paynters; and he like[s] our pictures very well, and so do I. Thence he and I to the Countesse of Sandwich to lead him to her to kiss her hands, and dined with her. And told her the news (which Sir W. Penn told me today) that expresse is come from my Lord with letters, that by a great Storme and tempest the Mole of Argier is broken down, and many of their ships sunk in the mole; so that God Almighty hath now ended that unlucky business for us[2] – which is very good news.

After dinner to the office – where we stayed late; and so I home and late writing letters to my father and Dr. Fairebrother and an angry letter to my brother John for his not writing to me. And so to bed.

2. *Lords day*. To church in the morning; and then home and dined with my wife; and so both of us to church again – where we had an Oxford man give us a most impertinent* sermon upon "Cast your bread upon the waters,"[3] &c; so home – to read – supper and to prayers; and then to bed.

3. After musique practice I went to the office, and there with the two Sir Wms. all the morning about business. At noon I dined with Sir W. Batten with many friends more, it being his Wedding=day. And among other Froliques, it being their

a l.h. repl. s.h. 'all'

---

1. Fellow of King's College.
2. Sandwich's expedition in the previous summer had failed to subjugate this pirates' stronghold: above, ii. 184 & n. 2. For the storm, see *CSPVen. 1661–4*, p. 108; Tanner 47, f.139*r*. The Algerines lost 11 men-of-war and several merchantmen besides suffering damage to the mole. The storms were widespread and also affected the English Channel.

3. *Recte* 'Cast thy bread . . .' Eccles., xi, 1.

third year, they had three pyes, whereof the middlemost was
made of an ovall form in an Ovall hole within the other two,
which made much mirth and was called the middle peace; and
above all the rest, we had great striving to steal a spoonefull out of
it; and I remember Mrs. Mills the minister's wife did steal one for
me and did give it me; and to end all, Mrs. Shippman did fill
the pie full of White wine (it holding at least a pint and a half)
and did drink it off for a health to Sir Wm. and my Lady,
it being the greatest draught that ever I did see a woman drink
in my life.

Before we had dined came Sir G. Carteret, and we went all*a*
three to the office and did business there till night.   And then to
Sir Wm. Batten again, and I went along with my Lady and the
rest of the gentlewomen to Major Holmes's, and there we had a
fine supper; among others, excellent lobsters, which I never eat
at this time of the year before.   The Major hath good lodgings
at the Trinity-house.   Here we stayed late, and at last home.
And being in my chamber, we do hear great noise of mirth at Sir
Wm. Battens, tearing the ribbands from my Lady and him.[1]
So I to bed.

4.   To Westminster-hall, where it was full terme.   Here all
the morning; and at noon to my Lord Crewes – where one Mr.
Templer (an ingenious [man] and a person of honour he seems to
be) dined; and discoursing of the nature of Serpents, he told us
of some that in the waste places in Lancashire do grow to a great
bigness, and that do feed upon larkes, which they take thus –
they observe when the lark is soared to the highest, and do crawle
till they come to be just underneath them; and there they place
themselfs with their mouths uppermost, and there (as is conceived)
they do eject poyson up to the bird; for the bird doth suddenly
come down again in its course of a circle, and falls directly into the
mouth of the serpent – which is very strange.*b*[2]   He is a great

a l.h. repl. s.h. 'back'   *b* repl. 'pl'-

1. Cf. above, i. 27, n. 2.
2. This story may be based on a
misunderstanding of the fact that
birds often attack snakes: see, e.g.,
E. Topsell, *Hist. Serpents* (1608),
pp. 25+.   It has not been traced elsewhere.   Pepys's informant may have
been Benjamin Templer, ex-Fellow of
Trinity College, Cambridge, whose
Northamptonshire living at Ashley
was not far from the Crews' country
house at Stene.

traveller; and speaking of the Tarantula, he says that all the harvest long (about which time they are most busy) there are fidlers go up and down in the fields everywhere, [in] expectation of being hired by those that are stung.[1]

Thence to the office, where late; and so to my chamber and then to bed, my mind being a little troubled how put things in order to my advantage in the office in obedience to the Dukes orders lately sent to us, and of which we are to treate at the office tomorrow morning. ⟨This afternoon, going into the office, one met me and did serve a subpoene upon me from one Fielde, whom we did commit to prison the other day for some ill words he did give the office. The like he hath for others, but we shall scowre him for it.⟩[a][2]

5. earely at the office; Sir G. Carteret, the two Sir Wms.

a addition crowded in small symbols into bottom of page

---

1. In S. Italy the bite of the tarantula spider was supposed to cause a disease which, according to tradition, could be cured by music and dancing. (Hence the dance 'tarantella'.) The Royal Society examined the evidence in 1672 and found it 'fabulous': *Philos. Trans.*, vii. 4066. Another story was that the victims both sang and danced expertly: E. Topsell, *Hist. four-footed beasts* (1658), p. 1061.

2. This was the beginning of a series of disputes lasting until the end of 1663. Edward Field of Wapping had accused the Board of failing to act on information he had given them about the alleged embezzlement of timber by one Turpin. 'Spleen' or 'hopes . . . of reward', as Pepys wrote, might well inspire such allegations (*Further Corr.*, p. 4), and Turpin was in fact later acquitted in the Admiralty Court. Field, now committed for slander, successfully sued for wrongful arrest on the technical ground that the Board had no authority as magistrates within the city. The diary tells the rest of the story. In October 1662 he brought an action against Pepys and was awarded £30 damages; in November 1663 he sued the whole Board and obtained £20 damages plus costs, after demanding an out-of-court settlement of £250. Meanwhile, on an order from the Duke of York, Batten brought an action in the Exchequer on the original charge of slander and on 3 June 1663 was awarded £10 damages. This, *inter alia*, led to the act of 1664 giving the Board powers of magistracy within the city: below, iv. 82 & n. 1. None of the papers concerning Field have survived among Pepys's collections.

and myself all alone, reading over the Duke's Institucions[1] for the Settlement of our office.   Whereof we read as much as concerns our owne duties, and left the other officers for another time.   I did move several things for my purpose, and did ease my mind.

At noon Sir W. Pen dined with me; and after dinner, he and I and my wife to the Theater[2] and went in; but being there very earely, we went out again to the next door and drank some Renish wine and Sugar; and so to the House again and there saw *Rule a Wife and have a Wife*[3] – very well done; and here also I did look long upon my Lady Castlemayne, who, notwithstanding her late sickness, continues a great beauty.

Home, and supped with Sir W. Pen and played at Cards with him; and so home and to bed – putting some cataplasme to my testicle, which begins to swell again.

6.   At my musique practice.   And so into my sellar to my workmen, and I am very much pleased with my alteracion there.[4]

About noon comes my uncle Thomas to me to aske for his Annuity.[5]   And I did tell him my mind freely.   We had some high words, but I was willing to end all in peace; and so I made him dine with me, and I have hopes to work my ends upon him. After dinner the Barber trimmed me; and so to the office, where I do begin to be exact in my duty there and exacting my privileges – and shall continue to do so.

None but Sir W. Batten and me here tonight; and so we broke up earely, and I home and to my chamber to put things in order, and so to bed.   My swelling, I think, doth begin to go away again.

1. Normally known as 'Instructions'.   More or less stereotyped by this time, they were issued by each Lord High Admiral at the outset of his term of office, and detailed the duties of all his officers at the Navy Board and in the dockyards.   The Duke of York's Instructions of 1662 (28 January; based on those of 1640) remained substantially in force until Nelson's day, but the theory that the Board could do only what was authorised by them or by special warrants was not observed.   Many MS. copies survive; Pepys preserved two: PL 2611 (in Hewer's hand), PL 2867 (in Hayter's).   Printed (imperfectly, from a copy originally in the Admiralty Library, now PRO, Adm. 7/633) in *Oeconomy of . . . navy-office* (1717); analyses in *Cat.*, i. 20+; Tedder, pp. 48+.

2. The TR, Vere St.   (A).

3. A comedy by Fletcher: see above, ii. 64 & n. 1.   (A).

4. See above, p. 14.

5. Under the will of his brother Robert Pepys.

7. Among my workmen this morning. By and by, by water to Westminster with Comissioner Pett (landing my wife at Blackfriers), where I hear the prisoners in the Tower that are to die are come to the parliament-house this morning.[1]

To the Wardrobe to dinner with my Lady – where a Civitt= Catt, parrot, Apes, and many other things are come from my Lord by Captain Hill, who dined with my Lady with us today. Thence to the painter's, and am well pleased with our pictures; so by coach home – where I find the Joyners setting up my chimny-piece in the dining roome, which pleases me well; only, the frame for a picture they have made so massy and heavy that I cannot tell what to do with it.[2]

This evening came my she-Cosen Porter to see us (the first time that we have seen her since we came to this end of the towne) and after her Mr. Hunt, who both stayed with us a pretty while, and so went away.

By and by, hearing that Mr. Turner was much troubled at what I do in the office,[3] and doth give ill words to Sir W. Pen and others of me, I am much troubled in my mind, and so went to bed – not that I fear him at all, but the natural aptnesse I have to be troubled at anything that crosses me.

8. All the morning in the sellar with the Colliers, removing the Coles out of the old coal-hole into the new one, which cost

1. These were the regicides who had voluntarily surrendered to the Restoration government, and were now held at parliament's mercy, having escaped execution with most of the others in October 1660. A bill for their execution had passed the Commons (cf. above, p. 16) and was now before the Lords. Eleven were examined by the Lords this morning, but the bill never passed, and the men lived out their lives in imprisonment. *LJ*, xi. 380–1.

2. Throughout the 17th century pictures had been inset over fireplaces. They were often the only pictures in rooms which were hung with tapestry or panelled in an old-fashioned style. In Pepys's time pictures (almost invariably of *genres* other than the portrait) were being set over doors and fireplaces as integral parts of the decoration. Particularly good examples can be seen in the rooms redecorated by the Duke and Duchess of Lauderdale at Ham House in the 1670s: Whinney and Millar, pp. 272–3. (OM).

3. About the payments for petty provisions: see above, ii. 54 & n. 1; below, p. 27; v. 320.

me 8s. the doing; but now the cellar is done and made clean, it
doth please me exceedingly, as much as anything that was ever
yet done to my house. I pray God keep me from setting my
mind too much upon it.

About 3 a-clock, the Colliers having done, I went up to dinner
(my wife having often urged me to come, but my mind is so set
upon these things that I cannot but be with the workmen to see
things done to my mind; which if I am not there is seldom done);
and so to the office, and thence to talk with Sir W. Penn, walking in the dark in the garden some turns, he telling me of the ill
management of our office and how Wood the Timber=merchant
and others were very Knaves, which I am apt to believe.

Home, and wrote letters to my father and my brother John,
and so to bed – being a little chillish – entending to take physique
tomorrow morning.

9. *Lordsday.* I took physic this day, and was all day in my
chamber – talking with my wife about her laying out of 20l.,
which I had long since promised her to lay out in clothes against
Easter for herself. And composing some ayres (God forgive
mee).[1]

At night, to prayers and to bed.

10. Musique practice a good while. Then to Pauls churchyard, and there I met with Dr: Fullers *Englands worthys*[2] – the
first time that I ever saw it; and so I sat down reading in it, till
it was 2 a-clock before I thought of the time's going. And
so I rose and went home to dinner, being much troubled that
(though he had some discourse with me about my family and
armes) he says nothing at all, nor mentions us either in Cambrige

1. For Pepys's anxiety over Sabbath indulgence in music, see above,
i. 270. (E).

2. See above, ii. 21, n. 1; PL 2438
(folio, 1662).

or Norfolke. But I believe endeed, our family were never considerable.[1]

At home all the afternoon; and at night to bed.

11. Musique. Then my brother Tom came; and spoke to him about selling of Sturtlow,[2] which he consents to; and I think it*ª* will be the best for him, considering that he needs money and hath no mind to marry.

Dined at home, and at the office in the afternoon. So home to Musique, my mind being full of our alteracions in the garden[3] and my getting of things in the office settled to the advantage of my Clerkes, which I find Mr. Turner much troubled at. And myself am not quiet in mind – but I hope by degrees to bring it to it. At night begun to compose songs, and begin with *Gaze not on Swans*.[4] So to bed.

12. This morning, till 4 in the afternoon, I spent abroad, doing of many and very considerable businesses at Mr. Phillips's

a MS. 'I'

---

1. Pepys knew almost nothing about the history of the medieval Pepyses: see below, viii. 261 & n. 4. They had been settled in and around Cottenham (Cambs.) from at least the 14th century – in Bryant's words (i. 2, 3) 'villeins in breed and tenure' and occasionally 'rural bureaucrats' (e.g. reeves of Crowland Abbey). Since Elizabethan times they had acquired more substance – the main line, from the diarist's great-grandfather, John Pepys, onwards, being owners of Impington manor. John had a son and a grandson who served as recorders and M.P.'s for Cambridge. No Pepys had held high county office. In the marriage market the outstanding successes were the Elizabethan John who married a small fortune (with which he is said to have bought his manor), and the diarist's

great-aunt who married into the Mountagus. Arms had been confirmed to Thomas Pepys of South Creake, Norf. (cousin of Pepys's great-grandfather) in 1563.

2. Part of Pepys's Uncle Robert's estate in Huntingdonshire, near Brampton; sold in the following year: below, iv. 119, 308.

3. See above, p. 17 & n. 3.

4. Finished and largely composed by Birchensha: below, p. 46. Pepys's source of the words may have been Henry Lawes's first *Ayres and dialogues* (1653), where they are ascribed to Henry Noel; they have later been attributed to William Strode: *Poet. Works* (ed. Dobell), pp. 128-9. To 'compose' could mean to put words and music together. (E).

the lawyer, with Prior – Westminster, my Lord Crewes, Wardrobe – &c.¹ And so home, about that time of day, to dinner; with my mind very highly contented with my day's work – wishing I could do so every day. Then to my Chamber, drawing up writings against tomorrow, in expectacion of my uncle Thomas's coming. So to my Musique and then to bed.

This night I had a 100 poore Jack sent me by Mr. Adis.²

13. After Musique comes my Cosen Tom. Pepys the Executor; and he did stay with me above two houres, discoursing about the difference between my uncle Thomas and me, and what way there may be to make it up, and I have hopes we may do good of it for all this. Then to dinner. And then came Mr. Kennard, and he and I and Sir W. Pen went up and down his house to view what may be the contrivance and alterations there to the best advantage.³

So home, where Mr. Blackburne (whom I have not seen a long time) was come to speak with me; and among other discourses, he doth tell me plain of the Corrupcion of all our Treasurer's officers, and that they hardly pay any money under 10 per cent; and that the other day, for a mere assignacion of 200*l* to some Countys, they took 15*l* – which is very strange.⁴ So to the office till night; and then home and to write by the post about many businesses, and so to bed. Last night dyed the Queene of Bohemia.⁵

14. *Valentine's day.* I did this day purposely shun to be seen at Sir W. Battens – because I would not have his daughter to be my Valentine,⁶ as she was the last year, there being no great

1. For Pepys's work at the Wardrobe, see above, ii. 113, n. 2.
2. Navy victualler, Plymouth.
3. Thomas Kinward was the Master-Joiner in the office of the King's Works. For the progress of the work, see below, pp. 41, 134; for its cost, below, iv. 293 & n. 1.
4. The Lord Treasurer had paid money to the Navy Treasurer by means of tallies struck on the land-tax

returns from several counties. For this transaction, see *CTB*, i. 360, 362. Robert Blackborne was now Secretary to the Customs Commissioners.
5. Elizabeth, 'Winter Queen' of Bohemia, aunt of Charles II, died at Leicester House in the early hours of the morning of the 13th.
6. Custom required her to choose the first person she saw: cf. above, i. 55 & n. 3.

friendship between us now as formerly. This morning in comes W. Bowyer, who was my wife's Valentine, she having (at which I made good sport to myself) held her hands all the morning, that she might not see the paynters that were at work in gilding my chimny-piece and pictures in my dining-room.

By and by she and I by coach with him to Westminster, by the way leaving at Tom's and my wife's father's lodgings each of them some poore Jack, and some she carried to my father Bowyers, where she stayed while I walked in the hall; and there, among others, met with Serjeant Pierce, and I took him aside to drink a cup of ale and he told me the basest things of Mr. Mountagus and his man Eschars going away in debt, that I am troubled and ashamed, but glad to be informed of. He thinks he hath*a* left 1000*l* for my Lord to pay, and that he hath not laid out 3000*l* of the 5000*l* for my Lord's use, and is not able to make an account of any of the money.[1]

My wife and I to dinner to the Wardrobe, and then to talk with my Lady; and so by coach, it raining hard, home. And so to do business and to bed.

15. With the two Sir Wms. to the Trinity-house; and there in their society had the business debated of Sir Nicholas Crisps Sasse at Deptford.[2] Then to dinner; and after dinner I was sworne a younger Brother,[3] Sir W. Rider being Deputy-Maister for my Lord of Sandwich; and after I was sworn, all the elder Brothers shake me by the hand; it is their Custome it seems.

Thence to the office, and so to Sir Wm Battens all three; and there we stayed till late, talking together in complaint of the Treasurers instruments – above all, Mr. Waith[4] – at whose child's

a repl. 'is'

---

1. This story appears to have been exaggerated: see below, iv. 47, for the settlement of Edward Mountagu's accounts. Serjeant Pierce (Pearse) seems to have been brother of James, the navy surgeon.
2. See above, p. 18 & n. 1.
3. Pepys kept a copy of the oath:

HMC, *Eliot Hodgkin*, pp. 157-8 (where the year is misdated); cf. *Mar. Mirr.*, 19/219. He became an Elder Brother in 1672, Younger Warden in 1675, and served as Master in 1676-7 and 1685-6, resigning from the corporation in 1689.
4. Robert Waith, paymaster.

christening our wifes and we should have been today, but none
of them went and I am glad of it – for he is a very rogue.   So
home and drew up our[a] report for Sir N. Crisp's Sasse,[1] and so
to bed.

No news yet of our fleet gone to Tanger, which we now begin
to think long.[2]

16.   *Lords day.*   To Church[b] this morning, and so home and
to dinner.   In the afternoon I walked to St. Brides to church,
to hear Dr. Jacomb preach upon the recovery, and at the request
of Mrs. Turner, who came abroad this day, the first time since
her[c] long sickness.   He preached upon Davids words ("I shall not
die, but live and declare the works of the Lord") and made a[d]
pretty good sermon, though not extraordinary.[3]   After sermon
I led her home and sat with her, and there was the Doctor got
before us.   But strange what a command he hath got over Mrs.
Turner, who was so carefull to get him what he would, after his
preaching, to drink; and he, with a cunning gravity, knows how
to command and have it.   And among other things, told us that
he heard more of the Common-prayer this afternoon (while he
stood in the vestry, before he went up into the pulpitt) then he
had heard this 20 years.

Thence to my uncle Wight to meet my wife, and with other
friends of hers and his, met by chance, we were very merry and
supped.   And so home – not being very well, through my usuall
pain, got by Cold.

So to prayers and to bed.   And there had a good draught of
mulled ale brought me.

17.   This morning, both Sir Wms., myself, and Captain

a repl. 'the'   *b* l.h. repl. s.h. 'this'   *c* l.h. repl. s.h. ? 'this'   *d* repl. 'the'

---

1. Navy Board to Lord Treasurer,
19 February (copy in PL 2871, pp.
657–9), advising against use of the
site, and proposing instead the cutting
of a channel from Blackwall through
the Isle of Dogs to Limehouse.   For
the report from Trinity House, see
HMC, *Rep.*, 8/1/1/250 *b*.

2. It had arrived on 29 January:
Sandwich, p. 117.

3. The text was from Ps. 118, xvii;
the preacher (Thomas Jacombe,
Rector of St Martin's, Ludgate Hill) a
Presbyterian.   Jane Turner had been
ill since at least November 1661:
above, ii. 214.

Cock and Captain Tinker (of the *Convertine*, which we are
going to look upon, being entended [to go] with these ships
fitting for the East Indys) down to Deptford; and thence, after
being on ship-board, to Woolwich – and there eat something.
The Sir Wms. being unwilling to eat flesh, Captain Cock and
I had a breast of veale roasted. And here I drank wine upon
necessity, being ill for want of it. And I find reason to fear that
by my too sudden leaving off wine, I do contract many evils
upon myself.

Going and coming, we played at Gleeke, and I won 9s-6*a*d clear,
the most that ever I won in my life.*b* I pray God it may not
tempt me to play again.

Being come home again, we went to the Dolphin, where
Mr. Alcock and my Lady and Mrs. Marth. Batten came to us,
and after them many others (as it always is where Sir W. Batten
goes); and there we had some pulletts to supper. I eat, though
I was not very well; and after that left them, and so home and
to bed.

18. Lay long in bed. Then up to the office (we having
changed our days to Tuseday and Saturday*c* in the morning and
Thursday at night);[1] and by and by, with Sir Wm. Pen, Mr.
Kenard and others to Survey his house again and to contrive for
the alterations there – which will be handsome I think.

After we had done at the office, I walked to the Wardrobe,
where with Mr Moore and Mr Lewes Phillips, after dinner
we did agree upon the agreement between us and Prior, and I
did seal and sign it.[2]

Having agreed with Sir Wm. Pen and my wife to meet them
at the Opera, and finding by my walking in the streets, which
were everywhere full of brick battes and tyeles flung down by the

a repl. '9' *b* l.h. repl. s.h. 'mind' *c* l.h. repl. l.h. 'Thursday'

---

1. Pepys's office memorandum-
book has a note under this date: 'We
altered our sittings to Tuesd. &
Saturday mornings and Thursd.
afternoones': PRO, Adm. 106/3520,
f.6r.

2. This concerned the purchase of
a house at Brampton: see above,
ii. 204 & n. 2.

extraordinary Winde the last night[1] (such as hath not been in memory before, unless at the death of the late Protector),[2] that it was dangerous to go out*a* of doors; and hearing how several persons have been killed today by the fall of things in the streets and that the pageant in Fleetstreete[3] is most of it blown down, and hath broke down part of several houses, among others Dick Brigdens, and that one Lady Sanderson,[4] a person of Quality in Covent garden, was killed by the fall of the house in her bed last night, I sent my boy home to forbid them to go forth. But he bringing me word that they are gone, I went thither and there saw *The Law against Lovers*,[5] a good play and well performed, especially the Little Girle's (who I never saw act before) dancing and singing; and were it not for her, the losse of Roxalana[6] would spoil the house. So home and to Musique, and so to bed.

19. Musique practice. Thence to Trinity-House to conclude upon our report of Sir N. Crisps project; who came to us to

a repl. 'through'

---

1. Dr D. J. Schove writes: ' "Windy Tuesday" was certainly the best documented, and in S. England perhaps the worst, storm between 1362 and 1703. It was associated with the death of the Queen of Bohemia, all Europe being affected by the gales about this time. Rugge (ii, f.12*r*) estimated the damage at £1m. and described the London streets as full of "brick bats, tileshards, spouts, sheets of lead . . . hats and feathers and perriwigs". Cf. below, p. 35 & n. 5; Evelyn, 17 February; *Mirabilis annus secundus* (1662); *A full and certain account of the last great wind* (1661/2); C. E. Britton in *Met. Mag.*, (1939)/22–4.'

2. Cromwell had died on 3 September 1658. The storm in which the Devil ' "*took Bond*" for Oliver's appearance' occurred on 30 August: Wood, *L. & T.*, i. 258, 259.

3. Erected for the coronation of April 1661.

4. *Recte* Lady Saltonstall; (? widow of Sir Richard, nephew of Sir Richard Saltonstall, Lord Mayor, 1597–8).

5. The play was Davenant's adaptation of Shakespeare's *Measure for measure*, with Beatrice, Benedick and the singing Balthasar imported from *Much ado about nothing*; acted for the first time this month and published in Davenant's *Works* in 1673. The identity of the actress playing the little girl is not known; Mrs Norton has been suggested. (A).

6. Mrs Hester Davenport, so called after her part in *The siege of Rhodes*. She had been one of the leading actresses in the Duke of York's Company, but had left the stage to live with Aubrey de Vere, Earl of Oxford: see Gramont, pp. 233–4. (A).

answer objeccions, but we did give him no eare, but are resolved to stand to our report – though I could wish we had shown him more Justice and had heard him.

Thence to the Wardrobe and dined with my Lady, and talked after dinner as I used to do; and so home and up to my chamber to put things in order to my good content; and so to Musique practice.

20. This morning came Mr. Childe to see me, and set me something to my Theorbo.[1]   And by and by comes letters from Tanger from my Lord, telling me how, upon a great defeate given to the Portugeses there by the Moores, he had put in 300 men into the Towne, and so hee*ᵃ* is in possession;[2] of which we are very glad, because now the Spaniards designes of hindering our getting that place are frustrated.   I went with the letters inclosed to my Lord Chancellor to the House of Lords, and did give it him in the House.   And thence to the Wardrobe with my Ladys; and there would not stay dinner, but went by promise to Mr. Savills and there sot the first time for my picture in little,[3] which pleaseth me well.   So to the office till night and then home.

21. All the morning putting things in my house in order and packing up glass to send into the country to my father, and books to my brother John; and then to my Lord Crewes to dinner.   And thence to Mr. Lewes Filipps's chamber, and there made even with him for business, and received 80*l.* upon Jespar Trices account.[4]   So home with it; and so to my chamber for all this evening, and then to bed.

22. At the office busy all the morning; and thence to dinner to my Lady Sandwiches.   And thence with Mr. Moore to our

a l.h. repl. s.h. 'in'

---

1. William Child (one of the King's private musicians) was probably providing theorbo tablature: cf. above, i. 302 & n. 2, 324. (E).

2. Sandwich to Pepys, 20/30 January; printed in HMC, *Eliot Hodgkin*, p. 157 (mistakenly ascribed to 1661). The Portuguese defeat had occurred on 12 January and is described in

Sandwich, pp. 114–15. On the 14th Sandwich sent 80 men from his own ship into the lower castle, and stronger parties went ashore on the 17th and the 23rd. See Sandwich, loc. cit.; Routh, pp. 9–10.

3. Untraced. (OM).

4. Cf. above, ii. 134, n. 2.

Atturny, Wallpooles, and there find that Godfry hath basely taken out a Judgement against us for the 40*l* – for which I am vexed.[1] And thence to buy a pair of stands and a hanging shelf for my wife's chamber, and so home; and thither came Mr. Savill with the pictures and we hung them up in our dining-room; it comes now to appear very handsome with all my pictures.

This evening I wrote letters to my father; among other things, acquainting him with the unhappy accident which hath happened lately to my Lord of Dorsetts two eldest sons; who, with two Bellasses and one Squire Wentworth, were lately apprehended for killing and robbing of a Tanner about Newington on Wednesday last, and are all now in Newgate.[2] I am much troubled for it and for the grief and disgrace it bring to their families and friends. After this, having got a very great cold, I got something warm tonight, and so to bed.

23. *Lords day.* My cold being increased, I stayed at home all day, pleasing myself with my dining-room, now graced with pictures, and reading of Dr. Fullers *worthys.* So I spent the day; and at night comes Sir W. Pen and supped and talked with me. This day, by God's mercy I am 29 years of age, and in very good health and like to live and get an estate; and if I have a heart to be contented, I think I may reckon myself as happy a man as any is in the world – for which God be praised. So to prayers and to bed.

24. Long with Mr. Berchenshaw in the morning at my Musique practice, finishing my song of *Gaze not on swans* in

1. This was a debt owed by Robert Pepys of Brampton at his death: PL (unoff.), Freshfield MSS, nos 8, 9. Pepys (as executor) paid it on the following 9 May: below, p. 80.
2. The incident had occurred on the 18th, at Stoke Newington, Middlesex. The men concerned were Charles, Lord Buckhurst and Edward Sackville, sons of Richard, 5th Earl of Dorset; Sir Henry Belasyse, eldest son of Lord Belasyse; John Belasyse, brother of Lord Fauconberg; and Thomas, only son of Sir G. Wentworth. They had killed the man while pursuing a band of four or five highwaymen, and were later charged with manslaughter and acquitted. See below, pp. 35–6; HMC, *Var. Coll.*, viii. 66.

two parts, which pleases me well.[1]   And I did give him 5*l* for
this month or five weeks that he hath taught me, which is a great
deal of money and troubled me to part with it.   Thence to the
painter's and sat again for my picture in little.   And thence over
the water to Southwarke to Mr. Berchenshaws house and there
sat with him all the afternoon, he showing me his great Card of
the body of Musique, which he cries up for a rare thing; and I
do believe it cost much pains, but is not so usefull as he would
have it.[2]   Then we sat down and set *Nulla nulla sit formido*,[3] and
he hath set it very finely.   So home and to supper; and then
called Will up and chid him before my wife for refusing to go to
church with the maids yesterday, and telling his mistress that he
would not be made a slave of – which vexes me.   So to bed.[a]

25.   All the morning at the office.   At noon with Mr.
Moore to the Coffee-house – where among other things, the
great talk was of the effects of this late great wind;[4] and I heard
one say that he hath five great trees standing together blown
down, and going to lop them – one of them, as soon as the lops
were cut off, did by the weight of the root rise again and fasten.
We have letters from the Forrest of Deane, that above 1000 oakes
and as many beeches are blown down in one walke there.[5]   And
letters from my father tells me of 20 hurt to us down at Brampton.
    This day in the news-booke,[6] I find that my Lord Buckhurst

a entry crowded into bottom of page

---

1. Pepys began the song on 11
February, but Birchensha probably
did most of the composition: see
below, p. 46.   As it was for two
voices it probably followed Birchensha's 'rule', which Pepys used 'to
compose a duo of counterpoint' on
15 October 1665.   (E).
2. Sir John Hawkins (*Gen. hist.
music*, 1776, iv. 447+) refers to a
single sheet by Birchensha, 'Rules and
Directions for composing in Parts'.
(E).
3. Copy in PL 2591, ff. 166*v*-167*v*.
(E).

4. See above, p. 32 & n. 1.
5. D. Furzer to Navy Board, 21
February, Lydney: PRO, SP 29/50,
no. 76: summary in *CSPD 1661-2*,
p. 281.   The gale had occurred on
the 18th, and altogether 3000 trees
were destroyed: *CSPD 1661-2*,
p. 296; H. G. Nicholls, *Forest of Dean*,
p. 39.   A survey of the damage was
made in March–April: PRO, SP 46/
136, no. 30.   It was the largest of the
English nurseries of naval timber.
Cf. PL 2265, no. 56.
6. *Kingd. Intell.*, 24 February, pp.
116-18.   See above, p. 34 & n. 2.

and his fellows have printed their case as they did give in, upon examinacion, to a Justice of peace.   Wherein they make themselfs a very good tale, that they were in pursuite of thiefs and that they took this man for one of them, and so killed him; and that he himself confessed that it was the first time of his robbing and that he did pay dearly for it, as he was a dead man.   But I doubt things will be proved*a* otherwise as they say.

Home to dinner; and by and by comes Mr. Hunt and his wife to see us, and stayed a good while with us.   Then parted, and I to my study in the office – the first time since the alteracion that I have begun to do business myself there, and I think I shall be well pleased with it.[1]

At night home to supper and to bed.

26.   Mr. Berchensha with me all the morning, composing of musique to *This cursed Jeaulousy, what is it?*, a song of Sir W. Davenants.[2]

After dinner I went to my Bookesellers, W. Joyces and several other places, to pay my debts and do business – I being resolved to cast up my accounts within a day or two, for I fear I have run out too far.

In coming home, I met with a face I knew and challenged him, thinking it had been one of the Theatre=musique, and did enquire for a song of him.   But finding it a mistake and that it was a gentleman that comes sometimes to the office,[3] I was much ashamed but made a pretty good excuse, that I took him for a gentleman of Greys Inne who sings well – and so parted. Home for all night and set things in order, and so to bed.

27.   This morning came Mr. Berchensha to me; and in our discourse, I finding that he cries up his rules for most perfect (though I do grant them to be very good, and the best I believe

a   MS. s.h. 'preeved'

---

1. There was now a separate office for Penn and Batten: below, p. 41. For the carpenters' bills (for over £50), see PRO, Adm. 20/4, p. 291.
2. From *The siege of Rhodes* (1656),

p. 28; music untraced.   *Recte* 'what is't'.   (E).
3. Presumably William Pritchard, ropemaker: cf. below, ix. 37.   (E).

that ever yet were made) and that I could not persuade him to
grant wherein they were somewhat lame, we fell to angry
words, so that in a pet he flung out of my chamber and I never
stopped him, being entended to have put him off today whether
this had happened or no, because I think I have all the rules that
he hath to give, and so there remains nothing but practice now to
do me good – and it is not for me to continue with him at 5*l.* per
mensem.

So I settled to put his rules all in fair order in a book,[1] which
was my work all the morning till dinner. After dinner to the
office till late at night; and so home to write by the post, and
so to bed.

28. The boy failing to call us up as I commanded, I was
angry and resolved to whip him for that and many other faults
today. earely with Sir W. Pen by coach to White-hall, to the
Duke of Yorkes chamber; and there I presented him from my
Lord a fine map of Tanger, done by one Captain Beckman, a
Swede that is with my Lord.[2] We stayed looking it over a
great while with the Duke after he was ready.

Thence I by water to the painter's and there sat again for my
face in little; and thence home to dinner – and so at home all
the afternoon. Then came Mr. Moore and stayed and talked
with me; and then I to the office, there being all the Admiralty
papers brought hither this afternoon from Mr. Blackburnes,
where they have lain all this while, ever since my coming into
this office.

This afternoon Mr. Hater received half a year's salary for me,[3]
so that now there is nothing owing me but this Quarter, which will
be out the next month.

---

1. Untraced. (E).
2. This map is now in BL, King's
Maps, CXVII, 78. Martin Beckman
was a military engineer in the English
service. He had accompanied Sandwich on his voyage to take over
Tangier, and was appointed Engineer-
General there in August 1662.
Sandwich's letter to Pepys (20/30
January) entrusting him with the
'little longe box' containing Beck-

man's map, and enjoining him to
show it to no one but to deliver it
himself into the Duke's hands, is in
HMC, *Eliot Hodgkin*, p. 157. Beckman's work on the Tangier fortifica-
tions later brought him into contact
with Pepys. See also his views of
Tangier in BL, Add. 33233, ff. 16–21.
3. PRO, Adm. 20/2, p. 145 (warrant, 25 December 1661, for £87 10s.).

Home; and to be as good as my word, I bid Will get me a rod, and he and I called the boy up to one of the upper rooms of the Controllers house toward the garden, and there I reckoned all his faults and whipped him soundly; but the rods were so small that I fear they did not much hurt to him, but only to my arme, which I am already, within a Quarter of an houre, not able to stir almost. After supper, to bed.

MARCH.

1. This morning I paid Sir Wm. Batten 40*l*, which I have owed him this half year, having borrowed it of him.[1]

Then to the office all the morning. So dined at home. And after dinner comes my uncle Thomas, with whom I have some high words of difference; but ended quietly, though I fear I shall do no good by fair means upon him.

Then my wife and I by coach, first to see my little picture that is a-drawing,[2] and thence to the Opera and there saw *Romeo and Julett*, the first time it was ever acted.[3] But it is the play of itself the worst that ever I heard in my life, and the worst acted that ever I saw these people do; and I am resolved to go no more to see the first time of acting, for they were all of them out more or less.[4] Thence home, and after supper and wrote by the post – I settled to what I have long entended, to cast up my accounts with myself; and after much pains to do it and great fear, I do find that I am 500*l* in money beforehand in the world, which I was afeared I was not. But I find that I have spent above 250*l*[a] this last half year, which troubles me much. But by God's blessing, I am now resolved to take up, having furnished myself with all things for a great while, and tomorrow to think upon some rules and obligacions upon myself to walk by.

So with my mind eased of a great deal of trouble, though with no great content to find myself above 100*l* worse now then I was half a year ago, I went to bed.

2. *Lords day*. With my mind much eased, talking long in bed with my wife about our frugall life for the time to come,

a repl.? '290*l*'

1. It had been borrowed on 31 July 1661.

2. Savill's miniature: see above, p. 33 & n. 3. (OM).

3. I.e. since the Restoration. Shakespeare's tragedy was written about 1595 and published in 1597 (in a garbled form) and in the 1623 Folio. (A).

4. The cast listed by Downes (p. 22) includes Harris as Romeo, Betterton as Mercutio, Mrs Saunderson as Juliet and Price as Paris. For the poor memorising of parts, see above, ii. 8 & n. 2. (A).

proposing to her what I could and would do if I were worth 2000*l*; that is, be a Knight and keep my coach[1] – which pleased her; and so I do hope we shall hereafter live to save something, for I am resolved to keep myself by rules from expences.

To church in the morning; none in the pew but myself. So home to dinner. And after dinner came Sir Wm and talked with me till church-time; and then to church, where at our going out I was at a loss by Sir W. Pen's putting me upon it whether to take my wife or Mrs*a* Martha (who alone was there); and I begun to take my wife, but he jogged me and so I took Martha and led her down before him and my wife. So set her at home, and Sir Wm and my wife and I to walk in the garden; and anon, hearing that Sir G. Carteret hath sent to see whether we were at home or no, Sir Wm and I went to his house; where we waited a good while, they being at prayers, and by and by we went up to him; there the business was about hastening the East India ships, about which we are to meet tomorrow in the afternoon.[2]

So home to my house and Sir Wm. supped with me and so to bed.

3d.   All the morning at home about business with my brother Tom and then with Mr. Moore; and then I set to make some strict rules for my future practice in my expenses, which I did bind myself in the presence of God by oath to observe, upon penaltys therein set down. And I do not doubt but hereafter to give a good account of my time and to grow rich – for I do find a great deal more of content in those few days that I do spend well about my business then in all the pleasures of a whole week, besides the trouble which I remember I always have after them for the expense of my money.

Dined at home and then up to my chamber again about

a repl. 'is' (i.e. his)

---

1. The coach came in 1668 (when he was worth about £8000); the knighthood never: cf. above, i. 318, n. 2.

2. A squadron of five ships sailed in early April to take possession of Bombay as part of the dowry of Catherine of Braganza: *Cal. court mins E. India Co., 1660-3* (ed. E.B. Sainsbury), pp. xxii–xxiii. The Duke of York in a letter this day had ordered the Board to hasten their victualling: PRO, Adm. 106/6, f.299r.

business; and so to the office – about despatching of the East
India ships, where we stayed till 8 at night; and then after I had
been at Sir Wm. Pens awhile, discoursing with him and Mr.
Kenard the Joyner about the new building in his house,[1] I went
home, where I find a vessel of oysters sent me from Chatham.
And I fell to eat some and then to supper; and so after the
barber had done, to bed.

I am told that this day the Parliament hath voted 2s per annum
for every chimney in England, as a constant Revenue for ever to
the Crowne.[2]

4th.[a] At the office all the morning. Dined at home at noon.
And then to the office again in the afternoon to put things in
order there, my mind being very busy in settling the office to
ourselfs, I having now got distinct offices for the other two.[3]

By and by, Sir W. Penn and I and my wife in his Coach to
Moore-fields, where we walked a great while, though it was
no fair weather and cold; and after our walk we went to the
Popeshead and eat cakes and other fine things, and so home.
I up to my chamber to read and write, and so to bed.

5. In the morning to the paynters about my little picture.
Thence to Toms about business; and so to the pewterers to buy
a poore's box to put my forfeites in, upon breach of my late vowes.
So to the Wardrobe and dined, and thence home and to my
office and there sat looking over my papers of my voyage when
we fetched over the King, and tore so many of those that were
worth nothing, as filled my closet as high as my knees. I stayed
doing this till 10 at night; and so home and to bed.

6. Up earely, my mind full of business. Then to the office,
where the two Sir Wms and I spent the morning passing the

a MS. '4d'

---

1. See above, p. 28 & n. 3.
2. The Chimney-Money (Hearth-Tax) Bill was this day given a second reading, and committed: *CJ*, viii. 378. It became law in July. It was designed to supply the amount by which the revenue was calculated to fall short of the £1,200,000 p.a. agreed on in 1660 as an adequate income. It

proved unpopular and hard to collect, and was repealed in 1689.
3. Penn and Batten; they now presumably shared an office: in 1667 Penn was attempting to get one to himself: below, viii. 30. Their clerks would occupy the other new office.

Victuallers accounts – the first I have had to do withal.¹ Then home, where my uncle Thomas (by promise, and his Son Tom) was come to give me his answer whether he would have me go to law or arbitracion with him.² But he is unprovided to answer me and desires two days more.

I left them to dine with my wife, and myself to Mr. Gawden and the two Knights at dinner at the Dolphin; and thence after dinner to the office back again till night – we having been these four or five days very full of business, and I thank God I am well pleased with it – and hope I shall continue of that temper – which God grant.

So after a little being at Sir W. Battens with*ᵃ* Sir G. Carteret talking, I went home; and so to my chamber and then to bed – my mind somewhat troubled at Brampton affaires. This night my new Camelott riding Coate to my coloured cloth suit came home. More news today of our losses at Brampton by the late storm.³

7. early to White-hall to the Chappell; where by Mr. Blagraves's⁴ means, I got into his pew*ᵇ* and heard Dr Creeton, the great Scoch man, preach – before the King and Duke and Duchesse – upon the words of Michah: "Roule yourselves in dust."⁵ He made a most learned sermon upon the words; but in his applicacion, the most Comicall man that ever I heard in my life – just such a man as Hugh peters.⁶ Saying that it had been better for the poor Cavalier never to have come in with the King into England again; for he that hath the impudence to deny

1. Denis Gauden had been appointed contractor for navy victualling in 1660. A summary of his accounts, 1 November 1660–c. 31 March 1662, is in BL, Add. 9296, ff. 131*v*–132*r*.

2. In the dispute over the Brampton inheritance: see above, ii. 135, n. 2.

3. See above, p. 32.

4. Thomas Blagrave, court musician and member of the Chapel Royal. (E).

5. A loose recollection of Micah, i. 10. Robert Creighton, chaplain to the King, was Dean (later Bishop) of Bath and Wells, and Professor of Greek and Public Orator at Cambridge. Pepys always enjoyed his verve and humour in the pulpit; Evelyn found him 'extravagant' but 'very eloquent' (17 November 1661, 29 May 1663). For his 'strange bold sermon' on adultery (preached before the King), see below, viii. 362.

6. The Independent preacher, popular during the 'fifties. For a reference to the style of one of his sermons, see below, iv. 93.

obedience to the lawful magistrate and to swear to the oath of allegeance &c, were better treated nowadays in newgate then a poor Royalist that hath suffered all his life for the King is at White-hall among his friends.[1]   He discoursed much against a man's lying with his wife in Lent, saying that he might be as incontinent during that time with his own wife as at another time in another man's bed.

Thence with Mr. Moore to Westminster-hall and walked a little; and so to the Wardrobe to dinner, and so home to the office about business till late at night, by myself; and so home and to bed.

8. By coach with both Sir Wms. to Westminster – this being a great day there in the House, to pass the business for Chimney=mony – which was done.[2]

In the hall I met with Serjeant Pierce; and he and I to drink a cup of ale at the Swan, and there he told me how my Lady Monke[3] hath disposed of all the places which Mr. Edw. Mountagu hoped to have had, as he was Maister of the horse to the Queene.[4] Which I am afeared will undo him, because he depended much upon the profit of what he should make by those places.   He told me also many more Scurvy stories of him and his Brother Ralph, which troubles me to hear of persons of Honour, as they are.

About one a-clock, with both Sir Wms and another, one Sir Rich. Brames, to the Trinity-house; but came after they had dined, so we had something got ready for us.   Here Sir W. Batten was taken with a fit of coughing that lasted a great while and made him very ill, and so he went home sick upon it.

Sir W. Penn and I to the office, whither afterward came Sir G. Carteret, and we sent for Sir Tho. Allen, one of the Aldermen of the City – about the business of one Collonell Appesley,[5]

1. A common complaint: the court lacked the means of compensation. Relief of needy royalist soldiers by taxation was provided by two acts (one of which had just passed the Commons) of May 1662. *CJ*, viii. 376.

2. The bill, passed through Committee on this day, received royal assent on 19 May: *CJ*, viii. 382; *LJ*, xi. 471.

3. Her husband (Albemarle) was

Master of the Horse to the King.

4. The Queen Mother.

5. The Officers of the Navy Board (although J.P.'s for Middlesex) lacked until 1664 the power to issue warrants for arrest within the city (below, iv. 82 & n. 1); hence their sending for a magistrate.   The records of the city courts are defective for this period, and nothing more has been discovered about this case.

who we had taken counterfeiting of bills with all our hands and the officers of the yards, so well counterfeit that I should never have mistrusted them. We stayed about this business at the office till 10 at night, and at last did send him with a Constable to the Counter.[1]   And did give warrants for the seizing of a complice of his, one Blinkinsopp.

So home and wrote to my father, and so to bed.

9.   *Lords day.*   Church in the morning. Dined at home. Then to church again and heard Mr. Naylor (whom I knew formerly, of Keyes College)[2] make a most eloquent sermon. Thence to Sir W. Batten to see how he did.   Then to walk an houre with Sir W. Penn in the garden; then he into supper with me at my house, and so to prayers and to bed.

10.   At the office, doing business all the morning.   And my wife being gone to buy some things in the City, I dined with Sir W. Batten; and in the afternoon met Sir W. Pen at the Treasury Office and there paid off the *Guift* – where late at night, and so called in and eat a bit at Sir W. Battens again; and so home and to bed, tomorrow being washing-day.

11.   At the office all the morning.   And all the afternoon rumaging of papers in my chamber, and tearing some and sorting others till late at night, and so to bed – my wife being not well all this day.   This afternoon Mrs. Turner and The. came to see me – her mother not having been abroad many a day before, but now is pretty well again and hath made me one of the first visitts.

12.   At the office from morning till night, putting of papers in order, that so I may have my office in an orderly condition. I took much pains in sorting and folding of papers.[3]   Dined at home, and there came Mrs. Goldsborough about her old business,[4] but I did give her a short answer and sent her away.

This morning we have news from Mr. Coventry that Sir

---

1. A city prison.

2. Oliver Naylor, Prebendary of Exeter, had been a Fellow of Caius College, Cambridge, 1651-9.

3. Pepys usually wrote a summary of each paper on the outer fold.

4. A debt owed to Robert Pepys of Brampton: see above, ii. 195, n. 3.

G. Downing (like a perfidious rogue, though the action is good and of service to the King, yet he cannot with any good conscience do it) hath taken Okey, Corbet, and Barkestead at Delfe in Holland and sent them home in the *Blackmore*.[1]

Sir Wm. Pen, talking to me this afternoon of what a strange thing it is for Downing to do this – he told me of a speech he made to the Lords States of Holland, telling them to their faces that he observed that he was not received with the respect and observance now, that he was when he came from that Traitor and Rebell, Cromwell – by whom I am sure he hath got all he hath in the world – and they know it too.[2]

13. All day either at*ª* the office or at home, busy about business till late at night – I having lately fallowed my business much. And I find great pleasure in it, and a growing content.

14. At the office all the morning. At noon Sir W. Penn and I making a bargaine with the workmen about his house. In which I did see things not so well contracted for as I would have, and I was vexed and made him so too, to see me so criticall in the agreement. Home to dinner. In the afternoon came the German, Dr Kuffler, to discourse with us about his Engine to blow up ships. We doubted not [the] matter of fact, it being

a l.h. repl. s.h. 'all'

---

1. John Okey, Miles Corbet and John Barkstead, regicides who had taken flight, had been arrested by special command of Downing, ambassador to Holland, himself an ex-rebel. According to a contemporary pamphleteer, Downing had once been preacher to Okey's regiment, and he is said, moreover, to have given Okey an assurance that he would not be arrested: Ludlow, ii. 330–1; *The speeches . . . of Col. John Barkstead* (1662), pp. 1–2. He chose to act first and inform the Dutch afterwards. But he had obtained Clarendon's assent to this method

beforehand: Lister, iii. 151–2, 155, 169. Cf. also R. C. H. Catterall in *AHR*, 17/268+.

2. Since October 1661 Downing had refused to attend any conferences with the deputies of the States General because they denied him the courtesies which he claimed they had always in the past given to ambassadors, himself included. See his despatches to Clarendon (25 October, and 8 November: Bodl., Clar. 105, ff. 86+, 108+), in which he blamed de Witt and the republicans. Downing had previously served in The Hague, 1657–60.

tried in Cromwells time, but the safety of carrying them in ships; but he doth tell us that when he comes to tell the King his Secret (for none but the Kings successively, and their heires, must know it), it will appear to be of no danger at all.[1]

We concluded nothing, but shall discourse with the Duke of Yorke tomorrow about it.

In the afternoon, after we had done with him, I went to speak with my uncle Wight and find my aunt to have been ill a good while of a miscarriage. I stayed and talked with her a good while.

Thence home – where I find that Sarah my mayd hath been very ill all day, and my wife fears that she will have an ague, which I am much troubled for.

Then to my lute, upon which I have not played a week or two; and trying over the two songs of *Nulla nulla*, &c and *Gaze not on Swans*, which Mr. Berchinsha set for me a little while ago, I find them most incomparable songs as he hath set them – of which I am not a little proud, because I am sure none in the world hath them but myself, not so much as he himself that set[a] them.[2]

So to bed.

a repl. 'made'

---

1 For mines, see e.g. *Tangier Papers*, p. 44. The inventor of this 'Engine' was Cornelis van Drebbel (d. 1633). His son Jacob and son-in-law Johannes Siberius Kuffeler now asked for a trial, and for a reward of £10,000 if it were successful: *CSPD 1661–2*, p. 327. It is described by Monconys (ii. 40), who visited 'Dr. Keiffer' at Stratford-atte-Bowe in 1663, as 'un instrument d'environ neuf pouces en quarré, lequel se met au bout d'eun baston de 20 pieds de long, lequel si-tost qu'il est appliqué contre un Vaisseau, le ressort se desbandant allume une poudre de telle force, & vertu, qu'à l'instant mesme elle fait perir ce Vaisseau, de quelque grandeur qu'il puisse estre, sans endommager celuy qui l'a appliqué, parce que tout son effet se fait en avant, & non pas en haut ny en arriere, dont il fit voir l'experience à Cromwell, lequel estoit en traitte avec luy pour l'acheter lors qu'il mourut. Despuis on a desconseillé le Roy de l'auoir, de crainte qu'il ne se communiquast, & ne fût plus preiudiciable qu'avantageux à l'Angleterre, comme il le seroit à tout le genre humain.' Monconys alleges that Kuffeler had added nothing to the work of his father-in-law. There was also a design for a submarine: Birch, ii. 362. See also S. de Sorbière, *Relation d'un voyage en Angleterre* (Cologne, 1667), p. 50.

2. Cf. above, pp. 27, 34–5. (E).

15. With Sir G. Carteret and both the Sir Wms. at White-hall to wait on the Duke in his chamber, which we did, about getting money for the navy – and other things. So back again to the office all the morning. Then to the Exchange to hire a ship for the Maderas,[1] but could get none. Then home to dinner, and Sir G. Carteret and I all the afternoon by ourselfs upon business in the office, till late at night: so to write letters and home to bed – troubled at my maid's being ill.

16. *Lords day.* This morning, till Churches[a] were done, I spent going from one church to another and hearing a bit here and a bit there. So to the Wardrobe to dinner with the young ladies, and then into my Lady's chamber and talked with her a good while. And so walked to White-hall, an houre or two in the parke – which is now very pleasant. Here the King and Duke came to see their fowle play.[2] The Duke took very civil notice of me. So walked home, calling at Tom's, giving him my resolution about my boy's Livery. Here I spent an houre walking in the garden with Sir W. Penn: and then[b] my wife and I thither to supper – where his son Wm. is at home, not well. But all things, I fear, do not go well with them; they look discontently, but I know not what ales them. Drinking of cold small beer here, I fell ill and was forced to go out and vomit; and so was well again, and went home by and by to bed.[c] Fearing that Sarah would continue ill, wife and I removed this night to our matted chamber and lay there.

17. All the morning at the office by myself, about setting things in order there; and so at noon to the Exchange to see and be seen; and so home to dinner and then to the office again till night; and then home, and after supper and reading a while, to bed.

Last night the *Blackmore* pinke brought the three prisoners, Barkstead, Okey, and Corbet, to the tower – being taken at Delfe in Holland; where the Captain tells me the Dutch were a

_a_ l.h. repl. s.h. 'children'   _b_ symbol blotted
_c_ This entry up to this point, and the preceding one, are crowded into the bottom of the page.

---

1. See below, p. 51.   2. For the birds in the park, see above, ii. 157, n. 1.

good while before they could be persuaded to let them go, they being taken prisoners in their land.[1]   But Sir G. Downing would not be answered so – though all the world takes notice of him for a most ungratefull villaine for his pains.

18.   All the morning at the office with Sir W. Pen.   Dined at home, and Luellin and Blurton with me.   After dinner to the office again, where Sir George Carteret and we stayed awhile, and then[a] Sir W. Pen and I on board some of the ships now fitting for East Indys and Portugall, to see in what forwardness they are.   And so back home again.   And I to write to my father by the post about Brampton Court, which is now coming on.   But that which troubles me is that my father hath now got an Ague that I fear may endanger his life.   So to bed.

19.   All the morning and afternoon at my office, putting things in order.   And in the evening I do begin to digest my uncle the Captain's papers into one book, which I call my *Brampton=booke*,[2] for my clearer understanding things how they are with us.

So home and supper and to bed.

This noon came a letter from T. Pepys the Turner, in answer to one of mine the other day to him, wherein I did cheque him for not coming to me, as he had promised, with his and his father's resolucion about the difference between us.   But he writes to me in the very same slighting terms that I did to him, without the least respect at all, but word for word as I did him – which argues a high and noble spirit in him; though it troubles me a little that he should make no more of my anger, yet I cannot blame him for doing so, he being the elder brother's son[3] and not depending upon me at all.

20.   At my office all the morning.   At noon to the Exchange, and so home to dinner; and then all the afternoon at the office,

a preceded by symbol rendered illegible

1. The provincial government of Holland tried to shift the responsibility to the municipal magistrates of Delft: *Speeches . . . of Col. John Barkstead . . .* (1662), p. 3; A. L. Pontalis, *de Witt* (trans., 1885), i. 269.
2. Untraced.
3. I.e. son of the elder brother of Capt. Robert Pepys, whose estate was in dispute.

till late at night. And so home and to bed. My mind in good ease when I mind business, which methinks should be a good argument to me never to do otherwise.

21. With Sir W. Batten by water to White-hall, and he to Westminster. I went to see Sarah and my Lord's Lodgeings, which are now all in dirt, to be repaired against my Lord's coming from sea with the Queene. Thence to Westminster-hall and there walked up and down and heard the great difference that hath been*a* between my Lord Chancellor and my Lord of Bristoll, about a proviso that my Lord Chancellor would have brought into the bill for Conformity, that it shall be in the power of the King, when he sees fit, to dispence with the act of Conformity. And though it be carried in the House of Lords, yet it is believed it will hardly pass in the Commons.[1] Here I met with Chetwind, Parry, and several others, and went to a little house behind the Lords' house to drink some Wormewood ale, which doubtless was a bawdy house – the mistress of the house having that look and dress. Here we stayed till noon and then parted. I by water to the Wardrobe to meet my wife; but my Lady and they had dined, and so I dined below with the servants; and then up to my Lady, and there stayed and talked a good while; and then parted and walked into Chepside and there saw my little picture, for which I am to sit again the next

a repl. 'like to be'

---

1. The bill of uniformity (ultimately passed on 19 May) was now being debated, and this proviso, introduced by Clarendon, would have allowed, to those ministers who wanted it, freedom not to wear the surplice, and (in the baptismal service) freedom to omit the sign of the cross. It was one of the concessions to moderate Presbyterians which Clarendon now favoured, and which Bristol opposed in a series of bitter speeches on 19-21 March. The account of the Venetian Resident (21 March) is almost the same as Pepys's: 'Even if it should be carried by virtue of the authority of the Chancellor, who, though no Presbyterian, supports that party because it is strong, to have it on his side in case of need, there is not the smallest sign that it would be passed by the Commons, on account of the animosity of the majority there against the Presbyterians, and of their rancour against the Chancellor . . .'; *CSPVen. 1661-4*, pp. 124-5. The proviso passed the Lords on 9 April and was defeated in the Commons on the 22nd. For Clarendon's attitude, see G. R. Abernathy in *Journ. Eccles. Hist.*, 11/55+.

week. So home, and stayed late writing at my office; and so home and to bed – troubled that now my boy is also fallen sick of an ague we fear.

22. At the office all the morning. At noon, Sir Wms both and I by water down to the *Lewes*, Captain Dekins his ship, a merchantman – where we met the owners, Sir John Lewes and Alderman Lewes and several other great merchants; among others, one Jefferys, a merry man that is a fumbler; and he and I called brothers,[1] and he made all the mirth in the company. We had a very fine dinner, and all our wifes' healths with seven or nine guns apiece.[2] And exceeding merry we were, and so home by barge again; and I vexed to find Griffin leave the office door open, and had a design to have carried away the Screw or the carpet in revenge to him; but at last I would not, but sent for him and chid him; and so to supper and to bed – having drank a great deal of wine.

23. *Lords day.* This morning was brought me my boyes fine livery, which is very handsome, and I do think to keep to black and gold lace upon gray, being the colour of my armes, for ever.[3] To church in the morning. And so home*a* with Sir W. Batten and there eat some boiled great oysters; and so home, and while I was at dinner with my wife, I was sick and was forced to vomitt up my oysters again, and then I was well.

a repl. 'at'

---

1. He was childless – hence a 'fumbler' and a 'brother' of Pepys.

2. An even number signalled a funeral.

3. He later changed the colour of the livery: below, 22 November 1668. Pepys now used the arms confirmed to Thomas Pepys of South Creake, Norf., in 1563: J. Foster, *Grantees of arms* (ed. Rylands), p. 197. They were sable, on a bend or, between two nags' heads erased argent, three fleurs de lys of the field. They are still to be seen on the monument he put up to his wife in St Olave's after her death in 1669, and on the rosewater cup and dish he gave as Master to the Clothworkers' Company in 1677: *Pepysiana*, p. 43. The arms of Samuel Pepys illustrated in John Guillim's *Display of heraldry* (1679, p. 291) are those of Pepys quartered with those of Talbot – a version deriving from the marriage of John Pepys (the diarist's great-grandfather) with the heiress Edith Talbot. Pepys seems to have used this version in later life.

By and by a Coach came to call me, by my appointment, and so my wife and I carried to Westminster to Mrs. Hunts; and I to White-hall, Worster-house, and to my Lord Treasurers to have found Sir G. Carteret, but missed in all those places. So back to White-hall and there met with Captain Isham, this day come from Lisbone with letters from the Queene to the King. And did give me letters which speak that our fleet is all at Lisbon; and that the Queene doth not entend to embarque sooner then tomorrow come fortnight.[1]

So having sent for my wife, she and I to my Lady Sandwich; and after a short visit, away home, she home and I to Sir G. Carterets about business, and so home too. And Sarah having her fit, we went to bed.

24. earely, Sir G. Carteret, both Sir Wms, and I on board the *Experiment* to dispatch her away, she being to carry things to the Maderas with the East India fleet.[2] Here (Sir W. Penn going to Deptford to send more hands), we stayed till noon, talking and eating and drinking a good ham of English bacon; and having put things in good order, home – where I find Jane, my old maid, come out of the country; and I have a mind to have her again.[3]

By and by comes *la Belle* Perce to see my wife and to bring her a pair of peruques of hair, as the fashion now is for ladies to wear – which are pretty and*a* are of my wife's own hair, or else I should not endure them. After a good while stay, I went to see if any play was acted, and I*b* find none upon the post,[4] it being passion weeke. So home again and took water with them towards Westminster; but as we put off with the boate, Griffen came after me, to tell me that Sir G. Carteret and

a repl. 'is'   *b* repl. 'and not till'

---

1. She embarked on 13 April: Sandwich, pp. 130-2. Isham had left Lisbon on 6 March: ib., p. 123. These last-mentioned letters are not among the Lisbon letters from John Creed to Pepys in BL, Add. 38849; but his letter of 26 March/5 April (ib., f. 23r–v) also mentions the delay.

2. See above, p. 40 & n. 2.
3. Jane Birch served the Pepyses from August 1658 to August 1661, from March 1662 to February 1663, and from March 1666 to March 1669.
4. Playbills were displayed outside the theatres and on posts in the streets. (Hence 'poster'.)   (A).

the rest were at the office; so I entended to see them through
the bridge and come back again, but the tide being against us
when we were almost through, we were carried back again with
much danger, and Mrs. Pierce was much afeared and frighted.
So I carried them to the other side and walked to the beare and
sent ⟨them⟩ away; and so back again myself to the office.   But
finding nobody there, I went again to the old swan and thence
by water to the New Ex[c]hange and there find them; and thence
by coach carried my wife to Bowes to buy something; and
while they were there, went to Westminster-hall and there
bought Mr. Grant's book of observations upon the weekely bills
of Mortality[1] – which appear to me, upon first sight, to be very
pretty.

So back again and took my wife, calling at my brother
Tom's, whom I find full of work, which I am glad of; and
thence at the New Exchange and so home.   And I to Sir W.
Battens and supped there, out of pure hunger and to save getting
anything ready at home, which is a thing I do not nor shall not
use to do.

So home and to bed.

25. *Lady day*. All the morning at the office. Dined with
my wife at home.   Then to the office, where (while Sir Wms
both did examine the Victuallers account)[2] I sat in my closet
drawing letters and other businesses – being much troubled for
want of an order of the Councells lately sent us, about making
of boates for some ships now going to Jamaica.[3]   At last, late at
night, I had a Copy sent me of it by Sir G. Lane[4] from the Council
Chamber. With my mind well at ease, home and to supper
and bed.

1. John Graunt, *Natural and political
observations . . . made upon the bills of
mortality* (1662); one of the earliest
English treatises on vital statistics;
PL 891 (1) (5th ed., 1676). The long-
held view that Graunt's friend, Sir
William Petty, should have the credit
for the book is now discounted:
D. V. Glass in *Proc. Roy. Soc.* B 159/
14 +. Cf. also Dr de Beer's review
of the evidence in Evelyn, iv. 60, n. 3.

2. See above, p. 42 & n. 1.
3. On the 12th the Council's Committee for Jamaica had asked the Navy
Board for an estimate for this purpose.
Pepys and Batten now sent it: its
receipt was acknowledged on 4
April.   PRO, PC 6/1, pp. 27, 28–9;
Acts of Privy Council Col. 1613–80,
pp. 324–5, 327–8.   For the voyage to
Jamaica, see below, p. 63.
4. Clerk of the Council.

26.   Up earely – this being, by God's great blessing, the fourth solemne day of my cutting for the stone this day four year.   And am by God's mercy in very good health, and like to do well, the Lord's name be praised for it.   To the office and Sir G. Carterets all the morning, about business.   At noon came my good guest[s] Madam Turner, The, and Cosen Norton, and a gentleman, one Mr. Lewin of the King's life-guard; by the same token he told us of one of his fellows, killed this morning in the dewell.   I had a pretty dinner for them – *viz*: a brace of stewed Carps, six roasted chicken, and a Jowle of salmon hot, for the first course – a Tanzy and two neats' tongues and cheese the second.   And were very merry all the afternoon, talking and singing and piping on the Flagelette.   In the evening they went with great pleasure away; and I with great content, and my wife, walked half an houre in the garden; and so home to supper and to bed.

We had a man-cook to dress dinner today, and sent for Jane to help us.   And my wife and she agreed at 3*l* a year (she would not serve under) till both could be better provided; and so she stays with us – and I hope we shall do well if poor Sarah were but rid of her ague.*a*

27.   earely, Sir G. Carteret, both Sir Wms. and I by Coach to Deptford, it being very windy and rainy weather – taking a Codd and some prawnes in Fishstreete with us.

We settled to pay the *Guernsy* – a small ship, but came to a great*b* deal of money, it having been unpaid ever since before the King came in[1] – by which means, not only the King pays wages while the ship hath lain still, but the poor men have most of them been forced to borrow all*c* the money due for their wages before they receive it, and that at a dear rate, God knows. So that many of them had very little to receive at the table – which grieved me to see it.

To dinner, very merry.   Then Sir George to London, and

a 'and I ...' crowded into bottom of page   b repl. 'great'
c l.h. repl. s.h. 'their'

1. Her pay (for 24 June 1660-27   £3000: PRO, Adm. 20/2, p. 186
March 1662) amounted to almost   She was a 5th-rate.

we again to the pay; and that done, by Coach home again – and to the office, doing some business, and so home and to bed.

28. *Good friday*. At home all the morning. And dined with my wife, a good dinner. At my office all the afternoon. At night to my chamber to read and sing; and so to supper and to bed.

29. At the office all the morning. Then to the Wardrobe; and there coming late, dined with the people below. Then up to my Lady and stayed two houres, talking with her about her family business, with great content and confidence in me. So calling at several places, I went home; where my people are getting the house clean against tomorrow. I to the office and wrote several letters by post; and so home and to bed.

30. *Easterday*. Having my old black suit new-furbished, I was pretty neat in clothes today – and my boy, his old suit new-trimmed, very handsome. To church in the morning. And so home, leaving the two Sir Wms. to take the Sacrament – which I blame myself that I have hitherto neglected all my life, but once or twice at Cambridge.[1] Dined with my wife, a good shoulder of veal, well dressed by Jane and handsomely served to table – which pleased us much and made us hope that she will serve our turns well enough.

My wife and I to church in the afternoon and seated ourselfs, she below me; and by that means the precedence of the pew

---

1. At this period there was monthly communion at St Olave's (GL, MS. 863), but in the whole of the diary Pepys never once records receiving it. At Christmas of this year he intended to, but 'came a little too late'; on Easterday of both 1662 and 1665 he went to church but left it to his companions to stay on for communion. It is unlikely that he failed to record his attendances. But speaking in the Commons on 16 February 1674 and defending himself against the charge of Popery, he is reported to have affirmed, 'without ostentation', that he 'received the communion seven or eight times, and not less than six times a year, in twenty years': Grey, ii. 426. And in 1681 Dr Milles, Rector of St Olave's, certified that he had been a constant communicant, and from June 1660 until Whitsunday 1681 had missed only two of the principal celebrations: Rawl. A175, f.266r. Pepys dictated the form of the certificate: Rawl. A194, f.248v. Milles seems to have given him a similar certificate in 1672 on the occasion of his candidature for parliament: Smith, i. 142.

which my Lady Batten and her daughter takes, is confounded.[1]
And after sermon she and I did stay behind them in the pew and
went out by ourselfs a good while after them – which we judge
a very fine project hereafter, to avoyd contention.

So my wife and I to walk an hour or two on the leads; which
begins to be very pleasant, the garden being in good condition.

So to supper, which is also well served in. We had a lobster
to supper, with[a] a crabb Pegg Pen sent my wife this afternoon;
the reason of which we cannot think, but something there is of
plot or design in it – for we have a little while carried ourselfs
pretty strange to them.

After supper, to bed.

31. This morning Mr. Coventry and all our company met
at the office about some business of the victualling; which being
dispatched, we parted.

I to my Lord Crewes to dinner (in my way calling upon my
brother Tom, with whom I stayed a good while and talked, and
find him a man like to do well, which contents me much), where
used with much respect. And talking with him about my Lord's
debts and whether we should make use of an offer of Sir G.
Carteret's to lend my Lady 4 or 500*l*[b], he told me by no means,
we must not oblige my Lord to him. And by the by he made
a Question whether it were not my Lord's interest a little to appear
to the King[c] in debt, and for people to clamour against him
as well as others for their money, that by that means the King
and the world may see that he doth lay out for the King's honour
upon his own main stock – which many, he tells me, do.[2] But
in fine, if there be occasion, he[3] and I will be bound for it.

Thence to Sir Tho. Crewes lodgings: he hath been ill and
continues so, under fits of appoplexy. Among other things, he
and I did discourse much of Mr. Mountagu's base doings and

---

a MS.'which with'   *b* figure smudged   *c* MS.'Lord'

---

1. There were three pews in the
Navy Board gallery; the one below
would be at the front. Cf. below,
p. 177.

2. The reference here is perhaps

principally to the expenses of Sandwich's embassy to Portugal: cf.
below, p. 121, n.1 .

3. Crew.

the dishonour that he will do my Lord, as well as cheating him of 2 or 3000*l*:, which is too true.

Thence to the play; where, coming late and meeting with Sir W. Pen, who had got room for my wife and his daughter in the pit, he and I into one of the boxes, and there we sat and heard *The Little thiefe*,[1] a pretty play and well done.

Thence home and walked in the garden with them; and then to my house to supper and sat late talking, and so to bed.[a]

a entry crowded into bottom of page

---

1. A comedy by John Fletcher and James Shirley: see above, ii. 65 & n. 1. As this play was now in the repertoire of the King's Company, Pepys evidently saw it at the TR Vere St. (A).

APRILL.

1. Within all the morning and at the office. At noon, my wife and I (having paid our mayde Nell her whole wages, who hath been with me half a year and now goes away for altogether) – to the wardrobe – where my Lady and company had almost dined. We sat down and dined. Here was Mr. Herbert, son to Sir Charles Herbert,[1] that lately came with letters from my Lord Sandwich to the King. After some discourse, we remembered one another to have been together at the taverne when Mr. Fanshaw took his leave of me at his going to Portugall with Sir Richard.[2]

After dinner he and I and the*a* two young ladies[3] and my wife to the playhouse, the Opera, and saw *The Mayd in the mill*,[4] a pretty good play. In the middle of the play, my Lady Paulina, who had taken physique this morning, had need to go forth; and so I took the poor lady out and carried her to the Grange,[5] and there sent the mayde of the house into a room to her, and she did what she had a mind to. And so back again to the play. And that being done, in their coach I took them to Islington; and there, after a walk in the fields, I took them to the great Chescake-house[6] and entertained them, and so home; and after an hour stay with my Lady, their coach carried us home; and so, weary to bed.

2. Mr. Moore came to me and he and I walked to the Spittle, an hour or two before my Lord Mayor and the Blewe coate boys came, which at last they did, and a fine sight of charity it is

a repl. 'two'

---

1. Charles, son of Sir Charles Harbord.

2. See above, ii. 163.

3. Sandwich's daughters, Jemima and Paulina.

4. A comedy by Fletcher and

Rowley (q.v. above, ii. 25, n. 4). A.

5. An inn close by, near Portugal Row, Lincoln's Inn Fields. (R).

6. The King's Head; an inn much favoured by Pepys: cf. above, ii. 125 & n. 2.

endeed.[1] We got places and stayed to hear a sermon; but it being a presbyterian one, it was so long, that after above an hour of it we went away;[2] and I home and dined, and then my wife and I by water to the Opera and there saw *The Bondman* most excellently acted; and though we had seen it so often, yet I never liked it better then today, Ianthe acting Clerora's part very well now Roxalana is gone.[3] We are resolved to see no more plays till Whitsontide, we having been three days together. I met Mr. Sanchy, Smithes, Gale and Edlin at the play;[4] but having no great mind to spend money, I left them there. And so home and to supper; and then dispatch some business, and to bed.

3. At home and the office all the day. At night to bed.

4. By barge, Sir George, Sir Wms. both, and I, to Deptford; and there fell to pay off the *Drake* and *Hampshire*.[a] Then to dinner. Sir George to his Lady at his house and Sir W. Pen to Woolwich, and Sir Wm. Batten and I to the taverne, where much company came to us, and our dinner somewhat short, by

a repl. '*Sophia*'

---

1. The occasion was one of the 'Spital' (Hospital) sermons, usually on charity, given at Easter in Spital Sq., Spitalfields, and attended by Bluecoat boys of Christ's Hospital, with representatives of four other royal hospitals—St Bartholomew's, Bridewell, Bethlehem (Bedlam) and St Thomas's. The sermons, originally five in number, dwindled in the later 17th century to three, later to two, and nowadays to one. For their history (continuous since Richard II's time except for the Interregnum), see E. H. Pearce, *Annals Christ's Hosp.*, pp. 217–27; A. R. Wright, *British cal. customs: Engl.* (ed. Lones), i. 113–14. The Lord Mayor was Sir John Frederick.

2. The sermons were usually long. Isaac Barrow once preached for $3\frac{1}{2}$ hours: W. Pope, *Seth Ward* (1697), p. 148.

3. For the play, see above, ii. 47, n. 2; now at the LIF. Mary Saunderson, later Mrs Betterton, was one of the leading actresses in the Duke of York's company, and is here called 'Ianthe' after the part she played in *The siege of Rhodes*. 'Roxalana' was Hester Davenport, and was so-called after her part in the same work. She had been enticed from the stage by the Earl of Oxford; see above, p. 32; below, p. 86. (A).

4. All parsons, and Cambridge friends.

reason of their taking part away with them. Then to pay the rest of the *Hampshire* and the *Paradox*, and were at it till 9 at night;[1] and so by night home by barge safe. And took Tom Hater with some money that the clerks had to carry home along with us in the barge, the rest staying behind to pay tickets. But came home after us that night. So being come home, to bed.

I was much troubled today to see a dead man lie floating upon the waters; and had done (they say) these four days and nobody takes him up to bury him, which is very barbarous.

5. At the office till almost noon; and then broke up. Then came Sir G. Carteret, and he and I walked together alone in the garden, taking notice of some faults in the office, perticularly of Sir Wm. Batten's. And he seemed to be much pleased with me, and I hope will be the ground of a future interest of mine in him, which I shall be glad of. Then with my wife abroad; she to the Wardrobe and there dined, and I to the Exchange. And so to the Wardrobe, but they had dined. After dinner my wife and the two ladies to see my aunt Wight, and thence met me at home; from whence (after Sir W. Batten and I had viewed our houses with a workeman, in order to the raising of our roofes higher to enlarge our houses)[2] I went with them by coach, first to moore fields and there walked, and thence to Islington and had a fine walk in the fields there; and so after eating and drinking, home with them; and so by water with my wife home. And after supper, to bed.

6. *Lords day.* By water to White-hall to Sir G. Carteret, to

---

1. The pay of the *Drake* (£591), *Weymouth* (£1652) and *Paradox* (£1813) – but not of the *Hampshire* – is recorded in PRO, Adm. 20/2, pp. 186–7 (warrants of 27 March, 4 April).

2. This work (completed by the end of November) was to be the most extensive done to Pepys's house during his tenancy. He gained four extra rooms, including a new wains-

cotted dining-room: PRO, Adm. 20/4, p. 216. The cost cannot be stated exactly because the entries in the Navy Treasurer's ledger do not sufficiently particularise the work, but a rough estimate (for the houses of Pepys and Batten) is something over £320. The main timber structures were made in Deptford dockyard: see below, p. 102.

give him an account of the backwardnesse of the ships we have
hired to Portugall.[1]

At which he is much troubled. Thence to the Chappell and
there, though crowded, heard a very honest sermon before the
King by a Canon of Christ Church – upon these words: "Having
a forme of godlinesse but denying," &c.[2] Among other things,
did much insist upon the sin of adultery – which methought
might touch the King and the more because he forced it into his
sermon, methought besides his text.

So up and saw the King at dinner; and thence with Sir G.
Carteret to his lodgings, to dinner with him and his Lady – where
I saluted her – and was well received as a stranger by her – she
seems a good lady. And all their discourse, which was very
much, was upon their sufferings and services for the King.
Yet not without some trouble, to see that some that have been
much bound to them do now neglect them, and others again
most civil that have received least from them.

And I do believe that he hath been a good servant to the King.[3]
Thence to walk in the parke, where the King and Duke did
walk round the park. After I was tired, I went and took boat
to milford-stairs. And so to grayes Inne walkes, the first I
have been there this year, and it is very pleasant and full of good
company. When tired, I[a] walked to the Wardrobe and there
stayed a little with my Lady; and so by water from Pauls wharfe
(where my boat[4] stayed for me) home. And supped with my
wife with Sir W. Pen; and so home and to bed.

7. By water to White-hall; and thence to Westminster and
stayed at the parliament-door long, to speak with Mr. Coventry,
which vexed me. Thence to the Lords' house and stood within
the House while the Bishops and Lords did stay till the Chan-

a MS. 'and'

---

1. These were to transport men,
horses etc. to the war in Portugal
against Spain. Several ships were
sent from England, Scotland and
Dunkirk: PRO, Adm. 20/3, p. 79.
2. 2 Tim., iii. 5. The preacher
was Dr Jasper Mayne, Archdeacon of

Chichester and chaplain to the King:
PRO, LC 3/73, p. 81.
3. Particularly as Governor of Jersey (1643-51), base of the royalist navy.
4. The office boat. Watermen
were not allowed to ply for hire on
Sundays.

cellors coming; and then we were put out – and they to prayers.

There comes a Bishop; and while he was rigging himself, he bid his man listen at the door whereabout in the prayers they were; but the man told him something, but could not tell whereabouts it was in the prayers, nor the Bishop neither, but laughed at the conceit – and so went in. But God forgive me, I did tell it by and by to people, and did say that the man said that they were about something of saving their souls, but could not tell whereabouts in the prayer that was.

I sent in a note to my Lord Privy Seale, and he came out to me and I desired that he would make another deputy for me, because of my great business of the navy this month: but he told me he could not do it without the King's consent – which vexed me. So to Dr. Castles[1] and there did get a promise from his Clerke that his master should officiate for me tomorrow.

Thence by water to Toms and there with my wife took coach and to the old Exchange; where, having bought six *a* large holland bands, I sent her home; and myself found out my uncle Wight and Mr. Rawlinson, and with them went to the latter's house to dinner, and there had a good dinner of cold meat *b* and good wine. But was troubled in my head after the *c* little wine I drank; and so home to my office and there did promise to drink no more wine but one glass a meal till Whitsuntide next upon any score.

Mrs. Bowyer and her daughters being at my house, I forbore to go to them, having business and my head disturbed, but stayed at my office till night. And then to walk upon the leads with my wife, and so to my chamber. And thence to bed.

The great talk is that the Spaniard and Hollander do entend to set upon the Portugais by sea at Lisbone so soon as our fleet is come away; and that means our fleet is not likely to come yet these two months or three – which I hope is not true.[2]

a MS. '6' (possibly s.h. 'us')   *b* MS. 'me'   *c* repl. 'a'

---

1. Of the Privy Seal Office.

2. De Ruyter, with a fleet of 17 sail, had been in the Mediterranean since the end of the previous August, under orders to protect the Spanish treasure fleet. These suspicions that he meant to attack the Portuguese seem to have been unfounded: G. Brandt, *Michel de Ruiter* (trans., Amsterdam, 1698), pp. 159, 161, 173–4. The main part of the English fleet left the Tagus in early April.

8. Up very earely and to my office, and there continued till noon. So to dinner, and in comes Uncle Fenner and the two Joyces; I sent for a barrel of oysters and a breast of veal roasted, and were very merry but I cannot down with their dull company and impertinent. After dinner to the office again. So at night by coach to White-hall, and Mr. Coventry not being there, I wrote my business of the office to him, it being almost dark and so came away – and took up my wife by the way home. And on Ludgate-hill, there being a stop, I bought two cakes and they were our supper at home; and so to bed.*a*

9. Sir G. Carteret, Sir Wms. both, and myself all the morning at the office, passing the Victualler's accounts;[1] and at noon to dinner at the Dolphin – where a good Chine of beef and other good cheer.

At dinner Sir George showed me an account in french of the great Famine,[2] which is to the greatest extremity in some part of France at this day – which is very strange.

So to the Exchange, Mrs. Turner (who I find sick in bed), and several other places about business, and so home. Supper and to bed.

10. To Westminster with the two Sir Wms by water – and did several businesses. And so to the Wardrobe with Mr. Moore to dinner. Yesterday came Collonell Talbot with letters from Portugall – that the Queene is resolved to embarque for England this week.[3]

Thence to the office all the afternoon. My Lord Windsor came to us to discourse of his affairs and to take his leave of us,

a   entry crowded into bottom of page

---

1. See above, p. 42 & n. 1.

2. ? one of the appeals for money issued during the famine by the ladies of the *Compagnie du Saint-Sacrement*: list in *Revue d'hist. écon. et soc.*, 12/69, n. 95. This famine was for France one of the worst of the century and caused many deaths, especially in Normandy, the Loire valley and Paris (ib., pp. 53+; C. W. Cole, *Colbert*, ii. 503+): parts with which Carteret (a Jersey man and recently an exile in France)

had several contacts. At the time of this entry, starvation was at its worst, and the authorities – King, churches, towns – were busy with measures of relief.

3. She embarked on Sunday, 13 April, after mass: Sandwich, p. 132. Col. Richard Talbot (Groom of the Bedchamber to the Duke of York; later Earl of Tyrconnel) appears to have left the fleet in the Tagus on 27 March: ib., p. 128.

he being to go Governor*a* of Jamaica with this fleet that is now going.[1]

Late at the office. Home, with my mind full of business, and so to bed.

11. Up early to my lute and a song. Then about 6 a–clock with Sir W. Pen by water to Deptford and among the ships now going to Portugall with men and horse, to see them dispatched. So to Greenwich; and had a fine pleasant walk to Woolwich, having in our company Captain Minnes,[2] with whom I was much pleased to hear him talk, in fine language but pretty well for all that. Among other things, he and the other Captains that were with us tell me that Negros drownded look white and lose their blacknesse – which I never heard before.[3]

At Woolwich, up and down to do the same business and so back to Greenwich by water; and there, while something is dressing for our dinner, Sir Wm and I walked into the Parke, where the King hath planted trees and made steps in the hill up to the Castle, which is very magnificent.[4] So up and down the house, which is now repayring in the Queenes lodgings.[5]

So to dinner at the Globe, and Captain Lambert of the Dukes pleasure-boat[6] came to us and dined with us. And were merry

a l.h. repl. l.h. 'Emb'-

---

1. The new Governor had been negotiating with the Navy Board for boats and yawls: above, p. 52 & n. 3. He arrived in Jamaica in July: *CSPCol. 1661–8*, p. 99.

2. Christopher Myngs.

3. The removal of the epidermis by putrefaction makes the body paler, but not white.

4. The park had suffered some deforestation during the Interregnum, and in 1661 replanting had begun. In 1664, 6000 elms were planted (E. Hasted, *Hist. Kent*, ed. Drake, i. 65–6); in 1667 there is mention of a 'dwarf orchard and wilderness' (*CTB*, ii. 204). See also Mundy, v. 158–9; *CTB*, i. 294, 449, 556; G. H. Chettle, *The Queen's House, Greenwich*, p. 41.

The castle had been built at the end of the 15th century and was converted by Charles II into an observatory in 1675-6: Hasted, loc. cit.

5. Later this summer, before moving to Somerset House, the Queen Mother stayed in the Queen's House, built for her (1616–39) by Inigo Jones to replace the original gate-house. The main body of the old palace by the riverside had also been renovated in 1660–1 and a new building was being added. Below, v. 75 & n. 3; *Merc. Pub.*, 31 July 1662; *CTB*, i. 291, 385, 441; Hasted, op. cit., i. 65; *CSPVen. 1661-4*, p. 184; Monconys, ii. 83; Chettle, op. cit., esp. p. 41.

6. The *Anne*: see above, ii. 14, n. 4.

and so home.   And I in the evening to the Exchange and spoke with Uncle Wight; and so home and walked with my wife on the leads late; and so the barber came to me; and so to bed very weary, which I seldom am.

12.   At the office all the morning.   Where among other things, being provoked by some impertinence of Sir W. Battens, I called him "unreasonable man".   At which he was very angry and so was I, but I think we shall not much fall out about it.

After dinner to several places about business; and so home and wrote letters at my office, and one to Mr. Coventry about business, and at the close did excuse my not waiting on him myself so often as others do, for want of leisure.   So home and to bed.

13.   *Lords day.*   In the morning to Pauls, where I heard a pretty good sermon; and thence to dinner with my Lady at the Wardrobe; and after much talk with her after dinner, I went to the Temple to church, and there heard another.   By the same token, a boy, being asleep, fell down a high seat to the ground, ready to break his neck – but got no hurt.

Thence to grayes Inn walkes; and there met Mr. Pickering and walked with him two houres till 8 a-clock, till I was quite weary.   His discourse most about the pride of the Duchesse of Yorke[1] and how all the ladies envy my Lady Castlemaine.   He entends to go to Portsmouth to meet the Queene this week – which is now the discourse and expectation of the towne.

So home; and no sooner come but Sir W. Batten*ᵃ* comes to me to bring me a paper of Fieldes (with whom we have lately had a great deal of trouble at the office), being a bitter petition to the King against our office, for not doing Justice upon his complaint to us of embezzlement of the King's stores by one Turpin.[2]   I took Sir Wm to Sir W. Pens (who was newly come from Walthamstowe), and there we read it and discoursed; but we do not much fear it, the King referring it to the Duke of Yorke.   So we drank a glass or two of wine; and so home and I to bed – my wife being in bed already.

a MS. 'Warren'

----

1. Cf. Burnet, i. 298: '[she] took state on her, rather too much.'
2. The petition has not been traced; for the case, see above, p. 23 & n. 2.

14. Being weary last night, I lay very long in bed today – talking with my wife, and persuaded her to go to Brampton, and take Sarah with her, next week, to cure her ague by change of ayre; and we agreed all things therein.

We rose, and at noon dined. And then we to the paynters and there sot the last time for my little picture,[1] which I hope will please me. Then to Paternoster rowe to buy things for my wife against her going.

So home and walked upon the leads with my wife. And whether she suspects anything or no, I know not, but she is quite off of her going to Brampton. Which something troubles me, and yet all my design was that I might the freer go to Portsmouth when the rest go to pay off the yards there, which will be very shortly. But I will get off if I can.

So to supper and to bed.

15. At the office all the morning. Dined at home. Again at the office in the afternoon to dispatch letters; and so home and with my wife by Coach to the New Exchange to buy her some things; where we saw some new-fashion pettycoates of Sarcenet, with a black broad lace printed round[a] the bottom and before, very handsome; and my wife hath a mind to one of them – but we did not then buy one. But thence to Mr. Bowyers, thinking to have spoke to them for our Sarah to go to Huntsmore for a while to get away her ague. But we had not opportunity to do it, and so home – and to bed.

16. Up earely and took my physique; it wrought all the morning well. At noon dined; and all the afternoon, Mr. Hater to that end coming to me, he and I did go about my abstracting all the Contracts made in the office since we came into it.[2] So at night to bed.

a   repl. incorrect symbol for 'round'

---

1. See above, p. 33 & n. 3.
2. They were compiling an abstract (untraced) which Pepys kept for his personal use. The book was finished on 16 May and its index on 11 June. The official contract-books

(eight in number, covering 1660–86) were in the office of the Clerk of the Acts at 12 October 1688 and are listed in BL, Add. 9303, ff. 53r, 124v. The first covered 27 July 1660–3 July 1662. All seem now to have disappeared.

17.   To Mr. Holliards in the morning, thinking to be let blood, but he was gone out.[1]   So to White-hall, thinking to have had a Seal at Privy Seale; but my Lord did not come and so I walked back home.   And stayed within all the afternoon, there being no office kept*a* today.   But in the evening Sir W. Batten sent for me to tell me that he had this day spoke to the Duke about raising our houses, and he hath given us leave to do it; at which being glad, I went home merry; and after supper, to bed.

18.   This morning, sending the boy down into the cellar for some beer, I fallowed him with a cane, and did there beat him for his staying of arrands and other faults, and his sister came to me down and begged for him: so I forebore.   And afterwards in my wife's chamber did there talk to Jane how much I did love the boy for her sake and how much it doth concern to correct the boy for his faults, or else he would be undone.[2]   So at last she was well pleased.

This morning Sir G. Carteret, Sir W. Batten and I met at the office and did conclude of our going to Portsmouth next week.   In which, my mind is at a great loss what to do with my wife, for I cannot persuade her to go to Brampton and I am loath to leave her at home.   All the afternoon in several places to put things in order for my going.

At night home and to bed.

19.   This morning before we sat, I went to Allgate; and at the Corner shop, a drapers, I stood and did see Barkestead, Okey, and Corbet drawne toward the gallows at Tiburne; and there they were hanged and Quarterd.   They all looked very cheerfully.   But I hear they all die defending what they did to the

a MS. 'keep'

---

1. Hollier performed the operation on 4 May: below, pp. 76–7.

2. Wayneman Birch was dismissed in July 1663, and in the following November was packed off to Barbados: below, iv. 382. He was a 'pretty well-looked boy' and had been in Pepys's service since September 1660. His escapades included one small explosion, an attempt at running away and 'strange things ... not fit to name': below, p. 207.

King to be just – which is very strange.[1] So to the office. And then home to dinner. And Captain David Lambert came to take his leave of me, he being to go back to Tanger, there to lie.

Then abroad about businesse and in the evening did get a bever, an old one but a very good one, of Sir W. Batten; for which I must give him something, but I am very well pleased with it. So after writing by the post, to bed.

20. *Lords day.* My intention being to go this morning to White-hall to hear Zouth, my Lord Chancellors Chaplin, the famous preacher and oratour of Oxford (who the last Lord's-day did sink down in the pulpitt before the King and could not proceed),[2] it did rain and the wind against me, that I could by no means get a boat or Coach to carry me; and so I stayed at Pauls, where the Judges did all meet, and heard a sermon, it being the first Sunday of the Terme; but they had a very poor sermon. So to my Lady's and dined; and so to White-hall to Sir G. Carteret, and so to the Chappell, where I challenged my place as Clerke of the Privy Seale, and had it.[3] And then walked home with Mr. Blagrave to his old house in the Fish yard, and there he had a pretty kinswoman that sings and we

1. For their arrest, see above, p. 45 & n. 1. For their execution, see *Kingd. Intell.*, 21 April, pp. 252+; *The speeches, discourses and prayers of Col. John Barkstead etc . . . upon the 19th of April . . .* (1662), pp. 49+. Okey, unlike the others, did not attempt to defend regicide; he alone therefore was given Christian burial: *CSPD 1661–2*, p. 344.

2. Robert South was a Student of Christ Church and Public Orator of the University; later (1663) a canon of Westminster; a popular preacher whose sermons were often printed and reprinted. A puritan pamphleteer, reporting the occasion, noted that the preacher (handling the text 'Say not thou what is the cause that the former days were better than these . . .?') was struck dumb just as he was about to prove that the days

of the rebellion were worse than the present. 'It pleased God that he was suddenly taken with a Qualm, Drops of Sweat standing in his Face as big as Pease, and immediately he lost the Use of his Speech . . . the Expectations of all being thus sadly disappointed, they were contented with the Divertisement of an Anthem, and so the Solemnity for the Service of that Day was ended': qu. Wood, *Ath. Oxon.* (ed. Bliss), iv. 635–6. According to the same pamphlet, South had been struck dumb during an attack on the sectaries some years before at Oxford: ib., p. 632.

3. Clerks of the privy seal (and their deputies) were entitled to seats on the Dean's side of the Chapel Royal: Household Ordinances [c. 1660–70], BL, Stowe 562, f.8*v*.

did sing some holy things;[1] and afterward others came in and so I left them and by water through the bridge (which did trouble me)[2] home.   And so to bed.

21. This morning I attempted to persuade my wife in bed to go to Brampton this week; but she would not, which troubles me.   And seeing that I could keep it no longer from her, I told her that I was resolved to go to Portsmouth tomorrow.   Sir W. Batten goes to Chatham today and will be back again to come for Portsmouth after us on Thursday next.

I went to Westminster and several places about business. Then at noon dined with my Lord Crew; and after dinner went up to Sir Tho. Crew's chamber, who is still ill.   He tells me how my Lady Duchess of Richmond[3] and Castlemayne had a falling out the other day; and she call[ed] the latter Jane Shoare,[a] and did hope to see her come to the same end that she did.[4]

Coming down again to my Lord, he told me that news was come that the Queene is landed; at which I took leave, and by coach hurried to White-hall, the bells ringing in several places; but I find there no such matter, nor anything like it.   So I went by appointment to Anthony Joyces, where I sat with his wife and Mall Joyce an hour or two; and so, her husband not being at home, away I went and in Cheepeside spied him and took him into the coach home; and there I find my Ladys Jemimah and Anne and Madamoiselle come to see my wife.

a blots below name

---

1. In the PL certain MS. songs are classified as 'Compositions: Grave'. (E).

2. See *Comp.*: 'London Bridge'.

3. Dowager Duchess, and daughter of Lady Castlemaine's great-uncle, the 1st Duke of Buckingham.

4. Jane Shore (who died c. 1527) was Edward IV's mistress. Popular legend had it that she died in poverty, and that her body was cast on a dunghill: see esp. Deloney's ballad: Percy, *Reliques* (ed. H. B. Wheatley), ii. 263-73. Lady Castlemaine was often compared to her. One evening in 1664 she was accosted by 'trois gentils-hommes . . . masquez qui luy firent la plus forte et rude reprimande que l'on se puisse imaginer, jusques à luy dire que la quatrièsme maîstresse d'Edouard estoit morte sur un fumier, mesprisée et abandonnée de tout le monde': de Cominges to de Lionne, 22 September/2 October 1664; PRO, PRO 31/3/113, ff. 324-5. Cf. *A dialogue between the D[uchess] of C[leveland] and the D[uchess] of P[ortsmouth] at their meeting . . . with the ghost of Jane Shore* (1682). Pepys retained in his library a biography of her: *The history of Mrs. Iane Shore* (n.d.): PL 362 (11).

Whom I left, and to talk with Joyce about a project I have of his and my joyneing to get some money for my brother Tom and his kinswoman,[1] to help forward with her portion if they should marry: I mean, in buying of tallow of him at a low rate for the King, and Tom should have the profit. But he tells me the profit will not be considerable, at which I was troubled. But I have agreed with him to serve some in in my absence.[2]

He went away, and then came Mr. Moore and sat late with me, talking about businesses; and so went away and I to bed.

22. After taking leave of my wife, which we could hardly do kindly, because of her mind to go along with me – Sir W. Penn and I took coach and so over the bridge to Lambeth – W. Bodham and Tom Hewet going as clerks to Sir W. Penn, and my Will for me.[3] Here we got a dish of buttered eggs, and there stayed till Sir G. Carteret came to us from White-hall, who brought Dr Clerke[4] with him, at which I was very glad. And so we set out. And I was very much pleased with his company, and were very merry all the way. He, among [other] good Storys, telling us a story of the monkey that got hold of the young lady's cunt as she went to stool to shit, and run from[a] under her coats and got upon the table, which was ready laid for supper after dancing was done. Another about a Hectors crying "God damn you, rascall!" We came to Gilford and there passed our time in the garden cutting of Sparagus for supper, the best that ever I eat in my life but in that house[5] last year. Supped well, and the Doctor and I to bed together – calling Cosens, from his name and my office.

23. Up earely and to Petersfield, and there dined well; and thence got a contry-man to guide us by Havan, to avoid going through the forrest;[6] but he carried us much out of the way. And upon our coming, we sent away an express to Sir W. Batten

a repl. 'und'-

---

1. See above, ii. 242.
2. See below, p. 96 & n. 2.
3. Travelling charges for this trip came to c. £88: PRO, Adm. 20/3, p. 62.
4. Timothy Clarke, physician to the

King's Household (1660); an original F.R.S. (1661).
5. The Red Lion, where he had stayed on 4–6 May 1661.
6. The Forest of Bere, to the north and north-west of Havant, Hants.

to stop his coming, which I did project to make good my oath
that my wife should come if any of our wifes came, which my
Lady Batten did entend to do with her husband.   The Doctor
and I lay together at Wiards the Chyrurgeons in Portsmouth –
his wife a very pretty woman.   We lay very well and merrily.
In the morning, concluding him to be of *a* the eldest blood and
house of the Clerkes, because that all the fleas came to him and
《24》   not to me.   Up and to Sir George Carterets lodging at
Mrs. Stephens, where we keep our table all the time we
are here.   Thence all of us to the pay-house; but the books not
being ready, we went to church to the Lecture,* where there was
my Lord Ormond and Manchester and much London company,
though not so much as I expected.   Here we had a very good
sermon upon this text – "in love serving one another"[1] – which
pleased me very well.

No news of the Queene at all.   So to dinner and then to the
pay all the afternoon:[2] then Sir W. Penn and I walked to the
Kings-yard, and there lay at Mr. Tippets's,[3] where exceeding
well treated.

25.   All the morning at Portsmouth at the pay; and then to
dinner and again to the pay; and at night got the Doctor to go
lie with me, and much pleased with his company; but I was
much troubled in my eyes, by reason of the healths*b* I have this
day been forced to drink.

26.   Sir G and I and his clerk, Mr. Stephens, and Mr. Holt
our guide, over to Gosport, and so rode to Southampton.
In our way, besides my Lord Southamptons parks and lands,[4]
which in one viewe we could see 6000*l* per annum, we observed
a little churchyard, where the graves are accustomed to be all

---

a MS. 'the of'   *b* repl. 'drink'

---

1. A loose recollection of Gal., v.
13.
2. The principal work was to pay
the 16 ships (including two hulks and
a hoy) kept on the ordinary establishment in the dock.   Details in
PRO, Adm. 20/4, pp. 38+.
3. John Tippets, Master-Shipwright of the yard.
4. Around Titchfield House, Hants.

Sowed with Sage.[1] At Southampton we went to the Mayors[2] and there dined, and had Sturgeon of their own catching the last week, which doth not happen in 20 year, and it was well ordered.[a] They brought us also some Caveare, which I attempted to order, but all to no purpose, for they had neither given it salt enough nor are the seedes of the roe broke, but are all in berryes. The towne is one most gallant street – and is walled round with stone,[3] and Bevis's picture upon one of the gates.[4] Many old walls of religious houses, and the Keye well worth seeing. After dinner to horse again, being in nothing troubled but the badness of my hat, which I borrowed to save my beaver. Home by night and wrote letters to London, and so with Sir W. Penn to the docke to bed.

27. *Sunday.* Sir W. Penn got trimmed before me, and so took the coach to Portsmouth to wait on my Lord Steward[5] to church. And sent the coach for me back again; so I rode to church and met my Lord Chamberlaine[6b] upon the walls of the Garrison, who owned and spoke to me. I fallowed him in the Crowde of gallants through the Queenes lodgings to Chappell; the rooms being all rarely furnished – and escaped hardly being set on fire yesterday.[7] At Chappell we had a most excellent

a l.h. repl. s.h.'dr'-   *b* l.h. repl. symbol rendered illegible

---

1. A country custom long surviving in, e.g., Wales: see J. Brand, *Pop. Antiq.* (ed. Hazlitt), i. 240–1. Jerusalem or Bethlehem sage (longwort) has white spots on its leaves which were said to have been caused by the Virgin's tears.

2. William Stanley.

3. The walls and gates still served a useful purpose: visitors were closely examined on entering the town. Description (c. 1682) in HMC, *Rep.*, 13/2/286–7.

4. Bargate; on which were displayed panel paintings of Sir Bevis of Hampton and the Giant Ascapart, figures derived from a legend of about the 10th century, whose popularity in the 14th century was reflected in the

metrical romance of 'Sir Beves of Hamtoun'. Sir Bevis was the son of Guy, Earl of Southampton, and was renowned for the many feats of chivalry he performed in Edgar's reign. J. Speed, *Hist. Southampton* (ed. Aubrey), p. 123; J[ohn] S. Davies, *Hist. Southampton*, p. 66.

5. Duke of Ormond, Steward of the King's Household.

6. Earl of Manchester, a distant relative of Pepys by marriage.

7. Lodgings had been prepared for Catherine of Braganza in Government House ('God's House'), residence of the Governor. Charles and his Queen were married there by proxy on 21 May: *Mem. Lady Fanshawe* (1829), p. 144; Sandwich, p. 139.

and eloquent sermon.   And here I spied and saluted Mrs. Pierce; but being in haste, could not learn of her where her lodgings are, which vexes me.   Thence took Ned Pickering to dinner with us; and the two Marshes, father and son, dined with us, and very merry.   After dinner, Sir W. Penn and I, the Doctor, and Ned Pickering by coach to the Yard; and there, on board the *Swallow* in the Dock, hear our Navy Chaplin[1] preach a sad sermon, full of nonsense and false Latin – but prayed for the Right Honourable the Principal Officers: after sermon took him to Mr. Tippets to drink a glass of wine.   And so we four back again by coach to Portsmouth, and there visited the Mayor, Mr. Timbrell our Anchorsmith, who showed us the present they have for the Queene; which is a salt-sellar of silver, the walls Christall, with four Eagles and four greyhounds standing up at top to bear up a dish – which endeed is one of the neatest pieces of plate that ever I saw – and the case is very pretty also.[2]

This[a] evening came a Merchantman in the harbour, which we hired at London to carry horse to Portugall; but Lord, what running there was to the seaside to hear what news, thinking it had come from the Queene.   In the evening, Sir George, Sir W. Penn and I walked round the walls; and thence we two with the Doctor to the yard; and so to supper and to bed.

28.   The Doctor and I begun Philosophy discourse, exceeding pleasant.   He offers to bring me into the college of the Virtuosoes and my Lord Brunkard's acquaintance.[3]   And to show me some

a repl. 'good'

---

1. Thomas Bragg, chaplain to the dockyard.
2. One of the finest salts of its period; now known as the Seymour salt because it passed into the possession of Thomas Seymour (? in 1692 when Catherine returned to Portugal), who in 1693 presented it to the Goldsmiths' Company, the present owners; 10½ ins. high; artist unknown. The case has now disappeared.   Description (by C. Oman) and illust. in *Caroline Silver, 1625–88*

(1970), p. 48, pl. 49. Great salts (placed in front of the host at table) were almost obsolete.
3. This 'college of the Virtuosoes' became the Royal Society, its first charter being granted on 15 July 1662. Cf. above, ii. 22 & n. 1.   Brouncker became the first President.   Clarke had been a fellow since at least 16 January 1661, and was a member of the Council in 1662 and 1663. Pepys was elected a fellow on 15 February 1665.

anatomy, which makes me very glad. And I shall endeavour it when I come to London. Sir W. Penn much troubled, upon letters come last night; and this morning showed me one of Dr Owens to his son, whereby it appears his son is much perverted in his opinion by him;[1] which I now perceive is one thing that hath put Sir Wm so long off of the hookes. By coach to the Pay-house, and so to work again. And then to dinner. And to it again, and so in the evening to the yard and supper and bed.

29. At the pay all the morning, and so to dinner and then to it again in the afternoon. And after our work was done, Sir G. Carteret, Sir W. Penn and I walked forth, and I spied Mrs. Pierce and another lady passing by; so I left them and went to the ladies, and walked with them up and down and took them to Mrs. Stephens's, and there give them wine and sweetmeats and were very merry; and then comes the Doctor and we carried them by coach to their lodging; which was very poor, but the best they could get and such as made much mirth among us. So I appointed one to watch when the gates of the towne were ready to be shut and to give us notice; and so the Doctor and I stayed with them, playing and laughing; and at last was forced to bid good-night, for fear of being locked into the towne all night. So we walked to the yard, designing how to prevent our going to London tomorrow, that we might be merry with these ladies, which I did. So to supper, and merrily to bed.

30. This morning Sir G came down to the yard, and there we mustered over all the men and determined of some regulacions in the yard. And then to dinner, all the officers of the yard with us; and after dinner walk to Portsmouth – there to pay off the *Successe*,[2] which we did pretty earely; and so I

1. William Penn, jun. (the future Quaker leader) had been sent down from Christ Church, Oxford, for nonconformity in October 1661. Among his mentors had been Dr John Owen, the Independent divine, who, after resigning the deanery of Christ Church in March 1660 (some months before Penn matriculated there), had stayed on in Oxford. For Penn's 'convincement', see below, ix. 595 & n. 3. His father was always distressed by his religious opinions and twice sent him away from home on that account.

2. A frigate; paid £3076 for 24 June 1660–30 April 1662: PRO, Adm. 20/2, p. 187.

took leave of Sir W. Penn – he desiring to know whither I went, but I could not tell him. I went to the ladies, and there took them and walked to the Mayors¹ ⟨to show them the present, and then to the⟩ Dock, where Mrs. Tippets made much of them; and thence back again, the Doctor being come to us to their Lodgeings, whither came our supper by my appointment, and we very merry, playing at Cards and laughing very merry, till 12 a-clock at night. And so having stayed so long (which we had resolved to stay till they bid us be gone), which yet they did not do; but by consent we bid them good-night. And so passed the guards and went to the Doctor's lodgings, and there lay with him – our discourse being much about the Quality of the lady with Mrs. Pierce, she being some old and handsome and painted and fine, and hath a very handsome maid with her – which we take to be the marks of a bawd. But Mrs. Pierce says*ª* she is a stranger to her and met by chance in the coach, and pretends to be a dresser. Her name is Eastwood. So to sleep in a bad bed, about one a-clock in the morning.

This afternoon, after dinner, comes Mr. Stephenton, one of the Burgeses of the towne, to tell me that the Mayor and burgesses did desire my acceptance of a Burgessshipp and were ready at the Mayor['s] to make me one.² So I went and there they were all ready and did with much civility give me my oath; and after the oath, did by custom shake me all by the hand. So I took them to a taverne and made them drink; and paying the reckoning, went away – they having first in the taverne made Mr. Waith³ also a burgesse, he coming in while we were drinking. It cost me a piece in gold to the Towne Clerke and 10s to the bayliffes, and spent 6s.

a   repl. 'since'

---

1. John Timbrell, anchor-smith.
2. In May 1661 the Mayor had refused Pepys the honour: above, ii. 93 & n. 4. For this occasion, see R. East, *Extracts from records of Portsmouth*, p. 357. On the following day the Duke of Ormond and other notables were made free: ib., loc. cit. Pepys's election qualified him for choice as M.P. for Portsmouth in February 1679, but he withdrew in order to sit for Harwich. St John Steventon was Clerk of the Cheque at the dockyard.
3. Robert Waith, clerk and paymaster to the Navy Treasurer (Carteret, M.P. for the borough).

MAY.

1. Sir G. Carteret, Sir W. Pen, and myself, with our clerks, set out this morning from Portsmouth very early and got by noon to Petersfield, several of the officers of the yard accompanying us so far. Here we dined and were merry.

At dinner comes my Lord Carlingford from London, going to Portsmouth; tells us that the Duchess of Yorke is brought to bed of a girle,[1] at which I find nobody pleased. And that Prince Robert, the Duke of Buckingham and   [2] are sworne of the Privy Councell.

He himself made a dish with egges of the butter of the Sparagus; which is very fine meat, which I will practise hereafter.

To horse again after dinner, and got to Gilford – where after supper I to bed, having this day been offended by Sir Wm Pens foolish talk, and I offending him with my answers; among others, he in discourse complaining of want of Confidence, did ask me to lend him a grain or two, which I told him I thought he was better stored with then myself, before Sir George. So that I see I must keep a greater distance then I have done. And I hope I may do it, because of the interest which I am making with Sir George.

To bed all alone, and my Will in the truckle-bed.

2. earely to coach again and to Kingston, where we baited a little; and presently to coach again and got earely to London; and I find all well at home, and Mr. Hunt and his wife had dined with my wife today – and been very kind to my wife in my absence. After I had washed myself, it having been the hottest day that hath been this year, I took them all by coach to Mrs. Hunts; and I to Dr Clerkes lady and give her her letter and token. She is a very fine woman, and what with her person and the number of fine ladies that were with her, I was

1. Princess Mary, later Queen: born at St James's Palace on 30 April.
2. Rupert, Buckingham and the Earl of Middleton (Commander-in-) Chief and Commissioner to Parliament in Scotland) were admitted to the Council on 28 April: PRO, PC 2/55, p. 618.

75

much out of countenance and could hardly carry myself like a man among them. But however, I stayed till my courage was up again; and talked to them and viewed her house, which is most pleasant; and so drank and good-bye. And so to my Lord's lodgings,*a* where*b* by chance I spied my Lady's coach, and find her and my Lady Wright there; and so I spoke to them. And they being gone, went to Mr. Hunts for my wife, and so home. And to bed.

3. Sir W. Penn and I by coach to St. James's, and there to the Dukes chamber, who hath been a-hunting this morning and is come back again. Thence to Westminster, where I met Mr. Moore and hear that Mr. Watkins[1] is suddenly dead since my going. To dinner to my Lady Sandwich; and Sir Tho. Crewes children coming thither, I took them and all my Lady's to the Tower and showed them the lions[2] and all that was to be shown, and so took them to my house and there made much of them; and so saw them back to my Lady's – Sir Th. Crewes children being as pretty and the best behaved that ever I saw of their age.

Thence, at the goldsmiths took my picture in little,[3] which is now done, home with me; and pleases me exceedingly, and my wife. So to supper and to bed, it being exceeding hot.

4. *Lords day.* Lay long, talking with my wife. Then up and Mr. Holliard came to me and let me blood, about 16 ounces,

a   repl. 'where my'   b   repl.? 'and'

---

1. Clerk in the Privy Seal Office.
2. Lions had been kept in the Tower since the 13th century; they were now in the 'Lion Tower', which was 'very small and without any beauty of structure': Magalotti, p. 177. The menagerie was removed to the Zoological Gardens in Regent's Park in 1834. J. Howell, *Londino-polis* (1657), p. 24; G. Loisel, *Hist. des menageries*, ii. 12–15.
3. Savill's miniature which had presumably just been framed: cf. above, p. 33 & n. 3. (OM).

I being exceeding full of blood, and very good.[1] I begun to
be sick; but lying upon my back, I was presently well again
and did give him 5s for his pains; and so we parted. And I to
my chamber to write down my Journall from the beginning of
my late Journy to this houre.

Dined well. And after dinner, my arm tied up with a black
ribbon, I walked with my wife to my Brother Toms, our boy
waiting on us with his sword, which this day he begins to
wear to out-do Sir W. Pens boy, who this day, and Sir W.
Batten['s] too, begin to wear new liverys. But I do take mine
to be the neatest of them all.[2]

I led my wife to Mrs. Turners pew; and the church[3] being
full, it being to hear a Doctor who is to preach a probacion
Sermon,[4] I went out to the Temple and there walked; and so
when church was done went to Mrs. Turners; and after a stay
there, my wife and I walked to Grayes Inne to observe fashions
of the ladies, because of my wife's making some clothes. Thence
homewards and called in at Ant: Joyces, where we found his
wife brought home sick from church, and was in a Convulsion
fit. So home and to Sir W. Penn and there supped; and so
to prayers at home and to bed.

5. My arme not being well, I stayed within all the morning
and dined alone at home, my wife being gone out to buy some
things for herself and a gowne for me to dress myself in. And
so all the afternoon looking over my papers; and at night
walked upon the leads, and so to bed.

---

1. This operation (which Pepys
had hoped to have on 17 April) was
common. Cupping and leeching
were used as well as venesection.
The aim was to normalise the balance
of the body's 'humours'; in Pepys's
case, presumably to relieve his
kidney condition. The amount of
blood was not unusual (anything up
to 20 oz. being normal); on 13 July
1668 he had 14 oz. removed. Cf.
V. Woodall, *Surgeons Mate* (1639),
pp. 18–20.

2. For the Pepys livery, see above,
p. 50 & n. 3; for dress swords,
above, ii. 29 & n. 2. Fashion was
too strong for the proclamation of
September 1660 which forbade pages,
footmen and lackeys to wear swords
or weapons in London and Westminster: Steele, no. 3261.

3. St Bride's, Fleet St.

4. Cf. below, p. 259.

6. This morning I got my seat set up on the leads, which pleases me well. So to the office, and thence to the Change but could not meet with my uncle Wight; so home to dinner. And then out again to several places to pay money and to understand my debts; and so home and walked with my wife on the leads; and so to supper and to bed.

I find it a hard matter to settle to business after so much leisure and pleasure.

7. Walked to Westminster; where I understand the news that Mr. Mountagu is this last night come to the King, with news that he left the Queene and fleet in the bay of Biscay, coming this way-ward, and that he believes she is now at the Isle of Scilly.[1] So at noon to my Lord Crewes and there dined; and after dinner Sir Tho. Crew and I talked together; and among other instances of the simple light discourse that sometimes is in the Parliament-house, he told me how in the late business of Chymny-money, when all occupyers were to pay, it was questioned whether women were under that name to pay, and somebody rose and said that they were not occupiers, but occupied.[2]

Thence to Pauls Churchyard; where seeing my Lady Sandwich and Carteret and my wife (who this day made a visit the first time to my Lady Carteret) come by Coach and going to Hide parke, I was resolved to fallow them; and so went to Mrs. Turners and thence found her out at the Theatre, where I saw the last act of *The Knight of the Burning Pestle*[3] (which pleased me not at all); and so after the play done, she and The and Mr. Lue[ll]in and I in her coach to the Parke and there find them out and spoke to them, and observed many fine ladies and stayed till all were gone almost, and so ⟨to⟩ Mrs. Turners. And there supped and so walked home; and by and by comes my wife home, brought by my Lady Carteret to the gate. And so to bed.

1. Edward Mountagu left the fleet on 26 April in the *Princess*, bringing news of the Queen's approach; she was in fact off St Michael's Mount at this moment: *CSPVen. 1661–4*, pp. 140–1; Sandwich, pp. 134, 137.

2. The Hearth-Tax Bill, made statutory on 19 May, had been sent to a committee of the whole House on 3 March: *CJ*, viii. 378.

3. A burlesque comedy by Beaumont, first acted c. 1608, and published in 1613. Now at the TR, Vere St. (A).

8. At the office all the morning, doing business alone. And then to the Wardrobe, where my Lady going out with the children to dinner, I stayed not but returned home; and was overtaken in St. Paul's churchyard by Sir G. Carteret in his coach, and so he carried me to the Exchange, where I stayed awhile. He told me that the Queene and the fleet were in Mounts bay on monday last – and that the Queene endures her sickness pretty well.[1] He also told me how Sir John Lawson hath done some execution upon the Turkes in the Straight,[2] of which I am glad and told the news the first on the Exchange. And was much fallowed by merchants to tell it. So home and to dinner. And by and by to the office, and after the rest gone (my Lady Albemarle being this day at dinner at Sir W. Batten), Sir G. Carteret comes and he and I walked in the garden; and among other discourse, he tells me that it is Mr. Coventry that is to come to us as a Comissioner of the Navy.[3] At which he is much vexed, and cries out upon Sir W. Penn and threatens him highly; and looking upon his lodgings, which are new enlarging, he in passion cried *"guarda mi spada!*[4] for by God, I may chance to keep him in Ireland when he is there" – for Sir W. Penn is going thither with my Lord Lieutenant;[5] but it is my design to keep much in with Sir G. and I think I have begun very well towards it. So to the office, and was there late doing business; and so, with my head full of business, I to bed.

9. Up and to my office. And so to dinner at home. And then to several places to pay my debts, and then[a] to Westminster

a repl. 'this'

---

1. She had been sea-sick: Sandwich, p. 132.

2. During 22-29 March Lawson had attacked the Algerines at Bougie and sunk several of their ships under the very guns of Algiers itself: *Kingd. Intell.*, 12 May. 'The news was received at Court with great rejoicing, and confirmation is eagerly awaited': Venetian resident, 9/19 May; *CSPVen. 1661-4*, pp. 139, 141-2.

3. William Coventry was formally appointed on the 14th.

4. 'Beware of my sword'; a Spanish phrase which had some currency in England at this time: cf. E. Gayton, *Pleasant notes upon Don Quixot* (1654), p. 87.

5. For Penn's departure, see below, p. 134. He had estates in co. Cork and was Governor of Kinsale, the principal naval base in Ireland, as well as Vice-Admiral of Munster. The Lord-Lieutenant was Ormond; Penn was put in charge of the squadron accompanying him: HMC, *Portland*, ii. 101.

to Dr Castle, who discoursed with me about Privy Seale business, which I do not much mind, it being little worth. But by Watkins's late sudden death we are like to lose money. Thence to Mr. De Cretz and there saw some good pieces that he hath copyed of the King's pieces, some of Raphael and Michaell Angelo; and I have borrowed an *Elizabeth* of his copying to hang up in my house – and sent it home by Will.[1] Thence with Mr. Salsbury, who I met there, into Covent Garden to an alehouse to see a picture that hangs there, which is offered for 20s and I offered 14 but it is worth much more money, but did not buy it, I having no mind to break my oath. Thence to see an Italian puppet play that is within the rayles there, which is very pretty, the best that ever I saw, and great resort of gallants.[2] So to the Temple and by water home; and so walk upon the leads, and in the dark played there on my Flagelette, it being a fine still evening; and so to supper and to bed.

This day I paid Godfry's debt of 40 and odde pounds.[3] The Duke of Yorke went last night to Portsmouth; so that I believe the Queene is near.

10. By myself at the office all the morning, drawing up instruccions for Portsmouth yard in those things wherein we at our late being there did think fit to reforme. And got them signed this morning to send away tonight, the Duke being now there.[4]

At noon to the Wardrobe; there dined. My Lady told me

1. Emanuel de Critz may have had special facilities for copying the royal collection. No original paintings by Michelangelo belonged to Charles II, and the only original paintings by Raphael in the royal collection were the Cartoons of the *Acts of the Apostles*, now on loan to the Victoria and Albert Museum. (OM).

2. Puppet plays, permitted after the closing of the theatres in 1642 and during the revolution, continued to enjoy great popularity after the Restoration. The play on this occasion may have been *Polichinello*. The puppeteer at Covent Garden was an Italian. Signor Bologna: G. Speaight, *Hist. Engl. puppet theatre*, p. 73. The performance probably took place in the central open space within the Piazza. (A).

3. See above, p. 34 & n. 1.

4. Copy in PRO, Adm. 106/2507, no. 13. The Principal Officers expressed concern about the number and inefficiency of the boys employed as servants to boatswains and gunners, and directed that in future they should be over 15 and bound by indentures. The Duke had gone to Portsmouth to meet Charles II's new Queen.

how my Lady Castlemaine doth speak of going to lie in at Hampton Court;[1] which she and all our ladies are much troubled at,[a] because of the King's being forced to show her countenance in the sight of the Queene when she comes. Back to the office and there all afternoon; and in the evening comes Sir G. Carteret, and he and I did hire a ship for Tanger,[2] and other things together; and I find that he doth single me out to join with him apart from the rest; which I am much glad of. So home; and after being trimmed, to bed.

11. *Lordsday.* To our own church in the morning; where our Minister being out of town, a dull, flat Presbiter preached. Dined at home, and my wife's brother with us, we having a good dish of stewed beef of Janes own dressing, which was well done, and a piece of Sturgeon, of a barrel lately sent me by Captain Cocke. In the afternoon to White-hall and there walked an hour or two in the parke, where I saw the King now out of mourning[3] – in a suit laced with gold and silver, which it was said was out of fashion. Thence to the Wardrobe and there consulted with the ladies about our going to Hampton Court tomorrow; and thence home and after settled business there, my wife and I to the Wardrobe; and there we lay all night in Captain Ferrers chamber, but the bed so saft that I could not sleep that hot night.

12. Mr. Townsend called us up by 4 a-clock. And by 5 the three ladies, my wife and I, and Mr. Townsend, his son and daughter, were got to the barge and set out. We walked from Moreclacke to Richmond, and so to boat again; and from Teddington to Hampton Court, Mr. Townsend and I walked again – and there met the ladies and were showed the whole

---

a repl. 'it'

1. She did not go there. Her first son by the King (Charles Palmer, afterwards Fitzroy, cr. Duke of Southampton, 1675; d. 1730) was born in her house in King St, West-minster and was baptised at St Margaret's on 18 June: G. S. Stein-man, *A mem. of Duchess of Cleveland*, p. 33; cf. below, p. 146 & n. 4.

2. Several ships were now hired for the transport of soldiers and pro-visions to Tangier and Lisbon: PRO, Adm. 20/3, p. 339.

3. He had been in mourning for his aunt, Elizabeth, Queen of Bohemia (d. 13 February).

house by Mr. Marriot[1] – which endeed is nobly furnished –
perticularly the Queenes bed, given her by the States of Holland.
A Lookeing glase, sent by the Queene-Mother from France,
hanging in the Queens chamber.   And many brave pictures.[2]

So to Mr. Marriots, and there we rested ourselfs and drank.
And so to barge again, and there we had good victuals and wine
and were very merry.   And got home about 8 at night, very
well.   So my wife and I took leave of my Lady and home by
a hackny-coach, the easiest that ever I met with.   And so to bed.

13. At the office all the morning.   Dined at home alone, my
wife being sick of her *Mois* in bed.   Then to walk to Pauls
churchyard, and there[3] evened all reckonings to this day.   So
back to the office and so home.   And Will Joyce came with a
friend, a Cosen of his, to see me and I made them drink a bottle
of wine; and so to sing and read and to bed.

14. All the morning at Westminster and elsewhere about
business.   And dined at the Wardrobe, and after dinner sat an
hour or two talking alone with my Lady.   She is afeared that
my Lady Castlemayne will keep in still with the King; and I am
afeared she will not, for I love her well.   Thence to my brother's,
and finding him in a lie about the lining of my new morning
gowne, saying that it was the same with the outside, I was very
angry with him and parted so.   So home, after an hour stay at
Pauls churchyard; and there came Mr. MoreCocke of Chatham
and brought me a stately Cake, and I perceive he hath done the
same to the rest – of which I was glad.[4]   So to bed.

1. Richard Marriott, housekeeper
of the palace. Since October 1661
repair work had been in progress, and
some new building: *CTB*, i. 296, 320.
Pepys kept several prints and drawings
of Hampton Court: PL 2972, pp.
209-13.

2. After the recovery at the
Restoration of some of Charles I's
works of art, a number of pieces were
set up at Hampton Court, although
the finest pieces were perhaps reserved
for Whitehall. The inventory of
Charles II's pictures (c. 1667; see
above, i. 258, n. 1) lists over 200

pictures at Hampton Court, mainly
in the Queen's Gallery, the King's
Dressing Room, in Paradise and in the
King's Gallery. Perhaps the best
pictures then in the palace were
Mantegna's *Triumph of Caesar* and
Van Dyck's equestrian portrait of the
King's father with M. St Antoine.
(OM).

3. Sc. at Joshua Kirton's the bookseller's.

4. John Moorcock was a timber
merchant: for another of his cakes,
see below, v. 259.

15. To Westminster; and at the Privy Seale I saw Mr. Coventrys seal for his being Comissioner with us – at which I know not yet whether to be glad or otherwise.[1] So, doing several things by the way, I walked home;*a* and after dinner to the office all the afternoon. At night all the bells in the towne rung, and bonefires made for the joy of the Queenes arrivall;[2] who came and landed at Portsmouth last night. But I do not see much thorough joy, but only an indifferent one,[3] in the hearts of people, who are much discontented at the pride and luxury of the Court, and running in debt. So to bed.

16. Up earely; Mr Hater and I to the office, and there I made an end of my book of Contracts, which I have been making an abstract of.[4] Dined at home, and spent most of the day at the office. At night to supper and bed.

17. Upon a letter this morning from Mr. Moore, I went to my Cosen Turner's chamber, and there put*b* him upon drawing a replicacion to Tom Trices answer speedily.[5] So to White-hall and there met Mr. Moore; and I walk long in Westminster-hall and thence with him to the Wardrobe to dinner, where dined Mrs. Sanderson, the mother of the Mayds;[6] and after dinner my Lady and she and I on foot to Paternoster rowe to buy a petticoat against the Queenes coming for my Lady, of plain satin, and other things. And being come back again, we there met

a repl. 'o'-   *b* repl. 'up'

---

1. William Coventry was to prove Pepys's staunchest ally in the office. Pepys was now influenced perhaps by Carteret's dislike of Coventry: above, p. 79. Or he may have been nervous of some of the effects of Coventry's reforming zeal; see e.g. below, p. 104. For Coventry's patent of appointment, see above, p. 79, n. 3.

2. Cf. the account (16 May) in *CSPVen. 1661–4*, pp. 143–4.

3. Cf. Pepys's similar observation below, at p. 95.

4. See above, p. 65 & n. 2.

5. Cf. above, ii. 230. The dispute (now in Chancery) was about Robert Pepys's Brampton estate (above, ii. 134); the lawyer was John Turner of the Middle Temple.

6. *Recte* Lady Sanderson; Bridget, wife of Sir William, Gentleman of the Privy Chamber to the King. The Mother of the Maids was the household officer in charge of the maids-of-honour (in this case of the Queen). The post (established under Elizabeth) ceased to exist after 1689.

Mr. Nathaniel Crew at the Wardrobe with a young gentleman, a friend and fellow-student of his and of a good family, Mr. Knightly, and known to the Crews, of whom my Lady privately told me she hath some thoughts of a mach for my Lady Jemimah.[1] I like the person very well, and he hath 2000*l* per annum.   Thence to the office and there we sat; and thence, after writing letters to all my friends with my Lord at Portsmouth, I walked to my brother Toms to see a velvet Cloake which I buy of Mr. Moore; it will cost me 8*l*-10*s* – he bought it for 6*l*. 10*s* – but it is worth my money.   So home, and find all things made clean against tomorrow, which pleases me well.   So to bed.

18.   *Whitsunday.* By water to White-hall and there to Chappell in my pew, belonging me as Clerk of the Privy Seale.[2] And there I heard a most excellent sermon of Dr. Hacker,[3] Bishop of Lichfield and Coventry – upon these words: "Hee that drinketh*ᵃ* this water shall never thirst."[4] We had an excellent Anthemne sung by Captain Cooke and another, and brave Musique; and then the King Come down[5] and offered, and took the Sacrament upon his Knees – a sight very well worth seeing.   Thence with Sir G. Carteret to*ᵇ* his lodgeing to dinner,

a repl. ? 'S'-   b repl. 'home to'

1. Nathaniel Crew was Lady Sandwich's brother; Richard Knightley (a member of a well-known Northamptonshire family, and only son of Thomas Knightley, Rector of Byfield, Northants.) had been with Crew at Lincoln College, Oxford, and like him had taken holy orders. The proposed match did not come off: Knightley married in 1664 Sarah, daughter of John Wood of Hookland Park, Sussex; and in 1665 Lady Jemima married Philip, son of Sir George Carteret.

2. See above, p. 67 & n. 3.
3. *Recte* Hacket: now over 70, but still one of the most popular preachers of the day, in the elaborate style of preaching fashionable in the early part of the century.
4. A loose recollection of John, iv. 14. Two of his sermons on this text (both preached at Whitehall, but neither dated) were published in his *Century of sermons* (1675), pp. 893+, 902+.
5. From the King's closet where he sat during service.

with his Lady and one Mr. Brevin, a french divine.[1] We were
very merry, and good discourse, and I had much talk with my
Lady – after dinner; and so to Chappell again and there had
another good Anthemne of Captain Cookes. Thence to the
Councell Chamber; where the King and Council sat till almost 11
a-clock at night, and I forced to walk up and down the gallerys
till that time of night. They were reading all the bills over that
are to pass tomorrow at the House,[2] before the King's going
out of towne – and proroguing the House.

At last, the Council risen and Sir G. Carteret telling me what
the Council hath ordered about the ships designed to carry
horse from Ireland to Portugall, which is now altered,[3] I got a
Coach; and so home, sending the boat away without me. At
home, I find my wife discontented at my being abroad, but I
pleased her. She was in her new suit of black Sarcenet and
yellow petticoat, very pretty. So to bed.

19. Long in bed, sometimes scolding with my wife, and then
pleased again. And at last up and put on my riding cloth suit
and Camelot coat, new – which pleases me well enough. To
the Temple about my replicacion; and so to my brother Toms
and there hear that my father will be in town this week. So
home, the shops being but some shut and some open. I hear
that the House of Commons do think much that they should
be forced to huddle over business this morning, against the after-

1. Daniel Brevint, Canon of Dur-
ham, later (1681) Dean of Lincoln,
who had married Anne, Carteret's
sister. Not French, but like Carteret
a Jerseyman. He had been educated
in France (at Saumur) and had
spent his years of exile there during
the revolution, becoming spiritual
director of Turenne's wife, and had
returned from Normandy only a few
months before: *Corr. J. Cosin* (ed.
Ornsby), ii. 26. His visit to London
may have been connected with his
presentation to Brancepeth, co. Dur-
ham, a rectory in the royal gift, at
about this time: *CSPD 1661–2*,
pp. 256, 370.

2. John Browne, Clerk of Parlia-
ments, attended this meeting and read
12 bills: PRO, PC 2/55, pp. 637–8.
This was the normal procedure at the
end of session: E. R. Turner, *Privy
Council, 1603–1784*, ii. 129–31. The
last occasion on which it was done
was on 27 June 1685: BL, Add.
34349, f. 21r.

3. A previous order required
several merchant ships, employed to
carry horse-troops from England to
Portugal, to make the return journey
to Kinsale and there take on more
cavalry. They were now ordered to
sail back to Plymouth instead. PRO,
Adm. 106/6, f.453r.

noon, for the King to passe their acts, that he may go out of towne.[1] But he was, I hear since, forced to stay till almost 9 a-clock at night before he could have done; and then he prorogued them, and so to Gilford and lay there. Home, and Mr. Hunt dined with me, and were merry. After dinner, Sir W. Penn and his daughter and I and my wife by coach to the Theatre, and there in a box saw *The Little Thiefe*.[2] well done. Thence to Moore fields, and walked and eat some cheese cakes and gammon of Bacon; but when I was come home I was sick, forced to vomitt it up again. So [with] my wife walking and singing upon the leades till very late, it being pleasant and mooneshine, and so to bed.

20. Sir W. Penn and I did a little business at the office, and so home again. Then comes Deane*a* Fuller after we had dined, but I got something for him; and very merry we were for an houre or two, and I am most pleased with his company and goodness. At last parted, and my wife and I by coach to the Opera and there saw the second part of *Seige of Rhodes*,[3] but it is not so well done as when Roxalana was there – who, it is said, is now owned by my Lord of Oxford.[4] Thence to tower wharfe and there took boat; and we all walked to halfe-way-house and there eat and drunk – and were pleasant; and so finally home again in the evening, and so good-night – this being a very pleasant life that we now lead, and have long done; the Lord be blessed and make us thankful. But though I am much against too much spending, yet I do think it best to enjoy some degree of pleasure, now that we have health, money and opportunities, rather then to leave pleasures to old age or poverty, when we cannot have them so properly.

21. My wife and I by water to Westminster; and after she had seen her father (of whom lately I have heard nothing at all

a repl. 'Deane' (blotted)

---

1. To meet the Queen at Portsmouth. He had on the 15th requested the Commons to expedite business: *CJ*, viii. 29.

2. A comedy by Fletcher and Shirley (q.v. above, ii. 65 & n. 1); now at the TR, Vere St. (A).

3. See above, ii. 130 & n. 2; now at the LIF. (A).

4. See above, p. 58, n. 3. (A).

what he does, or her mother),[1] she came to me to my Lord's
Lodgeings, where she and I stayed, walking into White-hall
garden; and in the privy Garden saw the finest smocks and linen
petticoats of my Lady Castlemaynes, laced with rich[a] lace at the
bottomes, that ever I saw; and did me good to look upon them.
So to Wilkinsons, she and I and Sarah,[2] to dinner, where I had a
good Quarter of Lamb and a salat.   Here Sarah told me how
the King dined at my[b] Lady Castlemayne – and supped – every
day and night the last week.[3]   And that the[c] night that the bonefires were made for joy of the Queenes arrivall, the King was
there; but there was no fire at her door, though at all the rest
of the doors almost in the street; which was much observed.
And that the King and she did send for a pair of scales and weighed
one another; and she, being with child,[4] was said to be heavyest.
But she is now a most disconsolate creature, and comes not out
of doors – since the King's going.

But we went to the Theatre to *The French Dancing Maister*,[5] and
there with much pleasure we saw and gazed upon her.   But it
troubles us to see her look dejectedly, and slighted by people

a   repl. symbol rendered illegible   *b*   repl. 'supped'
c   l.h. repl. s.h. 'on'

---

1. They lived close by Westminster Hall until the autumn of
1662, when they moved near to
Covent Garden, possibly to the house
in Long Acre ('among all the bawdy-
houses') where Pepys found them on
17 February 1664.   What Alexandre
St Michel was working at is a
mystery.
2. Sandwich's housekeeper.
3. She then lived in King St,
Westminster.
4. See above, p. 81 & n. 1.
5. This piece (now at the TR,
Vere St) may have been the droll
entitled *The humours of M. Galliard*,
which was based upon two scenes of
The Variety, a comedy by William,
Duke of Newcastle, written c. 1641

and published in 1649. 'Drolls' –
short adaptations of full-length plays
– became popular during the Commonwealth period when dramatic
performances were given surrepti-
tiously at times despite the prohibition
of acting.   *The humours of M.
Galliard* was published in Francis
Kirkman's *The Wits, or Sport upon
sport* (1662).   M. Galliard, the French
dancing master, is one of the characters portrayed on the title-page of the
1672 edition of *The Wits*.   It is
possible, however, that Pepys may
have seen *The Variety* on this occasion
and that he is referring to it under a
title given to the droll: see *The Wits*
(ed. J. J. Elson), p. 388.   (A).

already. The play pleased us very well; but Lacy's part, the
Dancing Maister,[1] the best in the world.[a]

Thence to my brother Tom's in expectation to have met my
father there tonight, come out of the country. But he is not yet
come, but here we find my Uncle Fenner and his old wife, whom
I have not seen since the wedding dinner,[2] nor care to see her.
They being gone, my wife and I went and saw Mrs. Turner,
whom we find not well. And her two boys, Charles and Will,
come out of the country, grown very plain boys after three
years being under their father's care in Yorkshire. Thence to
Toms again and there supped well, my she-Cosen Scott being
there; and my father being not come, we walked home. And
to bed.

22. This morning comes an order from the Secretary of
State Nicholas, for me to let one Mr. Lee, a Councellor, to view
what papers I have relating to passages of the late times wherein
Sir H. Vanes hand is imployed – in order to the drawing up his
charge; which I did.[3] And at noon he, with Sir W. Penn and
his daughter, dined with me; and he to his work again and
we by coach to the Theatre and saw *Love in a maze*.[4] The play
hath[b] little in it but Lacys part of Contry fellow – which he did
to admiration.[5] So home and supped with Sir W. Penn – where
Sir W. Batten and Captain Cocke came to us – to whom I have
lately been a great stranger. This night we have each of us a

---

a There follow here two lines crossed out: 'Thence homeward, and were
overtaken by Sir W. Penn and his coach, and so we and he and his daughter to
the tower wharfe and thence by water to ...'.   *b* repl. 'as'

---

1. John Lacy was well suited to this
part, for he had been apprenticed to
a dancing master before he became a
comic actor. (A).

2. See above, p. 16.

3. Sir Henry Vane, jun., the republican, was brought to trial on
2 June and executed on the 14th: see
below, p. 104 & n. 1. The evidence
here referred to concerned his work
as Treasurer of the Navy during the
revolution, and was now used to
prove that he had levied war against
the King: *State Trials* (ed. Howell),
vi. 150.

4. *The Changes, or Love in a maze*;
a comedy by Shirley, licensed and
published in 1632; now at the TR,
Vere St. (A).

5. Lacy played Johnny Thump,
one of his most popular comic roles.
Wintersel played Sir Gervaise Simple.
(A).

letter from Captain Teddiman from the Streights, of a peace made upon good terms by Sir J. Lawson with the Argier-men – which is most excellent news.[1] He hath also sent each of us some anchoves, Olives and Muscatt; but I know not yet what that is, and am ashamed to ask.

After supper home and to bed – resolving to make up this week in seeing plays and pleasure, and so fall to business next week again for a great while.

23. At the office good part of the morning. And then about noon with my wife on foot to the Wardrobe. My wife went up to the dining roome to my Lady Paulina and I stayed below, talking with Mr. Moore in the parler, reading of the King and Chancellors late speeches at the prorogueing of the Houses of Parliament.[2] And while I was reading, news is brought me that my Lord Sandwich is come and gone up to my Lady – which put me into great[a] suspence of joy. So I went up, waiting my Lord's coming out of my Lady's chamber – which by and by he did, and looks very well and my soul is glad to see him. He very merry. And hath left the King and Queene at Portsmouth, and is come up to stay here till next Wednesday, and then to meet the King and Queen at Hampton Court.

So to dinner, Mr. Browne (Clerk of the House of Lords, and his wife and mother there also) and my Lord mighty merry – among other things, saying that the Queene is a very agreeable lady, and paints still.[3] After dinner I showed him my letter from Teddiman about the news from Argier, which pleases him

a repl. 'so'

1. This treaty, signed on 23 April/3 May and confirmed by the Sultan on 10 November, reduced the right of search which the Algerines claimed under the agreement made with the Earl of Winchilsea in 1660. It brought prestige to Lawson, but no solution to the problem of piracy, and was immediately dishonoured by the Algerines. Its terms were substantially repeated in Allin's treaty of 1664. Below, 28 November 1664; *Hist. memoirs of Barbary . . .* (1816),

pp. 102+; R. L. Playfair, *Scourge of Christendom*, pp. 85+; Sir G. Fisher, *Barbary Legend*, pp. 332+.

2. *His Majestie's most gracious speech, together with the Lord Chancellors to the two Houses of Parliament, at their prorogation . . . the nineteenth of May, 1662* (1662); reprinted in *LJ*, xi. 474–7.

3. Painting the face was commoner in most Mediterranean countries than in England: cf. J. Howell, *Epist. Ho-Elianae* (ed. Jacobs), i. 203.

exceedingly;[1] and he writ one to the Duke of Yorke about it and sent it express.

There coming much company after dinner to my Lord, my wife and I slunk away to the Opera, where we saw *Witt in a Constable*,[2] the first time that it is acted; but so silly a play I never saw I think in my life. After it was done, my wife and I to the puppet play in Covent garden, which I saw the other day, and endeed it is very pleasant. Here among the Fidlers I first saw a Dulcimore played on, with sticks[a] knocking of the strings, and is very pretty. So by water home. And supped with Sir W. Penn very merry; and so to bed.

24. To the Wardrobe and there again spoke with my Lord and saw W. Howe[3] – who is grown a very pretty and is a sober fellow. Thence abroad with Mr. Creede, of whom I informed myself of all I have a mind to know. Among other things – the great difficulty my Lord hath been in all this summer for lack of good and full orders from the King – and I doubt our Lords of the Council do not mind things as the late powers did, but their pleasures or profit more. That the *Huego de Toros* is a simple sport, yet the greatest in Spaine. That the Queene hath given no rewards to any of the Captaines or Officers, but only to my Lord Sandwich; and that was a bag of gold (which was no honourable present) of about 1400*l* Sterling. How recluse the Queene hath ever been, and all the voyage never came upon the deck, or put her head out of her Cabin[4] – but did love my Lord's musique; and would send for it down to the stateroom, and she set in her Cabin within hearing of it. That my Lord was forced to have some clashing with the Council of Portugall about payment of the porcion before he could get it – which was, besides

a repl. 'sticking'

1. Cf. Sandwich, p. 140.
2. A comedy by Henry Glapthorne, written between 1636 and 1638, and published in 1640; now at the LIF. (A).
3. Clerk to Sandwich.
4. She had always been shy. The English consul at Lisbon wrote to Secretary Nicholas on 19/29 July

1661 that she had hardly ventured outside the palace. 'In five years tyme shee was not out of doores, untill she harde of his Majesties intentions to make her Queen of Ingland, since which shee hath been to visit two saintes in the city . . .': qu. Lister, iii. 156.

Tanger and a free trade in the Indys, two millions of crownes –
half now, and the other half in twelve months. But they have
brought but little money; but the rest in Sugars and other
Comoditys, and bills of Exchange.[1] That the King of Portugall is
a very foole almost, and his mother doth all. And that he is a
very poor Prince.[2]

After a morning draught at the Starr in Cheapeside, I[a] took
him to the Exchange and thence home, but my wife having
dined, I took him to Fishstreet, and there we had a couple of
lobsters and dined upon them, and much discourse. And so I
to the office. And that being done, Sir W. Penn and I to Deptford by water to Captain Rooths to see him, he being very
sick; and by land home, calling at Halfe-way-house, where we
eat and drank. So home and to bed.

25. *Lords day.* To trimming myself, which I have this week
done every morning, with a pumice stone, which I learnt of Mr.
Marsh when I was last at Portsmouth; and I find it very easy,
speedy and cleanly,[b] and shall continue the practice of it.[3] To
church and heard a good sermon of Mr. Woodcockes at our
church. Only, in his later prayer for a woman in childbed, he
prayed that God would deliver her from the hereditary curse of
childebearing, which seemed a pretty strange expression. Dined
at home, and Mr. Creede with me. This day I had the first
dish of pease I have had this year. After discourse, he and I
abroad; and walked up and down and look into many churches –

a MS. 'my'   b repl. 'cleank'-

---

1. The dowry also included Bombay. The amount to be paid in cash
(2 m. crusados – c. £300,000 sterling)
was very large – too large for the
resources of Portugal – but Sandwich
exceeded his instructions in accepting,
in part payment, goods and bills as
well as money. It was never com-
pletely paid. See Sandwich, pp.
125+, and his letters to Clarendon,
in Lister, iii. 193, 196; E. Prestage,
Diplom. relations Portugal 1640–68,
pp. 142+; C. L. Grose in *Hispanic-
Am. Hist. Rev.*, 10/313+; Harris,
i. 195+, 210+.

2. Afonso VI reigned very feebly
from 1656 to 1683; in June of this
year he overthrew the regency of his
mother, Luisa, only to fall under the
domination of other advisers.

3. Previously Pepys had usually
been shaved by a barber. On 6 January 1664 he began to use a razor.

among other, Mr. Baxters at Blackefryers.[1] Then to the Wardrobe, where I find my Lord takes physic, so I did not see him.
But with Captain Ferrers (in Mr. George Mountagus coach) to
Charing-cross; and there at the Triumph taverne he showed
me some portugall Ladys which are come to towne before the
Queene. They are not handsome, and their farthingales[2] a
strange dress.[a] Many ladies and persons of Quality come to see
them. I find nothing in them that is pleasing. And I see they
have learnt to kiss and look freely up and downe already, and I do
believe will soon forget the recluse practice of their own country.
They complain much for lack of good water to drink.[3] So to
the Wardrobe back on foot, and supped with my Lady; and so
home, and after a walk upon the leads with my wife, to prayer
and bed.

The King's guards and some City companies do walk up and
down the towne these five or six days; which makes me think,
and they do say, there are some plots in laying.[4] God keep us.

26. Up by 4 a-clock in the morning and fell to the preparing
of some accounts for my Lord of Sandwich. By and by, by
appointment comes Mr. Moore; and by what appears to us at
present, we find that my Lord is above 7000*l* in debt and that
he hath money coming into him that will clear all; and so we

a preceding part of entry crowded into bottom of page

---

1. St Anne's, of which John Gibbon
was Rector, and where Richard
Baxter was employed as a preacher to
deliver a weekly Sunday sermon.
On this day Baxter preached his
farewell sermon before resigning
under the Act of Uniformity: M. Sylvester, *Reliq. Baxt.* (1696), bk i (pt ii),
p. 302.
2. These hooped petticoats had
gone out of fashion in England c.
1630. Clarendon remarks on the
'opiniatrety' of the Portuguese ladies-
attendant in retaining their own
fashion, and says that the Queen herself was only with difficulty persuaded

not to: *Life*, ii. 168. Evelyn found
them 'monstrous': 30 May 1662.
3. Household water in Westminster came mainly from wells and
carriers; in Lisbon it was mountain
water carried in by aqueducts. For
the city of London's supplies, see
below, iv. 295 n.3.
4. There were rumours of a plot
by the sectaries; especially in St
Giles Cripplegate, and All Hallows;
details in *CSPD 1661–2*, pp. 376, 385,
396, 397.

think him clear – but very little money in his purse.[1] So to my
Lord's; and after he was ready, we spent an houre with him,
giving him an account thereof. And he having some 6000*l* in
his hands remaining of the King's, he is resolved to make use
of that and get off of it as well as he can – which I like well
of – for else I fear he will scarce get*a* beforehand again a great
while. Thence home and to the Trinity-house, where the
Bretheren (who have been at Deptford today choosing a new
Maister; which is Sir J. Minnes, notwithstanding Sir W. Batten
did contend highly for it; at which I am not a little pleased,
because of his proud Lady) about 3 a-clock came hither, and so to
dinner. I seated myself close by Mr. Prin; who, in discourse
with me, fell upon what records he hath of the lust and wicked
lives of the Nuns heretofore in England,[2] and showed me out of
his pocket one wherein 30 Nuns for their lust were ejected of their
house, being not fit to live there, and by the Popes command
to be put, however, into other Nunnerys.

I could not stay to end dinner with them; but rise and privately
went out, and by water to my brother's; and thence to take*b*
my wife to the Redd bull,[3] where we saw *Dr. Faustus*;[4] but so
wretchedly and poorly done, that we were sick of it – and the
worse because by a former resolution it is to be the last play we
are to see till Michaelmas. Thence homewards by coach through
Moore-fields, where we stood a while and saw*c* the Wrestling.[5]
At home, got my lute upon the Leades and there played; and
so to bed.

27. To my Lord this morning and thence to my brother's,
where I find my father, poor man, come; which I was glad to

a repl. 'before'   *b* MS. 'took'   *c* MS. 'some'

---

1. For these accounts, see above,
ii. 113, n. 2; below, p. 121, n. 1.

2. William Prynne, the Presbyterian pamphleteer, was keeper of the
Tower records, and a rabid anti-
papist.

3. An old open-air playhouse in
St John's St, Clerkenwell; see above,
ii. 58 & n. 1. (A).

4. A tragedy by Marlowe, acted

c. 1592, and published in 1604.
Pepys probably saw the version
printed in 1663, which contained
several new scenes. It was probably
acted by a minor company managed
by George Jolly; certainly not by
the King's Company or the Duke of
York's Company. (A).

5. Cf. above, ii. 127, n. 2.

see. I stayed with him till noon and then he went to my Cosen Scotts to dinner, who had invited him. He tells me his altera-tions of the house and garden at Brampton, which please me well.[1]

I could not go with him, and so we parted at Ludgate, and I home to dinner. And to the office all the afternoon, and Musique in my chamber alone at night, and so to bed.

28. Up earely to put things in order in my chamber. Then to my Lord's, with whom I spoke about several things; and so up and down in several places about business with Mr. Creede; among others, to Mr. Wottons the shoemaker and there drank our morning draught. And then home about noon; and by and by comes my father by appointment to dine with me; which we did very merrily – I desiring to make him as merry as I can while the poor man is in towne. After dinner comes my uncle Wight and sat awhile and talk[ed] with us; and thence we three to the Mum-house at Leaden hall and there sat awhile; then I left them and to the Wardrobe, where I find my Lord gone to Hampton Court. Here I stayed all the afternoon, till late, with Creed and Captain Ferrers, thinking whether we shall go tomorrow together to Hampton Court; but Ferrers his wife coming in by and by to the house with the young ladies (with whom she had been*a* abroad), she was unwilling to go, where-upon I was willing to put off our going; and so home. But still my mind was hankering after our going tomorrow. So to bed.

29. At home all the morning. At noon to the Wardrobe and dined with my Lady. And after dinner stayed long, talk-ing with her. Then homeward; and in Lumberstreete was called out of a window by Alderman Backwell, where I went and saluted his lady, a very pretty woman. Here was Mr. Creede, and it seems they have been under some disorder, in feare of a fire at the next door, and have been removing their goods. But the fire*b* was over before I came. Thence home,

a repl. 'abr'-　　　*b* MS. 'fear'

---

1. Cf. below, pp. 97, 219. Nothing more is known of these alterations.

and with my wife and the two maids and the boy took boat and to Fox hall – where I have not been a great while – to the Old Spring garden. And there walked long and the wenches gathered pinks. Here we stayed; and seeing that we could not have anything to eat but very dear and with long stay, we went forth again without any notice taken of us; and so we might have done if we had had anything. Thence to the New=one,[1] where I never was before, which much exceeds the other. And here we also walked, and the boy creeps through the hedge and gather[s] abundance of roses. And after long walk, passed out of doors as we did in the other place. And so to another house, that was an ordinary house, and here we have cakes and powdered beef and ale; and so home again by water, with much pleasure.

This day, being the Kings birth-day,[2] was very solemnely observed; and the more for that the Queene this day comes to Hampton Court. In the evening bonefires were made, but nothing to the great number that was heretofore at the burning of the Rump.[3]

So to bed.

30. This morning I made up my accounts and find myself *de Claro* worth about 530*l.* and no more, so little have I encreased it since my last reckoning;[4] but I confess I have laid out much money in clothes.

Upon a Suddaine motion, I took my wife and Sarah and Will by water, with some victuals with us, as low as Gravesend, entending to have gone into the Hope to the *Royall James*[5] to have seen the ship and Mr. Sheply; but meeting Mr. Sheply in a hoy, bringing up my Lord's things, she and I went on board and sailed up with them as far as half-way tree – very glad to see Mr. Sheply. Here we saw a little Turke and a negro, which are entended for pages to the two young ladies. Many birds and other pretty noveltys there was. But I was afeared of being lowzy, and so took boat again and got to London before them.

1. The New Spring Garden, con-structed in 1661; see *Comp.*: 'Vaux-hall'.

2. Cf. above, i. 166, n. 2.
3. Cf. above, i. 52 & n. 4.

4. On 31 December 1661 he had put his wealth at c. £500: above, ii. 241.

5. Sandwich's flagship on his Mediterranean voyage, 1661–2.

All the way, coming and going, reading in *The Wallflower*[1] with great pleasure. So home; and thence to the Wardrobe, where Mr. Sheply was come with the things. Here I stayed talking with my Lady, who is preparing to go tomorrow to Hampton Court. So home, and at 10 a-clock at night Mr. Sheply came to sup with me; so we had a dish of Mackerell and pease, and so he bid us good-night, going to lie on board the Hoy, and I to bed.

31. Lay long in bed. So up to make up my Journall for these two or three days past. Then came Anthony Joyce, who duns me for money for the tallow which he served[a] in lately by my desire, which vexes me. But I must get it him the next by my promise.[2]

By and by to White-hall, hearing that Sir G. Carteret was come to towne; but I could not find him, and so back to Tom's; and thence I took my father to my house and there he dined with me – discoursing of our businesses with uncle Thomas and T. Trice. After dinner he departed, and I to the office, where we met.[3] And that being done, I walked to my Brother[b] – and the Wardrobe and other places about business, and so home. And had Sarah to comb my head clean, which I find so foul with poudering and other troubles, that I am resolved to[c] try how I can keep my head dry without pouder.[4] And I did also in a

a repl. 'several'   *b* repl. 'father'   *c* repl. 'how'

---

1. *Herba Parietis or The wall-flower, as it grew out of the stone chamber belonging to Newgate, being a history which is partly true, partly romantick, morally divine: whereby a marriage between reality and fancy is solemnized by divinity. Written by Thomas Bayly, D.D., whilst he was a prisoner there* (1650). Bayly had graduated from Magdalene in 1627. The frontispiece is in PL 2973 (p. 314*a*), but Pepys did not retain the book itself.

2. Joyce had served in 20 barrels of hard English tallow to Deptford stores, and his bill (for £92 6s. 3d.) had been registered in the Navy Treasury on 29 April: PRO, Adm. 20/3, p. 244. Shish, the Deptford shipwright, on 4 June sent Pepys 'with haist' a certificate of its good quality, possibly at Pepys's request: PRO, SP 29/56, no. 15. For Pepys's promise to Joyce, see above, p. 69.

3. Sc. the Principal Officers had a meeting.

4. Cf. below, p. 196.

sudden fit cut off all my beard, which I have been a great while bringing up, only that I may with my pumice-stone do my whole face, as I now do my chin, and so save time – which I find a very easy way and gentile. So she also washed my feet in a bath of hearbes; and so to bed.

This month ends with very fair weather for a great while together. My health pretty well, but only wind doth now and then torment me about the fundament extremely. The Queene is brought a few days since to Hampton Court; and all people say of her to be a very fine and handsome lady[1] and very discreet, and that the King is pleased enough with her: which I fear will put Madam Castlemaines nose out of Joynt. The Court is wholly now at Hampton. A peace with Argiers is lately made; which is also good news. My father is lately come to towne to see us, and though it hath cost and will cost more money, yet I am pleased with the alteracions on my house at Brampton. My Lord Sandwich is lately come with the Queene from Sea, very well and good repute. Upon an audit of my estate I find myself worth about 530*l de Claro*. [The] Act for Uniformity is lately printed, which it is thought will make mad work among the presbyterian ministers.[2] Spirits of all sides are

---

1. She was short, plump and of a good colour, with prominent front teeth, fine eyes and a pleasant expression. Opinions about her looks varied greatly, though probably there cannot have been any real ground for doubt. They are collected in Burnet, i. 307, n. 4; to which may be added Monconys, ii. 19–20 (May 1662); *Verney Mem.*, ii. 173; and James Yonge, *Journal* (ed. Poynter), pp. 43, 170. Charles himself wrote to Clarendon on 21 May that her eyes were 'excellent good', and that there was 'not any thing in her face that in the least degree can shoque one . . .': BM, Lansdowne 1236, f.124r. Pepys's view was critical: see below, p. 277. He preserved several engraved portraits of her:

J. Charrington, *Cat. engraved portraits in PL*, p. 29: PL 2973, p. 416. Later in life she 'waddled like a duck': Yonge, p. 43.

2. *An act for the uniformity of publick prayers . . .*; 13–14 Car. II c. 4; passed on 19 May; put into effect on 24 August; the Act usually held as marking the establishment of modern nonconformity. Much more severe than the Elizabethan law of uniformity, it imposed on all clergy a revised prayer-book and other tests, and led to the ejection in the following August of all those parsons (almost all Presbyterian) who were now unwilling to accept these terms. Close on 1000 were extruded without compensation, and the 'mad work' was particularly heavy in London.

very much discontented; some thinking themselfs used, contrary to promise, too hardly; and the other, that they are not rewarded so much as they expected by the King. God keep us all. I have by a late oath obliged myself from wine and playes, of which I find good effect.

JUNE.

1. *Lords day.* At church in the morning a stranger made a very good sermon. Dined at home, and Mr. Spong came to see me. So he and I set down a little to sing some French psalms,[1] and then comes Mr. Sheply and Mr. Moore; and so we to dinner – and after dinner to church again where a presbyter made a sad and long sermon, which vexed me, and so home. And so to walk on the leads, and sup and to prayers and bed.

2. Up earely about business. And then to the Wardrobe with Mr. Moore and spoke to my Lord about exchange of the Crusados into Sterling money[2] – and other matters. So to my father at Toms; and after some talk with him, away home; and by and by comes my father to dinner with me. And then by coach, setting him down in cheapeside, my wife and I to Mrs. Clarkes at Westminster, the first visit that ever we both made her yet. We find her in a *dishabillée* – entending to go to Hampton Court tomorrow. We had much pretty discourse, and a very fine lady she is. Thence by water to Salsbury Court and Mrs. Turner not being at home, home by Coach. And so after walking on the leads and supper, to bed. This day my wife put on her slashed wastecoate,[3] which is very pretty.

3. Up by 4 a-clock. And to my business in my chamber – to even accounts with my Lord and myself; and very fain I would become master of 1000*l.*, but I have not above 530*l* towards it yet.

At the office all the morning, and Mr. Coventry brought his patent and took his place with us this morning. Upon our making a Contract, I went, as I use to do, to draw the heads thereof; but Sir W Pen most basely told me that the Controller

---

1. See above, i. 140 & n. 3. (E).
2. Part of the dowry of Catherine of Braganza: see above, p. 91, n. 1. Her gift to Sandwich (worth c. £540) was included. Crusados were usually of gold. For their value, see below,

p. 102; E. Prestage, *Diplom. relations Engl. and Portugal*, p. 16.
3. A slashed garment was cut so as to reveal a colourful undergarment or lining.

99

is [to] do it, and so begun to imploy Mr. Turner about it, at
which I was much vexed and begun to dispute; and what with
the letter of the Dukes orders,[1] and Mr. Barlows letter,[2] and the
practice of our predecessors, which Sir G. Carteret knew best
when he was Comptroller, it was ruled for me.[3]   What Sir
J. Minnes will do when he comes I know not, but Sir W. Penn
did it like a base raskall, and so I shall remember him while I
live.

After office done, I went down to the Tower wharfe, where
Mr. Creed and Sheply was ready with three chests of Crusados,
being about 6000*l*, ready to bring on shore to my house; which
they did, and put it in my further cellar – and Mr. Sheply took
the key.   I to my father and Dr Williams and Tom Trice, by
appointment in the old Bayly, to Short's*ᵃ* the ale house, but
could come to no terms with T. Trice.   Thence to the Wardrobe, where I find my Lady come from Hampton Court, where
the Queene hath used her very civilly; and my Lady tells me is
a most pretty woman – at which I am glad.

Yesterday (Sir R. Ford told me) the Aldermen of the City did
attend her in their habitts, and did present her with a gold Cupp,
and 1000*l* in gold therein.[4]   But he told me that they are so
poor in their Chamber, that they were fain to call two or three

a   repl. l.h. 'Cap'-

---

1. The Instructions of January
1662.
2. Untraced. Thomas Barlow (appointed jointly with Fleming in
1639) was the only Clerk of the Acts
surviving from the pre-Civil War
period.
3. The Comptroller (whose duties
were miscellaneous and enormous)
had long ceased to draft contracts,
and the Clerk of the Acts, in taking
over this and other work, had assumed the major share of business
in the office.   See below, p. 145 for

Pepys's objection to merchants making contracts with Batten at his
house.   It was a far cry from the
position in 1600 and 1617 when the
duties of the Clerk were stated to
be merely those of registering the
decisions of the board: Oppenheim,
pp. 87, 190.
4. On 1 June Common Council
had voted to the Queen 1000 twenty-
shilling gold pieces 'in a rich purse'
(not cup) 'with all humble congratu-
lation' on her safe arrival: LRO,
Journals 45, f.215*r*.

Aldermen to raise fines to make up this sum – among which
was Sir W. Warren.[1]

Home and to the office; where, about 8 at night, comes Sir
G. Carteret and Sir W. Batten. And so we did some business.
And then home and to bed, my mind troubled about Sir W. Penn
– his playing the rogue with me today. As also about the
charge of money that is in my house, which I had forgot. But I
made the maids to rise and light a candle and set it in the dining
room to scare away thiefs. And so to sleep.

4. Up early. And Mr. Moore comes to me and tells me
that Mr. Barnwell is dead, which troubles me something, and
the more for that I believe we shall lose Mr. Sheply's company.[2]

By and by Sir W. Batten and I by water down to Woolwich
and there saw an experiment made of Sir R. Ford's holland's
yarne (about which we have lately had so much stir; and I have
much concerned myself for our Ropemaker, Mr Hughes, who
hath represented it as bad); and we found it to be very bad, and
broke sooner then, upon a fair triall, five threades of that against
four of Riga yarn; and also that some of it hath old Stuffe that
hath been tarred, coverd over with new hempe, which is such a
cheat as hath not been heard of.[3] I was glad of this discovery,
because I would not have the King's workmen discouraged (as

1. This was a financial device
commonly used at this period by all
municipalities. Warren (a timber
merchant) was nominated alderman
on 13 May, sworn on the 27th and
then discharged from service on the
same day on payment of a fine of £400
which protected him from all further
election to office: LRO, Repert. 68,
f.119r. Between 27 May and the end
of June a further £2080 was levied
from five other aldermen-elect by
the same method: ib., ff. 119-41.

2. Robert Barnwell was Sandwich's steward at Hinchingbrooke;
Edward Shipley held a similar office
in his London household.

3. William Hughes, ropemaker at

Woolwich yard, had written un-
favourably to Batten about Ford's
yarn on 17 May; on the other hand,
his subordinates Falconer and Bar-
tram had on 2 June reported a successful trial of it: *CSPD 1661-2*, pp. 374,
396. Hughes was dismissed by
Batten a few weeks later, and Ford
seems to have had his revenge on
Pepys in the autumn: below, p. 283.
For Riga yarn (generally reputed
the best) and for methods of rope-
making, see below, iv. 259 & n. 4;
vi. 34 & n. 3. Some fraudulent
practices of the trade are described in
John Hollond, *Discourses* (ed. Tanner),
pp. 187+. The one mentioned by
Pepys was not new.

Sir W. Batten doth most basely do) from representing the faults of merchants goods, when there is any.

After eating some fish that we had bought upon the water at Falconers, we went to Woolwich and there viewed our frames of our houses,[1] and so home; and I to my Lord's, who I find resolved to buy Brampton Mannor of Sir Peter Ball, at which I am glad.[2]   Thence to White-hall and showed Sir G Carteret the cheat; and so to[a] the Wardrobe and there stayed and supped with my Lady – my Lord eating nothing, but writes letters tonight to several places, he being to go out of town tomorrow. So late home and to bed.

5.   To the Wardrobe; and there my Lord did enquire my opinion of Mr. Moore, which I did give to the best advantage I could, and by that means shall get him joyned with Mr. Townesend in the Wardrobe business.[3]   He did also give me all Mr. Sheplys and Mr. Moores accounts to view – which I am glad of, as being his great trust in me, and I would willingly keep up a good interest with him.[4]   So took leave of him (he being to go this day) and to the office, where they were just set down. And I showed them yesterday's discovery, and have got Sir R. Ford to be my enemy by it; but I care not, for it is my duty; and so did get his bill stopped for the present.

To dinner, and find Dr Tho. Pepys at my house.   But I was called from dinner, by a note from Mr. Moore, to Alderman Backwells to see some thousands of my Lord's Crusados weighed. And we find that 3000 come to about 530 or 40l generally.

a   repl. 'home'

---

1. The wooden structures of the upper storeys that were to be added to the houses of Pepys and Batten: see above, p. 59 & n. 2.

2. See below, p. 176.

3. Cf. above, ii. 113, n. 2. Townshend proved to be a disastrously bad (or dishonest) accountant: below, 30 December 1667. Moore does not seem to have received any formal appointment, but may have acted informally.   William Godolphin, another of Sandwich's servants, found him an honest but slow accountant: Sandwich MSS, Letters from Ministers, ii, f.127r.

4. Throughout the diary period Pepys seems to have been employed by Sandwich to supervise his accounts, and had special responsibility for collecting Sandwich's naval pay. The accounts here mentioned do not appear to have survived. Some of 1670 are in Rawl. A 174, ff. 437-9, 446r.

Home again and find my father there. We talked a good while and so parted.

We met at the office in the afternoon to finish Mr. Gaudens accounts; but did not do them quite. In the evening with Mr. Moore to Backewells with another 12000 Crusados and saw them weighed, and so home. And to bed.

6. At my office all alone all the morning; and the smith, being with me about other things, did open a chest that hath stood ever since I came to the office in my office, and there we find the modell of a fine ship – which I long to know whether it be the King's or Mr. Turner's.[1]

At noon to the Wardrobe by appointment to meet my father; who did come and was well treated by my Lady – who tells me she hath some thoughts to send her two little boys to our house to Brampton. But I have got leave for them to go along with me and my wife to Hampton Court tomorrow or Sunday. Thence to my brother Toms, where we find a letter from Pall that my mother is dangerously ill, in fear of death; which troubles my father and me much, but I hope it is otherwise – the letter being four days old since it was writ.

Home and at my office, and with Mr. Hater set things in order till evening; and so home and to bed by daylight.

This day, at my father's desire, I lent my brother Tom 20*l.*, to [be] repaid out of the proceed of Stirtlow when we can sell it. I sent the money all in new money by my boy, from Alderman Backwells.

7. To the office, where all the morning. And I find Mr. Coventry is resolved to do much good and to inquire into all the miscarriages of the office. At noon with him and Sir W. Batten to dinner at Trinity-house – where among others, Sir J. Robinson, Lieutenant of the Tower, was; who says that yesterday Sir H. Vane had a full hearing at the Kings bench, and is

1. Since c. 1650 the navy authorities had ordered wooden scale models of ships under construction: R. C. and R. Anderson, *Sailing Ship*, p. 146. Pepys made a collection of them: see below, p. 163 & n. 1. Thomas Turner had been Clerk-General of the office in the 1650's.

found guilty.   And that he did never hear any man argue more*a*
simply then he in all his life, and so others say.¹

My mind in great trouble whether I should go as I entended
to Hampton Court tomorrow or no.   At last, resolved the
contrary because of the charge thereof and I am afeared now to
bring in any accounts for journys; and so will others I suppose
be, because of Mr. Coventry's prying into them.²

Thence sent for to Sir G. Carterets, and there talked with him
a good while.   I perceive, as he told me, were it not that Mr.
Coventry hath already feathered his nest in selling of places,³
he doth like him very well and hopes great good from him.
But he complains so of lack of money, that my heart is very sad,
under the apprehension of the fall of the office.   At my office
all the afternoon.   And at night hear that my father is gone
into the country; but whether to Richmond as he entended
and thence to meet me*b* at Hampton Court on Monday, I know
not, or to Brampton – at which I am much troubled.   In the
evening, home and to bed.

8.   *Lords day.*   Lay till church-time in bed; and so up and
to church and there I find Mr. Mills come home out of the
country again, and preached but a lazy sermon.   Home and
dined with my wife, and so to church again with her.

Thence walked to my Lady's and there supped with her; and

a MS. 'for'   *b* MS. 'be'

---

1. The republican Vane the
younger was not a regicide, but was
reckoned too dangerous to be allowed
to live.   Imprisoned since the Restoration, he had now been brought
to trial on 2 June on charges of high
treason against Charles II.   Found
guilty on the 6th, he was sentenced on
the 11th.   His arguments in his own
defence (being accused of treason, he
had no counsel) are in *State Trials* (ed.
Howell), vi. 152+.   They were
able, but were presented hesitantly:
Merc. Pub., 12 June; cf. Burnet, i.
286, n. 2.

2. Travelling charges continued to
be allowed, but had perhaps to be
more strictly justified.   Shortly afterwards, Batten found himself criticised
for taking his wife to Portsmouth on
official business: below, p. 145.   See
Treasurer's ledgers, PRO, Adm. 20,
passim.

3. Coventry had not exceeded the
normal practice of his office (as
Admiral's Secretary), but his per-
quisites had been large because many
commands had been filled at the
Restoration.   See above, i. 241 &
n. 1; below, iv. 156 & n. 4.

merry, among other things, with the Parrett which my Lord
hath brought from sea, which speaks very well and cries "Pall" so
pleasantly that made my Lord give it my Lady Paulina; but my
Lady her mother doth not like it.

Home, and observe my man Will to walk with his cloak flung
over his shoulder like a Ruffian; which whether it was that he
might not be seen to walk along with the footboy, I know not,
but I was vexed at it; and coming home, and after prayers, I did
ask him where he learned that immodest garb, and he answered
me that it was not immodest, or some such slight answer, at
which I did give him two boxes on the ear; which I never did
before, and so was after a little troubled at it; and to bed.

9. earely up and at the office with Mr. Hater, making my
Alphabet of Contracts,[1] upon the dispatch of which I am now very
intent, for that I am resolved much to inquire into the price of
commodities.

Dined at home; and after dinner to my brother's and several
other places; among the rest, to Gratorex's and with him and
another stranger to the Taverne, but I drunk no wine. He com-
mended Bond, of our end of the towne, to teach me to measure
Timber[2] – and some other things that I would learn in order to
my office. Thence back again to the office and there T. Hater
and I did make an end of my Alphabet, which did much please
me. So home to supper and to bed.

10. At the office all the morning. Much business and great
hopes of bringing things, by*a* Mr. Coventry's means, to a good
condition in the office. Dined at home, Mr. Hunt with us. To
the office again in the afternoon; but not meeting as was intended, I went to my brother's and booksellers and other places
about business, and paid off all for books to this day and do not
entend to buy any more of any kind a good while – though I
had a great mind to have bought the King's *works*, as they are

a l.h. repl. s.h. 'my'

---

1. See above, p. 65 & n. 2.
2. Henry Bond, an experienced
teacher of applied mathematics, and
author on the subject, now lived in
the Tower Bulwark. The measuring
of timber was difficult and often gave
rise to fraud: cf. below, pp. 151, 163,
169.

new-printed in folio,¹ and present it to my Lord.   But I think it
will be best to save the money.

So home and to bed.

11.   At the office all the morning, Sir W. Batten, Sir W. Penn
and I, about the Victuallers accounts.   Then home to dinner,
and to the office again all the afternoon, Mr. Hater and I writing
over my Alphabet faire, in which I took great pleasure to rule
the lines and to have the Capitall words writ with red inke.   So
home and to supper.   This evening Mr Savill the painter came
and did varnish over my wife's picture and mine, and I paid him
for my little picture 3*l-os-od*, and so am clear with him.   So
after supper, to bed.

This day I have a letter from my father that he is got down
well and finds my mother pretty well again – so that I am vexed
with all my heart at Pall for writing to him so much concerning
my mother's illnesse (which I believe was not so great), as that
he should be forced to hasten down on the sudden back into the
country, without taking leave or having any pleasure here.

12.   This morning I tried on my riding-cloth suit with close
knees, the first that ever I made, and I think they will be very
convenient – if not too hot to wear any other open-knees after
them.   At the office all the morning – where we have a full
Board, *viz.*, Sir G. Carteret, Sir John Mennes, Sir W. Batten,
Mr. Coventry, Sir W Pen, Mr. Pett and myself.   Among many
other businesses, I did get a vote signed by all concerning my
issuing of warrants, which they did not smell the use I entend to
make of it; but it is to plead for my clerks to have their right
of giving out all warrants, in which I am not a little pleased.²
But a great difference happened between Sir G. Carteret and Mr.
Coventry about passing the victuallers account, and whether Sir

1. ΒΑΣΙΛΙΚΑ;   *The workes of
King Charles the Martyr* . . . (2 vols);
licence for its publication was dated
this day: *Trans. Stat. Reg.*, ii. 311.
Pepys later bought a copy for himself:
below, vi. 101 & n. 3.

2. These warrants authorised payment by the Navy Treasurer for
supplies, and were now, by this order,
to be issued on Tuesday mornings
only, Thursday mornings being reserved for concluding contracts with
merchants.   Pepys's own memorandum of this vote does not mention
the question of who signed the warrants: PRO, Adm. 106/3520, f.6*v*.

George is to pay the Victualler*a* his money, or the Exchequer; Sir George claiming it to be his place to save his threepences.[1] It ended in anger, and I believe will come to be a Question before the King and Council. I did what I could to keep myself unconcerned in it, having some things of my own to do before I would appear high in anything.

Thence to dinner, by Mr. Gaudens invitation, to the Dolphin, where a good dinner. But which is to myself a great wonder, that with ease I passed the whole dinner without drink[ing] a drop of wine.

After dinner to the office, my head full of business, and so home, and it being the longest day in the year,[2] I made all my people go to bed by daylight. But after I was abed and asleep, a note came from my brother Tom to tell me that my Cozen Anne Pepys of Worstershire her husband is dead and [she] married again, and her second husband in town and entends to come and see me tomorrow.[3]

13. Up by 4 a-clock in the morning and read Cicero's *Second Oracion against Cataline*,[4] which pleased me exceedingly; and more I discern therein then ever I thought was to be found in him. But I perceive it was my ignorance, and that he is as good a writer as ever I read in my life.

By and by to Sir G. Carterets to talk with him about yesterday's difference at the office; and offered my service to look into any old books or papers that I have that may make for him. He was well pleased therewith – and did much inveigh against

a MS. 'Victuallers'

1. The Treasurer received from all payments he made a poundage of threepence, and the victualler's accounts were by far the largest he dealt with. For his victory in the struggle with the Exchequer, see below, p. 243. Coventry re-opened the issue with Carteret's successor in 1667: below, viii. 378 & n. 2. At about this time Carteret seems to have succeeded in reviving this system of payment by fees and allowances in place of the salary of £2000 intro-duced in 1660: *Cat.*, i. 8, n. 3. Payment by salary was re-established in 1671.

2. By the Old Style. See above, pp. x–xi.

3. Her first husband was named Hall, and her second Fisher.

4. PL 2291, pp. 117–291. An Aldine edition of Cicero's works (PL 2290–3; Venice, 1582–3, 4 vols, folio) was an early acquisition in the PL, having six of Pepys's own shelf-marks apart from that of his heir.

Mr. Coventry, telling me how he had done him service in the parliament, when Prin had drawn up things against him for taking of money for places; that he did, at his desire and upon his letters, keep him off from doing it.[1]   And many other things he told me, as how the King was referring* to him, and in what a miserable condition his family would be if he should die before he had cleared his accounts: upon the whole, I do find that he doth much esteem of me and is my friend.   And I may make good use of him.

Thence to several places about businesses; among others, to my Brother and there Tom Beneere the barber trimmed me.

Thence to my Lady's and there dined with her – Mr. Loxton, Gibbons, and Goodgroone with us, and after dinner some Musique, and so home to my business; and in the evening, my wife and I and Sarah and the boy, a most pleasant walk to Halfway-house; and so home and to bed.

14.   Up by 4 a-clock in the morning and upon business at my office.   Then we sat down to business; and about 11 a-clock, having a room got ready for us, we all went out to the Tower hill; and there, over against the Scaffold made on purpose this day, saw Sir Henry Vane brought.[2]   A very great press of people.   He made a long speech, many times interrupted by the Sheriffe and others there; and they would have taken his paper out of his hand, but he would not let it go.   But they caused all the books of those that writ after him[3] to be given the Sheriffe; and the Trumpets were brought under the scaffold, that he might not be heard.[4]

Then he prayed, and so fitted himself and received the blow. But the Scaffold was so crowded that we could not see it done.

---

1. This occasion has not been traced.   Coventry was attacked on the same score in May 1663 and February 1668; see below, iv. 156 & n. 4; ix. 86–7.

2. For his trial, see above, pp. 103–4.   For other descriptions of his execution, see *Merc. Pub.*, 19 June, pp. 370–1; *CSPVen. 1661–4*, p. 157; *The tryal of Sir H. Vane* . . . (1662).

3. I.e. the notes of his speech taken by his friends.   But some survived: *State Trials* (ed. Howell), vi. 195.

4. For the speech, see *State Trials*, vi. 193+.   The use of the musicians to drown the condemned man's speech appears to have been novel, and excited comment: Burnet, i. 286; Mundy, v. 143; Ludlow, *Mem.* (ed. Firth), ii. 338.

But Boreman,[1] who had been upon the Scaffold, came to us and told us that first he begun to speak of the irregular proceeding against him; that he was, against Magna Charta, denied to have his excepcions against the Endictment allowed. And that there he was stopped by the Sheriffe. Then he drow out his paper of Notes and begun to tell them; first, his life, that he was born a Gentleman, that he was bred up and had the Qualitys of a Gentleman, and to make him in the opinion of the world more a Gentleman, he had been, till he was seventeen year old, a Goodfellow. But then it pleased God to lay a*ᵃ* foundacion of Grace in his heart, by which he was persuaded against his worldly interest to leave all preferment and go abroad,[2] where he might serve God with more freedom. Then he was called home and made a member of the Long parliament; where he never did, to this day, anything against his conscience, but all for the glory of God. Here he would have given them an account of the proceedings of the Long parliament, but they so often interrupted him, that at last he was forced to give over; and so fell into prayer for England in Generall, then for the churches in England, and then for the City of London. And so fitted himself for the block and received the blow. He had a blister or Issue upon his neck, which he desired them not to hurt. He changed not his colour or speech to the last, but died justifying himself and the cause he had stood for; and spoke very confidently of his being presently at the right hand of Christ. And in all things appeared the most resolved man that ever died in that manner, and showed more of heate then cowardize, but yet with all humility and gravity. One asked him why he did not pray for the King: he answered, "Nay," says he, "you shall see I can pray for the King: I pray, God bless him."

The King had given his body*ᵇ* to his friends;[3] and therefore he told them that he hoped they would be civil to his body when dead; and desired they would let him die like a gentleman and a christian, and not crowded and pressed as he was.

a repl. 'of'   *b* MS. 'boy'

---

1. Probably George Boreman, recently appointed Keeper of the Privy Lodgings, Greenwich.
2. To Massachusetts (1635-7),

where he served in 1636 as Governor.
3. Probably because his brother Sir Walter (in 1664 made envoy to Brandenburg) had been a royalist.

So to the office a little, and so to Trinity-house all of us to dinner. And then to the office again, all the afternoon till night; and so home and to bed. This day I hear my Lord Peterborough [is come] unexpected from Tanger, to give the King an account of the place, which we fear is in none of the best condition.[1] We have also certain news today that the Spaniard is before Lisbone with thirteen sayle; six Duch, and the rest his own ships – which will, I fear, be ill for Portugall.[2]

I writ a letter of all this day's proceedings to my Lord at Hinchingbrooke, who I hear is very well pleased with the work there.[3]

15. *Lords day.* To church in the morning and home to dinner – where came my Brother Tom and Mr. Fisher, my Cosen Nan Pepys's second husband, who I perceive is a very good-humord man, an old Cavalier. I made as much of him as I could, and were merry. And am glad she hath light of so good a man. They gone, I to church again; but my wife not being dressed as I would have her, I was angry and she, when she was out of doors in her way to church, returned home again vexed. But I to church: Mr. Mills, an ordinary sermon. So home and find my wife and Sarah gone to a neighbour church – at which I was not much displeased. By and by she comes again and, after a word or two, good friends. And then her brother came to see her; and he being gone, she told me that she believed he was married and hath a wife worth 500*l* to him,[4] and did enquire how he might dispose that money to the best

1. Peterborough's 'unexpected arrival' is commented on by the Venetian resident: *CSPVen. 1661-4*, p. 156. He had landed on 8 June at Plymouth, and was to return in August to resume his work as Governor. Instead of a thriving port, Tangier turned out to be a liability – most of the Portuguese traders there chose to leave rather than live under English rule, and the local Moorish warlord immediately atttacked the garrison and was with difficulty bought off by an insecure truce. See Routh, ch. ii.

2. Cf. above, p. 61 & n. 2. The Dutch ships may have been the 'six or seven Holland merchantmen' reported to be fitting out at Cadiz for the Spanish service: Allin, i. 99. The Spaniards (at war with Portugal, 1641-68) were short of men-of-war.

3. For the work on the house, see above, ii. 49 & n. 1. The letter is untraced.

4. The marriage of Balthasar St Michel and Esther Watts seems to have taken place in this year: see above, ii. 177; below, p. 277.

advantage; but I forbore to advise her till she could certainly
tell me how things are with him, being*a* loath to meddle too soon
with him.   So to walk upon the leads and to supper and bed.

16.   Up before 4 a-clock; and after some business, took Will
forth and he and I walked over the Tower-hill; but the gate[1]
not being open, we walked through St. Catharines and Ratcliffe
(I think it is) by the waterside above a mile before we could
get a boat; and so over the water in a Scull (which I have not
done a great while) and walked finally to Deptford, where I
saw in what forwardness the work is for Sir W. Battens house
and mine,[2] and it is almost ready.   I also, with Mr. Davis, did
view my Cosen Joyces tallow and compared it with the Irish
tallow we bought lately; and find ours much more white, but
as soft as it; now what is the fault, or whether it be or no a
fault, I know not.

So walked home again as far as over against the tower, and so
over and home – where I find Sir W. Penn and Sir John Minnes
discoursing about Sir J. Mennes house and his coming to live
with us; and I think he entends to have Mr. Turners house
and he to come to his lodgings, which I shall be very glad of.
We three did go to Mr. Turners to view his house, which I
think was to the end that Sir J. Mennes might see it.

Then by water with my wife to the Wardrobe and dined
there; and in the afternoon with all the children by water to
Greenwich, where I showed them the King's Yacht,[3] the house
and the parke, all very pleasant; and so to the taverne and had
the Musique of the house, and so merrily home again; Will
and I walked home from the Wardrobe, having left my wife at
the tower-wharf coming by – whom I find gone to bed not
very well, she having her month's upon her.   So to bed.

a preceded by symbol rendered illegible

1. The gate at the s.-e. end of the
city wall in the range of buildings
reaching almost to the n. side of the
Tower of London. It separated
Great Tower Hill and Little Tower
Hill. (R).
2. I.e. the timber frames for the
new roof at the Navy Office: above,
pp. 59, 102.
3. Probably the *Catherine*.   £450
had just been spent on painting and
gilding her: Bodl., MS. Eng. hist.
c. 311, p. 153.

17. Up, and Mr. Maylard[1] comes to me and borrowed 30s of me, to be paid again out of the money coming to him in the *James* and *Charles* for his late voyage.

So to the office, where all the morning. So home to dinner, my wife not being well. But however, dined with me. So to the office again and at Sir W. Battens, where we all met by chance and talked; and they drank wine but I forebore all their healths. Sir John Minnes, I perceive, is most excellent company. So home and to bed betimes, by daylight.

18. Up earely; and after reading a little in Cicero, I made me ready and to my*ᵃ* office – where all the morning very busy. At noon Mr. Creede came to me about business, and he and I walked as far as Lincolnes Inne fields together; and after a turn or two in the walks there, we parted and I to my Lord Crews and dined with him – where I hear the Courage of Sir H. Vane at his death is talked on everywhere as a miracle. Thence to Somersett-house to Sir J. Winter's chamber by appointment and met Mr. Pett;[2] where he and I read over his last contract with the King for the Forest of Deane, whereof I took notes because of this new one that he is now in making.[3] That done, he and I walked to Lillys the painter's; where we saw, among other rare thing[s], the Duchesse of Yorke her whole body,

a l.h. repl. s.h. 'the'

---

1. One of the musicians who had accompanied Sandwich on the voyage to Portugal.

2. Christopher Pett, shipbuilder.

3. Sir John Winter was secretary to the Queen Mother and principal entrepreneur in the Forest of Dean. His last contract was that of March 1640, by which he had bought a lease of 18,000 acres of the Forest with all ironworks, mines, wood and timber (except ship timber). It had been cancelled by parliament on 21 March 1642 because of his delinquency. Now a new contract (concluded on the following 30 July) was in negotiation, by which he was given a lease of the wood and ironworks for 11 years. This in turn was cancelled by the King in 1668 in response to protests against his felling of timber made both by the Commoners of the Forest and in parliament. *CSPD 1639–40*, p. 567; below, iv. 193 & n. 3; C. E. Hart, *Commoners of Dean Forest*, pp. 54–70; id., *Free Miners*, pp. 204–14; *DNB*.

sitting in state in a chair in white Sattin.[1] And another of the King's[2] that is not finished; most rare things. I did give the fellow something that showed them us, and promised to come some other time and he would show me my Lady Castlemaynes, which I could not then see, it being locked up.[3]

Thence to Wrights the painter's:[4] but Lord, the difference that is between their two works. Thence to the Temple and there spoke with my Cosen Roger, who gives me little hopes in the business between my uncle Thom: and us. So Mr. Pett (who stayed at his son's chamber)[5] and I by coach to the Old Exchange, and there parted and I home and at the office till night. My windows at my office are made clean today, and a casement in my closet. So home; and after some merry discourse in the kitchen with my wife and maids, as I nowadays often do (I being well pleased with both my maids) to bed.

19. Up by 5 a-clock; and while my man Will was getting himself ready to come up to me, I took and played on my lute a little.

So to dress myself and to my*a* office to prepare things against we meet this morning.

a repl. 'the'

---

1. Lely painted many portraits of her. The only extant original full length by him is at Hampton Court, but seems not to have been painted as early as 1662 and shows the Duchess in a deep golden dress. Pepys may conceivably have been referring to Lely's finest portrait of the Duchess, now in the Scottish National Portrait Gallery (no. 1179); in this she is dressed in white, but is not seated in a chair of state and the canvas is not quite a full length. It was painted, c. 1660–2, with a companion portrait of the Duke of York, for the Earl of Clarendon. Cf. O. Millar, *Tudor, Stuart and early Georgian pictures in coll. H.M.Queen*, nos 242–3; R. B. Beckett, *Lely*, pp. 40–1. (OM).

2. Of Lely's original portraits of Charles II there is no certain extant original of this date. (OM).

3. She sat on many occasions to Lely 'who used to say, that it was beyond the compass of art to give this lady her due, as to her sweetness and exquisite beauty': T. Hearne, *Reliq. Hearnianae* (1869 ed.), ii. 57–8. Pepys bought a print of one of these portraits: below, vii. 359 & n. 3. (OM).

4. John Michael Wright. By 1669 he was working in a studio next to the Queen's Head in Great Queen St. (OM).

5. Peter Pett, the son, was a lawyer of the Middle Temple.

We sat long today and had a great private business before us, about contracting with Sir W Rider, Mr. Cutler, and Captain Cocke for 500 ton of hempe, which we went through and I am to draw up the conditions.[1]

Home to dinner, where I find Mr. Moore. And he and I did cast up our accounts together and even them. And then with the last chest of Crusados to Alderman Backwells; by the same token, his lady, going to take coach, stood in the shop and having a gilded glassful of perfumed comfits given her by Don Duarte de Silva, the Portugall merchant[2] that is come over with the Queene, I did offer at a taste, and so she poured some out into my hand; and though good, yet pleased me the better coming from a pretty lady.

So home and at the office, preparing papers and things; and endeed, my head hath not been so full of business a great while and with so much pleasure, for I begin to see the pleasure of it.[a] God[b] give me health. So to bed.

20. Up by 4 or 5 a-clock, and to the office and there drow up the agreement between the King and Sir John Winter about the forest of Deane; and having done it, he came himself (I did not know him to be the Queenes[3] Secretary before, but observed him to be a man of fine parts); and we read and both liked it well. That done, I turned to the forrest of Deane in Speedes mapps;[4] and there he showed me how it lies, and the Lea=bayly, with the great charge of carrying it to Lydny,[5] and many other things worth my knowing; and I do perceive that I am very

a MS. 'God'　　　　*b* l.h. repl. s.h. 'give'

---

1. It was this contract which later seems to have proved troublesome: below, iv. 194.

2. Da Silva had undertaken to convert into cash certain parts of the Queen's dowry supplied in sugar and bills of exchange, and was later, in October, imprisoned for his failure to do so: PRO, PC2/56, f.90*v*; Lister, iii. 193, 196.

3. Queen Mother's.

4. John Speed, *The theatre of the empire of Great Britaine* (1625), now bound up with his *A prospect of the most famous parts of the world* (1631): PL 2901.

5. The Lea Bailey was by this time the only well-wooded part of the forest. Lydney (Glos.) was the port from which the timber was shipped.

short in my business by not knowing many times the geographicall part of my business.[1]

At my office till Mr.*a* Moore took me out; and at my house looked over our papers again, and upon evening our accounts, did give full discharges one to the other. And in his and many other accounts, I perceive I shall be better able to give a true ballance of my estate to myself within a day or two then I have been this twelve months.

Then he and I to Alderman Backwells and did the like there, and I gave one receipt for all the money I have received thence upon the account of my Lord's Crusados. Then I went to the Exchange, and hear that the merchants have a great fear of a breach with the Spaniard; for they think he will not brook our*b* having Tanger, Dunkirke, and Jamaica, and our merchants begin to draw home their estates as fast as they can. Then to popes head ally and there bought me a pair of tweezers, cost me 14*s*, the first thing like a bawble I have bought a good while; but I do it with some trouble of mind, though my conscience tells me that I do it with an apprension of service in my office, [to] have a book to write memorandums in and a pair*c* of compasses in it.[2] But I confess myself the willinger to do it because I perceive by my accounts that I shall be better by 30*l* then I expected to be. But by tomorrow night I entend to see to the bottom of all my accounts. Then home to dinner, where Mr. Moore met me. Then he went away, and I to the office and dispatch much business. So in the evening my wife and I and Jane over the water to Half-way-house, a pretty pleasant walk, but the wind high. So home again and to bed.

21. Up about 4 a-clock and settled some private business of my own. Then made me ready, and to the office to prepare things for our meeting today.

By and by we met; and at noon Sir W. Penn and I to the

a repl. 'dinner'   *b* MS. 'I'   *c* repl. symbol rendered illegible

---

1. Pepys later made a large collection of maps, charts etc. PL 2700 is an index to them. In 1671 he paid his first visit to the Forest of Dean and helped to make a survey of its timber: PL 2265.

2. The notebook and compasses were aids to his study of marine architecture and the measuring of timber.

Trinity-house, where was a feast made by the Wardens – where great good cheer;[1] and much, but ordinary, company. The Lieutenant of the tower, upon my demanding how Sir H. Vane died, told me that he died in a passion; but all confess, with so much courage as never man died. Hence to the office, where Sir W. Rider, Captain Cocke and Mr. Cutler came by appointment to meet me to confer about the contract between us and them for 500 tonnes of hempe. That being done, I did other business and so went home; and there found Mr. Creede, who stayed talking with my wife and I an hour or two; and I put on my riding-cloth suit, only for him to see how it is, and I think it will do very well. He being gone, and I having from my wife and the maids complaints made of the boy, I called him up and with my whip did whip him till I was not able to stir, and yet I could not make him confess any of the lies that they tax him with. At last, not willing to let him go away a conqueror, I took him in task again and pulled off his frock to his shirt, and whipped him till he did confess that he did drink the Whay, which he hath denied. And pulled a pinke, and above all, did lay the candlesticke upon the ground in his chamber, which he hath denied this Quarter of this year. I confess it is one of the greatest wonders that ever I met with, that such a little boy as he could possibly be able to suffer half so much as he did to maintain a lie. But I think I must be forced to put him away.[2] So to bed, with my arme very weary.

22. *Lords day*. This day I first put on my slasht doublet,[3] which I like very well. Mr. Sheply came to me in the morning, telling me that he and my Lord came to town from Hinchingbrooke last night. He and I spent an hour in looking over his accounts, and then walked to the Wardrobe, all the way discoursing of my Lord's business. He tells me, to my great wonder, that Mr. Barnwell is dead, 500 in debt to my Lord.

By and by my Lord came from church and I dined, with

---

1. These and the official Trinity Monday feasts were usually gargantuan. Pepys (as Master of the Corporation) had the latter abolished in 1677 for that year: *EHR*, 44/578-9.

2. For Wayneman Birch's misdeeds, see, e.g., above, p. 66 & n. 2.

3. For slashed garments, see above, p. 99, n. 3.

some others, with him; he very merry, and after dinner took me aside and talked*a* of state and other matters. By and by to my brother Toms and took [him] out with me homewards (calling at the wardrobe to talk a little with Mr. Moore); and so to my house, where I paid him all I owed him and did make the 20*l* I lately lent him*b* up [to] 40*l*, for which he shall give bond to Mr. Sheply, for it is his money.

So my wife and I to walk in the garden, where all our talk was against Sir W. Penn; against whom I have lately had cause to be much prejudiced against. By and by he and his daughter came out to walk, so we took no notice of them a great while; at last, in going home spoke a word or two, and so good-night and to bed. This day I am told of a Portugall lady at Hampton Court, that hath dropped a child already, since the Queenes coming. But the King would not have them searched whose it is; and so it is not commonly known yet.[1] Coming home tonight, I met with Will Swan, who doth talk as high for the fanatiques as ever he did in his life; and doth pity my Lord Sandwich and me that we should be given up to the wickedness of the world, and that a fall is coming upon us all. For he finds that he and his company are the true spirit of the nation, and the greater part of the nation, too – who will have liberty of conscience in spite of this act of uniformity, or they will die; and if they may not preach abroad, they will preach in their own houses. He told me that certainly Sir H. Vane must be gone to Heaven, for he died as much a martyr and saint as ever any man died. And that the King hath lost more by that man's death then he will get again a good while.[2] At all which, I know not what to think; but I confess I do think that the Bishops will never be able to carry it so high as they do.

a repl. 'talking' *b* l.h. repl. s.h. 'up'

---

1. Cf. *Old cheque-book of Chapel Royal* (ed. E. F. Rimbault), p. 180: 'Lisbona, the daughter of unknowne parents, accidentally found shortly after its birth in a private place of Hampton Court, but conceived to be the child of a Portugall woman, was baptised in a private chamber there, June 20, 1662.' The birth was in fact reported in a letter (21 June): HMC, *Rep.*, 15/7/95.

2. Cf. Burnet (i. 286): 'It was generally thought the government had lost more than it had gained by his death.'

23. Up earely this morning; and my people are taking down
the hangings and things in my house, because of the great dust
that is already made by the pulling down of Sir W. Batten's
house, and will be by my own when I come to it.[1]   To my
office, and there hard at work all the morning.   At noon to
the exchange to meet Dr. Williams, who sent me this morning
notice of his going into the country tomorrow; but could not
find him.   But meeting with Fr. Moore, my Lord Lamberts
man formerly, he and two or three friends of his did go to a
taverne; and there they drank, but I nothing but small beer.
In the next room, one was playing very finely of the Dulcimer,
which well played I like well.   But one of our own company,
a talking fellow, did in discourse say much of this Act against
Seamen, for their being brought to account,[2] and that it was
made on purpose for my Lord Sandwich, who was in debt
100000*l* and had been forced to have pardon oftentimes from
Oliver for the same.   At [which I] was vexed at him but thought
it not worth my trouble to oppose what he said, but took leave
and went home; and after a little dinner, to my office again.
And in the evening Sir W Warren came to me about business;
and that being done, discoursing of Deales, I did offer to go
along with him among his deal ships, which we did,*a* to half a
scoare; where he showed me the difference between Dram,
Swinsound, Christiana[3] and others, and told me many pleasant
notions concerning their manner of cutting and sawing them
by watermills,[4] and the reason how deals become dearer and

a l.h. repl. s.h. 'do'

---

1. See above, p. 59 & n. 2.
2. 14 Car. II c. 14, requiring accounts of prize goods taken in 1642–
60 and not yet accounted for to be
brought into the Court of Admiralty.
3. The three principal varieties of
Norwegian fir-deals, named from the
ports of shipment: Drammen, Svine-
sund and Christiania. See R. G.
Albion, *Forests and seapower*, ch. iv, and
map opp. p. 140.   Other varieties are

listed in an account-book (c. 1683) in
BL, Add. 9303, f.74*v*.   Norwegian
timber was both cheaper and more
quickly accessible than other Eastland
supplies, partly because it did not have
to be shipped through the Sound,
where dues were payable to Denmark.
4. In England sawpits were not
replaced by the watermills common
on the Continent until the late 18th
century.

cheaper; among others, when the snow is not so great as to fill up the vallys, that they pass from hill to hill over the snow, then it is dear carriage.[1] From on board he took me to his yard, where vast and many piles of deals, sparres, and balkes and Euphroes[2] – the difference between which I never knew before. And endeed, am very proud of this evening's work. He had me into his house, which is most pretty and neat and well furnished. After a glass, not of wine, for I could not be tempted to drink any, but a glass of mum, I well home by water; but it being late, was forced to land at the custome-house, and so home – and to bed. And after I was abed, letters came from the Duke for the fitting out of four ships forthwith from Portsmouth (I know not yet for what), so I was forced to make Will get them writ, and signed them in bed and sent them away by expresse.[3] And so to sleep.

24. *Midsummer day.*[4]
Up earely and to my office, putting things in order against we sit. There came to me my Cosen Harry Alcocke, whom I much respect, to desire (by a letter from my father to me, where he had been some days) my help for him to some place. I proposed the sea to him, and I think he will take it and I hope do well.[5]

1. Transport was the main constituent of expense. Logs were hauled on sleds by oxen or horses. Albion, op. cit., p. 145; Ehrman, pp. 52–3.

2. Deals were used for ships' upperworks, decks and bulkheads; spars (of various sizes) were the fir-staging used in the rigging as booms, bowsprits etc.; balks were fir timbers roughly dressed before shipment; uphroes were large Norwegian spars, 28–32 ft long: *Naval Expositor* (1750), pp. 49–50, 155, 180; W. Sutherland, *Britain's Glory: or Ship-building Unvail'd* (1729), pp. 204, 213; *OED.* The yard was in Wapping. Warren was by this time probably the greatest timber merchant in England.

3. The Duke had written on 22 June from Hampton Court ordering two months' victualling and rigging for the *Lion, Dover, Princess* and *York*: PRO, Adm. 106/7, no. 144. Pepys added at the foot of the order: 'recd this warrt 23 June 62 eleaven at night and issued out warrts for the rigging and fitting of the abovesd shipps at the same time, as alsoe for their victuals'. The ships sailed to Portugal under Thomas Allin in August: Allin, ii. 99+.

4. This was Midsummer Day by legal, not astronomical, reckoning. See above, p. 107 & n. 2.

5. But see below, ix. 208.

Sit all the morning, and I bless God I find that by my diligence of late and still, I do get ground in the office every day.

At noon to the change, where I begin to be known also. And so home to dinner and then to the office, all the afternoon dispatching business. At night news is brought me that Field, the rogue, hath this day cast me at Guild hall in 30*l* for his imprisonment, to which I signed his commitment with the rest of the officers. But they having been parliament-men, he hath begun the law with me¹ and threatens more. But I hope the Duke of Yorke will bear me out.

At night home, and Mr. Spong came to me; and so he and I sat singing upon the leads till almost 10 at night; and so he went away (a pretty harmelesse and ingenious man), and I to bed in a very great content of mind – which I hope, by my care still in my business, will continue to me.

25. Up by 4 a-clock and put my accounts with my Lord into a very good order, and so to my office – where having put many things in order, I went to the Wardrobe but find my Lord gone to Hampton Court. After discourse with Mr. Sheply, we parted and I into Thames-street beyond the bridge and there enquired among the shops the price of tarr and oyle; and do find great content in it and hope to save the King money by this practice. So home to dinner and then to the Change; and so home again and at the office, preparing business against tomorrow all the afternoon. At night walked with my wife upon the leads; and so to supper and to bed. My [wife] having lately a great pain in her eare, for which this night she begins to take phisique; and I have got cold and so have a great deal of my old pain.

26. Up and took phisique, but such as to go abroad with, only to loosen me, for I am bound. So to the office – and there all the morning, setting till noon; and then took Comissioner Pett home with me to dinner, where my stomach was turned when my sturgeon came to table, upon which I saw very many little worms creeping, which I suppose was through the staleness of the pickle.

He being gone, comes Mr. Nicholson, my old fellow-student

---

1. M.P.'s were protected by privilege from actions of this sort during parliamentary sessions. For Field's case, see above, p. 23, n. 2.

at Magdalen, and we played three or four things upon violin and Basse; and so parted, and I to my office till night; and then came Mr. Sheply and Creede in order to setting some accounts of my Lord right; and so to bed.

27. Up early, not quite rid of my pain. I took more phisique, and so made myself ready to go forth. So to my Lord, who ris as soon as he heard I was there and in his night-gown* and shirt stood talking with me alone two houres, I believe – concerning his greatest matters of state and interest. Among other things, that his greatest design is: first to get clear of all debts to the King for the embassy-money, and then a pardon.[1] Then to get his land settled;[2] and then to discourse and advise what is best for him, whether to keep his Sea imployment longer or no. For he doth discern that the Duke would be willing to have him out, and that by Coventry's means. And here he told me how the terms at Algier were wholly his; and*a* that he did plainly tell Lawson and agree with him, that he would have the honour of them if they should ever be agreed to; and that accordingly they did come over hither entitled, *"articles concluded on by Sir J. Lawson, according to instruccions received from His Royal Highness James Duke of Yorke &c., and from His Excellence the Earle of Sandwich"* (which, however, was more then needed; but Lawson tells my Lord in his letter that it was not he, but the Councell of Warr that would have His Royal Highness put into the title, though he did not contribute one word to it): but the Duke of York did yesterday propose them to the Council, to be printed with this title: *"Concluded on by Sir*

a l.h. repl. s.h. 'but'

1. Sandwich, who had not troubled to take the free pardon offered at the Restoration, was now granted a pardon in October 1662 for 'all treasons etc. by him committed before 16 August last': Bodl., Clar. dep. c. 406, p. 92; PRO, C 66/3011, no. 4. In his embassy to Portugal in 1661 (see above, ii. 118 & n. 3) he had received not only the normal grant to an ambassador (£5000 in this case) but also some of the dowry money paid on the Queen's behalf. On 31 December 1662 he was allowed to keep the 25,000 crusados for which he stood accountable, 'in recompense of his charges'. See *CTB*, i. 267, 496.

2. The grant of land from the King, made in November 1660 to support his earldom, was not completed until 1663: above, i. 285, n. 4.

J. Lawson, Kt." – and my Lord quite left out.[1]   Now I find my
Lord very politique; for he tells me that he discerns they design
to set up Lawson as much as they can and that he doth counter-
plot them by setting him up higher still; by which they will
find themselfs spoiled of their design, and at last grow jealous of
Lawson: this he told me with much pleasure.[2]   And that several
of the Dukes servants; by name, my Lord Barkely, Mr. Talbot
and others, have complained to my Lord of Coventry, and would
have him out.   My Lord doth acknowledge that his greatest
obstacle is Coventry.   He did seem to hint such a Question as
this – Hitherto I have been supported by the King and Chancellor against the Duke; but what if it should come about that
it shall be the Duke and Chancellor against the King? – which,
though he said it in these plain words, yet I could not fully
understand it.   But may more hereafter.

My Lord did also tell me that the Duke himself at Portsmouth
did thank my Lord for all his pains and care; and that he per-
ceived it must be the old Captains that must do the business, and
that the new ones would spoil all.[3]   And that my Lord did very
discreetly tell the Duke (though quite against his judgment and
inclinacion) that, however, the King's new Captaines ought to be
borne with a little and encouraged.   By which he will oblige
that party and prevent, as much as may be, their envy; but he
says that certainly things will go to wrack if ever the old Captains should be wholly out, and the new ones only command.

Then we fell to talk of Sir J. Minnes, of whom my Lord hath
a very slight opinion, and that at first he did come to my Lord

---

1. They appear in the Privy Council Register as 'Articles of Peace between his Sacred Majestie Charles the
Second ... And the Citie & King-
dome of Algeir ... Concluded by Sr
John Lawson Knt the 23rd day of
Aprill 1662': PRO, PC 2/56, ff. 19–
20.   The official printed version and
the government newspaper account
(*Kingd. Intell.*, 30 June, pp. 413+)
employed the same title.   In the
confirmation of 1664 the name of the
Duke of York was added to Lawson's:
Somers Tracts (ed. Scott), vii. 555.

For the treaty, see above, p. 89 & n. 1.
For James's coolness towards Sandwich, see below, v. 162–3.

2. Sandwich remained jealous of
Lawson and of his influence with
the Duke and Coventry: cf. below,
v. 343; vi. 276.

3. Cf. Penn, ii. 293–5, and Coventry's similar views: below, p.
129.   This was the contemporary
version of the old controversy
about the rival merits of tarpaulins
and gentlemen-captains; cf. above,
ii. 114 & n. 2.

very displeased and sullen, and had[a] studied and turned over all his books, to see whether it had ever been that two flags should ride together in the main-top – but could not find it; nay, he did call his Captaines on board to consult them. So when he came by my Lord's side, he took down his flag and all that day did not hoyse it again; the next day my Lord did tell him that it was not so fit to ride without a flag, and therefore told him that he should wear it in the foretopp, for it seems my Lord saw his instruccions; which was that he should not wear his flag in the main-top in the presence of the Duke or my Lord.

But that after that, my Lord did caresse him, and he doth believe him as much his friend as his interest will let him.

I told my Lord of the late passage between Swan and me; and he told me another lately between Dr. Dell and himself, when he was in the country.[1]

At last we concluded upon despatching all his accounts as soon as possibly; and so I parted and to my office, where I met Sir W. Penn and he desired a turn with me in the garden; where he told me now the day was fixed for his going into Ireland, and that whereas I had mentioned some service he could do a friend of mine there, Sam Pepys,[2] he told me he would most readily do what I would command him. And then told me we must needs eat a dish of meat together before he went, and so invited me and my wife on Sunday next. To all which I did give a cold consent; for my heart cannot love or have a good opinion of him since his last playing the knave with me;[3] but he took no

a repl. 'did'

---

1. Cf. above, p. 117. William Dell (formerly Rector of Yelden, Beds.; removed from his living in June 1661 for Independency) was like Swan a strong Puritan. He was said to have declared in church that 'he would rather hear a plain countryman from the plough speak there than the best orthodox minister in the country', and that he had allowed 'one Bunyon of Bedford, a tinker, to speak in his pulpit . . .': A. G. Matthews, *Calamy Revised*, p. 161.

2. This Samuel Pepys (of Dublin) was a parson – the son of Sir Richard Pepys, Lord Chief Justice of Ireland (d. 1659), who was a first cousin of the diarist's father. He was now attempting to obtain some £5000-worth of soldiers' debentures owed to his father, and on 8 August 1662 Ormond, the Lord Lieutenant, recommended his case to the Trustees of the Commissioned Officers: HMC, *Ormonde*, n. s., iii. 21.

3. See above, pp. 99–100.

notice of our difference at all, nor I to him. And so parted; and I by water to Deptford,*a* where I find Sir W. Batten alone, paying off the yard, three Quarters pay. Thence to dinner; where too great a one was prepared, at which I was very much troubled and wished I had not been there; after dinner comes Sir J. Minnes and some Captains with him, who had been at a Council of Warr today, who tell us they have acquitted Captain Hall, who was accusd of cowardize in letting of old Winter, the Argier pyrate,[1] go away from him with a prize or two. And also Captain Diamond of the murther*b* laid to him of a man that he had struck, but he lived many months after; till, being drunk, he fell into the hold and there broke his jawe and died. But they say that there are such bawdy articles against him as never was heard of – one, that he should upon his knees drink the King and Queenes health at Lisbon, wishing that the King's pintle were in the Queenes cunt up to her heart, that it might cry "Knack,*c* knock" again.

To the pay again, where I left them and walked to Redriffe and so home; and there came Mr. Creede and Sheply to me, and stayed till night about my Lord's accounts our proceeding to set them in order. And so parted and I to bed.

Mr. Holliard hath been with my wife today and cured her of her pain in her eare, by taking out a most prodigious quantity of hard wax that had hardened itself at the bottom of the eare, of which I am very glad.

28. Up to my Lord's and my own accounts; and so to the office – where all the forenoon setting. And at noon by appointment to the Miter, where Mr. Sheply gave me and Mr. Creede, and I had my uncle Wight with us, a dish*d* of fish. Thence to the office again and there all the afternoon till night; and so home and after talking with my wife, to bed. ⟨This day a gentlewoman came to me, claiming kindred of me, as

a repl. 'Woolwich'   *b* MS. 'mother'   *c* repl. 'knock'
d repl. 'fish'

1. Pirates were often renegade Christians. Winter – widely known as 'old Winter' – seems to have been the foremost of the Algiers captains at this time: cf. HMC, *Finch*, i. 277. There are no records of courts martial at this period in the PRO.

she had once done before,[1] and borrowed 10s of me, promising to repay it at night, but I hear nothing of her. I shall trust her no more.⟩[a]

Great talk there is of a fear of a war with the Duch; and we have order to pitch upon 20 ships to be forthwith set out;[2] but I hope it is but a scarecrow to the world, to let them see that we can be ready for them; though God knows, the King is not able to set out five ships at this present without great difficulty, we neither having money, credit, nor stores.

My mind is now in a wonderful condition of quiet and content, more then ever in all my life – since my minding the business of my office, which I have done most constantly; and I find it to be the very effect of my late oaths against wine and plays; which, if God please, I will keep constant in. For now my business is a delight to me and brings me great credit, and my purse encreases too.

29. *Lords day.* Up by 4 a-clock, and to the settling of my own accounts, and I do find upon my monthly ballance (which I have undertaken to keep from month to month) that I am worth 650l., the greatest sum that ever I was yet master of.[3] I pray God give me a thankful spirit, and care to improve and increase it.

To church with my wife, who this day put on her green petticoate of[b] flowered satin, with five white and black gimp lace of her own putting on, which is very pretty. Home with Sir W. Penn to dinner by appointment, and to church again in the

a addition crowded into end of line   *b* l.h. repl. s.h. 'with'

---

1. ? Cf. above, ii. 193.

2. In pursuance of an order from the Privy Council, the Duke wrote on 27 June from St James's asking which 20 ships could most speedily be put to sea (two 2nd-rates, five 3rd-rates, ten 4th-rates and three 5th-rates), and for an estimate of the cost of a six-months' voyage: PRO, Adm. 106/7, no. 150. Cf. *CSPVen.*

1661–4, p. 167. More serious preparations for war were undertaken in the spring of 1664; hostilities began in that year, and war was declared in March 1665.

3. Perhaps Pepys now kept a monthly account because of his recent discovery that he had lately fallen behind in his saving: cf. above, p. 95.

afternoon. And then home, Mr. Sheply coming to me about my Lord's accounts; and in the evening parted and we to supper again to Sir W. Penn. Whatever the matter is, he doth much fawn upon me, and I perceive would not fall out with me, and his daughter mighty officious to my wife; but I shall never be deceived again by him, but do hate him and his traitorous tricks with all my heart. It was an invitation in order to his taking leave of us today, he being to go for Ireland in a few days.

So home to prayers and to bed.

30. Up betimes and to my office, where I find Griffens girl making it clean; but God forgive me, what a mind I have to her, but did not meddle with her. She being gone, I fell upon boring holes for me to see from my closet into the great office without going forth, wherein I please myself much.

So settled to business; and at noon with my wife to the Wardrobe and there dined and stayed talking all the afternoon with my Lord. And about 4 a-clock took coach with my wife and Lady and went toward my house, calling at my Lady Carteret's, who was within by chance (she keeping altogether at Deptford for a month or two) and so we sat with her a little. Among other things, told my Lady how my Lady Fanshaw is fallen out with her, only for speaking in behalf of the French; which my Lady wonders at, they having been formerly like sisters. But we see there is no true lasting friendship in this world.

Thence to my house, where I took great pride to lead her through the Court by the hand, she being very fine and her page carrying up her train.

She stayed a little at my house, and then walked through the garden and took water; and went first on board the King's pleasure-boat[1] – which pleased her much; then to Greenwich parke, and with much ado, she was able to walk up to the top of the hill. And so down again and took boat, and so through bridge to Black-friars and home – she being much pleased with the ramble – in every perticular of it. So we supped with her and then walked home, and to bed.

_____

1. See above, p. 111, n. 3.

Observations

This I take to be as bad a Juncture as ever I observed. The King and his new Queene minding their pleasures at Hampton Court. All people discontented; some that the king doth not gratify them enough; and the others, Fanatiques of all sorts, that the King doth take away their liberty of conscience; and the heighth of the Bishops, who I fear will ruin all again. They do much cry up the manner of Sir H. Vanes death, and he deserves it. They clamour against the Chimny-money and say they will not pay it without force. And in the meantime, like to have wars abroad – and Portugall to assist, when we have not money to pay for any ordinary layings-out at home.

Myself all in dirt about building of my house and Sir W. Batten's a storey higher. Into a good way; fallen on minding my business and saving money, which God encrease; and I do take great delight in it and see the benefit of it. In a longing mind of going to see Brampton, but cannot get three days time, do what I can.

In very good health, my wife and myself.

JULY.

1. To the office. And there we sat till past noon; and then Captain Cuttance and I by water to Deptford, where the *Royall James* (in which my Lord went out the last voyage, though came back in the *Charles*) was paying-off by Sir W. Batten and Sir W. Penn.

So to dinner, where I had Mr. Sheply to dine with us. And from hence I sent to my Lord to know whether she should be a first-rate, as the men would have her, or a second.[1] He answered that we should forbear paying the officers and such whose pay differed upon the rate of the ship till he could speak with his Royal Highness.

To the pay again after dinner; and seeing of Cooper the Mate of the ship, whom I knew in the *Charles*, I spoke to him about teaching the Mathematiques, and do please myself in my thoughts of learning of him. And bid him come to me in a day or two.

Towards evening I left them and to Redriffe by land, Mr Cowly the Clerk of the Cheque with me, discoursing concerning the abuses of the yard, in which he did give me much light. So by water home; and after half an hour's sitting talking with my wife, who was afeared I did entend to go with my Lord to fetch the Queene-Mother over,[2] in which I did clear her doubts – I went to bed by daylight, in order to my rising early tomorrow.

2. Up while the chimes went 4 – and to put down my

---

1. She was now rated as a 2nd-rate. The dividing line between 1st- and 2nd-rate ships (fixed by size and fighting power in most cases) was often narrow until the introduction of new rules in 1677. Both rates of ship were three-deckers. Pay for most officers was higher in 1st-rates; for others (e.g. lieutenants and bosuns' mates), there was no difference. The prevalent rating system – establishing six rates of ship – appears to have been introduced in 1653. The Duke of York on 1 September 1662 ordered a new establishment, with 'a Table of the Officers and Mates to be allowed to the Ships of several Rates': *Mem. (naval)*, p. 38. Rates and the details of pay (for 1653) are given in H. W. Hodges and E. A. Hughes (eds), *Select naval documents*, p. 57. Cf. *Cat.*, iv. 527–8; Oppenheim, pp. 216, 360; Ehrman, p. 34.

2. See below, p. 139 & n. 3.

Journall; and so to my office to read over such instruccions as
concern the officers of the yards; for I am much upon seeing
into the miscarriages*a* there.[1] By and by, by appointment comes
Comissioner Pett and then a messenger from Mr. Coventry,
who sits in his boat expecting us; and so we down to him at
the Tower and there took water all, and to Deptford (he in
our passage taking notice how much difference there is between
the old Captains for obedience and order, and the King's new
Captains, which I am very glad to hear him confess);[2] and there
we went into the Store-house and viewd, first the provisions
there and then his books (but Mr. Davis[3] himself was not there,
he having a kinswoman in the house dead; for which, when
by and by I saw him, he doth trouble himself most ridiculously,
as if there was never another woman in the world); in which
so much lazinesse, as also in the Clerkes of the Cheque and Survey[4]
(which after one another we did examine), as that I do not
perceive that there is one-third of their duties performed. But
I perceive, to my great content, Mr. Coventry will have things
reformed.

So Mr. Coventry to London and Pett and I to the pay, where
Sir Wms. both were paying-off the *Royall James* still;[5] and so
to dinner and to the pay again – where I did reliefe several of
my Lord Sandwiches people, but was sorry to see them so
peremptory, and at every word would complain to my Lord,
as if they shall have such a command over my Lord. In the
evening I went forth and took a walk with Mr. Davis, and told
him what had passed at his office today, and did give him my
advice; and so with the rest by barge home and to bed.

3. Up by 4 a-clock and to my office till 8 o'clock, writing
over two Copys of our contract with Sir Wm Rider &c. for

a repl. 'mis'-

1. The Admiral's Instructions of
January 1662 defined the duties of the
officers of the yards, and required the
Principal Officers of the Navy to see
that they were performed.

2. Cf. above, p. 122 & n. 3.

3. John Davis, Storekeeper at
Deptford.

4. Thomas Cowley and John
Uthwayt respectively. For Pepys's
note about some of the subsequent
reforms, see below, p. 234.

5. PRO, Adm. 20/2, p. 187 (£9593,
covering 29 March 1661 – 1 July
1662).

500 ton of Hempe; which, because it is a secret, I have the trouble of writing over, as well as drawing.

Then home to dress myself and so to the office – where another fray between*a* Sir Rich: Ford and myself about his yarne,[1] wherein I find the board to yield on my side; and was glad thereof, though troubled that the office should fall upon me of disobliging Sir Richard.[2]

At noon, we all by invitation dined at the Dolphin with the Officers of the Ordinance; where Sir W. Compton and Mr. Oneale[3] and other*b* great persons were, and a very great dinner. But I drank, as I still do, but my allowance of wine.

After dinner was brought to Sir Wm. Compton a gun to discharge seven times, the best of those devices that ever I saw, and very serviceable and not a bawble, for it is much approved of and many thereof made.[4]

Then to my office all the afternoon, as long as I could see – about setting many businesses in order. In the evening came Mr. Lewes to me, and very ingeniously did inquire whether I did ever look into the business of the Chest at Chatham;[5] and after my readiness to be informed did appear to him, he did produce a paper wherein he stated the government of the Chest to me; and upon the whole did tell me how it hath ever been abused, and to this day is, and what a meritorious act it would be to look after it; which I am resolved to do, if God bless me – and do thank him very much for it.[6]

So home; and after a turn or two upon the leads with my wife, who hath lately had but little of my company since I

a repl. 'against'   b repl. 'other'

---

1. See above, p. 101 & n. 3.

2. A neighbour as well as a contractor.

3. Compton was Master of the Ordnance; Daniel O'Neill (Postmaster-General and an influential courtier) held a contract for the supply of gunpowder to the Ordnance.

4. Repeaters were occasionally made but never widely used. Some were revolvers; others employed a

succession of charges loaded down the barrel. See C. Singer *et al.*, *Hist. Technol.*, iii. 258–9, 362 & n.; John N. George, *Engl. Pistols*, pp. 33+. Cf. also Birch, i. 396; below, v. 75 & n. 1.

5. The Chatham Chest was the organisation for the relief of wounded and maimed seamen. Thomas Lewis was a clerk in the Victualling Office.

6. See below, p. 257 & n. 2.

begun to fallow my business; but is contented therewith since she sees how I spend my time. And so to bed.

4. Up by 5 a-clock; and after my Journall put in order, to my office about my business, which I am resolved to fallow, for every day [I] see what ground I get by it. By and by comes Mr. Cooper, Mate of the *Royall Charles*, of whom I entend to learn Mathematiques; and so begin with him today, he being a very able man and no great matter, I suppose, will content him. After an hour's being with him at Arithmetique, my first attempt being to learn the Multiplicacion table,[1] then we parted till to-morrow: and so to my business at my office again – till noon; about which time Sir W. Warren did come to me about busi-ness and did begin to instruct me in the nature of Firre, timber and deals, telling me the nature of every sort; and from that, we fall to discourse of Sir W. Batten's corruption and the people that he imploys, and from one discourse to another of that kind; I was much pleased with his company and so stayed talking with him all alone at my office till 4 in the afternoon, without eating or drinking all day; and then parted and I home to eat a bit, and so back again to my office. And toward the evening came Mr. Sheply, who is to go ⟨out⟩ of*a* town tomorrow; and so he and I with much ado settled his accounts with my Lord; which though they be true and honest, yet so obscure that it vexes me to see in what manner they are kept. He being gone, and leave taken of him as of a man likely not to come to London again a great while, I eat a bit of bread and butter, and so to bed. This day I sent my brother Tom, at his request, my father's old Basse viall which he and I have kept so long; but I fear Tom will do little good at it.

a l.h. repl. s.h. 'to'

---

1. This was not normally learned in childhood (at any rate beyond 5 × 5), but was occasionally taught in the mathematical schools and by the mathematical handbooks. Alter-native and often laborious methods of multiplication were often used. See J. Mellis, *Records Arithmetick* (1652), pp. 69–70; W. Leybourn, *Arith-metick* (1678), p. 27; E. Cocker, *Arithmetick* (1678), pp. 62–3; cf. Foster Watson in *Gent. Mag.*, 287 (1899)/257+; M. H. Nicolson, *Pepys' diary and the new science*, pp. 9–10.

5. To my office to get things ready against our sitting; and by and by we sat and did business all the morning; and at noon had Sir W. Penn (who I hate with all my heart for his base treacherous tricks, but yet I think it not policy to declare it yet) and his son Wm to my house to dinner, where was also Mr. Creede and my Cosen Harry Alcocke; I having some venison given me a day or two ago, and so I had a shoulder roasted, another baked, and the umbles baked in a pie, and all very well done. We were merry as I could be*a* in that company – and the more because I would not seem otherwise to Sir W. Penn, he being within a day or two to go for Ireland.

After dinner he and his son went away, and Mr. Creede would, with all his rhetorique, have persuaded me to have gone to a play; and in good earnest I found my nature desirous to have gone, notwithstanding my promise and my business, to ⟨which I⟩ have lately kept*b* myself so close, but I did refuse it and I hope shall ever do so; and above all things, it is considerable that my mind was never in my life in so good a condition of quiet as it hath been since I have fallowed my business and seen myself to get greater and greater fitness in my imployment and honor, every day more then other. So at my office all the afternoon and then my mathematiques at night with Mr. Cooper; and so to supper and to bed.

6. *Lords day.* Lay long in bed today with my wife, merry and pleasant. And then rose and settled my accounts with my wife for housekeeping, and do see that my kitchen, besides wine, fire, candle, soap, and many other things, comes to about 30s a week or a little over.

To church, where Mr. Mills made a lazy sermon; so home to dinner, where my brother Tom dined with me. And so my wife and I to church again in the afternoon. And that done, I walked to the Wardrobe and spent my time with Mr. Creede and Mr. Moore, talking about business; so up to supper with my Lady – who tells me with much trouble that my Lady Castlemayne is still as great with the King and that the King comes often to her as ever he did. At which, God forgive me, I am well pleased.

a MS. 'me'   *b* repl. 'keep'

It begun to rain, and so I borrowed a hat and cloak of Mr. Moore and walked home, where I found Captain Ferrer with my wife; and after spending a matter of an hour with him, he went home and we all to bed.

⟨Jack Cole, my old friend,[1] found me out at the Wardrobe; and among other things, he told me that certainly most of the chief Ministers of London would fling their livings;[2] and that soon or late the issue thereof would be sad to the King and Court.⟩*a*

7. Up and to my office early, and there all the morning alone till dinner and after dinner to my office again; and about 3 a-clock with my wife by water to Westminster, where I stayed in the hall while my wife went to see her father and mother; and she returning, we by water home again; and by and by comes Mr. Cooper, so he and I to our Mathematiques; and so to supper and to bed.

My morning's work at the office was to put the new books of my office into order and writing on the backsides what books they be and transferring out of some old books some things into*b* them.[3]

8. At the office all the morning, and dined at home; and after dinner in all haste to make up my accounts with my Lord, which I did with some trouble, because I had some hopes to have made a profit to myself in this account, above what was due to me (which God forgive me in); but I could not, but carried them to my Lord, with whom they passed well. So to the Wardrobe, where alone with my Lord above an hour, and

a addition crowded into bottom of page   *b* l.h. repl. s.h. 'from'

---

1. A schoolfellow, now in business in London.
2. See below, p. 166, n. 1.
3. A full list of the books remaining in the office on 12 October 1688 (but now untraced) is in BL, Add. 9303, ff. 124-5; printed in *Mar. Mirr.*, 34/269-70. At the time of this entry Pepys began his private collection of official letters (10 July 1662-29 April

1679), now NMM, LBK/8: three volumes bound as one; partially printed by J. R. Tanner in *Further Corr. of S. Pepys . . .* (1929) and by E. Chappell in *Shorthand Letters of S. Pepys* (1933). The memorandum book now in the PRO (Adm. 106/3520) begins with a series of notes in Pepys's hand (July 1660-24 July 1662) probably made at this time.

he doth seem still to have his old confidence in me; and tells
me to boot, that Mr. Coventry hath spoke of me to him^a to
great advantage; wherein I am much pleased. By and by comes
in Mr. Coventry to visit my Lord; and so my Lord and he and
I walked together in the great chamber a good while, and I find
him a most ingenuous man and good company. He being gone,
I also went home by water, Mr. Moore with mee^b for discourse
sake; and then parted from me, Cooper being there, ready to
attend me; so he and I to work till it was dark, and then eat a
bit and by daylight to bed.

9. Up by 4 a-clock and at my multiplication table hard, which
is all the trouble I meet withal in my arithmetique. So made me
ready and to my office – where all the morning busy. And Sir
W. Penn came to my office to take his leave of me; and desiring
a turn in the garden, did commit the care of his building to me
and offered all his services to me in all matters of mine. I did
(God forgive mee)^c promise him all my service and love, though
the rogue knows he deserves none from me, nor I entend to
show him any; but as he dissembles with me, so must I with
him.¹ Dined at home, and so to the office again, my wife with
me; and while I was for an hour making a hole behind my seat
in my closet, to look into the office, she was talking to me about
her going to Brampton – which I would willingly have her do
but for the cost of it; and to stay here will be very inconvenient
because of the dirt that I must have when my house is pulled
down.

Then to my business till night; then Mr. Cooper and I to our
business, and then came Mr. Mills the Minister to see me – which
he hath but rarely done to me, though every day almost to
others of us; but he is a cunning fellow and knows where the

---

a   phrase repl. 'of him to me'   b   repl. 'him'
c   repl. 'him'

---

1. For Penn's journey to Ireland,
see above, p. 79 & n. 5. In a letter
of 12 August Batten and Pepys
reported to Penn on the progress of
the alterations to the Principal
Officers' houses. They also expressed their exceeding gladness at his
safe arrival, and their 'hopes' of his
'speedy return': *Further Corr.*, p. 1.

good victualls is and the good drink, at Sir W. Batten.[1]   However, I used him civilly, though I love him as I do the rest of his coat.[2]   So to supper and to bed.

10.   Up by 4 a-clock; and before[a] I went to the office, I practised my arithmetique; and then when my wife was up, did call her and Sarah and did make up a difference between them – for she is so good a servant as I am loath to part with her.   So to the office all the morning, where very much business; but it vexes me to see so much disorder at our table, that, every man minding a several business, we despatch nothing.

Dined at home with my wife.   Then to the office again; and being called by Sir W. Batten, walked to the Victualling Office, there to view all the several offices and houses to see that they were imployed, in order to give the Councell an account thereof.[3] So after having taken an oath or two of Mr. Lewes and Captain Browne and others, I returned to the office and there sat despatching several businesses alone till night;   and so home and by daylight[b] to bed.

11.   Up by 4 a-clock, and hard at my multiplicacion table, which I am now almost maister of.   And so made me ready and to my office – where by and by comes Mr. Pett and then a messenger from Mr. Coventry, who stays in his boat at the Tower for us; so we to him and down to Deptford first and there viewed some Deales, lately served in at a low price;   which our

a repl. 'there'   b repl. 'late'

---

1. So did Pepys; he often made use of Batten's hospitality: e.g. dining there three days running on the following 26, 27 and 28 August.

2. The diary has many evidences of this view of the clergy, and Pepys maintained it throughout life, despite his later high churchmanship. Cf. his letter to Dryden (14 July 1699, inserted in his copy of the *Fables ancient and modern*, 1700: PL 2442), in which he thanks the author for the book and assures him that his version

of Chaucer's Good Parson has made 'some amends for the hourly offence I beare with, from the sight of soe many Lewd Originalls'.

3. The Victualling Office occupied a complex of storehouses, slaughterhouses, bakeries etc. in East Smithfield.   On 2 July the Council had ordered the Navy Board to inspect them, and in August almost £1000 was directed to be spent on their repair: PRO, PC 6/1, f.34*v*; *CSPD 1661–2*, p. 468.

officers, like knaves, would undervalue in their worth – but we find them good. Then to Woolwich and viewed well all the houses and stores there, which lie in very great confusion for want of storehouses.[1] And then to Mr. Ackworths and Sheldens[2] to view their books – which we find not to answer the King's service and security at all, as to the stores. Then to the Ropeyard and there viewed the hemp, wherein we find great corruption. And then saw a trial between Sir R. Fords yarn and our own, and find great oddes. So by water back again, about 5 in the afternoon, to Whitehall, and so to St. James's and at Mr. Coventrys chamber, which is very neat and fine, we had a pretty neat dinner; and after dinner fell to discourse of business and regulation and do think of many things that will put matters into better order. And upon the whole, my heart rejoices to see Mr. Coventry so ingenious and able and studious to do good, and with much frankness and respect to Mr. Pett and myself perticularly. About 9 ⟨a-clock⟩ we broke up, after much discourse and many things agreed on in order to our business of regulation; and so by water (landing Mr. Pett at the Temple) I went home and to bed.

12. Up by 5 a-clock – and put things in my house in order, to be laid up against my workmen come on Monday to take down the top of my house – which trouble I must go through now, but it troubles me much to think of it. So to my office – where till noon we sat; and then I to dinner and to the office all the afternoon, with much business. At night with Cooper at Arithmetique; and then came Mr. Creede about my Lord's accounts, to even them; and he gone, I to supper and to bed.

13. *Lords day*. Having by some mischance hurt my cods, I had my old pain all yesterday and this morning, and so keep my bed all this morning. So up, and after dinner and some of my people to church, I set about taking down my books and papers and making my chamber fit against tomorrow, to have

---

1. Estimates were made in the following August for an addition to the yarn house in the ropeyard, and in 1663 for repairing the storehouse: *CSPD 1663–4*, p. 235.

2. Storekeeper and Clerk of the Cheque respectively at Woolwich.

the people come to work in pulling down the top of my house.
In the evening I walked to the garden and sent for Mr. Turner
(who yesterday did give me occasion of speaking to him about
the differences between him and me), and I told him my whole
mind and how it was in my power to do him a discourtesy
about his place of petty-purveyance;[1] and at last did make him
see (I think) that it was his concernment to be friendly to me and
what belongs to me. After speaking my mind to him and he
to me, we walked down and took boat at the tower and to
Deptford, on purpose to sign and seal a couple of warrants, as
Justice of Peace in Kent, against one Annis, who is to be tried
next Tuesday at Maidstone assizes for stealing some lead out of
Woolwich yard.[2] Going and coming, I did discourse with
Mr. Turner about the faults of our management of the business
of our office; of which he is sensible, but I believe is a very
knave. Come home, I find a Rabbit at[a] the fire and so supped
well; and so to my Journall and to bed.

14. Up by 4 a-clock and to my Arithmetique; and so to my
office till 8 a-clock; then to Thames-street along with old Mr.
Greene among the tarr=men, and did instruct myself in the
nature and prices of tarr, but could not get Stockholme for the
use of the office under 10*l*:15*s* per last, which is a great price.[3]
So home and at my office all the morning; and at noon Dr

a   symbol blotted

---

1. See above, ii. 54 & n. 1.
2. Robert Annis was workman to
the King's plumber, and the alleged
offence had taken place in December
1661: *CSPD 1661–2*, p. 190; cf.
PRO, Adm. 20/3, p. 63. Pepys, in
common with the other Principal
Officers, was a J.P. for the counties
in which the royal dockyards were
situated. An act of 1664 (renewed
in 1666) simplified the procedure for
prosecutions in cases of embezzlement,
the Navy Board (or any two of them)
being given some of the powers of
magistrates: see below, iv. 82 & n. 1.

But filching persisted: for some of
the evidence, see *Cat.*, i. 186–7.
3. William Green was a tar merchant. The average price of tar in
1662 has been calculated at £10 3*s*. 4*d*.
per last (i.e. 12 barrels of 30 galls.
each), which was lower than the 1661
average: Sir W. Beveridge *et al.*,
Prices and wages in Engl., i. 673. It
rose to £15 in 1666. Stockholm tar
was generally reputed the best: other
varieties were from Norway (Bergen)
and Russia. Cf. Pepys's notes on the
subject (23 March 1664) in NWB,
pp. 25+.

T. Pepys¹ came to me, and he and I to the Exchange and so back
to dinner, where by chance comes Mr. Pierce the Chyrurgeon,
and then Mr. Batersby the Minister, and then Mr. Dun; and it
happened that I had a hanch of venison boiled, and so they were
very welcome and merry; but my simple Doctor doth talk so
like a fool that I am weary of him.   They being gone, to my
office again and there all the afternoon; and at night home and
took a few turns with my wife in the garden, and so to bed –
my house being this day almost quite untiled, in order to its
raising higher.   And this night I begun to put off my wastecoate.*
Too, also I find the pageant in Cornhill² taken down, which was
pretty strange.

15.   Up by 4 a-clock; and after doing some business as to
settling my papers at home, I went to my office, and there busy
till sitting time.   So at the office all the morning – where James
Southerne, Mr. Coventrys clerk, did offer me a warrant for an
officer to sign; which I denied – claiming it for my clerk's duty;
which however did trouble me a little to be put upon it, but I
did it.   We broke up late, and I to dinner at home; where
my brother Tom and Mr. Cooke came and dined with me, but
I could not be merry, for my business; but to my office again
after dinner, and they two and my wife abroad.   In the evening
comes Cooper, and I took him by water, on purpose to tell
me things belonging to ships, which was time well spent, and
so home again.   And my wife came home and tells me she hath
been very merry, and well pleased with her walk with them.
About bedtime it fell a-raining; and the house being all open
at top, it vexed me; but there was no help for it, and so to bed.

16.   In the morning I find all my ceilings spoiled with rain
last night, so that I fear they must be all new-whited when the
work is done.
Made me ready and to my office.   And by and by came Mr.
Moore to me, and so I went home and consulted about drawing
up a fair state of all my Lord's accounts; which being settled, he
went away and I fell to writing of it very neatly, and it was
very handsome and concisely done.   And at noon to my Lord's

1. Physician; son of Talbot Pepys   2. The naval arch erected for the
of Impington (Pepys's great-uncle).   coronation: above, ii. 77 & n. 2.

with it, but find him at dinner and some great company with him, Mr. Edwd. Mountagu and his brother and Mr. Coventry; and after dinner went out with them, and so I lost my labour. But dined with Mr. Moore and the people below, who after dinner fell to talk of Portugall rings, and Captain Ferrers offered five or six to sell; and I seeming to like a ring made of a Coco= nutt, with a stone done in it, he did offer and would give it me. By and by we went to Mr. Creedes lodging, and there got a dish or two of sweetmeats; and I seeing a very neat leather standish, to carry paper, pen, and ink in when one travels,[1] I also got that of him; and that done, I went home by water and to finish some of my Lord's business; and so early to bed.

This day I was told that my Lady Castlemayne (being quite fallen out with her husband) did yesterday go away from him with all her plate, Jewells and other best things; and is gone to Richmond to a brother of hers;[2] which I am apt to think was a design to get out of town, that the King might come at her the better. But strange it is, how for her beauty I am willing to conster all this to the best and to pity her wherein it is to her hurt, though I know well enough she is a whore.

17. To my office; and by and by to our sitting – where much business. Mr. Coventry took his leave, being to go with the Duke over for the Queene-Mother.[3] I dined at home and so to my Lord's, where I presented him with a true state of all his accounts to last Monday, being the 14 of July – which did please him; and to my great joy, I continue in his great esteem and opinion. I this day took a general acquittance from my Lord to the same day – so that now I have but very few persons to deal withal for money in the world.

Home, and find much business to lie upon my hand; and was late at the office, writing letters by candle-light, which is rare at this time of the year. But I do it with much content and joy,

1. Cf. below, vi. 312.

2. She went in fact to her uncle, Col. Edward Villiers, who lived in Richmond Palace: G. S. Steinman, *Duchess of Cleveland*, p. 34.

3. I.e. to France. Sandwich sailed too: hence the 'general acquittance' with Pepys which follows. This was Henrietta-Maria's last visit to England: she returned finally to France in June 1665, and died there in 1669.

and then I do please me to see that I begin to have people direct themselfs to me in all businesses.

Very late, I was forced to send for Mr. Turner, Smith, Young, about things to be sent down early tomorrow on board the King's pleasure-boat.[1]   And so to bed, with my head full of business but well contented in mind as ever in my life.

18.   Up very early and got a-top of my house, seeing the design of my work; and like it very well, and it comes into my head to have my dining-[room] wainscoated, which will be very pretty. By and by, by water to Deptford to put several things in order, being myself now only left in town; and so back again to the office and there doing business all the morning and the afternoon also, till night, and then came Cooper for my Mathematiques; but in good earnest, my head is so full of business that I cannot understand it as otherwise I should do.

At night to bed, being much troubled at the rain coming into my house, the top being open.

19.   Up early and to some business; and my wife coming to me, I stayed long with her, discoursing about her going into the country; and as she is not very forward, so am I at a great loss whether to have her go or no, because of the charge; and yet in some[a] considerations, I could be glad she was there, because of the dirtiness of my house and the trouble of having of a family there.   So to my office, and there all the morning; and then to dinner, and my brother Tom dined with me, only to see me.   In the afternoon I went upon the River to look after some tarr I am sending down and some Coles, and so home again.   It raining hard upon the water, I put ashore and sheltered myself while the King came by in his barge, going down toward the Downes to meet the Queene,[2] the Duke being gone yesterday.   But methought it lessened my esteem of a king, that he should not be able to command the rain.

Home, and Cooper coming (after I had despatch[ed] several letters), to my Mathematiques.   And so at night to bed, to a chamber in Sir W. Pens – my own house being so foule that I

a   symbol smudged

---

1. The yachts of the King and of   with the flotilla to France.
the Duke of York were now to sail   2. The Queen Mother.

cannot lie there any longer. And then the chamber lies so as that I come into it over my leads without going about. But yet I am not fully content with it, for there will be much trouble to have servants running over the leads to and fro.

20. *Lordsday.* My wife and I lay talking long in bed; and at last she is come to be willing to stay two months in the country, for it is her unwillingness to stay till the house is quite done that makes me at a loss how to have her go or stay.

But that which troubles me most is that it hath rained all this morning, so furiously that I fear my house is all over wet; and with that expectation I rose and went into my house, and I find that it is as wet as the open street, and that there is not one dry footing above nor below in my house. So I fitted myself for dirt and removed all my books to the office, and all day putting up and removing things, it raining all day long as hard within doors as without. At last to dinner; we had a calf's head and bacon at my chamber at Sir W Pens, and there I and my wife concluded to have her go, and her two maids and the boy; and so there shall be none but Will and I left at home, and so the house will be free, for it is impossible to have anybody come into my house while it is in this condition; and with this resolution, all the afternoon we were putting up things in the further cellar against next week, for them to be gone. And my wife and I went into the office and there measured a silk flag that I have found there, and hope to get it to myself, for it hath not been demanded since I came to the office. But my wife is not hasty to have it, but rather to stay a while longer and see the event, whether it will be missed or no.

At night to my office and there put down this day's passage*a* in my Journall and read my oaths, as I am obliged every Lord's day; and so to Sir W. Pens to my chamber again, being all in dirt and foule, and in fear of having ketched cold today with dabbling in the water.

That which hath most vexed me today was that by carrying the key to Sir W. Pens last night, it could not, in the midst of all my hurry to carry away my books and things, it could not be found; and at last they found it in the fire that we made last night.*b* So*c* to bed.

a repl. 'page'   *b* repl. 'not'   *c* repl. 'to'

21. Up early; and though I found myself out of order and cold and the weather cold and likely to rain, yet upon my promise and desire to do what I entended, I did take boat and down to Greenwich to Captain Cockes, who hath a most pleasant seat, and neat.[1]   Here I drank wine and eat some fruit off the trees; and he showed me a great rarity, which was two or three of a great number of silver dishes and plates which he bought of an Embassador that did lack money, in the edge or rim of which was placed silver and gold medalls, very ancient and I believe writ, which if they be, they are the greatest rarities that ever I saw in my life – and I will show Mr. Crumlum[2] them.

Thence to Woolwich to the Ropeyard; and there looked over the several sorts of hemp, and did fall upon my great survey of seeing the working[a] and experiments of the strength and the charge in the dressing of every sort; and I do think have brought it to so great a certainty as I have done the King great service in it.   And do purpose to get it ready against the Dukes coming to towne, to present to him.[3]

I breakfasted at Mr. Falconer's[4] well, and much pleased with my inquiries.

Thence to the Dock, where we walked in Mr. Sheldens garden, eating more fruit and drinking and eating figs, which were very good, and talking, while the *Royall James* was bringing towards the docke; and then we went out and saw the manner and trouble of dockeing such a ship; which yet they could not do,

a repl. 'work'

---

1. For the gardens of 'Herr Cox, a rich dealer in flax [? John, his son] ... three miles out of London', see Z. C. von Uffenbach, *London in 1710* (ed. Quarrell and Mare), p. 110.

2. Samuel Cromleholme, High Master of St Paul's School, 1657–72.

3. Pepys's memorandum has not been traced. He has a good note on the subject (23 December 1663) in NWB, p. 33. Hemp was amongst the most important and costly of naval supplies. The best dressing was with Stockholm tar: above,

p. 137 & n. 3. The principal varieties were Königsberg, Riga (the best), and Russian. Milanese and English hemp (which Pepys at 3 August 1663 puts second-best only to Riga), were less frequently used and cheaper. Cf. J. Hollond, *Discourses* (ed. Tanner), pp. 74, 190; R. W. K. Hinton, *Eastland trade and commonweal in 17th cent.*, p. 97; prices in Sir W. Beveridge *et al.*, *Prices and wages in Engl.*, i. 635–6.

4. Clerk of the Ropeyard, Woolwich.

but only brought her head into the docke and so shored her up till next tide. But, good God, what a deal of company was there from both yards to help to do it, when half the company would have done it as well; but I see it is impossible for the King to have things done as cheap as other men.[1]

Thence by water; and by and by, landing at the riverside somewhere among the reeds, we walked to Greenwich, where to Cockes house again and walked in the garden; and then in to his lady, who I find still pretty, but was now vexed and did speak very discontented and angry to the Captain for disappointing a gentleman that he had invited*a* to dinner, which he took like a wise man and said little. But she was very angry – which put me clear out of countenance, that I was sorry I went in. So after I had eat still some more fruit, I took leave of her in the garden, plucking appricotes for preserving, and went away; and so by water home, and there, Mr. Moore coming and telling me that my Lady goes into the country tomorrow, I carried my wife by coach to take her leave of her father, I staying in Westminster-hall, she going away also this week; and thence to my Lady's – where we stayed and supped with her, but find that my Lady was truly angry, discontented with us and angry for our neglecting to see her*b* as we used to do; but after a little, she was pleased as she was used to be, at which we were glad. So after supper, home and to bed.

22. Among my workmen early. Then to the office and there I have letters from the Downes from Mr. Coventry, who tells me of the foul weather they had last Sunday, that drove them back from near Bologne,*c* where they were going for the Queene, back again to the Downes, with the loss of their Cables, sayles, masts. But are all safe; only, my Lord Sandwich, who went before with the Yachts, they know not what is become of him;

---

a   short line between lines   *b*   repl. 'us'   *c*   word smudged

---

1. The Navy Treasurer had later to pay £1 16s. for two barrels of beer for the Deptford workmen who came to help: PRO, Adm. 20/3, p. 60.

which doth trouble me much.   But I hope he got ashore before the storm begun – which God grant.[1]

All day at the office, only at home at dinner.   Where I was highly angry with my wife for her keys being out of the way; but they were found at last, and so friends again.   All the afternoon answering letters and writing letters; and at night to Mr. Coventry, an ample letter in answer to all his and the Dukes business.[2]

Late at night at my office, where my business is great, being now all alone in towne; but I shall go through it with pleasure. So home and to bed.

23.   After being angry a little in the morning, and my house being so much out of order makes me a little pettish, I went to the office and there despatched business by myself; and so again in the afternoon – being a little vexed that my Brother Tom, by his neglect, doth fail to get a coach for my wife and maid this week, by which she will not be at Brampton feast[3] to meet my Lady at my father's.   At night, home; and late packing up things in order to their going to Brampton tomorrow, and so to bed – quite out of sorts in my mind, by reason that the weather is so bad and my house all full of wet and the trouble of going from one house to another, to Sir W. Pens upon every occasion. Besides, much disturbed by reason of the talk, up and down the towne, that my Lord Sandwich is lost; but I trust in God the contrary.

24.   Up early this morning, sending the things to the Carriers,

---

1. The storm overtook the flotilla close by the Goodwin Sands on the way to France. Cf. the description in *Diary of Henry Townshend* (ed. Willis Bund), i. 92–3: the King's 'barque struck ground and was in very great danger, but through God's providence, and his own skill and Prince Rupert and some others ... stood into Quimborough Castle. The Duke of York ... lost his mast in pieces, and the Vice-Admiral, Lord Montagu [*sic*] driven into the seas again. But all at last safe.' Coventry's letters referred to here have not been traced.

2. Copy (in Hewer's hand) in NMM, LBK/8, pp. 9–11; reporting measures taken to fit out and victual ships, and briefly recounting Pepys's visit on the 21st to Woolwich. Copies of six other letters, dated this day, are in ib., pp. 6–9.

3. A parish feast: cf. below, iv. 237. A similar village feast, that at Broughton, not far away, is mentioned in *Huntington Divertisement* (1678), p. 31.

and my boy, who goes today, though his mistress doth not till next Monday.

All the morning at the office, Sir W^a Batten being come to towne last night. I hear, to my great content, that my Lord Sandwich is safe, landed in France. Dined at our chamber, where Will Bowyer with us. And after much simple talk with him, I left him and to my office, where all the afternoon busy till 9 at night; among other things, improving my late experiment at Woolwich about Hempe. So home and to bed.

25. At my office all the morning, reading Mr. Holland's discourse of the Navy, lent me by Mr. Turner; and am much pleased with them, they hitting the very diseases of the Navy which we are troubled with nowadays. I shall bestow writing of them over and much reading thereof.[1]

This morning Sir W Batten came in to the office and desired to speak with me. He begun with telling me that he observed a strangeness between him and me of late, and would know the reason of it – telling me that he heard I was offended with merchants coming to his house and making contracts there. I did tell him that as a friend I have spoke of it to Sir W. Pen and desired him to take a time to tell him of it, and not as a backbiter; with which he was satisfied, but I find that Sir W. Pen hath played the knave with me, and not told it from me as a friend but in a bad sense. He also told me that he heard that exceptions was taken at his carrying his wife down to Portsmouth, saying that the King should not pay for it; but I denied that I had spoke

a repl. 'where'

---

1. John Hollond (Surveyor of the Navy, 1649–52) had written two discourses on naval administration (dated 1638 and 1659) dealing with abuses in victualling, dead-pays, misuse of stores etc. The second (much the fuller) had been revised in 1661 and dedicated to the Duke of York. Both now circulated in MS. – Dr Tanner traced nine copies of the first, and two of the second. Pepys had copies made of each and had them bound: below, p. 286; PL 2193, 2835. The second seems to have been made from Coventry's copy now at Longleat. There is also a copy of the first discourse (in three clerical hands) in Pepys's papers in Rawl. A 192, ff. 222–56. For Pepys's use of them, see below, ix. 489 & n. 2. They were published for the first time by Dr J. R. Tanner in 1896 for the Navy Records Society.

of it, nor did I.　at last, he desired the difference between our
wifes might not make a difference between us; which I was
exceeding glad to hear, and do see every day the fruits of looking
after my business, which I pray God continue me in – for I do
begin to be very happy.　Dined at home, and so to the office
all the afternoon again; and at night home and to bed.

26.　Sir W. Batten, Mr. Pett and I at the office, sitting all the
morning.　So dined at home, and then to my office again,
causing the Modell[1] hanging in my chamber to be taken down
and hung up in my office, for fear of being spoiled by the workmen, and for my own convenience of studying it.　This afternoon I have a letter from Mr. Creede, who hath escaped narrowly
in the King's yacht, and got safe to the Downes after the late
storm; and that there the King doth tell him that he is sure that
my Lord is landed at Callis safe.　Of which being glad, I sent
news thereof to my Lord Crew, and by the post to my Lady
into the country.

This afternoon I went to Westminster and there hear that the
King and Queene entends to come to White-hall from Hampton
Court next week – for all winter.[2]　Thence to Mrs. Sarah and
there looked over my Lord's lodgings,[3] which are very pretty,
and White-hall garden and the bowling ally (where lords and
ladies are[a] now at bowles) in brave condition.　Mrs. Sarah
told me how the falling-out between my Lady Castlemayne
and her Lord was about christening of the child lately; which
he would, and had done by a priest; and some days after, she
had it again christened by a Minister, the King and Lord of
Oxford and Duchess of Suffolk being wittnesses, and christened
with a proviso that it had not already been christened.[4]　Since

a MS. 'at are'

---

1. Of the *Royal James*: see above,
ii. 121.
2. 'Being very welcome to the
tradesmen of all that part of the City,
which extremely did miss the whole
Court': *Diary of Henry Townshend*
(ed. Willis Bund), i. 93.
3. In Whitehall Palace.
4. The child was the son of Lady

Castlemaine and the King and had
been christened Charles on 18 June at St
Margaret's, Westminster: *Harl. Soc.
Reg.*, 64/15.　Castlemaine himself was
a Roman Catholic.　The proviso does
not appear, of course, in the register.
'Duchess' of Suffolk is a mistake for
'Countess'; wife of the 3rd Earl, and
aunt of Lady Castlemaine.

that, she left her Lord, carrying away everything in the house; so much as every dish and cloth and servant but the porter. He is gone discontent into France, they say, to enter a Monastery.[1] And now she is coming back*a* again to her house in Kingstreete. But I hear that the Queene did prick her out of the list presented her by the King,[2] desiring that she might have that favour done her or that he would send her from whence she came; and that the King was angry and the Queene discontented a whole day and night upon it; but that the King hath promised to have nothing to do with her hereafter. But I cannot believe that the King can fling her off so, he loving her too well; and so I writ this night to my Lady to be my opinion, calling*b* her "my Lady" and "the lady I admire". Here I find that my Lord hath lost the garden to his lodgings, and that it is turning into a tennis Court.[3]

Thence by water to the Wardrobe to see how all doth there; and so home to supper and to bed.

27.*c* *Lords day*. At church, alone in the pew, in the morning. In the afternoon, by water I carried my wife to Westminster; where she went to take leave of her father and I to walk in the parke, which is now every day more and more pleasant, by the new works upon it.[4] Here meeting with Laud Crispe, I took him to the further end and sot under a tree in the corner and there sung some songs; he singing well, but no skill and so would sing false sometimes. Then took leave of him and find my wife at my Lord's lodgings; and so took her home by water

a repl. 'beck'   *b* MS. 'she calling'   *c* repl. '29'

---

1. He travelled in France and Italy and in 1664 served in the Venetian navy.

2. The composition of the Queen's Household was still in dispute – Charles refusing to make any appointments at all unless Lady Castlemaine were admitted to a place. The Countess of Suffolk had been nominated First Lady of the Bedchamber to the Queen, for instance, on 2 April, but was not yet appointed: *CSPD 1661–2*, p. 329. On 1 June 1663 the warrant ordering the appointment of Lady Castlemaine and four others was issued. See G. S. Steinman, *Duchess of Cleveland*, Add., p. 1; *CSPD 1663–4*, p. 160; Clarendon, *Life*, ii. 171+.

3. The garden had in turn been made from an older tennis court ('The Brake') in the 1650s. (R).

4. See above, i. 246 & n. 2.

and to supper in Sir W Pens balcony, and Mr. Keene with us; and then came my wife's brother. And then broke up and to bed.

28.   Up early; and by 6 a-clock, after my wife was ready, I walked with her to the George at Holborne conduict, where the Coach stood to carry her and her maid to Bugden; but that not being ready, my brother Tom stayed with them to see them gone; and so I took a troubled, though willing, godbwy, because of the bad condition of my house to have a family in it. So I took leave of her and walked to the waterside, and there took boat for the Towre, hearing that the Queene-Mother is come this morning already as high as Woolwich and that my Lord Sandwich was with her; at which my heart was glad (and I sent the waterman, though yet not very certain of it, to my wife to carry news thereof to my Lady): so to my office all the morning, abstracting the Dukes instruccions in the Margin thereof.[1]

So home all alone to dinner, and then to the office again, and in the evening Cooper comes; and he being gone, to my chamber a little troubled and melancholy; to my lute late, and so to bed – Will lying there at my feet,[2] and the wench in my house in Will's bed.

29.   Early up, and brought all my money, which is near 300*l*, out of my house into this chamber. And so to the office. And there we sat all the morning, Sir George and Mr. Coventry being come from Sea.

This morning, among other things, I broached the business of our being abused about Flaggs – which I know doth*a* trouble Sir W. Batten, but I care not.[3]

At noon, being invited, I went with Sir G. and Mr. Coventry to Sir W. Batten's to dinner, and there merry; and I very friendly

a l.h. repl. s.h. 'will'

---

1. Several later copies of the Instructions survive, with abstracts in the margins: PL 2867, ff. 352+; BL, Harl. 7464, ff. 5 + ; Rawl. A 466, ff. 9+. For the Instructions, see above, p. 24 & n. 1.

2. Sc. in a truckle-bed.

3. The flagmakers were overcharging: below, p. 164 & n. 2. John Young, a principal contractor, was a friend of Batten, and served later as an overseer of his will.

to Sir Wm and he to me, and complies much with me, but I know he envies me, and I do not value him.

To the office again, and in the evening walked to Deptford (Cooper with me, talking of Mathematiques) to send a fellow to prison for cutting of boy=ropes[1] and to see the difference between the flags sent in nowadays; and find the old ones, which were much cheaper, to be wholly as good. So I took one of a sort[2] with me home, and Mr. Wayth[3] accompanying[a] of me a good way, talking of the faults of the Navy, walked to Redriffe back, and so home by water; and after having done late at the office, I went to my chamber and to bed.

30. Up early and to my office; where Cooper came to me and begun his lecture upon the body of a ship – which my having of a modell in the office is of great use to me, and very pleasant and useful it is.

Then by water to White-hall, and there waited upon my Lord Sandwich; and joyed him, at his lodgings, of his safe coming home after all his danger, which he confesses to be very great.[4] And his people do tell me how bravely my Lord did carry himself in it, while my Lord Crofts[5] did cry; and I perceive it is all the town-talk how poorly he carried himself. But the best was of ⟨one⟩ Mr. Rawlins, a Courtier that was with my Lord; and in the greatest danger cried, "God damn me, my Lord, I won't give you 3*d* for your place now;"[b] but all ends in the honour of the pleasure-boats,[6] which, had they[c] not been very good boats, they could never have endured the sea as they did.

a   l.h. repl. s.h. 'leading'
b   phrase in quotation marks enclosed by square brackets
c   l.h. repl. s.h. 'not'

---

1. This case has not been traced.
2. One of each sort. Pepys has a note of this visit in NWB, p. 48.
3. Robert Waith, Paymaster to the Navy Treasurer.
4. For the storm, see above, pp. 143–4.
5. Master of Horse to the Duke of York.

6. The yachts belonging to the King and the Duke of York. As a result of their proved seaworthiness, yachts were used in the following November to transport from Calais the money obtained from the sale of Dunkirk.

Thence with Captain Fletcher of the *Eagl* in his ship's boat with eight oares (but every ordinary oares[1] outrowed us) to Woolwich, expecting to find Sir W. Batten there upon his Survey, but he is not come; and so we got a dish of steaks at the Whitehart, while his Clarkes and others were feasting of it in the best room of the house[2] and after dinner playing at Shuffleboard; and when at last they heard I was there, they went about their Survey; but God help the King, what surveys shall be taken after this manner.

I, after dinner, about my business to the Ropeyard, and there stayed till night, repeating several trialls of the strength, wayte, waste, and other things of Hemp, by which I have furnished myself enough to finish my intended business, of stating the goodness of all sorts of hemp.

At night home by boat (with Sir W Warren, who I landed by the way) and so being come home, to bed.

31. Up early and among my workmen and ordering my roomes above – which will please me very well. So to my office. And then we sat all the morning, where I begin more and more to grow considerable there. At noon, Mr. Coventry and I by his coach to the Exchange together and in Lumbardstreete met Captain Browne of the *Rosebush*; at which he was cruel angry and did threaten to go today to the Duke at Hampton Court and get him turned out because he was not sailed.[3] But at the Exchange we resolved of eating a bit together, which we did at the Shipp, behind the exchange; and so took boat at Billingsgate, and went down on board the *Rosebush* at Woolwich and find all things out of order; but after frighting the officers there, we left them, to[a] make more haste; and so on shore to the yard and did the same to the officers of the yard, that the ship was not despatched. Here we find Sir W Batten going

a repl. ? 'more'

---

1. Rowed by two watermen with one oar each.
2. The clerks' expenses were paid by the office. The White Hart may have been the inn of that name which once existed (? at this period) in Hare St. (Inf. from C. H. Turner.)

3. To Jamaica: cf. *CSPD 1661-2*, p. 338. In later years, Pepys, as Secretary to the Admiralty, had on many occasions to order captains ashore back to their ships: *Further Corr.*, p. 357; *Cat.*, iv. 52, 201 etc.

about his Survey; but so poorly and unlike a survey of the Navy, that I am ashamed of it and so is Mr. Coventry. We found fault with many things; and among others, the measure of some timber now serving in, which Mr. Day the assistant told us of.[1] And so by water home again, all the way talking of the office business and other very pleasant discourse, and much proud I am of getting thus far into his books – which I think I am very much in.

So home late; and it being the last day of the month, I did make up my accounts before I went to bed, and find myself worth about 650*l*, for which the Lord God be praised.[2] And so to bed.

I drank but two glasses of wine this day, and yet it makes my head ake all night, and indisposed me all the next day – of which I am glad. I am now in town only with my man Will and Jane; and because my house is in building, I do lie at Sir W Pen's house, he being gone to Ireland. My wife, her maid and boy gone to Brampton. I am very well entered into the business and esteem of the office, and do ply it close and find benefit by it.

1. On 30 October the timber measurers at both Woolwich and Deptford were dismissed and the work given to the storekeepers: Duke of York, *Mem. (naval)*, pp. 61–2. 'Day' is a slip for 'Deane': cf. below, p. 163. Anthony Deane, now Assistant-Shipwright at Woolwich, was to become a distinguished naval architect and a close friend of Pepys. For fraudulent measuring of timber, see below, p. 169 & n. 3.

2. His savings had recently increased: cf. above, pp. 95, 125.

AUGUST

1. Up, my head akeing, and to my office; where Cooper read me another lecture upon my modell, very pleasant.

So to my business all the morning, which encreases by people's coming now to me to the office. At noon to the Exchange; where meeting Mr. Creede and Moore, we three to a house hard by (which I was not pleased with) to dinner; and after dinner and some discourse ordinary, by coach home, it raining hard. And so at the office all the afternoon, till evening to my chamber; where, God forgive me, I was sorry to hear that Sir W Pens maid Betty was gone away yesterday, for I was in hopes to have had a bout with her before she had gone, she being very pretty. I have also a mind to my own wench, but I dare not, for fear she should prove honest and refuse and then tell my wife.

I stayed up late, putting things in order for my going to Chatham tomorrow. And so to bed – being in pain in my cods with the little riding in a coach today from the exchange[a] – which doth trouble me.

2. Up earely and got me ready in my riding clothes; and so to my office and there wrote letters to my father and wife against night. And then to the business of my office – which being done, I took boat with Will and down to Greenwich; where Captain Cocke not being at home, I was vexed and went to walk in the park till he came thither to me. And Wills forgetting to bring my boots in the boat did also vex me, for I was forced to send the boat back again for them. I to Captain Cockes, along with him to dinner; where I find his lady still pretty, but not so good a humour as I thought she was. We had a plain, good dinner, and I see they do live very frugally. I eat, among other fruit, much mulberrys, a thing I have not eat of these many years, since I used to be at Asted at my Cosen Pepys's.[1]

a l.h. repl. s.h. 'ch'-

---

1. John Pepys (a distant cousin who died c. 1652), confidential secretary to Chief Justice Coke. He had a large house at Ashtead, near Epsom, Surrey.

After dinner we to boate and had a pleasant passage down to Gravesend; but it was 9 a-clock before we got thither, so that we were in great doubt what to do, whether to stay there or no; and the rather because I was afeared to ride, because of my paine in my cods; but at the Swan,¹ finding Mr. Hemson and Lieutenant Carteret of the *Foresight* come to meet me, I borrowed Mr. Hempsons horse and he took another, and so we rode to Rochester in the dark. And there at the Crowne,² Mr. Gregory, Barrow,³ and others stayed to meet me. So after a glass of wine, we to our barge, that was ready for me, to the hill house,⁴ where we soon went to bed. Before we slept, I telling upon discourse Captain Cocke the manner of my being cut of the stone, which pleased him much. So to sleep.

3. *Lords day.* Up earely, and with Captain Cocke to the Docke yard, a fine walk and fine weather. Where we walked till Comissioner Pett came to us and took us to his house and showed us his garden and fine things,⁵ and did give us a fine breakfast of bread and butter and sweetmeats and other things, with great choice, and strong*ᵃ* drinks, with which I could not avoyde making my head ake, though I drank but little. Hither came Captain Allen of the *Foresight* and the officers of the yard to see me.

Hence by and by to church⁶ by coach with the Comissioner, and had a dull sermon; a full church and some pretty women in it; among others, Beck Allen, who was a bridemayde to a new-married couple that came to church today; and, which was pretty strange, sat in a pew hung with mourning for a mother of the brides, which methinks should have been taken down. After dinner, going out of the church, saluted Mrs. Pett, who

a MS 'stronger'

---

1. This inn had been shut for several years by 1737: R. P. Cruden, *Hist. Gravesend* (1843), p. 403.

2. An old inn, close to the bridge: Frederick F. Smith, *Hist. Roch.*, pp. 338–9, pl. 39.

3. Edward Gregory, sen., Clerk of the Cheque, and Philip Barrow, Storekeeper, Chatham.

4. A large house used for official business and for the accommodation of official visitors.

5. For the house, see above ii. 69 & n. 7.

6. St Mary's, Chatham; on the hill above the dockyard.

came after us in the coach to church, and other officers' wifes.[a]
The Comissioner stayed at dinner with me; and we had a
good dinner, better then I would have had, but I see there is
no helping of it.

After dinner the Comissioner and I left the company and
walked in the garden at the Hill-house, which is very pleasant,
and there talked of our businesses and matters of the navy.   So
to church again, where quite weary; and so after sermon walked
with him to the yard up and down and the fields, and saw the
place designed for the wet-dock.[1]   And so to his house and had
a syllabub and saw his closet, which came short of what I expected; but there was fine models of ships in it endeed, whose
worth I could not judge of.   At night walked home to the hill-
house, Mr. Barrow with me, talking of the faults of the yard,
walking in the fields an hour or two, and so home to supper
and so Captain Cocke and I to bed.

This day, among other stories, he told me how despicable a
thing it is to be a hangman[b] is in poleland, although it be a place
of credit.[2]   And that in his time there was some repairs to be
made of the gallowes there, which was very fine of stone; but
nobody could be got[c] to mend it till the Burgo-Maister or Mayor
of the towne, with all the companies of those trades which were
necessary to be used about those repairs, did go in their habits,
with flags, in solemn procession to the place, and there the Burgo-
Maister did give the first blow with the hammer upon the
wooden work, and the rest of the Maisters of the Companies
upon the works belonging to their trades, that so, workmen
might not be ashamed to be imployed upon doing of the gallows-
works.

a   preceded by blot   c   MS. 'god'
b   MS. 'hangman is'

1. See below, iv. 226 & n. 1.

2. Cocke had lived in Danzig c.
1656, trading in hemp and other naval
stores.   (It was there he met his first
wife.)   The office of executioner had
been introduced into Poland with
other municipal institutions from
Germany, and was regarded with
abhorrence.   The hangman often had

difficulty in finding a wife: in Cracow
females under sentence of death were
spared if they would marry an executioner.   Towns which had no hang-
men would employ other criminals or
the accuser. See Z. Gloger in
Encyklopedia Staropolska (1900–3 ed.):
'Kat'.

4. Up by 4 a-clock in the morning and walked to the Docke, where Comissioner Pett and I took barge and went to the Guardshipps and mustered them, finding them but badly manned. Thence to the *Souveraigne*, which we find keeped in good order and very clean, which pleased us well; but few of the officers on board. Thence to the *Charles*, and were troubled to see her kept so neglectedly by the boatswain Clements, who I always took for a very good officer. It is a very brave ship. Thence to Upner Castle, and there went up to the top; where there is a fine prospect, but of very small force.[1] So to the yard and there musterd the whole ordinary;[2] where great disorder by multitude of servants and old decrepitt men, which must be remedyed: so to all the store-houses and viewed the stores of all sort and the hempe; where we find Captain Cockes (which he came down to see along with me) very bad, and some others. And with much content (God forgive me) I did heare[a] by the Clerk of the Rope-yard how it was by Sir W Batten's private letter that one parcel of Alderman Barkers was received.[3]

At 2 a-clock to dinner to the hill-house; and after dinner despatched many people's business, and then to the yard again and looked over Mr. Gregorys and Barrowes houses, to see the matter of difference between them concerning an alteracion that Barrow would make;[4] which I shall report to the board.

a l.h. repl. s.h. 'by'

1. Upnor Castle, on the left bank of the Medway, a little downstream from Chatham, had been built under Elizabeth for the defence of the river. Ineffective against the invading Dutch fleet of 1667, it was much strengthened afterwards. By 1719 there were three smaller forts attached to it: John Harris, *Hist. Kent* (1719), i. 386. Plans in BL, King's MSSS 43, ff. 36–8 [1698]; ib., King's Maps, xviii. 57, 2 [1725].

2. The muster-book made on this occasion, mostly in a clerk's hand, with a few notes in Pepys's, is in Rawl. A 187, ff. 321+. Pepys and Pett charged £6 5s. for their travel-ling expenses: PRO, Adm. 20/3, p. 63.

3. It was probably this hemp to which Coventry referred in a letter to Pepys (3 March 1665) as 'bad hemp' bought of Barker 'by some of our own eyes': Rawl. A 174, ff. 454–5. On 28 July 1662 the Board had ordered Carteret not to pay the £1000 still owing to Barker for his Milan and Riga hemp until he had provided securities for the completion of his contract: PRO, Adm. 106/3520, f.7r. Cf. Pepys's recent suspicions of Batten's collusion with the flagmakers: above, p. 148 & n. 3.

4. Cf. below, iv. 149 & n. 2.

But both their houses very pretty, and deserve to be so, being well kept. Then to a tryall of several sorts of hemp; but could not perform it here so well as at Woolwich, but we did do it pretty well.

So took barge at the Docke and to Rochester; and there Captain Cocke and I and our two men took coach about 8 at night, and to Gravesend, where it was very dark before we got thither to the Swan; and there meeting with Doncaster, an old water=man of mine above bridge, we eat a short supper, being very merry with the drolling drunken coachman that brought us; and so took water – it being very dark and the wind rising and our waterman unacquainted with this part of the River, so that we were presently cast upon the Essex shoare; but got off again and so, as well as we could, went on; but I in such fear that*a* I could not sleep till we came to Erith; and there it begun to be calme and the stars to shine, and so I begun to take heart again and the rest, too; and so made shift*b* to slumber a little.

Above Woolwich, we lost our way and went back to Black-wall and up and down, being guided by nothing but the barking ⟪5⟫ of a dog which we had observed in passing by blackewall; and so got right again with much ado, after two or three circles, and so on and at Greenwich set in, Captain Cocke and I set forward, hailing to all the King's ships at Deptford, but could not wake any man, so that we could have done what we would with their ships. At last waked one man; but it was a merchant-ship, the *Royall Catharin*. So to the tower docke and home, where the girle sat up for me; it was about 3 a-clock. And putting Mr. Boddam[1] out of my bed, went to bed and lay till 9 a-clock; and so to the office, where we sat all the morning and I did give some accounts of my service. Dined alone at home, and was glad my house is begun tiling; and to the office again all the afternoon, till it was so dark that I could not see hardly what it is that I now set down when I write this word;*c* and so went to my chamber and to bed, being sleepy.

a MS. 'but'   b repl. 'ship'
c This comment must relate to a prior form of the diary. The s.h. is as neat here as in the preceding and following entries.

---

1. Clerk of the Ropeyard, Woolwich.

6. Up early; and going to my office, met Sir G. Carteret in coming through the garden and so walked a good while talking with him about Sir Wm. Batten; and find that he is going down the wind in everybody's esteem, and in that of his honesty by this letter that he writ to Captain Allen concerning Alderman Barkers hemp. Thence by water to White-hall and so to St. James's; but there find Mr. Coventry gone to Hampton=court. So to my Lord's and he is also gone, this being a great day at the Council about some business at the Council before the King.[1] Here I met with Mr. Pierce the Chyrurgeon, who told me how Mr. Edwd. Mountagu hath lately had a duell with Mr. Cholmely, that is first Gentleman-usher to the Queene and was a messenger from the King to her in Portugall, and is a fine gentleman but hath received many affronts from Mr. Mountagu (and some unkindnesses from my Lord upon his score, for which I am sorry).[2] Hee proved too hard for Mountagu and drove him so far backward that he fell into a ditch and dropped his sword; but with honour would take no advantage over him, but did give him his life; and the world says that Mr. Mountagu did carry himself very poorly in the business and hath lost his honour for ever with all people in it – of which I am very glad, in hopes that it will humble him. I hear also that he hath sent to my Lord to borrow 400*l*, giving his Brother Harvey's[3] security for it, and that my Lord will lend it him, for which I am sorry.

Thence home, and at my office all the morning and dined at home; and can hardly keep myself from having a mind to my wench, but I hope I shall not fall to such a shame to myself. All the afternoon also at my office and did business. In the evening came Mr. Bland the Merchant to me, who hath lived long in Spayne and is concerned in the business of Tanger, who did discourse with me largely of it; and after he was gone, did send me three or four printed things that he hath writ of trade in general

---

1. Presumably a committee meeting; the council register records no council meeting on this day.

2. Edward Mountagu (Sandwich's first cousin) was Master of the Horse to the Queen, and had accompanied Sandwich on the voyage which had brought her from Portugal. There is a brief account of the duel in PRO, SP 29/58, no. 59.

3. Sir Daniel Harvey; his brother-in-law.

and of Tanger perticularly.[1]   But I do not find much in them.
This afternoon Mr. Waith was with me and did tell me much
concerning the Chest, which I am resolved to look into; and I
perceive he is sensible of Sir W. Batten's carriage and is pleased
to see anything work against him[2] – who, poor man, is I perceive
much troubled, and did yesterday morning walk in the garden
with me and did tell me that he did see there was a design of
bringing another man in his room, and took notice of my sorting myself with others, and that we did business by ourselfs
without him – part of which is true; but I denied, and truly,
any design of doing him any such wrong as that.   He told me
he did not say it perticularly of me, but he was confident there
was somebody entended to be brought in.   Nay, that the trayne
was laid before Sir W Pen went,[3] which I was glad to hear him
say.   Upon the whole, I see he perceives himself tottering and
that he is suspected and would be kind to me; but I do my business in the office and neglect him.

At night, writing in my Study, a mouse run over my table,
which I shut up fast under my shelfe's upon my table till tomorrow.   And so home and to bed.

7.   Up by 4 a-clock and to my office; and by and by Mr.[a]
Cooper comes and to our modell – which pleases me more and
more.   At this till 8 a-clock, and so we sat in the office and stayed

a repl. 'comes'

---

1. John Bland is known to have
written *Trade Revived, or A way proposed to restore . . . the . . . trade of this
our English nation . . .* (first pub.
1659); and *To the King's most excellent
Majesty, the humble remonstrance of John
Bland . . .* (1661).   Another work –
*A short discours of the late forren acquests
which England holds, viz. of Dunkirk
. . ., Tangier . . ., Boombay . . ., Jamayca
. . . etc., By J. B.* (1662) – is sometimes doubtfully ascribed to him.
Pepys read one of his works (below, p.
291), but retained none in the PL.
Bland was a London merchant who
had traded in Seville (*CSPD 1664–5*,
p. 346), and now had a half-share in

the cargo of the *Peter and Andrew*, sent
to Tangier in September: BL, Sloane
1955, f.137r.   He went to Tangier in
October 1664 after failing to obtain
the contract for supplying it with
victuals.   There he became Mayor in
1668 and 1670.

2. Batten was chairman of the
governors of the Chatham Chest;
Robert Waith the Navy Treasurer's
paymaster.   The affairs of the Chest
were now about to be investigated:
below, p. 172 etc., esp. p. 257 & n. 2.
For the other complaints against
Batten, see above, p. 155 & n. 3.

3. To Ireland: above, p. 123.

all the morning, my interest still growing, for which God be praised. This morning I got unexpectedly the *Reserve* for Mr. Cooper to be Maister of, which was only by taking an opportune time to motion, which is one good effect of my being constant at the office; that nothing passes without me, and I have the choice of my own times to propose anything I would have. Dined at home and to the office again at my business all the afternoon till night, and so to supper and to bed – it being become a pleasure to me nowadays to fallow my business, and the greatest part of it may be imputed to my drinking no wine and going to no plays.

8. Up by 4 a-clock in the morning and at 5 by water to Woolwich, there to see the manner of Tarring; and all the morning looking to see the several proceedings in making of Cordage and other things relating to that sort of works, much to my satisfaccion. At noon came Mr. Coventree on purpose from Hampton Court to see the same. And dined with Mr. Falconer; and after dinner, to several experiments of Hempe and perticularly some Millan hemp that is brought over ready-dressed.[1]

Thence we walked, talking, very good discourse all the way to Greenwich; and I do find most excellent discourse from him. Among other things, his rule of suspecting every man that proposes anything to him to be a knave, or at least to have some ends of his own in it – being led thereto by the story of Sir John Millicent, that would have had a patent from King James for every man to have had leave to have given him a shilling and that he might take it of every man that had a mind to give*ᵃ* it.[2] And being answered that that was a fair thing, but what needed he a patent for it and what he would do to them that would not give him – he answered, he would not force them, but that they should come to the Council of State to give a reason why they would not.[3]

a MS. 'take'

---

1. For hemp and the methods of stoving it, see above, p. 142, n. 3; below, vi. 34 & n. 3; vii. 132 & n. 3. John Falconer was Clerk of the Ropeyard at Woolwich.

2. Millicent, of Barham, Cambs., was said to be 'the best extemporary fool' at James's court: A. Weldon,

Court ... *of James I* (1650), p. 92. James's monopolies had been notorious.

3. The Privy Council of the early Stuarts (not the 'Council of State' of the Interregnum) had in that way coerced their unwilling subjects.

Another rule is a proverb that he hath been taught, which is that a man that cannot sit still in his chamber (the reason of which I did not understand him) and he that cannot say no (that is, that is of so good a nature that he hath, cannot deny anything or cross another in doing anything) is not fit for business. The last of which is a very great fault of mine, which I must amend in.

Thence by boat. I being hot, he put the Skirt of his cloak about me. And it being rough, he told me the passage of a Frenchman through London bridge; where when he saw the great fall, he begun to cross himself and say his prayers in the greatest fear in the world; and as soon as he was over, he swore *"Morbleu c'est le plus grand plaisir du mond"* – being the most like a French humour in the world.

To Deptford and there surprized the yard and called them to a muster,*a* and discovered many abuses, which we shall be able to understand hereafter and amend.[1] Thence walked to Redriffe and so to London bridge, where I parted with him. And walked home. And did a little business, and to supper and to bed.

9. Up by 4 a-clock or a little after, and to my office, whither by and by comes Cooper, to whom I told my getting for him the *Reserve*, for which he was very thankful; and fell to work upon our Modell and did a good morning's work upon the Rigging, and am very sorry that I must lose him so soon. By and by comes Mr. Coventry, and he and I alone sat at the office all the morning upon business. And so to dinner to Trinity-house, and thence by his coach toward White-hall; but there being a stop at the Savoy, we light and took water. And my Lord Sandwich being out of towne, we parted there – all the way having good discourse; and in short, I find him the most in-genuous person I ever found in my life. And am happy in his acquaintance and my interest in him. Home by water and did business at my office – writing a letter to my brother John to disswade him from being Moderator of his year,[2] which I hear is

a repl. 'musterd'

1. Surprise musters were a normal means of inspection and discipline: cf. below, p. 164 & n. 5; p. 179 & n. 2.

2. John Pepys was now in his second year at Christ's College, Cambridge. Moderators presided over academic disputations.

proffered him, of which I am very glad. By and by comes Cooper, and he and I by Candle light at my Modell, being willing to learn as much of him as is possible before he goes.

So home and to bed.

10. *Lords day.*ᵃ Being to dine at my brother's, I walked to St. Dunstans, the church being now finished and is a very fine church;¹ and here I heard Dr Bates, who made a most eloquent sermon. And I am sorry I have hitherto had so low an opinion of the man – for I have not heard a neater sermon a great while, and more to my content.² So to Toms, where Dr Fairebrother, newly come from Cambrige, met me – and Dr Tom. Pepys. I framed myself as pleasant as I could, but my mind was another way. Hither came my uncle Fenner, hearing that I was here, and spoke to me about Pegg Kites business of her portionᵇ which her husband demands; but I will have nothing to do with it.³ I believe he hath no mind to part with the money out of hisᶜ hand, but let him do what he will in it. He told me the New Service=booke (which is now lately come forth) was laid upon their Deske at St. Sepulchers for Mr. Gouge to read; but he laid it aside and would not meddle with it.⁴ And I perceive the Presbyters do all prepare to giveᵈ over it all against Bartholmewtide.

---

a 'y' smudged   *b* repl. 'portion'   *c* l.h. repl. s.h. 'is'   *d* MS ? 'go'

---

1. St Dunstan-in-the-West; an account book for the repairs to roof, steeple, battlements, walls etc., is in Camb. Univ. Lib., MS., SSS. 4. 9. The work, costing c. £2000, was decided on at a vestry held in April 1659, and the accounts were closed in October 1663.

2. William Bates was Rector of St Dunstan's and a great Presbyterian preacher; he was ejected from his living by the Act of Uniformity a fortnight later. For his calm and equable style of preaching, see W. Fraser Mitchell, *Engl. pulpit oratory*, pp. 274–5.

3. Peg Kite (Pepys's first cousin)

had inherited most of her mother's estate under a will of which Thomas Fenner and Pepys were joint executors. Pepys, however, seems to have resigned the charge: above, ii. 179, n. 3. Peg was 'a troublesome carrion' and had married a 'beggarly rogue': above, ii. 179, 209.

4. Thomas Gouge was a leading Presbyterian. The newly revised Prayer Book was now enforced on all the clergy, who had to accept it by St Bartholomew's Day, 24 August. Gouge was extruded from the living on his refusal. On the question of the date of the publication of the book, see Burnet, i. 328.

Mr. Herring, being lately turned out at St. Brides,[1] did read
the psalm to the people while they sung at Dr. Bates's, which
methought is a strange turn.

After dinner to St. Brides and there heard one Carpenter, an
old man who they say hath been a Jesuite priest and is come
over to us.[2]   But he preaches very well.   So home with Mrs.
Turner, and there hear that Mr. Calamy[3] hath taken his farewell
this day of his people.   And that others will do so the next
Sunday.   Mr. Turner the Draper I hear is Knighted, made Alderman and pricked for Sheriffe with Sir Thomas Bluddell for the
next year by the King; and so are called with great honour the
Kings sheriffes.[4]

Thence walked home, meeting Mr. Moore by the way; and
he home with me and walked till it was dark in the garden, and
so good-night.   And I to my closet in my office, to perfect my
Journall and to read my solemne vowes, and so to bed.

11.   All the morning at the office.   Dined at home all alone,
and so to my office again, whither Deane Fuller came to see me;
and he having business about a ship to carry his goods to Dublin,

1. Relations between John Herring,
Vicar of St Bride's since c. 1656, and
his churchwardens and vestry had
been uneasy for some time, and this
may have caused him to relinquish
the living earlier than the last day
allowed by law. The church was
also served by a lecturer.

2. Richard Carpenter (d. ? 1670)
now an Anglican, had been an Independent, and three times joined the
Roman church. He was the author
of *A new play call'd the pragmatical
Jesuit newleven'd* (? 1669). 'A fan-
tastical man that changed his mind
with his clothes, and that for his
juggles and tricks in matters of religion . . . was esteemed a theological
mountebank': Wood, *Ath. Oxon.*
(ed. Bliss), ii. 419-20.

3. Edmund Calamy, sen., a leading
Presbyterian, Rector of St Mary
Aldermanbury. He preached his

farewell sermon on the 17th: PL.
1168, sig. B.

4. Cf. Sharpe, ii. 396, 470. This
appointment of the sheriffs virtually
by royal command derived from the
special and temporary powers exer-
cised under the Corporation Act
of 1661.   For the King's orders addressed to the Lord Mayor and to the
Commissioners on (16 June), see
CSPD 1661-2, p. 408.   Cf. also ib.,
p. 362 (a royal order, 15 June, for the
election of Bludworth – 'Bluddell' –
as alderman).   Sir William Turner
the draper (Lord Mayer 1668-9) was
brother-in-law to Mrs Turner, a
relative of Pepys. He had been
knighted on 19 July.   Both he and
Bludworth had previously paid fines
rather than accept office as aldermen,
but had recently been nominated to
the office by the Commissioners in
place of two Puritans, Milner and
Love.

whither he is shortly to return, I went with him to the Hermitage, and the ship happening to be Captain Hollands, I did give order for them to be well looked after. And thence with him to the Custome-house about getting a passe for them; and so to the Dolphin taverne, where I spent 6*d* on him, but drank but one glass of wine and so parted. He tells me that his neece that sings so well (whom I have long longed to see) is married to one Mr. Boys, a wholesayle man at the Three Crownes in Cheapeside.

I to the office again, whither Cooper came and read his last lecture to me upon my modell, and so bid me god-bwy – he being to go tomorrow to Chatham to take charge of the ship I have got him. So I to my business till 9 at night, and so to supper and to bed – my mind a little at ease because my house is now quite tiled.

12. Up earely at my office. And I find all people beginning to come to me. Among others, Mr. Deane the assistant of Woolwich, who I find will discover to me the whole abuse that his Majesty suffers in the measuring of timber, of which I shall be glad. He promises me also a modell of a ship, which will please me exceedingly, for I do want one of my owne.[1] By and by we sat. And among other things, Sir W Batten and I had a difference about his Clerkes making a warrant for a Maister; which I would not suffer, but got another signed; which he desires may be referred to a full board, and I am willing to it. But though I did get another signed of my own clerk's, yet I will give it to his Clerke, because I would not be judged unkinde,

1. Deane delivered it on 29 September. Pepys went on to assemble a fine collection of ship models (in handsome glass cases: *Further Corr.*, p. 296) which he bequeathed to William Hewer 'recommending it to him to consider how these also together with his own may be preserved for publick benefit': *Pepysiana*, p. 264. The fate of this collection is unknown. It was seen a few years after Pepys's death (John Aubrey, *Nat. hist.... Surrey*, 1719, v. 332), but may have been dispersed later. Some models may have found their way into Charles Sergison's collection and thence into the possession of an American collector, whose models certainly did include some from Pepys's period at the Admiralty: see H. A. Balridge, 'Ship models: the collections of Rogers, Sergison and Pepys', in *Proc. U.S. Naval Inst.*, November 1938, pp. 1553+; E. Keble Chatterton, *Ship models*, p. 21. It may be that some were lost when Hewer's house at Clapham was pulled down in the 1750s.

though I will stand upon my privilege.[1]   At noon home and to dinner alone; and so to the office again.

Where busy all the afternoon till 10 a-clock at night, and so to supper and to bed – my mind being a little disquieted about Sir W. Batten's dispute[a] today; though this afternoon I did speak with his man Norman at last, and told him the reason of my claim.

13.   Up earely and to my office – where people came to me about business, and by and by we met on purpose to inquire into the business of the Flaggmakers, where I am the person that doth chiefly manage the business against them on the King's part; and I do find it the greatest cheat that I have yet found – they having 8*d* per yard allowed them by pretence of a contract, when no such thing appears; and it is 3*d* more then was formerly paid and then I now offer the Board to have them done. We did not fully end it, but refer it to another time.[2]

At noon Comissioner Pett and I by water to Greenwich and on board the pleasure-boats to see what they wanted, they being ordered to sea; and very pretty things I still find them. And so on shore, and at the Shipp had a bit of meat and dined – there waiting upon us a barber of Mr. Petts acquaintance, that plays very well upon the viallin.[3]   Thence to Lambeth and there saw the little pleasure-boat in building by the King, my Lord Brunkard, and the virtuosos of the towne, according to new lines; which Mr. Pett cries up mightily, but how it will prove we shall soon see.[4]

So by water home.   And busy at my study late, drawing a letter to the yards of reprehension and direction for the board to sign; in which I took great pains.[5]   So home and to bed.

a   repl. ? 'matter'

---

1. Cf. above, p. 106 & n. 2.
2. On 18 September the Board decided to allow the contractors the higher price for what they had already served in: PRO, Adm. 106/3520, f.8*r*. Cf. above, p. 148 & n. 3.
3. Golding of Greenwich: cf. below, vi. 263, 279. (E).
4. The *Jemmy* (25 tons); for her race with the Dutch yacht, see below, p. 188. She was built by Commis-

sioner Pett. The Royal Society appears to have had no part in this enterprise.
5. Copy (21 August) in BL, Add. 9311, ff. 83–4. Cf. Duke of York, *Mem.* (*naval*), pp. 28–32; above, p. 129, n. 1. Coventry, on 5 August, had agreed with Pepys that a letter of this sort should be written: BL, Add. 9314, f.4*r*.

14. Up early and to look over my works, and find my house to go on apace. So to my office to prepare business; and then we met and sat till noon. And then Comissioner Pett and I being invited, went by Sir John Winter's coach, sent for us, to the Miter in Fanchurch-street – to a venison-pasty; where I find him a very worthy man and good discourse – most of which was concerning the Forrest of Deane and the timber there and Iron workes, with their great antiquity and the vast heaps of cinders which they find, and are now of great value, being necessary for the making of Iron at this day and without which they cannot work[1] – with the age of many trees there left at a great fall in Edwd the Thirds time, by the name of "forbid trees," which at this day are called "Vorbid trees."[2]

Thence to my office about business till late, and so home and to bed.

15. Up very early, and up about seeing how my work proceeds, and am pretty well pleased therewith; especially, my wife's closet will be very pretty. So to my office and there very busy all the morning, and many people coming to me. At noon to the Change and there hear of some Quakers that are seized on, that would have blown up the prison in Southwarke where they[a] are put.[3] So to the Swan in old Fish streete, where Mr. Brigden and his father-in-law Blackbury, of whom we have bought timber in the office but hath not dealt well with us, did make me a fine dinner, only to myself. And after dinner comes in a Jugler, which showed us very pretty tricks. I seemed very pleasant, but am no friend to the man's dealings

a repl. 'there'

---

1. Slags of Roman and medieval bloomeries, which had been only lightly smelted, could still be used both as ore and flux. Rhys Jenkins in *Trans. Newcomen Soc.*, 6/42+.

2. A 'forbid' was an order of the Mines Law Court: the miners were not to cut down these trees. The gale was that of 1362.

3. About 80 Quakers had been incarcerated in the White Lion prison, Southwark, for attending a conventicle on 3 August: J. Besse, *Coll. of sufferings* (1753), i. 690. They were released in the following January: N. Penney (ed.), *Extracts from state papers*, p. 164. The reported plot has not been traced; if it existed its authors were more likely to have been the Anabaptists who were in Southwark prison than the Quakers. The two sects were often confused.

with us in the office.   After an hour or two's sitting after dinner, talking about office business, I went to Pauls churchyard to my booksellers, where I have not spent any time a great while.   And there I hear the next Sunday will be the last of a great many Presbyterian ministers in towne, who I hear will give up all.[1] I pray God the issue may be good, for the discontent is great. Home to my office till 9 at night, doing business; and so to bed – my mind well pleased with a letter that I find at home from Mr. Coventry, expressing his satisfaction in a letter I writ last night and sent him this morning, to be corrected by him in order to its sending down to all the yards as a Charge to them.

16.   Up by 4 a-clock.   And up looking over my work, what they did yesterday; and am pretty well pleased, but I find it will be long before they have done, though the house is cover'd and I free from the weather.

We met and sat all the morning, and at noon was sent for by my Uncle Wight to Mr. Rawlinson's, and there we had a pigg, and Dr Fairebrother came to me to see me and dined with us.   And after dinner he went away, and I by my uncles desire stayed; and there he begun to discourse about our difference with Mr. Young about Flaggs, pleading for him, which he did desire might be made up; but I told him how things was, and so he was satisfied and said no more.   So home and above with my workmen, who I find busy and my work going on pretty well.   And so to my office till night; and so to eat a bit and so to bed.

17.   *Lords=day.*   Up very earely, this being the last Sunday that the Presbyterians are to preach, unless they read the new Comon Prayer and renounce the Covenant, and so I had a mind to hear Dr Bates's farewell sermon,[2] and walked thither – calling first at my brother, where I find that he is come home after being a week abroad with Dr Pepys, nobody knows where;[3] nor I, but by chance, that he was gone, which troubles me.   So I

---

1. Cf. above, p. 97 & n. 2. Fifty ministers in London and Middlesex were expropriated: A. G. Matthews, *Calamy Revised*, p. xii. Cf. below, v. 190 & n. 1.

2. For Dr William Bates, see above, p. 161 & n. 2.

3. They had been bride-hunting on Tom's behalf: below, p. 176 & n. 1.

called only at the door, but did not ask for him; but went to
Madam Turners to know whether she went to church and to tell
her that I would dine with her. And so walked to St. Dunstans,
where, it being not 7 a-clock yet, the doors were not open; and
so I went and walked an hour in the Temple garden, reading
my vows; which it is a great content to me to see how I am a
changed man, in all respects for the better, since I took them –
which the God of Heaven continue to me and make me thankful for.

At 8 a-clock I went and crowded in at a back door among
others, and the church being half-full almost before any doors
were open publicly; which is the first time that I have done so
these many years, since I used to go with my father and mother.
And so got into the Gallry besides the pulpit and heard very
well. His text was, "Now the god of peace" – the last*a* *Hebrews*
and the 20 verse – he making a very good sermon and very little
reflections in it to anything of the times.[1] Besides the sermon, I
was very well pleased with the sight of a fine lady that I have
often seen walk in Grayes-Inn walks. And it was my chance to
meet her just at the door going out, and very pretty and sprightly
she is; and I believe the same that my wife and I some years
since did meet at Temple barr gate and have sometimes spoke of.
So to Madam Turner's and dined with her. She had heard
parson Herring[2] take his leave; though he, by reading so much
of the Common Prayer as he did, hath cast himself out of the
good opinion of both sides.

After dinner to St. Dunstan's again, and the church quite
crouded before I came, which was just at one a-clock; but I got
into the gallery again, but stood in a crowd and did exceedingly
sweat all the while. He pursued his text again very well, and
only at the conclusion told us after*b* this manner – "I do believe
that many of you do expect that I should say something to you
in reference to the time, this being the last time that possibly I
may appear here. You know*c* it is not my manner to speak
anything in the pulpit that is extraneous to my text and business.

a repl. 'll'   *b* repl. 'that at'   *c* MS. 'not it'

---

1. The sermon (on Heb., xiii. 20–1)   *farewel sermons*... (1663); PL 1168.
was printed in *A compleat collection of*   2. See above, p. 162 & n. 1.

Yet this I shall say, that it is not my opinion, faction, or humour that keeps me from complying with what is required of us, but something which after much prayer, discourse and study yet remains unsatisfied and commands me herein. Wherefore, if it is my unhappinesse not to receive such an illuminacion as should direct me to do otherwise, I know no reason why men should not pardon me in this world, and am confident that God will pardon me for it in the next." [1] And so he concluded.

Parson Herring read a psalme and Chapters before sermon; and one was the Chapter in the *Acts* where the story of Ananias and Saphira is.[2] And after he had done, says he, "This is just the case of England at present; God, he bids us to preach, and men bid us not to preach; and if we do, we are to be imprisoned and further punished: all that I can say to it is that I beg your prayers and the prayers of all good Christians for us." This was all the exposition he made of the chapter, in these very words and no more.

I was much pleased with Dr Bates's manner of bringing in the Lord's Prayer after his owne, thus – "In whose comprehensive words we sum up all our imperfect desires; saying – Our Father" &c. Church being done and it raining, I took a hackney-coach and so home, being all in a sweat and fearful of getting cold.

To my study at my office, and thither came Mr. Moore to me and walked till it was quite dark. Then I writ a letter to my Lord Privy Seale as from my Lord, for Mr. [Moore] to be Sworne directly as Deputy to my Lord, he denying to swear him as Deputy together with me. So that I am now clear of it, and the profit is now come to be so little[3] that I am not displeased at my getting off so well.

---

1. Pepys had a MS. copy of the sermon, or had taken notes himself. The printed version (op. cit., n.p.) ran: 'I know you expect I should say something, as to my nonconformity. I shall onely say thus much, it is neither fancy, faction, nor humour, that makes me not to comply, but meerly for fear of offending God. And if after the best means used for my illumination, as prayer to God, discourse, study, *I* am not able to be satisfied concerning the lawfulness of what is required; if it be my unhappiness to be in error, surely *men* will have no reason to be angry with me in this world, and *I* hope *God* will pardon me in the next.'

2. Ch. v.

3. Cf. above, i. 213 & n. 1.

He being gone, I to my study and read; and so to eat a bit of bread and cheese and so to bed.

I hear most of the Presbyters took their leaves today. And the City is much dissatisfied with it. I pray God keep peace among us and make the Bishops careful of bringing in good men in their room,[1] or else all will fly a-pieces; for bad ones will not down with the City.

18. Up very earely, and up upon my house to see how work goes on, which doth please me very well. So about 7 a-clock took horse and rode to Bowe, and there stayed at the Kingshead and eat a breakfast of eggs till Mr. Deane of Woolwich came to me; and he and I rid into Waltham Forrest[2] and there we saw many trees of the King's a-hewing and he showed me the whole mystery of off=square,[a][3] wherein the King is abused in the timber that he buys, which I shall with much pleasure be able to correct. After we had been a good while in the wood, we rode to Ilford; and there, while dinner was getting ready, he and I practised measuring of the tables and other things till I did understand measure of timber and board very well. So to dinner; and by and by, being sent for, comes Mr. Cooper, our officer in the Forrest, and did give me an account of things there and how the country is backward to come in with their carts.[4] By and by comes one Mr. Marshall, of whom the King hath many carriages for his timber, and they stayed and drank with me. And while I am here, Sir Wm. Batten passed by in

a l.h. repl. l.h. 'over'-

---

1. For complaints made later on this score, see below, v. 190 & n. 1.

2. Epping Forest.

3. A fraudulent method of measuring timber: see W. Leybourn, *Compleat Surveyor* (1674), p. 350. Cf. above, p. 151 & n. 1.

4. A recent act of May 1662 (14 Car. II c. 20) required parishes to provide horse- or ox-carts for the carriage of timber for the navy at a charge of 1s. a mile. Warrants to this effect were to be issued to the constables of the hundreds and parishes by J.P.'s acting at the request of the naval purveyor. In the case here reported the authorities may have met with resistance because it was harvest-time: cf. *CSPD 1663-4*, pp. 258-9. The system was always unpopular and was abolished by an act of 1695, after which the Navy Office bore the full charge.

his coach homeward from Colchester, where he hath been seeing his son-in-law Lemon, that lies a-dying; but I would take no notice of him, but let him go.   By and by I got a-horse-back again and rode to Barking, and there saw the place where they ship this timber for Woolwich; and so Deane and I home again.   And parted at Bow, and I home just before a great showre of rain as God would have it.

I find Deane a pretty able man, and able to do the King service; but I think more out of envy to the rest of the officers of the yard (of whom he complains much) then true love, more then others, to the service.   He would fain seem a modest man, and yet will commend his own work and skill and vie with other persons, especially the Petts.   But I let him alone, to hear all he will say.[1]

Whiled away the evening at my office, trying to repeat my rules of measuring learnt this day; and so to bed – with my mind very well pleased with this day's work.

19.   Up betimes and to see how my work goes on.   Then Mr. Creede came to me, and he and I walked an hour or two till 8 a-clock in the garden, speaking of our accounts one with another, and then things public.   Among other things, he tells me that my Lord hath put me into commission with himself and many noblemen and others for Tanger; which if it be, is not only great honour but may be of profit too, and I am very glad of it.[2]

By and by to sit at the office; and Mr. Coventry did tell us of the duell between Mr. Jermin, nephew to my Lord St. Albans, and Collonell Giles Rawlins, the latter of whom is killed and the first mortally wounded as it is thought.[3]   They fought against

1. Anthony Deane rose to become Master-Shipwright (Portsmouth) in 1668, and Navy Commissioner and knight in 1675. Pepys came to have a lasting admiration for him, though in the diary he often refers to his conceit (below, iv. 176 etc.): cf. *Tangier Papers*, p. 231. The 30 ships he built under the act of 1677 Pepys regarded as the best in the world: *Naval Minutes*, p. 227.

2. See below, p. 238 & n. 3. Similar committees existed for a few but not all other colonies: C. M. Andrews, *Brit. committees of trade and plantations*, p. 80.

3. This was a quarrel over the Countess of Shrewsbury: the duels were fought on the 17th, and are described in Gramont, pp. 113+; Rugge, ii, ff. 42r, 51r; PRO, SP 29/58, no. 59. Jermyn survived.

Captain Tho Howard, my Lord Carliles brother, and another unknown[1] – who they say had armor on, that they could not be hurt, so that one of their swords went up to the hilt against it. They had horses ready and are fled. But what is most strange, Howard sent one challenge, but they could not meet, and then another; but did meet yesterday at the old Pall Mall at St. James's, and would not to the last tell Jermyn what the quarrell was. Nor doth anybody know. The Court is much concerned in this fray; and I am glad of it, hoping that it will cause some good laws against it.[2]

After sitting, Sir G. Carteret and I walked a good while in the garden; who told me that Sir W Batten hath made his complaint to him that some of us have a mind to do him a bad turn. But I do not see that Sir George is concerned for him at all, but rather against him. He professes all love to me, and did tell me how he hath spoke of me to my Lord Chancellor, and that if my Lord Sandwich[a] would ask my Lord Chancellor, he should know what he hath said of me to him to my advantage – of which I am very glad, and do not doubt but all things will grow better and better every day for me.

Dined at home alone; then to my office, and there till late at night doing business. And so home, eat a bit, and to bed.

20. Up earely and to my office. And thence to my Lord Sandwich, who I find in bed and he sent for me in; and among other talk, doth tell me that he hath put me into commission with a great many great persons in the business of Tanger, which is a very great Honour to me and may be of good concernment to me. By and by comes in Mr. Coventry to us, who my Lord tells that he is also put into the commission, and that I am there; of which he said he was glad and did tell my Lord that I was endeed the life of this office, and much more to my commenda-

a MS. 'Sandwiches'

---

1. Pepys's acquaintance Col. Cary Dillon.
2. Duelling was prohibited by royal proclamations and (for officers of the armed services) by the articles of war. The most recent proclamation (13 August 1660: Steele, no. 3245) had been ineffective. The King actually pardoned the Duke of Buckingham for his part in the worst duel of the reign in 1668: below, ix. 52 & n. 1. Proclamations (often repeated) remained futile until manners changed.

tion, beyond measure. And that whereas before he did bear me respect for his sake, he doth do it now much more for my own – which is a great blessing to me – Sir G. Carteret having told me what he did yesterday concerning his speaking to my Lord Chancellor about me. So that on all hands, by God's blessing, I find myself a very rising man. By and by comes my Lord Peterborow[1] in, with whom we talked a good while, and he is going tomorrow towards Tanger again. I perceive there is yet little hopes of peace with Guyland,[2] which is of great concernment to Tanger. And many other things I heard which yet I understand not, and so cannot remember.

My Lord and Lord Peterborough going out to the Sollicitor-Generall about the drawing up this commission, I went to Westminster-hall with Mr. Moore; and there meeting Mr. Townsend, he would needs take me to Fleetestreete to ⟨one⟩ Mr. Barwell, Squire Sadler to the King, and there we and several other Wardrobe-men dined. We had a venison pasty, and other*a* good plain and handsome dishes. The mistress of the house a pretty well-carriaged woman, and a fine hand she hath. And her maid a pretty brown lass. But I do find my nature ready to run back to my old course of drinking wine and staying from my business; and yet, I thank God, I was not fully contented with it, but did stay at little ease. And after dinner hasted home by water and so to my office till late at night. In the evening Mr. Hayward came to me to advise with him about the business of the Chest, which I have now a mind to put in practice, though I know it will vex Sir Wm. Batten – which is one of the ends, God forgive me, that I have in it.[3]

So home and eat a bit, and to bed.

a repl. ? 'good'

---

1. Governor of Tangier.

2. 'Abdallah al-Ghailan (d. 1673), known to the English as 'Guyland' etc., one of a number of war-lords now struggling for supremacy in Morocco. He controlled the region around Tangier, where, with an army mostly of Berbers and encouraged by Spanish patronage, he made sporadic attacks on the garrison. His offers of peace were usually to be distrusted; in the present case they led to nothing: Routh, pp. 24–5.

3. Edward Hayward (now of the Surveyor's department) had been Treasurer of the Chatham Chest in the 1650s; Batten was chairman of the Governors. For the sequel, see below, p. 257 & n. 2.

21. Up earely and to my office; and by and by we sat all the morning. At noon, though I was envited to my uncle Fenners to dinner to a hanch of venison I sent him yesterday, yet I did not go but chose to go to Mr. Rawlinsons, where my uncle Wight and my aunt and some neighbour=couples were at a very good venison pasty. Hither came, after we were set down, a most pretty young lady (only her hands were not white nor handsome), which pleased me well; and I found [her] to be sister to Mrs. Anne Wight that comes to my Uncle Wights. We were good company, and had a very pretty dinner – and after dinner some talk, I with my aunt and this young lady about their being [at] Epsum, from whence they came today. And so home and to my office, and there doing business till past 9 at night; and so home and to bed. But though I drank no wine today, yet how easily was I of my own accord stirred up to desire my aunt and this pretty lady (for it was for her that I did it) to carry them to Greenwich and see the pleasure-boats.[1] But my aunt would not go – of which since I am much glad.

22. About 3 a-clock this morning I waked with the noise of the rayne, having never in my life heard a more violent shower. And then the Catt was locked in the chamber and keeped a great mewing, and leapt upon the bed, which made me I could not sleep a great while. Then to sleep, and about 5 a-clock rose and up to my office. And about 8 a-clock went down to Deptford and there with Mr. Davis did look over most of his stores; by the same token, in the great storehouse, while Captain Badily[2] was talking to us, one from a trap-doore above let fall unawares a coyle of cable, that it was 10000 to one it had not broke Captain Bodily's neck, it came so near him – but did him no hurt.

I went on with looking and informing myself of the Stores, with great delight; and having done there, I took boat home again and dined. And after dinner sent for some of my workmen and did scold at them, so as I hope my work will be hastened. Then by water to Westminster-hall; and there I hear that

---

1. The royal yachts: see above, ii. 179 & n.1.

2. William Badiley, Master-Attendant at Deptford and Woolwich yards.

old Mr. Hales[1] did lately die suddenly in an hour's time. Here I met with Will Bowyer and had a[a] promise from him of a place to stand tomorrow at his house to see the show. Thence to my Lord's, and thither sent for Mr. Creede, who came; and walked together talking about business, and then to his lodgings at Clerkes the Confectioner's. Where he did give me a little banquet, and I had liked to have begged a parrett for my wife, but he hath put me in a way to get a better from Steventon[2] at Portsmouth. But I did get of him a Draught of Tanger to take a Copy by; which pleases me very well.[3] So home by water and to my office, where late; and so home and to bed.

23. Up earely and about my works in my house to see what is done and design more. Then to my office; and by and by we sat till noon at the office. After sitting, Mr. Coventry and I did walk together a great while in the garden, where he did tell me his mind about Sir G. Carteret's having so much the command of the money, which must be removed.[4] And endeed, it is the bane of all our business. He observed to me also how Sir W. Batten begins to struggle and to look after his business; which he doth indeed a little, but it will come to nothing. I also put him upon getting an order from the Duke for our inquiries into the Chest, which he will see done.[5] So we parted; and Mr. Creede by appointment being come, he and I went out together, and at an ordinary in Lumbardstreete dined together; and so walked down to the Styll yard and so all along Thames streete, but could not get a boat: I offered 8s for a boat to attend me this afternoon and they would not, it being the day of the

a repl. 'agreement'

1. Probably Thomas Hailes of the Exchequer; buried at St Margaret's, Westminster, in the week beginning 14 August.

2. St John Steventon, Clerk of the Cheque, Portsmouth.

3. Sandwich had done a drawing of Tangier roads, November 1661: it survives in BL, King's Maps, CXVII 77. Pepys's copy has not been traced.

4. Cf. Coventry's proposal to transfer payment of the Navy Victualler from the Navy Treasurer to the Exchequer: above, p. 107 & n. 1; below, p. 243.

5. The order was issued that day: PRO, Adm. 106/7, no. 196. See below, pp. 179, 257 & n. 2.

Queenes coming to town from Hampton Court.*a* So we fairly walked it to White-hall; and through my Lord's lodgings we got into White-hall garden, and so to the bowling-greene and up to the top of the new banquetting-house*¹ there over the Thames, which was a most pleasant place as any I could have got. And all the show consisted chiefly in the number of boats and barges – and two Pageants, one of a King and another of a Queene, with her maydes of honour sitting at her feet very prettily. And they tell me the Queene is Sir Rich. Fords daughter. Anon came the King and Queene in a barge under*b* a Canopy, with 10000 barges and boats I think, for we could see no water for them – nor discern the King nor Queen.² And so they landed at White-hall bridge,³ and the great guns on the other side went off.

But that which pleased me best was that my Lady Castlemayne stood over against us upon a piece of White-hall – where I glutted myself with looking on her. But methought it was strange to see her Lord and her upon the same place, walking up and down without taking notice one of another; only, at first entry, he put off his hat and she made him a very civil salute – but afterwards took no notice one of another. But both of them now and then would take their child,⁴ which the nurse held in her armes, and dandle it. One thing more; there happend a scaffold below to fall, and we feared some hurt but there was none; but she, of all the great ladies only, run down among the common rabble to see what hurt was done, and did take care of a child that received some little hurt; which methought was so noble.

Anon there came one there, booted and spurred, that she talked long with. And by and by, she being in her haire, she put on his*c* hat, which was but an ordinary one, to keep the

a followed by two blank pages stuck together   *b* repl. 'without'   *c* repl. 'is'

---

1. Not the main Banqueting Hall: see *Comp.* ('Whitehall Palace').

2. Evelyn witnessed the spectacle and called it 'the most magnificent Triumph that certainly ever floted on the *Thames* . . . far exceeding . . . all the *Venetian Bucentoro's* & . . . when they go to Espouse the *Adriatic*'. See also Mundy, v. 145; Rugge, ii, ff. 43*v*–44*v*. For a full description, see J. Tatham, *Aqua Triumphalis . . . 23 August 1662* (1662). Pepys kept a copy of Dirk Stoop's engraving of the occasion: PL 2972, pp. 234–5 (reproduced in R.T.D. Sayle, *Barges of Merchant Taylors' Co.*, opp. p. 51).

3. The public pier and landing stage for the palace.

4. Anne, born 25 February 1661.

wind off. But methought it became her mightily, as everything else do.

The show being over, I went away, not weary with looking on her; and to my Lord's lodgings, where my brother Tom and Dr Tom Pepys were to speak with me. So I walked with them in the garden and was very angry with them both, for their going out of towne without my knowledge. But they told me the business, which was to see a gentlewoman for a wife for Tom of Mr. Cooke's providing, worth 500l, of good education; her name Hobell and lives near Banbury; demands 40l per annum joynter. Tom likes her; and they say had a very good reception, and that Cooke hath been very serviceable therein and that she is committed to old Mr. Young of the Wardrobes' tuition.*1

After I had told them my mind about their folly in going so unadvisedly, I then begun to enquire after the business; and so did give no answer as to my opinion till I have looked further into it by Mr. Young.

By and by, as we were walking in my Lord's walk, comes my Lord; and so we broke our discourse and went in with him. And after I had put them away, I went in to my Lord and he and I had half an hour's private discourse about the discontents of the times, which we concluded would not come to anything of difference, though the presbyters would be glad enough of it; but we do not think Religion will so soon cause another warr.

Then to his owne business; he asked my advice there, whether he should go on to purchase more land and borrow money to pay for it, which he is willing to do, because such a bargaine as that of Mr. Buggins's of Stukely will not be every day to be had,2 and Brampton is now perfectly granted him by the King, I mean the Reversion of it, after the Queenes death. And in the meantime buys it of Sir Peter Ball his present right.3

1. She was a kinswoman of Young. For the failure of these negotiations, see below, pp. 228, 232–3.

2. In c. 1665 John Buggins sold the manor of Stukeley, Hunts., to Anne Bigge: VCH, Hunts., ii. 235. No purchase of any of his land by Sandwich has been traced.

3. The grant of the reversion of the manor of Brampton was completed by December and the patent issued on the following 3 February: CSPD 1661–2, pp. 527, 578, 584; Bodl., Clar. dep. c. 399, p. 44; PRO, C66/3032/9. Sandwich now bought from the Queen Mother's trustees the right to enjoy the revenues immediately. Ball was her Attorney-General.

Then we fell to talk of Navy business. And he concludes, as I do, that he needs not put himself upon any more voyages abroad to spend money, unless a war comes; and that by keeping his family a while in the country, he shall be able to gather money.

He is glad of a friendship with Mr. Coventry, and I put him upon encreasing it, which he will do. But he (as Mr. Coventry doth) doth much cry against the course of our payments and the Treasurer to have the whole power in his own hand of doing what he will. But I think will not meddle in himself.

He told me also, that in the Comission for Tanger, Mr. Coventry had advised him that Mr. Puvy, who entends to be Treasurer and it is entended him, may not be of the Commission itself;[1] and my Lord, I think, will endeavour to get him to be contented to be left out of the Commission. And it is a very good rule indeed, that the Treasurer in no office ought to be of the Commission.[2] Here we broke off, and I bid him good-night. And so with much ado (the streets being at 9 a-clock at night crammed with people going home to the City, for all the borders of the River have been full of people as the King hath come, to a miracle) got to the palace-yard and there took boat and so to the Old Swan; and so walked home and to bed, very weary.

24. ⟨*Lord's day.*⟩ Slept till 7 a-clock today, which I have not done a very great while, but it was my weariness last night that caused it.

So rose and to my office till church-time, writing down my yesterday's observations; and so to church – where I all alone, and found Will Griffin and Tho. Hewett[3] got into the pew next to our backs, where our maydes sit; but when I came, they went out, so forward some people are to outrun themselfs. Here we had a lazy, dull sermon. So home to dinner, where my brother Tom came to me; and both before and after dinner he and I walked all alone in the garden, talking about his late

---

1. Thomas Povey (Treasurer to the Duke of York) became Treasurer to the Commission for Tangier and was in fact made a member of the Commission too: below, p. 238. In March 1665 he resigned the Tangier treasurership to Pepys.

2. This has reference to Carteret's position *vis-à-vis* the Navy Board.

3. Doorkeeper and clerk respectively at the Navy Office.

Journy and his mistress; and for what he tells me, it is like to do well. He being gone, I to church again; where Mr. Mills making a sermon upon Confession, he did endeavour to pull down auricular confession, but did set it up by his bad arguments against it and advising people to come to him to confess their sins when they had any weight upon their consciences, as much as is possible; which did vex me to hear. So home; and after an hour's being in my office alone, looking over the plattes and globes, I walked to my uncle Wight's. The truth is, in hopes to have seen and been acquainted with the pretty lady that came along with them to dinner the other day to Mr. Rawlinson,[1] but she is gone away. But here I stayed supper, and much company there was; among others, Dr Burnitt – Mr. Cole the lawyer – Mr. Rawlinson, and Mr. Sutton, a brother of my aunts that I never saw before. Among other things, they tell me that there hath been a disturbance in a church in Friday-street; a great many young [people] knotting together and crying out "porridge"[2] often and seditiously in the church; and took the Common Prayer-Book, they say, away; and some say did tear it.[3] But it is a thing which appears to me very ominous. I pray God avert it. After supper, home and to bed.

25. Up earely and among my workmen when they came, and set them in good order, at work on all hands; which though it at first begun with anger,[a] yet I pleased myself afterwards in seeing it put into a good posture; and so I left them and away by water to Woolwich (calling in my way in Ham creeke,[4] where I have never been before; and there find two of the

a MS. 'angrier'

---

1. See above, p. 173.
2. The Puritans' nickname for the prayer-book.
3. For the imposition of the Act of Uniformity, see above, p. 97, n. 2. The incident Pepys reports occurred at St Matthew's, whose Rector, Henry Hurst, had been ejected under the terms of the act. The reader was taking the service in his place. Pepys's account of the incident is one of the

very few which survive: see A. G. Matthews, *Calamy Revised*, p. 286. On the whole, there were not many such disturbances. A government newspaper suggested that they were the work of a few organised bands, not of the parishioners: *Merc. Pub.*, 28 August, p. 570; cf. below, p. 210 & n. 1.
4. Rented from William Mason at £18 p.a.: PRO, Adm. 20/4, no. 1011.

King's ships lie there without any living creature aboard, which troubled me, everything being stole away that can be); where I stayed, seeing a cable of 14 inches laid[1] – in which there was good variety.

Then to Mr. Falconers and there eat a bit of roast meat off of the spit. And so away to the yard and there, among other things, mustered the yard[2] and did things, that I perceive people do begin to value me and that I shall be able to be of command in all matters – which God be praised for. Then to Mr. Pett's and there eat some fruit and drank; and so to boat again and to Deptford, calling there about the business of my house only;[3] and so home – where by appointment I find Mr. Coventry, Sir W. Batten and Mr. Waith met at Sir W. Batten's; and thither I met, and so agreed upon a way of answering my Lord Treasurer's letter.[4] Here I find Mr. Coventry hath got a letter from the Duke, sent us for looking into the business of the Chest[5] – of which I am glad. After we had done here, I went home and up among my workmen; and find they have done a good day's work; and so to my office till late, ordering of several businesses; and so home and to bed – my mind, God be praised, full of business, but great quiett.

26. Up betimes and among my works and workmen, and with great [pleasure] seeing them go on merrily and a good many hands, which I perceive makes good riddance. And so to the office, where we sat all the morning. And at noon I dined alone with Sir W Batten (which I have not done a great while, but his Lady being out of the way I was the willinger to do it); and after dinner, he and I by water to Deptford and there found Sir G. Carteret and my Lady at dinner, so we sat down and eat another dinner of venison with them; and so we went to the

1. For methods of 'laying' (making) a cable, see below, vi. 34 & n. 3. Fourteen ins. was the measurement of the circumference.

2. Pepys's notes of the roll-call are in PRO, SP 29/58, no. 76. Thirty absentees were dismissed on the following day.

3. The rebuilding of the roof: cf. above, p. 59 & n. 2.

4. In a letter of the 22nd the Lord Treasurer, enclosing a royal warrant of the day before, asked for estimates of the cost of paying off ships, and an account of the state of stores: *CTB*, i. 419–20; *CSPD 1661–2*, p. 464.

5. See above, p. 174 & n. 5.

pay-house and there stayed till 10 a-clock at night paying off
the *Martin* and *Kingsale*, being small but most troublesome ships
to pay.[1]   And so in the dark, by water home to the Custome-
house and so got a lanthorn to light us home, there being Mr.
Morrice the Wine Cooper with us, he having been at Deptford
to view some of the King's Caske[s] we have to sell.

So to bed.

27. Up and among my workmen – my work going on still
very well. So to my office all the morning, and dined again
with Sir W Batten, his Lady being in the country. Among
other stories, he told us of the Mayor of Bristolls reading a passe
with the bottom upwards. And a barber that could not read,
that flung a letter in the kennel when one came to desire him to
read the superscripcion, saying, "Do you think I stand here to
read letters?" Among my workmen again, pleasing myself all
the afternoon there; and so to the office, doing business till
past 9 at night; and so home and to bed. This afternoon Mrs.
Hunt came to see me and I did give her a Muske millon. Today
my hogshead of Sherry I have sold to Sir W. Batten, and am glad
of my money instead of wine.

After I had wrote this at my office (as I have of late altogether
done, since my wife hath been in the country), I went into my
house; and Will having been making up books at Deptford with
other clerks all day, I did not think he was come home; but
was in fear for him, it being very late, what was become of him.
But when I came home I find him there at his ease in his study;
which vexed me cruelly, that he should no more mind me, but
to let me be all alone at the office waiting for him. Whereupon
I struck him and did stay up till 12 a-clock at night chiding him
for it; and did in plain terms tell him that I could not be served
so, and that I am resolved to look out some boy that I may have
the bringing up of after my own mind; and which I do entend
to do, for I do find that he hath got a taste of liberty since he
came to me that he will not leave. Having discharged my
mind,[a] I went to bed.

a repl. 'went'

1. Both were frigates. The former was paid from 24 June 1660 (c.
£2143); the latter from 22 November 1660 (£883): PRO, Adm. 20/3
p. 329.

28. I observe that Will, whom I used to call two or three times in a morning, could now wake of himself and rise without calling – which, though angry, I was glad to see. So I rose; and among my workmen, in my gown without a Dublett, an hour or two or more, till I was afeard of getting an ague. And so to the office, and there we sat all the morning; and at noon Mr. Coventry and I dined at Sir W Batten's (where I have now dined three days together); and so in the afternoon again we sat, which we entend to do two afternoons in a week, besides our other sitting.

In the evening we rose, and I to see how my work goes on; and so to my office, writing by the post and doing other matters; and so home and to bed late.

29. Up betimes and among my workmen, where I did stay with them the greatest part of the morning, only a little at the office; and so to dinner alone at home and so to my workmen again, finding my presence to carry on the work both to my mind and with*a* more haste. And I thank God, I am well pleased with it.

At night, the workmen being gone, I went to my office, and among other businesses, did begin tonight with Mr. Lewes to look into the nature of a pursers account and the business of victualling; in which there is great variety, but I find I shall understand it and be able to do service there also.[1] So being weary and chill, being in some fear of an Ague, I went home and to bed.

30. Up betimes among my workmen, and so to the office, where we sat all the morning; and at noon rose and had news that Sir W Pen would be in towne tonight from Ireland, which

a MS. 'without'

---

1. Thomas Lewis had been a clerk of the Victualling Office since the 1650s. In June 1662 he had been instructed by the Admiral to deliver papers on the victualling to Pepys: BL, Add. 9307, f.16r. In July the Admiral had addressed two letters to the Board about the importance of pursers' accounts: Rawl. A 466, ff. 37-39. Within a few years Pepys (as Surveyor-General, 1665-7) was to reorganise much of the wartime victualling, and to introduce innovations in pursers' accounts: below, vii. 1 & n. 1.

I much wonder at, he giving so little notice of it; and it troubled me exceedingly what to do for a lodging, and more what to do with my goods that are all in his house. But at last I resolved to let them lie there till Monday, and so got Griffin[1] to get me a lodging as near as he could; which is without-a-door of our back-door upon Tower-hill, a chamber where John Davis, one of our clerks, doth lie in; but he doth provide himself elsewhere and I am to have his chamber.[2] So at the office all the afternoon and the evening, till past 10 at night, expecting Sir W Pen's coming; but he not coming tonight, I went thither and there lay very well, and like my lodging well enough. My man Will., after he had got me to bed, did go home and lay there, and my maid Jane lay among my goods at Sir W Pen's.

31. *Lords day*. Waked earely; but being in a strange house, did not rise till 7 a-clock almost; and so rose and read over my oaths and whiled away an hour thinking upon businesses till Will came to get me ready. And so I got ready and to my office, and thence to church. After sermon, home and dined alone. News is brought me that Sir W Pen is come; but I would take no notice thereof till after dinner, and then sent him word that I would wait on him, but he is gone to bed. So to my office and there made my monthly [balance], and find myself worth in money about 686*l*. 19*s*. 02½*d*, for which God be praised.

And endeed, greatly I ought to thank Almighty God, who doth most manifestly bless me in my endeavours to do the duty of my office – I now saving money and my expenses being very little.

My wife is still in the country. My house all in dirt, but my work in a good forwardness and will be much to my mind at last.

In the afternoon to church and there heard a simple sermon of a stranger, upon Davids words, "Blessed is the man that walketh not in the way of the ungodly" &c,[3] and the best of his sermon was the degrees of walking, standing and sitting, ⟨showing⟩ how by steps and degrees sinners do grow in wickedness.

---

1. Office doorkeeper.   3. A loose recollection of Ps. i. 1.
2. Pepys lodged there until 30
September.

After sermon to my brother Tom's, who I found hath taken physic today. And I talked with him about his country mistress and read Cookes letter, wherein I am well satisfied and will appear in promoting it. So back and to Mr. Rawlinsons and there supped with him; and in came my Uncle Wight and my aunt. Our discourse of the discontents that are abroad among and by reason of the presbyters. Some were clapped up today, and strict watch is kept in the City by the train-bands, and letters of a plot are taken.[1] God preserve us, for all these things bode very ill. So home; and after going to welcome home Sir W Pen, who was unready, going to bed, I stayed with him a little while; and so to my lodging and to bed.[a]

a 'So home . . . bed' crowded into bottom of page

---

1. It had been feared that a rising had been fixed for 24 August (when the Act of Uniformity was to come into full force) or for the 28th. Alarms continued for the next two months: see the evidence summarised by W. C. Abbott in *AHR*, 14/512–13. Cf. below, p. 186 & n. 1.

SEPTEMBER.

1. Up betimes at my lodging, and to my office and among my workmen. And then with Sir W. Batten and Sir W Pen by coach to St. James's, this being the first day of our meeting there weekly by the Duke's order;[1] but when we came, we find him going out by coach with his Duchesse, and he told us he was to go abroad with the Queene today (to Durdans it seems, to dine with my Lord Barkely, where I have been very merry when I was a little boy).[2] So we went and stayed a little at Mr. Coventry's chamber and I to my Lord Sandwichs, who is gone to wait upon the King and Queene today. And so Mr. Paget being there, Will Howe and I and he played over some things of Lockes that we used to play at sea,[3] that pleased us three well – it being the first musique I have heard a great while – so much hath my business of late taken me off from all my former delights.

By and by, by water home and there dined alone; and after dinner, with my brother Tom's two men I removed all my goods out of Sir W. Pen's house into one room, that I have with much ado got[a] ready at my house. And so I am glad to be quit of any further obligation to him. So to my office; but missing my key, which I had in my hand just now, makes me very angry and out of order, it being a thing that I hate in others and more in myself, to be carelesse[b] of keys, I thinking another not fit to be trusted that leaves a key behind their heels. One thing more vexes me – my wife writes me from the country that her boy plays the rogue there and she is weary of him; and complains also of her maid Sarah, of which I am also very sorry.

a MS. 'god' *b* l.h. repl. s.h. 'careless'

---

1. See below, p. 192 & n. 1.
2. Durdans, a country house near Epsom, Surrey, was owned by Lord Berkeley of Berkeley. **Pepys would** have known it when staying as a boy with his cousins at Ashstead. Evelyn attended the dinner party referred to in this entry, and reports the presence of the King and Queen, the Duke and Duchess of York and Prince Rupert, Prince Edward 'and aboundanc of Noble men'.

3. Probably Matthew Locke's *Little consort of three parts* (1656); see above, i. 114 & n. 1. (E).

Being thus out of temper, I could do little at my office; but went home and eat a bit, and so to my lodgings to bed.

2. Up betimes and got myself ready alone; and so to my office, my mind much troubled for my key that I lost yesterday; and so to my workmen and put them in order; and so to my office, and we met all the morning and then dined at Sir W Battens with Sir W Pen; and so to my office again all the afternoon, and in the evening wrote a letter to Mr. Cooke in the country in behalf of my brother Tom, to his mistress – it being the first of my appearing in it; and if she be as Tom sets her out, it may be very well for him. So home and eat a bit, and so to my lodgings to bed.

3. Up betimes; but now the days begin to shorten and so whereas I used to rise by 4 a-clock, it is not broad daylight now till after 5 a-clock, so that it is 5 before I do rise. To my office; and about 8 a-clock I went over to Redriffe and walked to Deptford, where I find Mr. Coventry and Sir W Pen beginning the pay – it being my desire to be there ⟨to⟩day, because it is the first pay that Mr. Coventry hath been at and I would be thought to be as much with Mr. Coventry as I can. Here we stayed till noon, and by that time paid off the *Breda*;[1] and then to dinner at the Taverne, where I have obtained that our commons is not so large as they used to be, which I am glad to see. After dinner, by water to the office; and there we met and sold the *Weymouth*, *Successe*, and *Fellowship* Hulke.[2] Where pleasant to see how backward men are at first to bid; and yet when the candle is going out, how they bawl and dispute afterward who bid the most first.[3]

And here I observed one man cunninger then the rest, that was sure to bid the last man and to carry it; and enquiring the reason, he told me that just as the flame goes out the smoke

---

1. A frigate; her pay (from 21 May 1662) amounted to c. £3000: PRO, Adm. 20/3, p. 329.

2. Valued at just over £485, they were sold at £685: *CSPD 1661–2*, p. 472. The sale had been advertised by

poster at the Exchange: PRO, Adm. 106/3520, f.7*v*. The '*Successe*' was the *Old Success*.

3. For sales 'by inch of candle', see above, i. 284, n. 2.

descends,ᵃ which is a thing I never observed before, and by that he doth know the instant when to bid last – which is very pretty. In our discourse in the boat, Mr. Coventry told us how the Fanatiques and the Presbyters that did entend to rise about this times did choose this day as the most auspicious to them in their endeavours against monarchy – it being fatal twice to the King, and the day of Olivers death.¹ But blessed be God, all is likely to be quiet I hope.

After the sale I walked to my brother's, in my way meeting with Dr Fairbrother, of whom I enquired what news in church matters. He tells me, what I heard confirmed since, that it was fully resolved by the King and Council that an indulgence should be granted the presbyters; but upon the Bishop of Londons speech (who is now one of the most powerful men in England with the King), their minds was wholly turned.² And it is said that my Lord Albemarle did oppose him most; but that I do believe is only in appearance. He told me also, that most of the presbyters now begin to wish they had complied, now they see that no Indulgence will be granted them, which they hoped for.³ And that the Bishop of London hath taken good care that places are supplied with very good and able men, which is the only thing that will keep all quiet.⁴

I took him in the taverne at puddle docke, but neither he nor

ᵃ l.h. repl. s.h. 'goes'

---

1. The royalists had been defeated twice on 3 September – at Dunbar in 1650, and at Worcester in 1651 – and Cromwell had died on 3 September 1658. The government had similar frights on the same day of 1661 and of 1663. This time there appears to have been little justification for apprehension. Cf. above, p. 183 & n. 1.

2. A proposal to issue a royal declaration allowing moderate Presbyterian ministers to escape the rigour of the Act of Uniformity for three months had been defeated at a Privy Council meeting at Hampton Court on 28 August, principally by Gilbert Sheldon, Bishop of London, the only bishop present. The news, supposedly secret, had been 'leaked' to the government newspapers and published in *Kingd. Intell.*, 1 September, p. 578. Cf. G. R. Abernathy in *Journ. Eccles. Hist.*, 11/63.

3. Cf. Clarendon, *Life*, ii. 151.

4. But cf. below, v. 190 & n. 1. According to Burnet (i. 341), Sheldon undertook to provide the vacant livings with better men than the extruded, and thought that in fact few replacements would be needed.

I drank any of the wine we called for, but left it; and so after discourse, parted. And Mr. Townsend not being at home, I went to my brother's and there heard how his love matters proceeded, which doth not displease me; and so by water to White-hall to my Lord's lodgings, where he being to go to Hinchingbrooke tomorrow morning, I stayed and fiddled with Will Howe some new tunes, very pleasant; and then my Lord came in, and had much kind talk with him; and then to bed with Mr. Moore there alone;*a* and so having taken my leave of my Lord before I went to bed, I resolved to rise early and be gone without more speaking to him.

4. Which I did; and by water betimes to the tower and so home; where I shifted myself, being to dine abroad; and so, being also trimmed, which is a thing I have very seldom done of late,[1] I set to my office, and then met and sot all the morning. And at noon we all to the Trinity house, where we treated, very dearly I believe, the Officers of the Ordinance – where was Sir W. Compton and the rest, and the Lieutenant of the tower.

We had much and good Musique, which was my best entertainment. Sir W Compton I heard talk, with great pleasure, of the difference between the fleet now and in Queene Elizabeth's days – where in 88 she had but 36 sail, great and small, in the world; and ten rounds of pouder was their allowance at that time against the Spaniard.[2] After Sir Wm. Compton and Mr. Coventry and some of the best of the rest were gone, I grew weary of staying with Sir Wms both, and the more for that my Lady Batten and her crew, at least half-scoare, came into the room, and I believe we shall pay sauce for it;[3] but tis very pleasant

a MS. 'all'

---

1. Cf. above, p. 91 & n. 3.

2. There were 40 ships in the Royal Navy in 1588, out of a total of 197 in service during the campaign of that year: *Defeat of Span. Armada* (ed. Sir J. K. Laughton), vol. i, p. xli; J. S. Corbett, *Drake and Tudor navy*, ii. 146, 159. Another figure (34) given in

HMC, *Savile-Foljambe*, p. 122, is also the figure given by Pepys himself in a memorandum on the subject written c. 1701: *Priv. Corr.*, ii. 244-7. For the shortage of ammunition, see *Naval tracts of Sir W. Monson* (ed. Oppenheim), i. 175-6.

3. Sc. pay dearly.

to see her in her haire under her hood, and how by little and little she would fain be a gallant; but Lord, the company she keeps about her are like herself, that she may be known by them what she is. Being quite weary, I stole from them and to my office, where I did business till 9 at night; and so to my lodgings to bed.

5. Up by break-a-day at 5 a-clock, and down by water to Woolwich; in my way saw the Yacht lately built by our Virtuosoes, my Lord Brunkard and others, with the help of Comissioner Pett also, set out from Greenwich with the little Dutch *Bezan*, to try for mastery;[1] and before they got to Woolwich, the Dutch beat them half-a-mile (and I hear this afternoon that in coming home it got above three mile); which all our people are glad of.

Here I stayed and mustered the yard and looked into the Storehouses, and so walked all alone to Greenwich; and thence by water to Deptford and there examined some stores and did some of my own business in hastening my work[2] there, and so walked to Redriffe; being by this time pretty weary and all in a sweat, took boat there for the tower, which made me a little fearful, it being a cold windy morning.

So to my lodgings and there rubbed myself clean, and so to Mr. Bland's the merchant, by invitation (I alone of all our company of this office), where I find all the officers of the Customes;[3] very grave fine gentlemen, and I am very glad to know them; *viz.* Sir Job Harvy, Sir John Wostenham, Sir John Jacob, Sir Nicho. Crisp, Sir John Harrison and Sir John Shaw – very good company. And among other pretty discourse, some was of Sir Jerom Bowes, Embassador from Queene Elizabeth to the Emperor of Russia – who, because some of the noblemen there would go up the stairs to the Emperor before him, he would not go up till the Emperor had ordered those two men to be

1. The yacht built by Pett and the virtuosi was the *Jemmy*: above, p. 164 & n. 4. Next year the King tried another design: below, iv. 123, n. 1. For the *Bezan*, see above, ii. 177, n. 4.

2. Sc. joinery work for his house: cf. above, p. 59, n. 2.

3. Farmers of the Customs. Until 1671, when the Customs Board was established, the collection of customs revenue was farmed to a group of great merchants.

dragged downstair, with their heads knocking upon every stair till they were killed. And when he was come up, they demanded his sword of him before he entered the room; he told them, if they would have his sword, they should have his boots too; and so caused his boots to be pulled off and his night-gown and night-cap and slippers to be sent for, and made the Emperor stay till he could go in his night-dress, since he might not go as a soldier. And lastly, when the Emperor in contempt, to show his command over his subjects, did command one to leap from the window down and broke his neck in the sight of our Embassador, he replied that his mistress did set more by and did make better use of the necks of her subjects: but said that to show what her subjects would do for her, he would, and did, fling down his gantlett before the Emperor and challenged all the nobility there to take it up in defence of the Emperor against his Queene. For which, at this very day, the name of Sir Jer. Bowes is famous and honoured there.[1]

After dinner I came home and find Sir John Minnes come this day, and I went to him to Sir W. Batten's. Where it pleased me to see how Jealous Sir Wm's both are of my going down to Woolwich &c and doing my duty as I nowadays do, and of my dining with the Comissioners of the Customes.[a]

So to my office, and there till 9 at night; and so to my lodgings to bed. I this day heard that Mr. Martin Noell is knighted by

a l.h. repl. 'N'-

---

1. Bowes was appointed envoy to Ivan the Terrible in 1583. His report of the embassy (which does not include these incidents) is in *Cal. State Papers Foreign, 1584-5*, pp. 83–6; the Tsar's complaints against him, in a letter to Elizabeth, are in ib., pp. 692–3. For other stories of his remarkable exploits, see R. Hakluyt, *Voyages* (1903 ed.), iii. 315+. Samuel Collins (*Present state of Russia*, 1671, pp. 49–50) reports that Ivan once rewarded the French envoy's boldness in remaining covered in the royal presence by nailing his hat to his head. Bowes, at his next interview, defiantly wore his hat and in answer to the Tsar's threats, announced that he represented 'not a cowardly king of *France* . . . but the invincible Queen of *England*, who does not vail her Bonnet, nor bare her Head to any Prince living'. Milton reproduced some of Hakluyt's account in his *Brief hist. of Moscovia* (1682).

the King, which I much wonder at; but yet he is certainly a very useful man.[1]

6. Lay long; that is, till 6 and past before I rose, in order to sweat a little away the cold which I was afeared I might have got yesterday, but I bless God I am well. So up and to my office. And then we met and sat till noon, very full of business. Then Sir John Minnes, both Sir Wms. and I to the Trinity-house, where we had at dinner a couple of venison pasties, of which I eat but little, being almost cloyed, having been at five pasties in three days; *viz.*, two at our own feast and one yesterday and two today. So home, and at the office all the afternoon, busy till 9 at night; and so to my lodging and to bed.

This afternoon I had my new key and the lock of my office door altered, having lost my key the other day, which vexed me.

7. *Lords day.* Up betimes, and round about by the streets to the office and walked in the garden, and in my office till my man Will rose; and then sent to tell Sir J. Minnes that I would go with him to White-hall, which anon we did, in his coach; and to the Chappell, where I heard a good sermon of the Deane of Elys upon Returning to the old wayes[2] – and a most excellent Anthem (with Symphony's between) sung by Captain Cooke.[3] Then home with Mr. Fox and his lady and there dined with them, where much company came to them. Most of our discourse was what Ministers are flung out that will not conform. And the care of the Bishop of London that we are here supplied with very good men.

Thence to my Lord's, where nobody at home but a woman

1. Noell, knighted on 2 September, was a financier and W. India merchant, and a member of the Council of Trade and of the Council for Foreign Plantations. Pepys's surprise perhaps arose from the fact that he had been not only the principal financial agent of the revolutionary government but also a personal friend of Cromwell.

2. Francis Wilford was the preacher, and the text presumably Jer., vi. 16. The subject was the return of ecclesiastical uniformity.

3. For verse-anthems, see above, i. 220, n. 3. The symphonies were probably played on the organ, perhaps supported by wind instruments: cf. Evelyn, 21 December 1662. According to Pepys, 14 September 1662 was 'the first day of having Vialls and other Instruments to play a Symphony between every verse of the Anthem': below, p. 197. (E).

that let me in, and Sarah above; whither I went up to her and played and talked with her and, God forgive me, did feel her; which I am much ashamed of, but I did no more, though I had so much a mind to it that I spent in my breeches. After I had talked an hour or two with her, I[a] went and gave Mr. Hunt a short visit, he being at home alone. And thence walked homeward; and meeting Mr. Pierce the Chyrurgeon,[1] he took me into Somersett-house and there carried me into the Queene-Mother's presence-chamber, where she was, with our own Queene sitting on her left hand (whom I did never see before; and though she be not very charming, yet she hath a good modest and innocent look which is pleasing):[2] here I also saw Madam Castlemayne and, which pleased me most, Mr. Crofts[3] the King's bastard, a most pretty sparke of about 15 year old; who I perceive doth[b] hang much upon my Lady Castlemayne and is alway with her. And I hear the Queenes, both of them, are mighty kind to him. By and by, in comes[c] the King, and anon the Duke and his Duchesse; so that, they being all together, was such a sight as I could never almost have happened to see with so much ease and leisure. They stayed till it was dark and then went away, the King and his Queene and my Lady Castlemayne and young Crofts in one coach, and the rest in other coaches. Here were great store of great ladies, but very few handsome.

The King and Queene were very merry; and he would have made the Queen-Mother believe that his Queen was with child, and said that she said so; and the young Queen answered, "you lye"; which was the first English word that I ever heard her say. Which made the King good sport, and he would have taught her to say in English, "Confess and be hanged."

The company being gone, I walked home, with great content as I can be in for seeing the greatest rarity and yet a little troubled that I should see them before my wife's coming home, I having made a promise that I would not. Nor did I do it industriously and by design, but by chance only.

a repl. 'and'   *b* repl. 'did'   *c* repl. 'Mr.'

1. James Pearse was now surgeon to the Duke of York.
2. For opinions about the Queen's looks, see above, p. 97, n. 1.
3. James Crofts, aged 13, cr. Duke of Monmouth, February 1663 but known by that title for some time before it was bestowed. Cf. below, p. 301.

To my office to fit myself for waiting on the Duke tomorrow morning with the rest of our company. And so to my lodgings and to bed.

8. Up betimes and to my office, preparing an account to give the Duke this morning of what we have of late done at the office. About 7 a-clock I went forth, thinking to go along with Sir John Minnes and the rest, and I find them gone, which did vex me; so I went directly to the old Swan and took boat before them and to Sir G Carteret's lodgings at White-hall; and there staying till he was dressed, talking with him, he and I to St. James's, where Sir Wms both and Sir John were come; and so up with Mr. Coventry to the Duke, who after he was out of his bed, did send for us in; and when he was quite ready, took us into his closet and there told us that he doth entend to renew the old custom for the Admiralls to have their principal officers to meet them once a week to give them an account what they have done that week, which I am glad of;[1] and so the rest did tell his Royal Highness that I could do it best for the time past, and so I produced my short notes and did give him an account of all that we have of late done and proposed to him several things for his commands; which he did give us and so dismiss us. The rest to Deptford, I to the Exchequer to meet Mr. Townsend; where I hear he is gone to the Sun taverne, and there find him with some friends at breakfast, which I eat with him; and so we crossed the water together, and in walking I told him my brother Tom's intentions for a wife, which he would do me all favour in to Mr. Young, whose kinswoman he doth look after. We took boat again at the Falcon and there parted, and I to the Old Swan and so to the Change; and there meeting Sir W Warren, did step to a taverne and there sat and talked about price of masts and other things; and so broke up, and to my office to see what business; and so we took water again at the towre.

And I over to Redriffe, and there left him in the boat and walked to Deptford, and there up and down the yard, speaking with people; and so Sir W Pen, coming out of the payhouse,

1. These Monday morning meetings in the Duke's closet (usually at St James's Palace in summer and at Whitehall in winter) were regularly held during the diary period. They were a resumption of pre-revolution practice, and no formal order about them appears to have been made.

did single me out to tell me Sir J. Minnes's dislike of my blind-
ing his lights over his stairs (which endeed is very bad) and block-
ing up the house of office on the leads.   Which did trouble me,
so I went into the payhouse and took an occasion of speaking
with him alone and did give him good satisfaction therein, so as
that I am well pleased and do hope*a* now to have my closets on
the leads without any more trouble.   For he doth not object
against my having a door upon the leads, but that all my family*
should not make it a through-faire – which I am contented with.
    So to the pay,[1] and in the evening home in the barge; and so
to my office, and after doing some business there, to my lodgings.
And so to bed.

    9.   At my office betimes; and by and [by] we sat, and at
noon Mr. Coventry, Sir J. Mennes, Mr. Pett and myself by
water to Deptford, where we met Sir G. Carteret, Sir W. Batten
and Sir W. Penn at the pay of a ship;[2] and we dined together
on a haunch of good venison boiled, and after dinner returned
again to the office and there met several tradesmen by our appointment, to know of them their lowest rates that they will take for
their several provisions that they sell to us.   For I do resolve to
know that, and to buy no dearer; that so, when we know the
lowest rate, it shall be the Treasurer's fault and not ours that we
pay dearer.
    This afternoon, Sir John Minnes, Mr. Coventry, and I went
into Sir John's lodgings, where he showed us how I have blinded
all his lights and stopped up his garden-door; and other things
he takes notice of that he resolves to abridge me of, which doth
vex [me] so much, that for all this evening and all night in my bed,
so great a fool I am and little master of my passion, that I could
not sleep for the thoughts of my losing the privilege of the leads
and other things which in themselfs are small and not worth half
the trouble.   The more fool am I, and must labour against it for

a   repl. 'ent'-

---

1. This was the quarterly pay of
the officers of the yard, their clerks,
the watchmen, boatswains *et al.*, and,
in this case, of 29 ships. It took several
days: below, pp. 195, 198, 201.
Details in PRO, Adm. 20/4, pp. 54-7;
travelling expenses of the Principal
Officers in ib., 3, no. 368; muster-
book (9 September) in Rawl. A 187,
ff. 305+.
    2. The *Dartmouth:* PRO, Adm.
20/3, p. 330.

shame – especially I that use to preach up Epictetus's rule of τὰ
ἐφ ἡμῖν κὶ τὰ οὐχ ἐφ ἡμῖν.[1]

Late at my office, troubled in mind; and then to bed, but
could hardly sleep all night.

10.   Up and to my house, and there contrived a way how Sir
John shall come into the leads, and yet I save part of the closet
I hoped for – which if it will not please him, I am a madman to
be troubled at it.

To my office, and then at my house among my lazy workmen all day.   In the afternoon to the Wardrobe to speak with
Mr. Townesend, who tells me that he hath spoke with Mr.
Young about my brother Tom's business and finds that he hath
made enquiry of him and doth hear him so well spoke of
that he doubts not but the business will take, with ordinary
endeavours.   So to my brother's, and there finding both door
and hatch open, I went in and knocked three or four times and
nobody came to me, which troubled me mightily; at last came
Margaret, who complained of Peter;[2] who by and by came in,
and I did rattle him soundly for it.

I did afterward take occasion to talk seriously alone with
Margarett, who I find a very discreet good woman, and tells
me upon my demand that her master is a very good husband*
and minds his business well; but his fault is that he hath not
command over his two men, but they do what they list and
care not for his commands; and especially on Sondays they go
whither they please, and not to church – which vexes me mightily
and I am resolved to schoole him soundly for it – it being so
much unlike my father, that I cannot endure it in myself or him.

So walked home; and in my way, at the Exchange find my
uncle Wight, and he and I to an alehouse to drink a cup of beere;

1. Dr R. Luckett writes: Pepys is
loosely paraphrasing, or inaccurately
recalling, Epictetus (*Encheiridion* I. i):
τῶν ὄντων τὰ μέν ἐστιν ἐφ' ἡμῖν, τὰ
δὲ οὐκ ἐφ' 'ἡμῖν ('Of things, some
are in our power, others are not'). He
accidentally writes οὐχ for οὐκ (he intended τὰ ἐφ' ἡμῖν καὶ τὰ οὐκ ἐφ'
ημῖν); the slip is a natural one given

the extensive use of ligatures in the
seventeenth century. That it was a
consequence of accident rather than
ignorance is demonstrated by his
correct rendering of οὐκ at iv. 16.
2. One of Tom Pepys's two
apprentices; Margaret was his servant.

and so away, and I home. And at my office till 9 a-clock and past, and so to my lodgings.

I forgot that last night Mr. Cooke came to me to make his peace for inviting my brother lately out of towne without my leave; but he doth give me such a character of the Lady that he hath found out for him, that I do*a* much rejoice at; and did this night write a letter to her, which he enclosed in one of his. And by the report that I hear of her, I confess I am much pleased with the match.

11. Up, but not so soon as I have of late practised, my little trouble of mind and the shortness of the days making me to lie a little longer then I used to do, but I must make it up by sitting up longer a-nights. To my office – whither my brother Tom came, whom I chid sufficiently for yesterday's work. So we sat at the office all the morning. Some of us at Deptford paying the ordinary there.[1] At noon Sir Wm. Pen took me to his lodgings to dinner. And after dinner I to my office again, and now and then to see how my work goes on; and so to my office late and so to my lodgings; and after staying ⟨up*b* till past 12 at night at my⟩ Musique ⟨upon my lute⟩, to bed. This night Tom came to show me a civil letter sent him from his mistress. I am pleased well enough with the business.

12. Up betimes and to my office; and up to my workmen, which goes on slowly and troubles me much. Besides, my mind is troubled till I see how Sir J. Minnes will carry himself to me about my lodgings, for all my fear is that he will get my best chamber from me; for as for the leads, I care not a farthing for them.

At my office all the morning – Mr. Lewes teaching me to understand the method of making up pursers accounts, which is very needful for me and very hard. Dined at home, all in dirt and my mind weary of being thus out of order; but I hope in God it will away, but for the present I am very melancholy, as I have been a great while.

All the afternoon, till 9 at night, at my office; and then home and eat an egge or two, and so to my lodgings. And to bed.

a MS. 'to'   *b* repl. 'all'

1. See above, p. 193, n. 1.

This day, by letter from my father, I hear that Captain Ferrers, who is with my Lord in the country, was at Brampton (with Mr. Creede) to see him. And that a day or two ago, being provoked to strike one of my Lord's footemen, the footman drow his sword and hath almost cut the fingers of one of his hands off. Which I am sorry for, but this is the vanity of being apt to command and strike.

13. Up betimes and to my office, and we sat all the morning. And then at noon dined alone at home; and so among my workfolks, studying how to get my way sure to me to go upon the Leades, which I fear at last I must be contented to go without; but however, my mind is troubled still about it. We met again in the afternoon to set accounts even between the King and the masters of ships hired to carry provisions to Lisbon;*a* 1 and in the evening Mr. Moore came to me and did lie with me at my lodgings. It is *b* great pleasure to me his company and discourse. And did talk also about my law-business,2 which I must now fall upon minding again, the term coming on apace. So to bed.

14. *Lords day.* Up very earely; and Mr. Moore taking leave of me, the barber came to me and trimmed me (I having him now to come to me again, after I have used a pumice-stone a good while; not but that I like this where I cannot conveniently have a barber, but here I cannot keep my hair dry without one); and so by water to White-hall (by the way hearing that the Bishop of London hath given a very strict order against boats going on Sondys;3 and as I came back again, we were examined by the masters of the company in another boat, but I told them who I was);4 but the door not being open, to Westminster-stairs and there called in at the Legg and drank a cup of ale and a toast; which I have not done many a month before, but it served me

a   repl. 'Tanger'   b   MS. 'is was'

1. The merchant ships hired for the purpose (above, p. 60 & n. 1) had not returned all the naval stores lent to them: *CSPD 1661-2*, p. 483.

2. The dispute in Chancery with the Trices about Robert Pepys's will. See above, ii. 134 & n. 2.

3. Sheldon's injunctions about the observance of the Sabbath (12 September 1662) have no mention of boats: W. Wasse, *The loyal Protestant* (1667), pp. 23-4.

4. The Watermen's Company had charge of the hire of boats. Pepys could claim privilege as a royal servant.

for my two glasses of wine today.   Thence to St. James's to Mr.
Coventry and there stayed talking privately with him an hour
in his chamber of the business of our office, and find him to
admiration good and industrious, and I think my most true
friend in all things that are fair.   He tells me freely his mind
of every man and in everything.

Thence to White-hall chapel, where sermon almost done and
I heard Captain Cookes new Musique; this the first day of having
Vialls and other Instruments to play a Symphony between every
verse of the Anthem; but the Musique more full then it was the
last Sunday, and very fine it is.[1]   But yet I could discern Captain
Cooke to overdo his part at singing, which I never did before.
⟨Thence up into the Queenes presence and there saw the Queene
again as I did last Sunday, and some fine ladies with her; but
by my troth, not many.⟩[a]

Thence to Sir G. Carterets and find him to have sprained his
foot and is lame, but yet hath been at Chappell, and my Lady
much troubled for one of her daughters that is sick.   I dined
with them and a very pretty lady, their kinswoman, with them.
My joy is that I do think I have good hold in Sir George and
Mr. Coventry.   Sir George told me of a Chest of Drawers that
was given Sir W. Batten by Hughes the Ropemaker, whom he
hath since put out of his employment, and now the fellow doth
cry out upon Sir Wm for his Cabinet.[2]   So home again by
water and to church.   And from church, Sir Wms both and
Sir J. Minnes into the garden; and anon Sir W. Penn and I
did discourse about my lodgings and Sir J Minnes, and I did
open all my mind to him; and he told me what he had heard,
and I do see that I shall hardly keep my best lodging-chamber –
which troubles me.   But I did send for Goodenough the plasterer, who tells me that it did ever belong to my lodgings, but
lent by Mr. Payler to Comissioner Smith;[3] and so I will strive
hard for it before I lose it.

So to supper with them at Sir W Battens; and do counterfeit
myself well pleased, but my heart is troubled and offended at

a addition crowded between paragraphs

---

1. Cf. above, p. 190 & n. 3.   (E).
2. For Hughes's dismissal, see
above, p. 101, n. 3.

3. George Payler and Thomas
Smith had been Navy Commissioners during the Interregnum.

the whole company. So to my office to prepare notes to read to the Duke tomorrow morning; and so to my lodgings and to bed. ⟨My mind a little eased because I am resolved to know the worst concerning my lodgings tomorrow.⟩*a*

Among other things, Sir W. Penn did tell me of one of my servants looking into Sir J. Minnes's window when my Lady Batten lay there, which doth much trouble them, and me also, and I fear will wholly occasion my losing the leads. One thing more he told me, of my Janes cutting off a carpenters long Mustacho, and how the fellow cried and his wife would not come near him a great while, believing that he had been among some of his wenches. At which I was merry, though I perceive they discourse of it as a crime*b* of hers, which I understand not.

15. Up betimes to meet with the plasterer and bricklayer that did first divide our lodgings; and they do both tell me that my chamber now in dispute did ever belong to my lodgings – which doth put me into good quiet of mind.

So by water with Sir Wm. Pen to White-hall; and with much ado, was fain to walk over the piles through the bridge (while Sir W. Batten and Sir J Minnes were aground against the bridge and could not in a great while get through). At White-hall we hear that the Duke of Yorke is gone a-hunting today and so we returned – they going to the Duke of Albemarles, where I left them (after I had observed a very good picture or two there); and so home and there did resolve to give up my endeavours for accesse to the leads and to shut up my doors, lest that being open might give them occasion of longing for my chamber, which I am in most fear about.

So to Deptford, and took my Lady Batten and her daughter and Mrs. Turner along with me, they being going through the garden thither. They to Mr. Uthwaytes, and I to the pay and then about 3 a-clock went to dinner (Sir W. Penn and I); and after dinner to the pay again, and at night by barge home all together. And so to my lodgings and to bed, my mind full of trouble about my house.

16. Up and to my workmen. And then to the office and there we sat till noon. Then to the Exchange, and in my way

a addition crowded between paragraphs   *b* repl. 'thing'

met with the housekeeper of this office[1] and he did give me so good an account of my chamber in my house about which I am so much troubled, that I am well at ease in my mind. At my office all the afternoon, alone. In the evening Sir J. Mennes and I walked together a good while in the garden, very pleasant and takes no notice that he doth design any further trouble to me about my house. At night eat a bit of bread and cheese; and so to my lodgings and to bed, my mind ill at ease for these perticulars: my house in dirt – and like to lose my best chamber – my wife writes me from the country that she is not pleased there with my father nor mother nor any of her servants and that my boy is turned a very rogue – I have 30*l* to pay to the Cavaliers[a][2] – then a[b] doubt about my being forced to leave all my business here when I am called to the Court at Brampton – and lastly, my law-businesses, which vex me to the heart what I shall be able to do next terme, which is near at hand.

17. At my office all the morning. And at noon to the Exchange; where meeting Mr. Moore and Mr. Stucky of the Wardrobe, we to an ordinary to dinner. And after dinner, Mr. Moore and I about 3 a-clock to Paul's schoole to wait upon Mr. Crumlum[3] (Mr. Moore having a hopeful lad, a kinsman of his, there at school); who we took very luckily and went up to his chamber with him, where there was also an old fellow-student of Mr. Crumlums, one Mr. Newell, come to see him; of whom he made so much, and of me, that the truth is he with kindness did drink more then I believe he used to do, and did begin to be a little impertinent* – the more when, after all, he would in the evening go forth with us and give us a bottle of wine abroad. And at the taverne met with an acquaintance of his that did occasion impertinent discourse, that though I honour the man and he doth declare abundance of learning and worth, yet I confess my opinion is much lessened of him. And there-

a repl. ? 'cav'- *b* repl. 'the'

1. William Griffith.
2. By a recent act (14 Car. II c. 8) £60,000 was to be raised for distribution among indigent officers who had served in the King's forces, by a levy made on office-holders whose income

was over £5 p.a. cf. above, p. 43, n. 1. For Pepys's assessment, see below, p. 283 & n. 5.
3. Samuel Cromleholme, High Master; his visitor, Mr Newell, has not been identified with certainty.

fore, let it be a caution to myself not to love drink, since it hath such an affect upon others of greater worth in my own esteem. I could not avoyd drinking of five glasses this afternoon with him. And after I had parted with him, Mr. Moore and I to my house; and after we had eaten something – to my lodgings,[1] where the Maister of the house, a very ordinary fellow, was ready to entertain me and took me into his dining-room where his wife was, a pretty and notable lady, too fine surely for him, and too much wit too. Here I was forced to stay with them a good while and did drink again, there being friends of theirs with them. At last, being weary of his idle company, I bid good-night; and so to my chamber and Mr. [Moore] and I to bed – neither of us well pleased with our afternoon's work, merely from our being witnesses of Mr. Crumlums weakness.

This day my boy is come from Brampton. And my wife, I think, the next week.

18. At the office all the morning. And at noon Sir G Carteret, Mr. Coventry and I by invitation to dinner to Sheriffe Maynells, the great money-man – he and Alderman Backwell – much noble and brave company; with the privilege of their rare discourse, which is great content to me, above all other things in the world. And after a great dinner and much discourse, we rise and I took leave and home to the business of my office, where I thank God I take delight. And in the evening to my lodgings and to bed.

Among other discourse, speaking concerning the great Charity used in catholique countries – Mr. Ashburnham did tell us that this last year, there being great want of corne in Paris and so a collection made for the poore – there was two pearles brought in, nobody knew from whom (till the Queene seeing them, knew whose they were but did not discover it), which were sold for 200000 Crownes.[a][2]

19. Up betimes and to my office; and at 9 a-clock (none of the rest going) I went alone to Deptford and there went on

a paragraph crowded into bottom of page

1. Cf. above, p. 182.   elsewhere. For the famine, see above,
2. The story has not been traced   p. 62 & n. 2.

where they left last night to pay Woolwich yard; and so at noon dined well, being chief at the table, and do not see but everybody begins to give me as much respect and honour as any of the rest. After dinner to pay again and so till 9 at night – my great trouble being that I was forced to begin an ill practice of bringing down the wages of servants, for which people did curse me; which I do not love.[1] At night, after I had eaten a cold pullet, I walked by brave Mooneshine, with three or four armed [men] to guard me, to Redriffe – it being a joy to my heart to think of the condition that I am now in, that people should of themselfs provide this for me, unspoke to. I hear this walk is dangerous to walk alone by night, and much robbery committed here. So from thence by water home. And so to my lodgings to bed.

20. Up betimes and to my house, where I find my brother Tom; who tells me that his mistress's Mother hath wrote a letter to Mr. Lull of her full satisfaccion about Tom, of which I was glad and do think the business will take. All the morning we sat at the office, Sir J. Mince and I. And so dined at home, and among my workmen all the afternoon. And in the evening Tom brought Mr. Lull to me, a friend of his mistress, a serious man; with whom I spoke and he gives me a good account of her and of their satisfaction in Tom, all which pleases me well. We walked a good while in the garden together, and did give him a glass a' wine at my office and so parted.

So to write letters by the post and news of this to my father concerning Tom; and so home to supper and so to my lodgings and to bed.

Tonight my*a* barber sent me his man to trim me; who did live in King's-street in Westminster lately and tells me that three or four that I knew in that street, tradesmen, are lately fall[en] mad;*b* and some of them dead, and the others continue mad. They live all within a door or two one of another.

a l.h. repl. s.h. 'a'   *b* symbol blotted and uncertain

---

1. Details of the pay are in PRO, Adm. 20/4, pp. 78+. A saving of £100 was made on the previous quarter: ib., pp. 75+.

21. *Lords day.* Got up betimes and walked to St. James's; and there to Mr. Coventry and sat an hour with him, talking of business of the office with great pleasure. And I do perceive he doth speak his whole mind to me. Thence to the parke, where by appointment I met my brother Tøm and Mr. Cooke and there spoke about Tom's business, and to good satisfaction. The Queene coming by in her coach, going to her chapel at St. James's (the first time it hath been ready for her), I crowded after her; and got up to the room where her closet is and there stood and saw – the fine Alter, ornaments, and the fryers in their habits and the priests come in with their fine Copes.[1] And many other very fine things. I heard their Musique too; which may be good, but it did not appear so to me, neither as to their manner of singing nor was it good Concord to my eares, whatever the matter was. The Queene very devoute. But what pleased me best was to see my dear Lady Castlemayne; who though a pro-testant, did wait upon the Queene to chapel. By and by, after masse was done, a Fryer with his Coole did rise up and preach a sermon in Portuges; which I not understanding,[2] did go away and to the King's Chappell, but that was done; and so up to the Queenes presence-chamber, where[a] she and the King was expected to dine; but she staying at St James's, they were forced to remove the things to the King's presence, and there he dined alone. And I with Mr. Fox, very finely; but I see I must not make too much use of that Liberty, for my honour sake only – not but that I am very well received.

After dinner to Tom's and so home; and after walking a good while in the garden, I went to my uncle Whites, where I find my aunt in mourning and making sad stories for the loss of her dear Sister Nicholls; of which I should have been very weary but that pretty Mrs. Margtt. Wight came in; and I was much pleased with her company, and so all supper did vex my aunt, talking in commendation of the Masse which I had been at

a MS. 'which'

---

1. The chapel had been built by Inigo Jones, 1623–7, and used by Queen Henrietta-Maria for Roman Catholic services. It was now served by Benedictines and by a small group of Portuguese Observant Franciscans.

2. In 1667 Pepys managed to understand some of a sermon in Portuguese: below, viii. 116.

today. But excused it afterwards, that it was only to make mirth.[1] And so after supper, broke up and home; and after putting my notes in order against tomorrow, I went to bed.

22. Up betimes among my workmen, hastening to get things ready against my wife's coming. And so with Sir J. Mennes, Sir W. Batten and Sir W. Penn by coach to St. James's; and there with the Duke I did give him an account of all things passed of late. But I stood in great pain, having a great fit of the Collique, having ketched cold yesterday by putting off my stocking to wipe my toes. But at last it lessened, and then I was pretty*a* well again; but in pain all day more or less. Thence I parted from them and walked to Greatorex's, and there with him did overlook many pretty things, new invencions, and have bespoke a weather=glasse of him. Thence to my Lord Crews and dined with the servants, he having dined; and so after dinner, up to him and sat an hour talking with him of public and my Lord's private businesses with much content. So to my brother Toms, where Mr. Cooke expected me and did go with me to see Mrs. Young and Mrs. Lull in Blackfryers, kindred of Tom's mistress. Where I was very well used, and do*b* find things to go in that business to my full content. Thence to Mr. Townsend, and did there talk with Mr. Young himself also; and thence home and to my study, and so to my lodgings and to bed.

23. Up betimes and with my workmen, taking some pleasure to see my work come towards an end, though I am vexed every day enough with their delay.

We met and sat all the morning. Dined at home alone, and with my workmen all the afternoon; and in the evening, by water and land to Deptford to give order for things about my house. And came back again by coach with Sir G. Carteret and Sir W. Batten (who have been at a pay today); and so to my

a repl. 'well'   *b* repl. 'did'

1. Answering the charge of being a papist in 1674, Pepys, in a speech to the Commons, is reported to have challenged 'the whole world that he has not been once in his life at Mass': Grey, ii. 427. He was not counting the occasions on which he had been a spectator. Cf. also below, iv. 130.

office and did some business, and so to supper and to my lodgings, and so to bed.

In our coming home, Sir G. Carteret told me how in most *Cabaretts* in France they have writ upon the walls, in fair letters to be read, *Dieu te regarde*, as a good lesson to be in every man's mind.   And have also, as in Holland,[1] their poor's box; in both which places, at the making all contracts and bargains they give so much, which they call God's=penny.[2]

24. Up betimes and among my workmen. And among them all the morning – till noon; and then to my Lord Crews and there dined alone with him; and among other things, he doth advise me by all means to keep my Lord Sandwich from proceeding too far in the business of Tanger.   First, for that he is confident the King will not be able to find money for the building the Molle;[3] and next, for that it is to be done as we propose it, by the reducing of the garrison;[4] and then either my Lord must oppose the Duke of Yorke, who will have the Irish regiment under the command of Fitzgerard continued, or else my Lord Peterborough, who is concerned to have the English continued. And he it seems is gone back again merely upon my Lord Sandwich's encouragement.

Thence to Mr. Wotton the shoemaker's and there bought a pair of boots, cost me 30s.   And he told me how Bird hath lately broke his leg while he was fencing in *Aglaura*[5] upon the stage.   And that the new Theatre of all will be ready against next Terme.[6]

1. Cf. above, i. 146 & n. 3.

2. The *denier-à-Dieu*. Since 1656-7, when the *Hôpital-Général* had been founded in Paris, there had been a considerable movement for the building of poorhouses in France. In some places keepers of drinking-houses had to make contributions. C. W. Cole, *Colbert*, i. 263+.

3. For the building and cost of the mole, see *Comp.*: 'Tangier; the Mole'.

4. In April 1663 orders were issued for reducing it from four regiments to two, bringing down the total from 2800 to 2000: Routh, p. 310.

5. A play by Sir John Suckling, which he originally wrote as a tragedy, but transformed into a tragicomedy; first acted in 1637, and published in 1638.   The scene mentioned here is probably the one at the beginning of Act V, involving a fight between Ariaspes and Ziriff. (A).

6. The new Theatre Royal being built for Thomas Killigrew at a cost of £2400 between Drury Lane and Bridges St; opened on 7 May 1663. (A).

So to my brother's, and there discoursed with him and Mr. Cooke about their journy to Tom's mistress again. And I did speak with Mrs. Croxton about measuring of silk flags.[1]

So by water home and to my workmen; and so at night, till late, at my office endicting a letter from Tom to his mistress, upon his sending her a watch for a token. And so home and to supper, and so to my lodgings and to bed.

It is my content that by several hands today I hear that I have the name of a good-natured man among the poor people that come to the office.

25. Up betimes and to my workmen; and then to the office, where we sat all the morning. So home to dinner alone and then to my workmen till night; and so to my office till bedtime, and so after supper to my lodgings and to bed.

This evening I sat a while at Sir W. Batten's with Sir J. Mennes &c., where he told us, among many other things, how in portugall they scorn to make a seat for a house of office. But they do shit all in pots and so empty them in the river.

I did also hear how the woman formerly nurse to Mrs. Lemon (Sir W. Batten's daughter) her child was torn to pieces by two dogs at Walthamstow this week, and is dead – which is very strange.

26. Up betimes and among my workmen. By and by to Sir W. Batten, who with Sir J. Mennes are going to Chatham this morning. And I was in great pain till they were gone, that I might see whether Sir John doth speak anything of my chamber that I am afeared of losing or no. But he did not, and so my mind is a*ᵃ* little at more ease. So all day long till night among my workmen; and in the afternoon did cause the particion between the entry and the boy's room to be pulled down, to lay it all into one – which I hope will please me and make my coming in more pleasant.

Late at my office at night, writing a letter of excuse to Sir G. Carteret that I cannot wait upon him tomorrow morning to Chatham as I promised – which I am loath to do because of my

---

a repl. 'a'

1. Jane Croxton was a neighbour of Tom Pepys in Salisbury Court. She may have been a mercer. Pepys's enquiry presumably related to the dispute mentioned above, p. 148 & n. 3.

workmen and my wife's coming to town tomorrow.   So to my
lodgings and to bed.

27.   Up betimes and among my workmen, and with great
pleasure see the posts in my entry taken down, beyond expectation; so that now, the boy's room being laid into the entry doth
make my coming in very handsome, which was the only fault
remaining almost in my house.

We sat all the morning.   And in the afternoon I got many
jobbs done to my mind, and my wife's chamber put into a good
readiness against her coming – which she did at night, for Will
did, by my leave to go, meet her*a* upon the road and at night did
bring me word she was come to my brother's by my order.
So I made myself ready and put things at home in order, and so
went thither to her.   Being come, I find her and her maid and
dog very well – and herself grown a little fatter then she was.
I was very well pleased to see her; and after supper, to bed and
had her company with great content – and much mutual love.
Only, I do perceive that there hath been fallings-out between my
mother and she, and a little between my father and she; but I
hope all is well again.   And I perceive she likes Brampton house
and seat better then ever I did myself.   And tells me how my
Lord hath drawn a plot of some alterations to be made there,
and hath brought it up, which I saw and like well.[1]   I perceive
my Lord and Lady have been very kind to her.   And Captain
Ferrers, so kind that I perceive [I] have some jealousy of him; but
I know what is the Captain's manner of carriage, and therefore
it is nothing to me.   ⟨She tells me of a Court[2] like to be in a
little time, which troubles me, for I would not willingly go out
of towne.⟩*b*

28.   *Lords day.*   Waked earely, and fell talking one with
another with great pleasure of my house at Brampton and that
here, and other matters.*c*   She tells me what a rogue my boy is

a repl. 'here'   *b* addition crowded in between entries   *c* repl. ? 'ma'-

---

1. Cf. above, pp. 94, 97; below,
p. 219. Nothing appears to be
known of any such alterations. Sandwich had probably had a hand in
designing the alterations to his own
house, Hinchingbrooke: see above, ii.

49 & n. 1. His MS. journals (now
at Mapperton, Dorset) are embellished
with many sketches of buildings,
fountains etc.

2. A manorial court at Brampton:
see below, pp. 209, 222-3.

and strange things he hath been found guilty of, not fit to name, which vexes. But most of all, the unquiet life that my mother makes my father and herself lead, through her want of reason.

At last I rose, and with Tom to the French church at the Savoy, where I never was before – a pretty place it is.[1] And there they have the Common Prayer-Book read in French.[2] And, which I never saw before, the Minister doth preach with ⟨his⟩ hat off, I suppose in further conformity with our church.[3]

So to Toms to dinner with my wife, and there came Mr. Cooke. And Joyce Norton doth also dine there. And after dinner Cooke and I did talk about his journy and Toms within a day or two, about his mistress; and I did tell him my mind and gave him my opinion in it.

So I walked home and find my house made a little clean, and pleases me better and better. And so to church in the afternoon. And after sermon to my study and there did something against tomorrow, that I go to the Duke; and so walked to Tom's again. And there supped and to bed – with good content of mind.

29. *Michaelmas day.* This day my oaths for drinking of wine and going to plays are out,[a] and so I do resolve to take a liberty today and then to fall to them again. Up and by coach to White-hall, in my way taking up Mr. Moore and walked with him, talking a good while about business in St. James's parke. And there left him and to Mr. Coventry's, and so with him and Sir W. Penn up to the Duke; where the King came also and stayed till the Duke was ready. It being Collar day – we had

a repl. 'now'

---

1. In 1661 this congregation had moved from Somerset House to the 'little chapel' of the hospital of the Savoy (the chancel of the original chapel). Both this and the other Calvinist French church in Threadneedle St were favourite resorts for Londoners anxious to improve their French – the Westminster congregation being the more fashionable.

2. It had been translated by Dr John Durel, pastor of the congregation and later (1677) Dean of Windsor. See *Proc. Hug. Soc. London,* 22/96. Pepys retained a copy (PL 549; now missing).

3. Calvinist ministers kept their hats on during the sermon (though disapproving of the men in the congregation who did likewise), because to them preaching was a part of their work as teachers. See Evelyn, i. 75 & n.

no time to talk with him about any business. They went out together and so we parted; and in the parke Mr. Cooke by appointment met me, to whom I did give my thoughts concerning Tom's match and their journy tomorrow. And did carry him by water to Toms, and there taking up my wife, maid, dog and him, did carry them home – where my wife is much pleased with my house, and so am I fully. I sent for some dinner and there dined (Mrs. Margt Pen being by, to whom I had spoke to go along with us to a play this afternoon) and then to the King's Theatre, where we saw *Midsummers nights dreame*,[1] which I have never seen before, nor shall ever again, for it is the most insipid ridiculous play that ever I saw in my life. I saw, I confess, some good dancing and some handsome women, which was all my pleasure.

Thence set my wife down at Madam Turners and so by coach home; and having delivered Pegg Pen to her father safe, went home, where I find Mr. Deane of Woolwich hath sent me the modell he had promised me. But it so far exceeds my expectation that I am sorry almost he should make such a present to no greater a person; but I am exceeding glad of it and shall study to do him a courtesy for it.

So to my office and wrote a letter to Tom's mistress's mother, to send by Cooke tomorrow. Then came Mr. Moore, thinking to have looked over the business of my Brampton papers against the Court, but my mind was so full of other*ᵃ* matters (as*ᵇ* it is my nature when I have been a good while from a business that I have almost forgot it, I am loath to come to it again) that I could not set upon it; and so he and I passed the evening away in discourse, and to my lodgings and to bed.

30. We rose; and he about his business and I to my house to look over my workmen. But good God, how I do find myself by yesterday's liberty hard to be brought to fallow business again; but however, I must do it, considering the great sweet and pleasure and content of mind that I have had since I did leave drink and plays and other pleasures and fallowed my business.

a MS. 'over'   *b* repl. 'and'

1. Shakespeare's comedy; written c. 1595 and published in 1600. Pepys does not record seeing this play again during the diary period. (A).

So to my office – where we sat till noon, and then I to dinner with Sir W Pen; and while we were at it, coming my wife to the office, and so I sent for her up; and after dinner we took coach and to the Dukes playhouse, where we saw *The Duchesse of Malfy* well performed, but Baterton and Ianthe to admiration.[1] That being done, home again by coach, and my wife's chamber got ready for her to lie in tonight; but my business did call me to my office, so that staying late, I did not lie with her at home but at my lodgings.

Strange to see how easily my mind doth revert to its former practice of loving plays and wine, having given myself a liberty to them both these two days; but this night I have again bound myself to Christmas next, in which I desire God to bless me and preserve me, for under God I find it to be the best course that ever I could take to bring myself to mind my business.

I have also made up this evening my monthly ballance; and find that notwithstanding the loss of 30*l* to be paid to the Loyall and necessitous Cavaliers by act of Parliament,[2] yet I am worth about 680*l* – for which the Lord God be praised. My condition at present is this.

I have long been building; and my house, to my great content, is now almost done; but yet not so but that I shall have dirt, which troubles me too – for my wife hath been in the country at Brampton these two months, and is now come home a week or two before the house is ready for her.

My mind is somewhat troubled about my best chamber, which I Question whether*a* I shall be able to keep or no. I am also troubled for my journy which I must needs take suddenly to the Court at Brampton, but most of all for that I am not provided to understand my business, having not minded it a great while; and at the best shall be able but to make a bad matter of it. But God, I hope, will guide all to the best, and I am resolved to-

a   repl. 'which'

---

1. Webster's tragedy, first acted c. 1614, and published in 1623; one of the most popular tragedies in the repertoire of the Duke of York's Company. The cast listed by Downes (p. 25) includes Betterton as Bosola, Mrs Saunderson (Pepys's 'Ianthe', later Mrs Betterton) as the Duchess, Harris as Ferdinand and Young as the Cardinal. (A).

2. See above, p. 199 & n. 2.

morrow to fall hard to it: I pray God bless me therein, for my father and mother and all our well-doings do depend upon my care therein.

My Lord Sandwich hath lately been in the country, and very civil to my wife; and hath himself spent some pains in drawing a plot of some alteracions in our house there – which I shall fallow as I get money.

As for the office, my late industry hath been such, as I am become as high in reputation as any man there, and good hold I have of Mr. Coventry and Sir G. Carteret – which I am resolved, and it is necessary for me, to maintain by all fair means.

Things are all quiet, but the King poor and no hopes almost of his being otherwise, by which things will go to wrack, especially in the Navy.

The late outing of the presbyter=Clergy, by*a* their not renouncing the Covenant as the act [of] Parliament commands, is the greatest piece of state now in discourse. But for aught I see, they are gone out very peaceably and the people not so much concerned therein as was expected.[1]

My brother Tom is gone out of town this day to make a second journy to his mistress at Banbury – of which I have good expectations – and pray God to bless him therein. My mind, I hope, is settled to fallow my business again, for I find that two days' neglect of business doth give me more discontent in mind then ten times the pleasure thereof can repair again, be it what it will.

a l.h. repl. s.h. 'is'

---

1. For corroboration of this view of the effects of the Act of Uniformity, see the evidence in R. S. Bosher, *Making of Restoration settlement*, p. 266. It is significant that in London (strongest of all Puritan centres) the changes should have been made so quietly. Pepys had expressed his fears a little earlier: above, pp. 166, 178, 183.

OCTOBER.

1. Up, with my mind pretty well at rest about my accounts and other business, and so to my house, there put my work[men] to business and then down to Deptford to do the same there; and so back and with my workmen all the afternoon, and my wife putting a chamber in order – for us to lie in. At night to look over some Brampton papers against the Court, which I expect every day to hear of; and that done, home and with my wife to bed, the first time I have lain there these two months and more, which I am now glad to do again; and do so like the chamber as it is now ordered, that all my fear is my not keeping it. But I hope the best, for it would vex me to the heart to lose it.

2. Up and to the office, where we sat till noon. And then to dinner, and Mr. Moore came and dined with me; and after dinner, to look over my Brampton papers, which was a most necessary work, though it is not so much to my content as I could wish, I fear;[a] but it must be as it can and not as I would. He being gone, I to my workmen again. And at night by coach toward White-hall; took up Mr. Moore and set him at my Lord's, and myself. And hearing that there was a play at the Cockpitt[1] (and my Lord Sandwich, who came to town last night, at it) I do go thither; and by very great fortune did fallow four or five gentlemen who were carried[b] to a little private door in a wall, and so crept through a narrow place and came into one of the boxes next the King's; but so as I could not see the King nor Queene, but many of the fine ladies, who yet are not really so handsome generally as I use to take them to be, but that they are finely dressed. Here we saw *The Cardinall*,[2]

a MS. 'were'   *b* MS. 'carry'

---

1. The royal private theatre in Whitehall Palace, at which evening performances were given. (A).
2. A tragedy by James Shirley, first acted in 1641, and published in 1652.

The King's Company may have acted it, since it was in the repertoire of this company when Pepys saw it on 24 August 1667 and 27 April 1668. (A).

a tragedy I have never seen before, nor is there any great matter in it.   The company that came in with me into the box were all Frenchmen that could speak no English; but Lord, what sport they made to ask a pretty lady that they got among them, that understood both French and English – to make her tell them what the actors said.   Thence to my Lord's, and saw him; and stayed with him half an hour in his chamber, talking about some of mine and his own business; and so up to bed with Mr. Moore in the chamber over my Lord's.

3.   Rose, and without taking leave or speaking to my Lord, went out earely and walked home, calling at my brother's and Paul's churchyard; but bought nothing because of my oath, though I had a great mind to it.

At my office and with my workmen till noon, and then dined with my wife upon Herrings, the first I have eat this year.   And so to my workmen again.   By and by comes a Gentleman to speak with my wife, and I find him to be a gentleman that hath used her very civilly in her coming up out of the country, on which score I showed him great respect, and I find him a very ingenious gentleman – and sat and talked with him a great while.

He gone, to my workmen again; and in the evening comes Captain Ferrers and sat and talked with me a great while, and told me the story of his receiving his cut in the hand by falling out with one of my Lord's Footemen.[1]   He told me also of the impertinence and mischief that Ned Pickering[2] hath made in the country between my Lord and all his servants almost, by his finding of faults; which I am vexed to hear – it being a great disgrace to my Lord to have that fellow seen to be so great still with him.   He brought me a letter from my father that appoints the day for the Court at Brampton to be the 13th. of this Month. But I perceive he hath kept the letter in[a] his pocket these three days, so that if the day had been sooner, I might have been spoilt – so that it is a great folly to send letters of business by any friend that requires haste.   He being gone, I to my office all the

a repl. 'his'

1. See above, p. 196.
2. Sandwich's brother-in-law; 'a lying, bragging coxcombe' (vii. 295)

but knowledgeable about horses: below, ix. 391.

evening, doing business there till bedtime – it being now my manner since my wife is come to spend too much of my daytime with her and the workmen, and do my office business at night, which must not be after the work of my house is done. ⟨This night late, I have notice that Mr. Dekins the Merchant is dead this afternoon suddenly, for grief that his daughter, my *Morena*, who hath long been ill, is given over by the Doctors; for both which I am very sorry.⟩*a*

So home – and to bed.

4. To my office in the morning after I was up (my wife beginning to make me lie long a-mornings), where we sat till noon. And then dined at home; and after a little with my workmen, to my office till 9 at night. Among other things, examining the perticulars of the miscarriage of the *Satisfaccion*, sunk the other day on the Duch coast through the negligence of the pilott.[1] And then I wrote letters to my father (and my brother, now with his mistress at Banbury) of my intentions to be at Brampton next week. So home and to bed.

5. *Lords day.* Lay long in bed, talking with my wife; and among other things, fell out about my mayde Sarah, which my wife would fain put away, when I think her as good a servant as ever came into a house, but it seems my wife would have one that could dress a head well. But we were friends at last.

I to church; and this day the parson hath got one to read with a surplice on; I suppose himself will take it up hereafter – for a cunning fellow he is as any of his coate.[2] Dined with my wife; and then to talk again above, chiefly about her learning to dance,

a addition crowded in between paragraphs

1. The ship was a 5th-rate and had sunk on 19 September off Hellevoetsluis on its way to Jamaica. On 2 October the Duke of York had written to the Navy Board ordering an enquiry. The report (1 November) found that the pilot, John Lewis, was to blame: PRO, Adm. 196/7, nos 223, 232; Adm. 106/3520, f.10r–v; for Pepys's s.h. notes of his examination of the pilot ('a sober man') and others, see PRO, SP 29/61, no. 94 (1). See also below, p. 226 & n. 1.

2. For Pepys's anti-clericalism, see above, p. 135 & n. 2. The use of the surplice was gradually restored after 1660, and fairly quickly after the Act of Uniformity of 1662. Cf. above, i. 195; ii. 135–6; below, p. 235; J. H. Overton, *Life in Engl. church*, pp. 188–9.

against her going next year into the country; which I am willing she shall do.

Then to church to a tedious sermon. And thence walked to Toms to see how things are in his absence in the country; and so home and in my wife's chamber till bedtime, talking; and then to my office to put things in order to wait on the Duke tomorrow morning; and so home and to bed.

6. Sir W. Penn and I earely to St. James's by water, where Mr. Coventry; finding the Duke in bed and not very well, we did not stay to speak with him, but to White-hall and there took boat, and down to Woolwich we went – in our way, Mr. Coventry telling us how of late, upon enquiry into the mis-carriages of the Dukes family, Mr. Biggs his steward is found very faulty and is turned out of his imployment.[1] Then we fell to reading of a book which I saw the other day at my Lord Sandwiches, entended for the late King, finely bound up – a treatise concerning the benefit the Hollanders make of our fish-ing;[2] but whereas I expected great matters from*a* it, I find it a very impertinent* [book]; and though some things good, yet so full of tautologys that we were weary of it.

At Woolwich we mustered the yard and then to the Hart[3] to dinner; and then to the Ropeyard, where I did vex Sir W. Penn I know, to appear so well acquainted, I thought better then he, in the business of Hempe. Thence to Deptford and there looked over several businesses and wakened the officers there and so walked to Redriffe; and thence, landing Sir W. Penn at the tower, I to White-hall with Mr. Coventry and so to my Lord

a repl. 'for'

---

1. For this enquiry, see HMC, *Rep.*, 8/1/2/278a. Abraham Biggs was Clerk of the Kitchen.

2. Throughout the 17th century it was a common complaint that the Dutch herring fisheries exploited English seas, and many books had been written on the subject. Pepys's comments later in the entry suggest that this book was probably the short but prosy work by Tobias Gentleman ('Fisherman and Marriner'): *Englands*

way to win wealth . . . with a true rela-tion of the inestimable wealth that is yearely taken out of His Majesties seas by the Hollanders . . . (1614). Presum-ably this copy was specially bound for presentation to Charles I. There is no trace of it (or of anything similar) in the 1760 MS. catalogue of the Earl of Sandwich's library at Hinchingbrooke.

3. Probably the White Hart: above, p. 150 & n. 2.

Sandwiches lodgings; but my Lord was not within, being at a ball this night with the King at my Lady Castlemaynes at next door. But here to my trouble I hear that Mr. Moore is gone very sick to the Wardrobe this afternoon; which troubles me much, both for his own sake and for mine, because of the law businesses that he doth for me and also for my Lord's*a* matters. So hence by water, late as it was, to the Wardrobe; and there find him in a high feaver in bed, and much cast down by his being ill. So thought it not convenient to stay, but left him and walked home; and there, weary, went to supper, and then the barber came to me; and after he had done, to my office to set down my journall of this day; and so home and to bed.

7. At the office all the morning. Dined at home with my wife. After dinner, with her by coach to see Mr. Moore, who continues ill. I took his books of accounts and did discourse with him about my Lord's and my own businesses; and there being Mr. Battersby by, did take notice of my having paid him the*b* 100*l* I*c* borrowed of him, which they did confess and promise to return me my bond.[1] Thence by water with Will Howe to Westminster; and there staying a little while in the Hall (my wife's father and mother being abroad, and so she returning presently) thence by coach to my Lord's, and there I left money for Captain Ferrers to buy me two bands. So toward the New Exchange; and there, while my wife was buying things, I walked up and down with Dr. Williams, talking about my law businesses; and thence took him to my brother's and there gave him a glass of wine, and so parted; and then by coach with my wife home. And Sir J. Mennes and Sir W. Batten being come from Chatham pay, I did go see them for complaisance; and so home and to bed.

8. Up, and by water to my Lord Sandwich and was with him a good while in his Chamber; and among other things, to my extraordinary joy he did tell me how much I was beholding to the Duke of Yorke, who did yesterday of his own accord tell him that he did thank him for one person brought into the Navy, naming myself, and much more to my commendation; which

a l.h. repl. s.h. 'own'   *b* l.h. repl. s.h. 'my'   *c* word blotted

1. See above, ii. 215.

is the greatest comfort and encouragement that ever I had in my life, and do owe it all to Mr. Coventry's goodness and ingenuity. I was glad above measure of this.

Thence to Mr. Moore, who I hope is better then he was, and so home, and dined at home and all the afternoon busy at my office. And at night by coach to my Lord's again, thinking to speak with him; but he is at White-hall with the King, before whom the puppett plays I saw this summer in Covent garden are acted this night.[1] Hither this night my scallop, bought and got made by Captain Ferrer's lady, is sent, and I brought it home – a very neat one; it cost me about 3*l* – and 3*l* more I have given him to buy me another. I do find myself much bound to go hansome; which I shall do in linnen, and so the other things may be all the plainer.

Here I stayed playing some new tunes, two parts, with W. Howe; and my Lord not coming home, I came home late on foot, my boy carrying a linke. And so eat a bit and to bed – my head full of ordering of businesses against my journy tomorrow, that there may be nothing done to my wrong in my absence.

This day Sir W Pen did speak to me from Sir J. Mennes, to desire my best chamber of me; and my great joy is that I perceive he doth not stand upon his right, which I was much afeared of; and so I hope I shall do well enough with him for it, for I will not part with it by fair means, though I contrive to let him have another room for it.

9. Up earely about my business, to get me ready for my journy. But first to the office, where we sat all the morning till noon and then broke up; and I bid them Adieu for a week, having the Dukes leave got me by Mr. Coventry – to whom I did give thanks for my news yesterday of the Duke's words to my Lord Sandwich concerning me. Which he took well and doth tell me so freely his love and value of me, that my mind is now in as great a state of quiet, as to my interest in the office, as I could ever wish to be.

1. Cf. above, pp. 80 & n. 2, 90. In October 1662 a small stage was constructed in the Queen's Guard Chamber at Whitehall, probably for this performance by puppets; as a reward for the performance, 'Signor Bologna alias Pollicinella' was presented with a gold chain and medal: E. Boswell, *Restoration court stage*, pp. 56–7, 116. (A).

I should this day have dined at Sir W. Penn at a venison pasty with the rest of our fellows, but I could not get time but sent for a bit home; and so between one and two a-clock got on horseback at our back gate, with my man Will with me, both well mounted on two gray horses.

We rode and got to Ware before night, and so resolved to ride on to puckridge; which we did, though the way was bad and the evening dark before we got thither, by help of company riding before us; and among others, a Gentleman that took up at the same Inne, the Falcon,[1] with me, his name Mr. Brian, with whom I supped; and was very good company and a scholler.

He tells me that it is believed the Queene is with child,[2] for that the coaches are ordered to ride very easily through the streets.

After supper we paid the reckoning together; and so he to his chamber and I to bed, very well; but my feet, being much cramped by my new hard boots that I bought the other day of Wotton, were in much pain. Will lay in another bed in the chamber with me.

10. Up, and between 8 and 9 mounted again. But my feet so swelled with yesterday's pain, that I could not get on my boots, which vexed me to the blood; but was forced to pay 4*s* for a pair of old shoes of my landlord's, and so rid in shoes to Cambrige; but the way so good that but for a little rain I have got very well thither – and set up at the beare.[3] And there, being spied in the streets passing through the town, my Cosen Angier came to me, and I must needs to his house; which I did and there find Dr Fairebrother, with a good dinner – a barrel of good oysters – a couple of lobsters, and wine. But above all, telling me that this day there is a Congregacion for the choice of some officers in the University, he after dinner gets me a gowne, Capp, and hoode and carries me to the Schooles, where Mr. Pepper, my brother's Tutor, and this day chosen Proctor, did

1. Now (1969) the Crown and Falcon.

2. This rumour was unfounded, but widespread in London: cf. HMC, *Portland*, iii. 265; ib., *Rep.*, 7/4/ (*Stewart*), p. 111. The Queen remained barren, but hopeful rumours of her pregnancy were common in the early years of her marriage.

3. There were two Bear Inns in Cambridge at this time: see above, ii. 181, n. 2. Pepys's inn was probably the Black Bear: see below, p. 224 & n. 3.

appoint a Master of art to lead me into the Regent-house,[1] where I
sat with them and did [vote] by subscribeing papers thus: "*Ego
Samuel Pepys eligo Magistrum Bernardum Skelton*"[2] (and which
was more strange, my old schoolfellow and acquaintance, and
who afterwards did take notice of me and we spoke together)
"*alterum e taxatoribus hujus Academiae in annum sequentem.*" The
like I did for one Biggs[3] for the other Taxor and for other officers,
as the Vice-proctor, Mr. Covell, for Mr. Pepper, and which was
the gentleman that did carry me into the Regent-house.

This being done and the congregacion dissolved by the Vice-
Chancellor,[4] I did with much content return to my Cosen Angiers,
being much pleased of doing this jobb of work, which I have
long wished for and could never have had such a time as now to
do it with so much ease.

Thence to Trinity hall and there stayed a good while with
Dr John Pepys,[5] who tells me that brother Roger is gone out
of town to keep a Court; and so I was forced to go to Impington
to take such advice as my old uncle and his son Claxton could
give me – which I did, and there supped and talked with them,
but not of my business, till by and by after supper comes in
unlooked*a*-for my Cosen Roger, with whom by and by I discoursed largely; and in short, he gives me good counsel but
tells me plainly that it is my best way to study a composition with
my uncle Thomas, for the law will not help us and that it is
but a folly to flatter ourselfs. With which, though much to
my trouble, yet I was well satisfied, because*b* it told me what I
am to trust to. And so to bed.

11. Up betimes; and after a little breakfast and a very poor
one, like our supper and such as I cannot feed on, because of my

a repl. 'unk'-   *b* repl. 'though'

---

1. The Old Regent House, occupy-
ing part of the n. range of the Schools'
quadrangle. The modern Senate
House to the east of it (completed in
1730) now houses such functions.

2. Fellow of Peterhouse.

3. Thomas Bigg, Fellow of Trinity
College.

4. Theophilus Dillingham, Master
of Clare Hall.

5. Civil lawyer and Fellow of
Trinity Hall; son of Talbot Pepys of
Impington, Pepys's great-uncle.

she-Cosen Claxton's gouty hands – and after Roger had carried me up and down his house and orchards to show me them, I mounted and rode to Huntington and so to Brampton, where I find my father and two Brothers and Mr. Cooke, my mother and Sister. So we are now all together, God knows when we shall be so again. I walked up and down the house and garden, and find my father's alterations very handsome;[1] but not so but that there will be cause enough of doing more if ever I should come to live there; but it is, however, very well for a country [house], being as any little thing in the country.

So to dinner, where there being nothing but a poor breast of mutton, and that but ill-roasted, I was much displeased, there being Mr. Cooke there, who I invited to come over with my brother thither and for whom I was concerned to make much of.[2] I told my father and mother of it, and so had it very well mended for the time after, as long as I stayed – though I am very glad to see them live so frugally.

But now to my business; I find my uncle Thomas come into the country, and doth give out great words.[3] And forewarns all our people of paying us rent, and gives out that he will invalidate the Will, it being but conditional, we paying debts and legacies; which we have not done. But I hope we shall yet go through well enough.

I settled to look over papers and discourse of business against the Court till the evening; and then rid to Hinchingbrooke (Will with me), and there to my Lady's chamber and saw her. But it being night and my head full of business, stayed not long; but drank a cup of ale below and so home again and to supper and to bed – being not quiet in mind till I speak with Piggott to see how his business goes, whose land lies mortgaged to my late uncle; but never taken up by him and so I fear the heire-at-law will do it, and that we cannot; but my design is to supplant him by pretending bonds as well as a morgage for the same money, and so as executor have the beneffit of the bonds.

12. *Lords day.* Made myself fine with Captain Ferrer's laced

1. Cf. above, p. 94 & n. 1.

2. Cooke was arranging a match for Pepys's brother, Tom: above, p. 176.

3. Thomas Pepys, of St Alphage, London, was heir-at-law to the estate of Robert Pepys: for these disputes, see above, ii. 133 & n. 1.

band, being loath to wear ⟨my⟩ own new Scallop, it is so fine.
And after the barber had done with us, to church – where I saw
most of the gentry of the parish – among others, Mrs. Hanbury,
a proper lady – and Mr. Bernard and his lady with her father,
my late Lord St. John,[1] who looks now like a very plain grave
man.   Mr. Wells[2] preached a pretty good sermon, and they say
he is pretty well in his wits again.

So home to dinner.   And so to walk in the garden and then to
church againe.[a]   And so home, there coming several people
about business; and among others, Mr. Piggott, who gives me good
assurance of his truth to me and our business,[3] in which I am very
much pleased; and tells me what my uncle Thomas said to him
and what he designs, which (in fine) is to be admitted to the estate as
well as we[4] – which I must endeavour to oppose as well as I can.

So to supper.   But my mind is so full of our business that I
am no company at all; and then their drink doth not please me,
till I did send to Goody Stankes for some of hers, which is very
small and fresh, with a little taste of Wormewood, which ever after
did please me very well.   So after supper to bed, thinking of
business.   But every night getting my brother John to go up
with me for discourse sake while I was making unready.

13.   Up to Hinchingbrooke and there with Mr. Sheply did look
all over the house; and I do, I confess, like well of the alterations
and do like the staircase;[5] but there being nothing done to make
the outside more Regular and moderne, I am not satisfied with it,
but do think it to be too much to be laid out upon it.   Thence
with Sheply to Huntington to the Crowne, and there did sit and
talk and eat a breakfast of cold roast beef.   And so he to St. Ives
market and I to Sir Robt. Bernard[6] for counsel – having a letter
from my Lord Sandwich to that end.   He doth give it me with

a l.h. repl. s.h. 'again'

---

1. Oliver St John; 'my late Lord'
in that he had been one of Cromwell's
peers. His third daughter Elizabeth
had married John, son of Sir Robert
Bernard of Huntingdon.

2. William Wells, Vicar of Brampton until his death in 1664.

3. See above, ii. 137 & n. 4.

4. See below, p. 223 & n. 1.

5. For the alterations, see above,
ii. 49 & n. 1.   The staircase was
made in London: Carte 73, ff. 502r,
540r; ib., 74, f. 366r.

6. Lawyer; steward of Brampton
manor court; he was to preside over
its sittings.

much kindness in appearance, and upon my desire doth promise to put off my uncles admittance if he can fairly. And upon the whole, doth make my case appear better to me then my Cosen Roger did; but not so but that we are liable to much trouble and that it will be best to come to an agreement if possible. With my mind here also pretty well satisfied to see things proceed so well, I returned to Brampton and spent the morning in looking over papers and getting my Copys ready against tomorrow. So to dinner. And then to walk with my father, and other business. When by and by comes in my uncle Thomas and his son Thomas to see us, and very calme they were and we to them; and after a short "How do you" and drinking a cup of beer, they went away again. And so by and by my father and I to Mr. Phillips's and there discoursed with him in order to tomorrow's business of the Court, and getting several papers ready. When presently comes in my uncle Tho. and his son thither also; but finding us there, I believe they were disappointed, and so went forth again and went to the house that Prior hath lately bought of us (which was Bartons)[1] and there did make entry and forbid paying rent to us, as now I hear they have done everywhere else and that that was their intent in coming to see us this day. I perceive most of the people that do deal with us begin to be afeared that their title to what they buy will not be good – which troubled me also, I confess, a little; but I endeavoured to remove all as well as I could. Among other things, they make me afeared that Barton was never admitted himself to that that my uncle bought of him, but I hope the contrary.

Thence home, and with my father took a melancholy walk to Portholme, seeing the country-maids milking their Cowes there (they being there now at grasse) and to see with what mirth they come all home together in pomp with their milk, and sometimes they have musique go before them.[2]

---

1. See above, ii. 204 & n. 2.
2. Cf. below, viii. 193 & n. 2. Also cf. Dorothy Osborne's description of a similar scene in Bedfordshire (May 1653; *Letters*, ed. Parry, pp. 86–7): 'I walk out into a common . . . where a great many young wenches keep sheep and cows, and sit in the shade singing of ballads. I go to them and compare their voices and beauties to some ancient shepherdesses that I have read of . . . . I talk to them, and find they want nothing to make them the happiest people in the world but the knowledge that they are so.'

So back again home and to supper. And in comes Piggott with a counterfeit bond, which by agreement between us (though it be very just in itself) he hath made, by which I shall lay claim to the interest of the morgage=mony. And so waiting with much impatience and doubt the issue of tomorrow's court, I to bed. But hardly sleep half-an-hour the whole night, my mind did so run with fears of tomorrow.

14. Up, and did digest into a method all I could say in our defence, in case there should be occasion, for I hear he will have councell to plead for him at the Court. And so about 9 a-clock to the Court of^a the Lordshipp – where the Jury was called; and there being vacancys, they would have had my father, in respect to him, have been one of the Homage; but he thought fit to refuse it, he not knowing enough the customs of the towne. They being Sworne and the Charge given them – they fell to our business, finding the heire-at-Law to be my Uncle Thomas; but Sir Robert[1] did tell them that he had seen how the estate was devised to my father by my uncles Will, according^b to the custom of the Mannor – which they would have denied. First, that it was not according^b to the custom of the manor, proposing some difficulty about the half-acre of Land which is given the heire at law according^b to custome – which did put me into great fear lest it might not be in my Uncles possession at his death, but morgaged with other to T. Trice (who was there and was with my good will admitted to Taylors house mortgaged to him, it not being worth the money for which it was mortgaged; which I perceive he now, although he lately bragged the contrary, yet is now sensible of and would have us to redeem it with money and he would now re-surrender it to us rather then the heire-at-law) or else that it was part of goody Gorums, in which she hath a life and so might not be capable of being, according to the custom given to the heire-at-law. But Will Stankes tells me we are sure enough against all that.

a MS. 'at'

b At the first two occurrences this word is represented by the arbitrary symbol that normally represents 'knowledge'. At the third occurrence a symbol is used which represents 'according' phonetically.

---

1. Robert Bernard: see above, p. 220, n. 6.

Then they fell to talk of Piggotts land, mortgaged to my uncle but he never admitted to it, which they now as heire would be admitted to. But the Steward, as he promised me, did find pretensions very kindly and readily to put off their admittance; by which I find they are much defeated, and if ever, I hope will now listen to a treaty and agreement with us at our meeting at London.[1] So they took their leaves of the Steward and Court and went away; and by and by, after other businesses, many, brought in, they broke up to dinner. So my father and I home with great content to dinner – my mind now as full against the afternoon business – which we set upon after dinner at the Court, and did sue out a Recovery and cut off the Intayle; and my brothers there to joyne therein, and my father and I admitted to all the lands; he for life, and I for myself and my heires in reversion. And then did surrender, according to bargaine, to Prior, Greene and Sheppheard the three Cottages with their appurtenances that they have bought of us; and that being done and taken leave of the Steward, I did with most complete Joy of mind go from the Court with my father home; and in a Quarter of an houre did get on horseback with my brother Tom, Cooke and Will, all mounted; and without eating or drinking, take leave of father, mother, Pall (to whom I did give 10s but have shown no kind of kindness since I came, for I find her so very ill-natured that I cannot love her, and she so cruel an Hypocrite that she can cry when she please) and John, and away – calling in at Hinchingbrooke and taking leave in three words of my Lady and the young ladies; and so by Moonelight most bravely all the way to Cambrige with*a* great pleasure; whither we came at about 9 a-clock and took up at the beare, but the house being full of guests, we had very ill lodging, which troubled me. But had a supper and my mind at good ease, and so to bed. Will in another bed in my chamber.

a MS. 'which'

---

1. See above, ii. 137 & n. 4. Thomas Pepys surrendered to the executors the mortgaged lands on 16 September 1663: below, iv. 309. Pepys and the steward were presumably anxious not to prejudge a general settlement of Thomas Pepys's claims by a settlement of this single issue. The 'admittance' was the court process which gave the tenant possession as a copyholder. The deceased Robert Pepys had failed to get admittance, though he held the title-deeds of the land as mortgagee.

15. My mind, though out of trouble, yet intent upon my journy home; being desirous to know how all my matters go there, I could hardly sleep; but waked very earely, and when it was time did call up Will and we rose; and Musique (with a Bandore for the Base) did give me a Levett, and so we got ready; and while Breakefast was providing, I went forth (by the way finding Mr. George Mountagu and his lady, whom I saluted, going to take their coach thus earely to proceed on their journy, they having lodged in the chamber just under me all this night) and showed Mr. Cooke King's College Chappell, Trinity College, and St. Johns College Library;[1] and that being done, to our Inne again, where I met Dr[a] Fairebrother,[2] brought thither by my brother Tom, and he did breakfast with us – a very good-natured man he is. And told us how the room we were in was the room where Cromwell and his associated officers did begin to plot and act their mischiefs in those counties.[3]

Having eat well, only our oysters proving bad, we mounted – having a pair of boots that I borrowed and carry with me from Impington, my own to be sent from Cambrige to London. And took leave of all and begun our Journy – about 9 a-clock. After we had rode about 10 mile, we got out of our way into Royston roade; which did vex me cruelly, and the worst for that my brother's horse, which was lame yesterday, grows worse today, that he could not keep pace with us. At last, with much ado we got into the road again, having misguided also a gentle-mans man who had lost his master and thought us to be going the same way, did fallow us; but coming into the road again, we met with his master, by his coat a Divine. But I perceiving

a repl. 'Mr'

---

1. Pepys showed his wife these same buildings on 8 October 1667. See David Loggan's engravings (c. 1676–90) in his *Cantabrigia Illustrata* (n.d.), pls x, xii, xxix and xxvi. Evelyn (1 September 1654) thought St John's College Library (built 1623–5) the 'fairest' in the University.

2. Fellow of King's.

3. In the spring of 1643 the Grand Committee for the Eastern Association sat 'at the Bear next Sidney Street' (the Black Bear), and the sub-committee in a room 'next the Grand Committee Chamber': A. Kingston, *E. Anglia and Great Civil War*, p. 99. This inn was used at this period for meetings of the J.P.'s in quarter-sessions, and in 1662 for meetings of the commissioners appointed under the Corporation Act. Cf. *Proc. Camb. Antiq. Soc.*, 17/81 n. 1; above, ii. 181, n. 2.

Tom's horse not able to keep with us, I desired Mr. Cooke and him to take their own time, and Will and I, we rode before them, keeping a good pace; and came to Ware about 3 a-clock in the afternoon, the ways being everywhere but bad. Here I fell into acquaintance and eat and drank with the Divine, but know not who he is. And after an hour's bait to myself and horses, he, though resolved to have lodged there, yet for company would out again; and so we remounted at 4 a-clock, and he went with me as far almost as Tibbalds[1] and there parted with us, taking up there for all night. But finding our horses in good case and the night being pretty light (though by reason of clouds the moon did not shine out), we even made shift from one place to another to reach London, though both of us very weary; and having left our horses at their masters, walked home. Found all things well; and with full joy, though very weary, came home and went to bed. There happening nothing since our going to my discontent, in the least degree; which doth so please me, that I cannot but bless God for my journy, observing a whole course of successe from the beginning to the end of it. And I do find it to be the reward of my diligence, which all along in this hath been extraordinary, for I have not had the least kind of divertisement imaginable since my going forth, but merely carrying on my business, which God hath been pleased to bless.

So to bed, very hot and feverish by being weary; but ere morning the fever was over.

16. And so I rose in good temper, finding a good chimny-piece made in my upper dining-room chamber and the dining-room wainscote in a good forwardness, at which I am glad. And then to the office, where by T. Hater I find all things to my mind. And so we sat at the office till noon. And then at home to dinner with my wife. Then coming Mr. Creede, in order to some business with Sir J. Minnes about his accounts this after-noon, I took him to the Treasury Office, where Sir John and I did stay late, paying some money to the men that are saved out of the *Satisfaccion*, that was lost the other day. The King

1. Theobalds, near Cheshunt, Herts.; the house James I acquired in 1607 from the 2nd Earl of Salisbury; at this time in the possession of Albe-marle.

gives them half-pay, which is more then is used in such cases, for they never used to have anything; [1] and yet the men were most outrageously discontented and did rail and curse us till I was troubled to hear it and wished myself unconcerned therein. Mr. Creede, seeing us engaged, took leave of us. Here late and so home; and at the office set down my Journy=journall to this hour; and so shut up my book, giving God thanks for my good successe therein, and so home and to supper and to bed.

I hear Mr. Moore is in a way of recovery. Sir H. Bennett made Secretary of State in Sir Edwd. Nicholas's stead; not known whether by consent or not. [2]

My brother Tom and Cooke are come to town I hear this morning. And he sends me word that his mistress's Mother is also come, to treat with us about her daughter's portion and her ioynture, which I am willing should be out of Sturtlow=lands.

17. This morning Tom comes to me and I advise him how to deal with his mistress's mother about his giving her a joynture. But I entend to speak with her shortly and tell her my mind.

Then to my Lord Sandwich by water and told him how well things ⟨did⟩ go in the country with me, of which he was very glad, and seems to concern himself much for me. Thence with Mr. Creede to Westminster-hall, and by and by thither comes Captain Ferrer, upon my sending for him; and we three to Creedes chamber and there sat a good while and drank

1. For the wreck, see above, p. 213 & n. 1. The King's order (which refers to the rarity of this bounty) was transmitted to the Board by the Admiral on 14 October: PRO, Adm. 106/7, f.212r. The total paid was c. £420: Adm. 20/3, p. 330.

2. Sir Henry Bennet (cr. Baron Arlington, 1665, and Earl of Arlington, 1672) was appointed on 15 October. Nicholas was now close on 70, and had been Secretary for almost 20 years. He received a *douceur* of £10,000 from the King and kept his place in the Privy Council. The King had obtained his consent – 'he would not do it otherwise' (as Claren-

don later wrote) 'to so old and faithful a servant': *Life*, iii. 228–9. But Nicholas was said to have been loath to go and to have appealed to Clarendon to save him: Inchiquin to Fanshaw, 29 December, HMC, *Heathcote*, pp. 54–5. Nicholas's letters to Ormond and Winchilsea at the time show a reluctance to relinquish his hold until he was sure of his compensation: Lister, iii. 224–5; HMC, *Finch*, i. 221–2; cf. Clarendon's account in Lister, iii. 228–9. His resignation was a victory for the young royalists over the old guard led by Clarendon, Southampton and Ormond.

Chocolate. Here I am told how things go at Court; that the young men get uppermost, and the old serious lords are out of favour.[1] That Sir H. Bennet being brought into Sir Edwd. Nicholas place, Sir Ch. Barkely is made Privy purse[2] – a most vicious person, and one whom Mr. Pierce the surgeon today (at which I laugh to myself) did tell me that he offered his wife 300*l* per annum to be his whore. He also told me that none in Court hath more the King's eare now then Sir Ch. Barkely and Sir H. Bennet and my Lady Castlemayne, whose interest is now as great as ever. And that Mrs. Haslerigge,[3] the great beauty, is got with child and now brought to bed, and lays it to the King or the Duke of York. He tells me too, that my Lord St Albans is like to be Lord Treasurer;[4] all which things do trouble me much.

Here I stayed talking a good while. And so by water to see Mr. Moore, who is out of bed and in a way to be well. And thence home and with Comissioner Pett by water to view Woods masts that he proffers to sell; which we find bad.[5] And so to Deptford to look over some businesses; and so home and I to my office – all our talk being upon Sir J. Mennes and Sir W. Batten's base carriage against him at their late being at Chatham; which I am sorry to hear, but I doubt not but we shall fling Sir W. Batten upon his back ere long.

At my office; I hearing Sir W. Penn was not well, I went to him to see and set with him, and so home – and to bed.

18. This morning, having resolved of my brother's entertaining his mistress's Mother tomorrow, I sent my wife thither today to lie there tonight and to direct him in that business. And I all the morning at the office and the afternoon, intent upon my workmen, especially my Joyners, who will make my dining-room very pretty. At night to my office to dispatch business,

1. Cf. de Cominges to Louis XIV, London, 29 December 1662/8 January 1663: 'Le Chevalier Benet est fort bien avec son Maistre j'usques au point qu'il avoit donne quelque jalousie à la cabale du Chancelier . . .': PRO, PRO 31/3/110, f.456*r*.

2. Berkeley's patent was dated 16 October.

3. Unidentified.

4. Cf. W. Denton to Sir R. Verney, London, 16 October: 'Hear is a rumour as if my Lord Treasurer should have a writ of ease . . ., and the Bishop of London or St Alban's is named for it': HMC, *Rep.*, 7/1/463. Southampton, however, remained in office until 1667.

5. They were sap-rotten: PL 2874, p. 405.

and then to see Sir W. Penn, who continues in great pain; and
so home and alone to bed. But my head being full of my own
and my brother Toms business, I could hardly sleep – though
not in much trouble, but only multitude of thoughts.

19. *Lords day.* Got me ready in the morning and put on
my first new lace-band; and so neat it is, that I am resolved my
great expense shall be lace-bands, and it will set off anything
else the more. So walk to my brother's, where I met Mr.
Cooke; and discoursing with him, do find that he and Tom
have promised a joynture of 50*l* to his mistress and say that I
did give my consent that she should be joyntured in 30*l* per
annum for Sturtlow, and the rest to be made up out of her
portion.[1] At which I was stark-mad, and very angry the business should be carried with so much folly, and against my mind
and all reason. But I was willing to forbear discovering of it,
and did receive Mrs. Butler her mother, and Mr. Lull and his
wife, very civil people, very kindly and without the least discontent, and Tom had a good and neat dinner for us. We had
little discourse of any business; but leave it to one Mr. Smith
on her part, and myself on ours. So we stayed till sermon was
done; and I took leave and to see Mr. Moore, who recovers
well; and his doctor coming to him, one Dr Merritt,[2] we had
some of his very good discourse of Anatomy and other things,
very pleasant. By and by I with Mr. Townsend walked in the
garden, talking and advising with him about Toms business;
and he tells me he will speak with Smith, and says I offer fair to
give her 30*l* per annum joynture and no more.

Thence, Tom waiting for me, homewards toward my house,
talking and schooling[a] him for his folly, and telling him my mind
plainly what he hath to trust to if he goes this way to work, for
he shall never have her upon the terms they demand, of 50*l*.

He left me, and I to my uncle Wight and there supped;
and there was pretty Mrs. Margtt Wight, whom I esteem
very pretty and love dearly to look upon her. We were very

a ? 'scolding'

1. See below, p. 231 & n. 1.　　Librarian of the Royal College of
2. Christopher Merrett, Fellow and　　Physicians.

pleasant, I drolling with my aunt and them. But I am sorry to hear that the news of the selling of Dunkirke is taken so generally ill, as I find it is among the merchants;[1] and other things, as removal of officers at Court, good for worse; and all things else made much worse in their report among people then they are. And this night, I know not upon what ground, the gates of the City ordered to be kept*a* shut and double guards everywhere.[2] So home; and after preparing things against tomorrow for the Duke, to bed.

Endeed, I do find everybody's spirit very full of trouble and the things of the Court and Council very ill taken – so as to be apt to appear in bad colours if there should ever be a beginning of trouble – which God forbid.

20. Up and in Sir J. Mennes's coach with him and Sir W. Batten to White-hall, where now the Duke is come again to lodge,[3] and to Mr. Coventry's little new chamber there. And by and by up to the Duke, who was making himself ready; and there, among other discourse, young Killigrew did so commend *The Villaine*, a new play made by Tom Porter and acted only on Saturday at the Duke's house, as if there never had been any

a MS. 'keep' or 'kep'

1. Dunkirk had been acquired from Spain in 1658, and was now sold to the French for 5 m. livres by a treaty signed on 7/17 October. A deputation of London merchants went to Whitehall at about this time to protest that the surrender would make Dunkirk 'the Harbour of all the *Privateers*', and the King therefore asked Louis XIV to issue an edict against the corsairs: E. Combe, *Sale of Dunkirk* (1728), p. 126. Cf. HMC, *Rep.*, 11/5 (*Dartmouth*, pp. 10–11; 14 October) and *CSPVen. 1661–4*, p. 205 (23 October) for reports similar to Pepys's. But the privateers, based on Dunkirk and thereabouts, inflicted millions of pounds' worth of damage on English shipping during the

Anglo-French wars of the following hundred years. In the period 1656–1783 English prize goods totalling almost £6 m. were sold in Dunkirk prize-courts alone: *Journ. Mod. Hist.*, 5/1. Jean Bart, greatest of the privateers, flourished c. 1667–1702.

2. There is no trace of any order to this effect in the principal city records or in those of the Privy Council (which occasionally issued directions to this effect). There were rumours of a plot at this time: *CSPD 1661–2*, p. 519; PRO, PC 2/56, ff. 97–8.

3. The Duke used his lodgings in St James's Palace during the summer and those in Whitehall Palace during the winter: cf. above, p. 192, n. 1.

such play come upon the stage.[1]   The same yesterday was told
me by Captain Ferrers; and this morning afterward by Dr
Clerke, who saw it – insomuch, that (after I had done with the
Duke and thence gone with Comissioner Pett to Mr.*a* Lillys
the great painter, who came forth to us;[2] but believing that I
came to bespeak a picture, he prevented us by telling us that he
should not be at leisure these three weeks, which methinks is a
rare thing; and then to see in what pomp his table was laid for
himself to go to dinner.   And here among other pictures, I saw
the so much by me desired picture of my Lady Castlemayne,[3]
which is a most blessed picture and that that I must have a copy
of.   And having thence gone to my brother's, where my wife
lodged last night, and eat something there, I took her by coach to
the Duke's house; and there was the house full of company, but
whether it was our over-expecting or what, I know not, but I
was never less pleased with a play in my life – though there was
good singing and dancing, yet no fancy in the play.   But something that made it less contenting was my conscience, that I
ought not to have gone by my vowe;[4] and besides, my business
commanded me elsewhere.   But however, as soon as I came
home, I did pay my Crowne to the poor's box according*b* to my
vowe, and so no harm as to that is done, but only business lost
and money lost and my old habitt of pleasure wakened, which I
will keep down the more hereafter, for I thank God these pleasures
are not sweet to me now in the very enjoying of them.   So by
coach home; and after a little business at my office and seeing
Sir W. Penn, who continues ill, I went to bed.

Dunkirke, I am confirmed, is absolutely sold; for which I am
very sorry.

a l.h. repl. s.h. 'Mr.'   *b* MS. 'knowledge'

---

1. The first record of a performance of this play, a tragedy by
Thomas Porter, published in 1663.
Now at the LIF; cast in Downes,
p. 23. (A).

2. Lely had been established, possibly in 1650 and certainly in 1651, in
the house in the n.-e. corner of the
Piazza at Covent Garden in which he
was to pass the rest of his life. By
then he was extremely successful.

He was granted in October 1661 an
annual pension from the Crown of
£200 'as formerly to Sr Vandyke';
he had, in addition, come of a pros-
perous and property-owning family
in The Hague, and his famous collection of pictures and drawings was
probably already impressive. (OM).

3. See above, p. 113 & n. 3.
(OM).

4. See above, p. 209. (A).

21. Up; and while I was dressing myself, my brother Tom being there, I did chide him for his folly in abusing himself about this match. For I perceive he doth endeavour all he can to get her, and she and her friends* to have more then her portion deserves, which now, from 6 or 700*l*, is come to 450. I did by several steps show Tom how he would not be 100*l* the better for her according to the ways he took to joynture her.[1] After having done with him, to the office and there all the morning; and in the middle of our sitting, my workmen setting about the putting up of my rails upon my leads, Sir J. Mennes did spy them and fall a-swearing; which I took no notice of but was vexed, and am still to the very heart for it, for fear it should put him upon taking the closet and my chamber from me, which I protest I am now afeared of. But it is my very great folly to be so much troubled at these trifles, more then at the loss of 100*l* or things of greater concernment. But I forget the lesson I use to preach to others of τὰ ἐφ ἡμῖν χγ τὰ γχ ἐφ ἡμῖν.[2]

After dinner to my office, with my head and heart full of troublesome businesses. And then by water with Mr. Smith to Mr. Leechmore, the Counsellor at the Temple, about Fields business;[3] and he tells me plainly that there being a verdict against me, there is no help for it but it must proceed to judgment. It is 30*l* damage to me for my joining with others in committing Field to prison, we being not Justices of the Peace in the City, though in Middlesex; this troubled me, but I hope the King will make it good to us.

Thence to Mr. Smith the Scrivener upon Ludgate-hill, to whom Mrs. Butler doth commit her business concerning her daughter and my brother. He tells me her daughter's portion is but 400*l*, at which I am more troubled then before; and they find fault that his house is too little. So after I had told him my full mind, I went away; to meet again tomorrow, but I believe the business will be broke off – which for Toms sake I am much grieved for, but it cannot be helped without his ruin. Thence

1. Tom was offering £50 p.a.: above, p. 228. At this time the average ratio of jointure to portion was one to six; later in the century it was one to ten. See H. J. Habbakuk in *TRHS* (ser. 4), 32/15+; cf. below, 25 June 1665.

2. Epictetus's warning against worry: see above, p. 194 & n. 1.

3. For the case, see above, p. 23 & n. 2. Robert Smith, messenger to the Navy Office, was its principal police officer.

to see Mr. Moore, who is pretty well again, and we read over and discoursed about Mrs. Goldsboroughs business; and her son coming by my appointment thither, I did tell him our resolution as to her having her estate reconveyed to her.[1]

Hither also came my brother; and before Mr. Moore, I did advise and counsel him about his match, and how we had all been abused by Mr. Cookes folly. So home, and to my office and there settled many businesses; and so home and to supper, and so to bed – Sir W. Penn being still in great pain.

22. Up, and carrying my wife and her brother to Covent garden, near their father's new lodging,[2] by coach, I to my Lord Sandwichs; who receives me now more and more kindly, now he sees that I am respected in the world – and is my most noble patron.

Here I stayed and talked about many things with my Lord and Mr. Puvy, being there about Tanger businesses for which the Comission is in taking out.

Thence (after talking with Mr. Cooke, whom I met here, about Mrs. Butler's portion, he doth persist to say that it will be worth 600*l* certain, when he knows as well as I do now, that it is but 400*l*; and so I told him. But he is a fool, and hath made fools of us). So I by water to my brother's, and thence to Mr. Smith's, where I was last night; and there by appointment met Mrs. Butler, with whom I plainly discoursed, and she with me. I find she will give but 400*l* and no more, and is not willing to do that without a joynture, which she expects and I will not grant for that portion; and upon the whole, I do find that Cooke hath made great brags on both sides and so hath abused us both, but know not how to help it – for I perceive she had much greater expectations of Toms house and being then she finds. But however, we did break off the business wholly, but with great love and kindness between her and me. And would have been glad we had known one another's minds sooner, without being misguided by*a* this fellow, to both our shames

a l.h. repl. s.h. 'my'

---

1. Cf. above, ii. 195, n. 3: this was one of the disputes inherited with Robert Pepys's estate.

2. Possibly the house in Long Acre mentioned below, 17 February 1664.

and trouble. For I find her a very discreet, sober woman; and her daughter, I understand and believe, is a good lady; and if portions did agree, though she finds fault with Toms house and his imperfection*a* in his speech, I believe we should well agree in other matters. After taking a kind farewell, I to Toms and there did give him a full account of this sad news; with which I find he is much troubled, but doth appear to me willing to be guided herein, and apprehends that it is not for his good to do otherwise. And so I do persuade [him] to fallow his business again, and I hope he will. But for Cookes part and Dr Pepys, I shall know them for two fools another time.

Thence, it raining hard, by coach home (being first trimmed here by Benier; who being acquainted with all the players, doth tell me that Baterton is not married to Ianthe as they say;¹ but also that he is a very sober, serious man, and studious and humble, fallowing of his study, and is rich already with what he gets and saves); and there to my office till late, doing great deal of business and settling my mind in pretty good order as to my business, though at present they are very many. So home and to bed.

This night was buried, as I hear by the bells at Barking church, my poor *Morena*² – whose sickness being desperate did kill her poor father; and he being dead for sorrow, she said she could not recover nor desire to live, but from that time doth languish more and more, and so is now dead and buried.

23. Up and among my workmen; and so to the office and there sitting all the morning. We stepped all out to visitt Sir W. Batten, who it seems hath not been well all yesterday; but being let blood, is now pretty well. And Sir W. Penn, after office, I went to see; but he continues in great pain of the goute and in bed, cannot stir hand nor foot but with great pain. So to my office all the evening, putting things public and private in order; and so at night home and to supper and to bed – finding

a repl. 'bad'

---

1. Thomas Betterton did not marry Mary Saunderson (here called 'Ianthe': see above, p. 58 & n. 3)

until 24 December 1662. (A).

2. See above, p. 213.

great content since I am come to fallow my business again, which God preserve in me.

24.   After with great pleasure lying a great while, talking and sporting in bed with my wife (for we have [been] for some years now, and at present more and more, a very happy couple, blessed be God),[1] I got up and to my office; and having done there some business, and by water and then walked to Deptford to discourse with Mr. Cowly and Davis about my late conceptions about keeping books of the distinct works done in the yards,[2] against which I find no objection but their ignorance and unwillingness to do anything of pains and what is out of their old dull road. But I like it well,*a* and will proceed in it. So home and dined there with my wife upon a most excellent dish of tripes of my own directing, covered with mustard, as I have heretofore seen*b* them done at my Lord Crews; of which I made a very great meal and sent for a glass of wine for myself. And so to see Sir Wm Penn, who continues bed-rid, in great pain. And thence to the Treasury to Sir J. Mennes, paying off of tickets; and at night home; and in my study, after seeing Sir W. Batten (who also continues ill), I fell to draw out my conceptions about books for the Clerkes [of] the Cheques in the yards to keep, according *c* to the distinct works there, which pleases me very well and I am confident it will be of great use. At 9 at night home, and to supper and to bed.

This noon came to see me and sit with me a little after dinner, Mr. Pierce the Chyrurgeon – who tells me how ill things go at Court; that the King doth show no countenance to any [that] belong to the Queene, nor above all to such english as she brought over with her or hath here since, for fear they should tell her how he carries himself to Mrs. Palmer;[3] insomuch that though he hath

a MS. 'will'   *b* repl. 'some'   *c* MS. 'knowledge'

---

1. One of the few passages in the diary which may be taken as referring to their separation in the early years of their marriage: cf. above, ii. 153 & n. 3. Elizabeth's birthday was on 23 October. (The diary has no mention of it.)

2. These were the call-books which Pepys introduced into the royal dockyards within the next six months, and of which he was very proud. Below, p. 289 etc.

3. Lady Castlemaine.

a promise and is sure of being made her Chyrurgeon, he is at a loss what to do in it, whether to take it or no,[1] since the King's mind is so altered; and [no] favour to all her dependents, which she is fain to let go back again into Portugall (though she brought them from their friends against their wills with promise of preferment), without doing anything for them. But he tells me that her owne Physician did tell him, within these three days, that the Queene doth know how the King orders things, and how he carries himself to my Lady Castlemayne and others, as well as anybody; but though she hath spirit enough, yet seeing that she doth no good by taking notice of it, for the present she forbears it in policy; of which I am very glad. But I pray God keep us in peace; for this, with other things, doth give great discontent to all people.

25. Up and to the office, and there with Mr. Coventry sat all the morning; only we two, the rest being absent or sick. Dined at home with my wife upon a good dish of neats' feet and mustard, of which I made a good meal. All the afternoon alone at my office and among my workmen, who (I mean the joyners) have even ended[2] my dining-room; and will be very handsome and to my full content.

In the evening at my office about one business or another; and so home and to bed – with my mind every day more and more quiet since I come to fallow my business, and shall be very happy endeed when the trouble of my house is over.

26. *Lords day.* Up, and put on my new Scallop, and is very fine. To church and there saw, the first time, Mr. Mills in a Surplice; but it seemed absurd for him to pull it over his eares in the reading-pew after he had done before all the church, to go up to the pulpitt to preach without it.

Home and dined; and Mr. Sympson, my Joyner[3] that doth my dining-room, and my brother Tom with me to a delicate fat pig. Tom takes his disappointment of his mistress to heart, but

---

1. He was surgeon to the Duke of York, and became surgeon to the King's Household in 1672, but he does not appear to have served the Queen.
2. Sc. just ended.

3. Thomas Simpson, Master-Joiner of Deptford and Woolwich yards. In 1666 he made two of the bookcases now in the Pepys Library at Magdalene.

all will be well again in a little time.   Then to church again and
heard a simple Scott preach most tediously.   So home and then
to see Sir W. Batten, who is pretty well again; and then to my
uncle Wights to show my fine band and to see Mrs. Margtt
Wight, but she was not there.   All this day, soldiers going up
and down the towne, there being an alarme and many Quakers and
others clapped up; but I believe[a] without any reason.   Only,
they say in Dorsettshire there hath been some rising discovered.[b1]
So after supper home and then to my study; and making up my
monthly account to myself, I find myself, by my expense in
bands and clothes this month, abated a little of my last, and that
I am worth 679*l* still; for which God be praised.   So home and
to bed, with quiet mind, blessed be God, but afeared of my
candle's going out, which makes me write thus slubberingly.[c]

27.   Up, and after giving order to the plasterer now to set
upon the finishing of my house, then by water to wait upon
the Duke; and walking in the matted-gallery, by and by comes
Mr. Coventry and Sir John Minnes; and then to the Duke and
after he was ready, to his Closett, where I did give him my
usuall account of matters.   And afterwards, upon Sir J. Mennes's
desire to have one to assist him in his imployment, Sir[d] Wm. Pen

---

a repl. ill-formed s.h. 'believe'   *b* l.h. repl. s.h. 'disl'-
c The MS. is here as neat as elsewhere.   *d* repl. l.h. 'Comr.'

---

1. A company of foot and a troop
of horse had been sent into the city at
the Lord Mayor's request, and over
300 were arrested (though not all
were imprisoned) – Quakers from the
Bull and Mouth meeting in Alders-
gate, and Anabaptists from Glovers'
Hall.   Arrests continued throughout
November, many Quakers not being
released until January 1663: *CSPD
1661-2*, p. 541; W. C. Braithwaite,
Second period of Quakerism, pp. 23+;
N. Penney (ed.), *Extracts from state
papers*, p. 153; Ludlow, ii. 341-2.
The events of this day are described in
a letter from Ellis Hooke to Margaret
Fell, 28 October, in *Letters of early
Friends* (The Friends' Library, vol. xi,
ed. William and Thomas Evans,
Philadelphia, 1847), pp. 359-60.
There had been rumours of a plot in
Dorset since July: *CSPD 1661-2*, p.
439. Cf. W. Denton to Sir R.
Verney, London, 30 October 1662:
'Here hath been news of a plot and
rioting about Sherborne in Dorset-
shire . . . a hot alarm to King,
General and City . . .'.   In London,
he continued, Ludlow was to have
acted as leader, and the plan was to
time the rising for Lord Mayor's day,
the 29th, 'about noon, when all were
busy, or at night when all were
drunk': HMC, *Rep.*, 7/1/463. Cf.
below, p. 303, n. 5; W. C. Abbott in
AHR, 14/511+.

is appointed to be his, and Mr. Pett to be the Surveyor's Assistant.[1] Mr. Coventry did desire ⟨to⟩ be excused; and so I hope (at least it is my present opinion) to have none joyned with me, but only Mr. Coventry doth desire that I would find work for one of his Clerkes, which I did not deny; but however, I will think of it, whether without prejudice to mine I can do it.

Thence to my Lord Sandwich, who nowadays calls me into his chamber, and alone did discourse with me about the jealousys that the Court hath of people's rising; wherein he doth much dislike my Lord Monkes being so eagre against a company of poor wretches, dragging them up and down the street: but would have him rather to take some of the greatest ringleaders of them and punish them; whereas this doth but[a] tell the world the King's fears and doubts. For Dunkirke, he wonders any wise people should be so troubled thereat, and scornes all their talk against it, for that he says it was not Dunkirke, but the other places,[2] that did and would annoy us, though we had that as much as if we had it not. He also took notice of the new Ministers of State, Sir H. Bennet and Sir Ch. Barkely, their bringing in, and the high game that my Lady Castlemayne plays at Court (which I took occasion to mention as that that the people do take great notice of), all which he confessed. Afterward he told me of poor Mr. Spong, that being with other people examined before the King and Council (they being laid up as suspected persons; and it seems Spong is so far thought guilty as that they entend to pitch upon him to put to the wracke or some other torture), he doth take knowledge of my Lord Sandwich and said that he was well known to Mr. Pepys. But my Lord knew, and I told him, that it was only in matter of musique and pipes, but that I thought him to be a very innocent fellow. And

---

a MS. 'put'

---

1. The Comptroller's duties were miscellaneous, and recognised to be particularly difficult. Both Mennes and Batten resisted these appointments. Cf. below, iv. 61 & n. 1.

2. I.e. the other ports on that coast: cf. above, p. 229, n. 1. Sandwich had been one of those mainly responsible for the sale of Dunkirk: below, vii. 55 & n. 4.

endeed, I am very sorry for him.[1]   After my Lord and I had done in private, we went out and with Captain Cuttance and Bunn did look over their draught of a bridge for Tanger,[2] which will be brought by my desire to our office by them tomorrow.

Thence to Westminster-hall and walked there long with Mr. Creede; and then to the great half-Crowne ordinary at the King's-head near Charing Crosse, where we had a most excellent neat dinner and very high company, and in a noble manner.

After dinner he and I into another room over a pot of ale and talked. He showed me our commission, wherein the Duke of Yorke – Prince Robt., Duke of Albemarle, Lord Peterburgh, Lord Sandwich, Sir G. Carteret, Sir Wm. Compton, Mr. Coventry, Sir R. Ford, Sir Wm. Rider, Mr. Cholmly, Mr. Povy, myself, and Captain Cuttance, in this order, are joyned for the carrying on the service of Tanger – which I take for a great honour to me.[3]

He told me what great faction there is at Court.   And above all, what is whispered, that young Crofts is lawful son to the King, the King being married to his mother.[4]   How true this is, God knows.   But I believe the Duke of Yorke will not be fooled in this of three crowns.

1. John Spong, Chancery clerk, at his examination, deposed that he had been informed that the Fifth-Mon-archy men had bribed some of the Tower guard, and had planned to rise on Bartholomew's Day: PRO, SP 29/66, no. 36 (n.d.). Pepys wrote in November to Spong's friend, William Lilly the astrologer, saying that he had spoken to several privy councillors on Spong's behalf and could, regretfully, do no more: NMM, LBK/8, p. 28. Spong was released on 24 January 1663: HMC, *Rep.*, 11/7/5.

2. A jetty 100 ft long, equipped with a capstan crane. See PRO, CO 279/1, f.133r for an estimate of £572 10s. for its construction, under the guidance of Captains Cuttance and Bun, by Jonas Shish and Edward Rundalls, the Deptford shipwrights.

It is endorsed, in Pepys's hand, 'Octbr 31. 1662'. Cf. also a bill for the work (£307; 14 October 1663) in PRO, Adm. 20/4, p. 291.

3. PRO, C 66/3030 (dorse, 20 November); Routh, pp. 12, 31. Pepys was a member of the Committee until May 1679 and served as its Treasurer from March 1665.

4. This is an early appearance of this rumour – in July 1663 Clarendon was accused of spreading it in order to alienate the King and the Duke of York: *LJ*, xi. 556. The story be-came widespread in the 1670s with the growth of the movement to make Crofts (Monmouth) Charles's suc-cessor. It was solemnly denied by the King in three proclamations issued in 1679–80. His mother was Lucy Walter (d. 1658).

Thence to White-hall and walked long in the galleries till (as they are commanded to all strange persons) one came to tell us, we not being known and being observed to walk there four or five houres (which was not true, unless they count my walking there in the morning), he was commanded to ask who we were; which being told, he excused his Question and was satisfied. These things speak great fear and jealousys. Here we stayed some time, thinking to stay out the play before the King tonight, but it being *The Villaine*[1] and my wife not being there,*a* I had no mind.

So walk to the Exchange and there took many turnes with him. Among other things, observing one very pretty Exchange lass with her face full of ⟨black⟩ patches, which was a strange sight.[2] So bid him good-night and away by coach to Mr. Moore, with whom I stayed an hour and find him pretty well, and entends to go abroad tomorrow. And so it raining hard, by coach home; and having visited both Sir Wms, who are both sick but like to be well again, I to my office and there did some business; and so home and to bed.

At Sir Wm. Battens I met with Mr. Mills, who tells me that he could get nothing out of the mayde hard by (that did poison herself) before she died, but that she did it because she did not like herself, nor had not liked herself nor anything she did a great while. It seems she was well-favoured enough, but Crooked, and this was all she could be got*b* to say – which is very strange.

28. At the office, sitting all the morning; and then home to dinner with my wife. And after dinner, she and I passing an hour or two in harmless talk, and then I to my office, doing business there till 9 at night; and so home and to supper and bed.

a repl. 'here'   *b* repl. 'great'

---

1. See above, p. 230 & n. 1; now at the Cockpit theatre, Whitehall Palace. (A).
2. For patches, see Cunnington, p. 187, fig. 85 (*b*). Fifteen worn at once

were by no means unknown: H. Misson, *Mémoires et observations* (The Hague, 1698), p. 305. On 22 November 1660 Elizabeth Pepys wore two or three.

My house is now in its last dirt I hope, the plasterer and painter now being upon winding up all my trouble – which I expect will now, in a fortnight's time or a little more, be quite over.

29. *Lord=Mayors=day.* Entended to have made me fine and by invitation to have dined with my Lord Mayor today; but going to see Sir Wm. Batten this morning, I find Sir G. Carteret and Sir J. Mennes going*a* with Sir W. Batten and myself to examine Sir G. Carteret's accounts for the last year; whereupon I settled to it with them all the day long, only dinner time (which Sir George gave us); and by night did as good as finish them. And so parted and thence to my office and there set papers in order and business against tomorrow. I received a letter this day from my father, speaking more trouble about my uncle Tho. his business and ours, he proceeding to lay claim to Brampton and all my uncle left, because it is given condicionall that we should pay legacies, which to him we have not yet done; but I hope*b* that will do us no hurt. God help us if it should, but it disquiets my mind. I have also a letter from my Lord Sandwich, desiring me upon matter of concernment to be with him earely tomorrow morning, which I wonder what it should be. So, my mind full of thoughts and some trouble, at night home and to bed.

Sir G. Carteret, who had been at the examining most of the late people that are clapped up, doth say that he doth not think that there hath been any great plotting among them, though ⟨they⟩ have a good will to it; but their condition is so poor and silly and low, that he doth not fear them at all.

30. Could sleep but little tonight for thoughts of my business. So up by candlelight and by water to White-hall; and so to my Lord Sandwich, who was up in his chamber and all alone did acquaint me with his business, which was that our old acquaintance Mr. Wade (in Axe yard) hath discovered to him 7000*l* hid in the tower, of which he was to have two for discovery – my Lord himself 2, and the King the other 3 when it was found. And that the King's warrant runs for me on my Lord's part, and one Mr. Lee for Sir Harry Bennet, to demand leave of the

a repl. 'to'   *b* repl. 'help'

Lieutenant of the tower for to make search.[1]   After he had told me the whole business, I took leave and hastened to my office, expecting to be called by a letter from my Lord to set upon that business.   And so there I sat with the officers all the morning.   At noon, when we were up, comes Mr. Wade with my Lord's letter and tells me the whole business.   So we consulted for me to go first to Sir H. Bennett, who is now with many of the Privy Counsellors at the Tower, examining of their late prisoners,[2] to advise with him when to begin.

So I went; and the guard at the water-gate making me leave my sword at the gate, I was forced to stay so long in the ale-house hard by till my boy run home for my cloak,[3] that my Lord Mayor that now is, Sir John Robinson, Lieutenant of the Tower, with all his company, was gone with their coaches to his house in Minchen-lane.   So my cloak being come, I walk thither; and there by Sir G. Carteret's means did presently speak with Sir H. Bennett, who did show and give me the King's warrant to me and Mr. Leigh, and another to himself, for the paying of 2000*l* to my Lord, and other 2 to the discoverers. After a little discourse, dinner came in and I dined with them. There was my Lord Mayor, my Lord Lauderdale – Mr. Secretary Morrice, to whom Sir H. Bennet would give the upper hand[4] –

1. The treasure (of gold, silver and jewels) was supposed to have been hidden by John Barkstead, a goldsmith of the Strand, who had been Lieutenant of the Tower, 1652–60. Recently he had been arrested in Holland, and in April 1662 had been executed.   It was alleged that he had been unable to recover his hoard before he fled abroad at the Restoration.   Several attempts have been made since Pepys's time (e.g. in 1958) to find it.   For Pepys's attempt, see Richard Brooke to Secretary Bennet, 16 October: PRO, SP 29/61, no. 57. Brooke wrote on behalf of unnamed friends, and for his own share asked for the nomination to an under-clerkship in Bennet's gift.   He said

he had first revealed the facts to Sir Richard Browne, Clerk of the Council.   Two undated drafts of the royal warrant which Pepys mentions – the second in Sandwich's hand – are in SP 29/109, nos 4, 5: wrongly dated and inaccurately summarised in *CSPD 1664–5*, p. 138.   In the first (mostly in Pepys's hand) Sandwich is not mentioned.   Robert Leigh (Ley) appears in these documents, but not Wade.

2. See above, p. 236 & n. 1.

3. When out of doors, a gentleman was properly dressed only if he carried a sword or wore an upper garment.

4. Both were Secretaries of State, but Morice was the senior by appointment.

Sir Wm. Compton, Sir G. Carteret, and myself and some other
company, and a brave dinner.   After dinner Sir H. Bennett did
call aside the Lord Mayor and me and did break the business to
him; who did not nor darst appear the least averse to it, but did
promise all assistance forthwith to set upon it.   So Mr. Leigh
and I to our office and there walked till Mr. Wade and one Evett
his guide did come, and W. Griffin and a porter with his picke-
axes &c.; and so they walked along with us to the tower, and
Sir H. Bennett and my Lord Mayor did give us full power to
fall to work.   So our guide demands a candle, and down into the
cellars he goes, inquiring whether they were the same that
Baxter [1] alway had.   We went into several little cellars and then
went out-a-doors to viewe, and to the Coleharbour; [2] but none
did answer so well to the marks which was given him to find it
by as one arched vault.   Where after a great deal of counsel
whether to set upon it now or delay for better and more full
advice, we set to it; and to digging we went till almost 8 a-clock
at night – but could find nothing.   But however, our guides
did not at all seem discouraged; for that they being confident
that the money is there they look for, but having never been in
the cellars, they could not be positive to the place and therefore
will inform themselfs more fully, now they have been there, of
the party that doth advise them.   So locking the door after us,
we left work tonight and up to the Deputy-Governor [3] (my Lord
Mayor and Sir H. Bennett, with the rest of the company, being
gone an hour before); and he doth undertake to keep the key of
the cellar, that none shall go down without his privity.   But
Lord, to see what a young simple fantastic coxcombe is made
Deputy-Governor would make one mad.   And how he called
for his night-gown of silk, only to make a show to us; and
yet for half an hour I did not think he was the Deputy-Governor,
and so spoke not to him about the business but waited for
another man.   At last I broke our business to him; and he
promising his care, we parted and Mr. Leigh and I by coach to
White-hall – where I did give my Lord Sandwich an account of
our proceedings and some encouragement to hope for something
hereafter, and so bade him good-night; and so by coach home
again, where to my trouble I find that the painter hath not been

1. Barkstead.   3. George Wild (Weld), M.P. for
2. A stone gateway.   Much Wenlock, Salop.

here today to do anything – which vexes me mightily. So to my office to put down my Journall, and so home and to bed.

This morning, walking with Mr. Coventry in the garden, he did tell me how Sir G. Carteret hath carried the business of the Victuallers money to be paid by himself, contrary to old practice;[1] at which he is angry I perceive, but I believe means no hurt, but that things may be done as they ought. He expects Sir G. should*a* bespatter him privately in revenge, not openly – against which he prepares to bedawbe him and swears he will do it from the beginning, from Jersy to this day;[2] and as to his own taking of too large fees or rewards for places that he hath sold, he will prove that he was directed to it by Sir G. Carteret himself, among others. And yet he did not deny Sir G. Carteret his due, in saying that he is a man that doth take the most pains and gives himself the most to do business of any man about the Court, without any desire of pleasure or divertisements – which is very true. But, which pleased me mightily, he said, in these words, that he was resolved, whatever it cost him, to make an experiment and see whether it was possible for a man to keep himself up in Court by dealing plainly and walking uprightly without*b* any private game a-playing. In the doing whereof, if his ground doth slip from under him, he will be contented; but he is resolved to try and never to baulke taking notice of anything that is to the King's prejudice, let it fall where it will – which is a most brave resolution. He was very free with me; and by my troth, I do see more reall*c* worth in him then in most men that I do know.[3]

I would not forget two passages of Sir J. Mennes at yesterday's dinner. The one, that to the Question how it comes to pass that there are no boars seen in London, but many Sowes and pigs, it was answered that the Constable gets them a-nights. The other, Tho. Killegrew's way of getting to see plays when he was a boy. He would go to the Red-bull, and when the man cried to the boys, "Who will go and be a divell, and he shall see the play for

---

a MS. 'should not'   *b* MS. 'with'   *c* repl. 'him'

---

1. Cf. above, p. 107 & n. 1.
2. Carteret had been royalist Governor of Jersey, 1643–51. For some of the stories criticising his conduct there, see below, iv. 195.

3. Cf. Pepys's later admiration of Coventry (*Naval Minutes*, p. 338) and Burnet's (i. 478). Clarendon's praise (*Life*, ii. 202) is the more impressive for being written of a political enemy.

nothing?" – then would he go in and be a devil upon the stage, and so got to see [the] play.[1]

31. Lay pretty long in bed; and then up and among my workmen – the Carpenters being this day laying of my floor in my dining-room, with whom I stayed a good while; and so to my office and did a little business, and so home to dinner; and after dinner, all the afternoon with my carpenters, making them lay all my boards but one in my dining-room this day, which I am confident they would have made two good days' work of if I had not been there. And it will be very pleasant. At night to my office and there late doing of my office businesses; and so home to supper and bed.

Thus ends this month. I and my family in good health, but weary heartily of dirt; but now in hopes within two or three weeks to be out of it. My head troubled with much business, but especially my fear of Sir J. Minnes claiming my bed-chamber of me; but I hope now that it is almost over, for I perceive he is fitting his house to go into it the next week. Then my law businesses for Brampton make me mad almost, for that I want time to fallow them; but I must by no means neglect them. I thank God I do save money, though it be but a little; but I hope to find out some jobb or other that I may get a sum by to set me up.

I am now also busy in a discovery for my Lord Sandwich and Sir H. Bennett by Mr. Wade's means, of some of Baxter's money hid in one of his cellars in the tower. If we get it, it may be I may be 10 or 20*l* the better for it.

I thank God I have no crosses, but only much business to trouble my mind with. In all other things, as happy a man as any in the world, for the whole world seems to smile upon me; and if my house were done, that I could diligently fallow my business, I would not doubt to do God and the King, and myself, good service. And all I do impute almost wholly to my late

---

1. Before 1642 the Red Bull playhouse in St John's St, Clerkenwell, had catered for plebeian tastes, and one type of production especially favoured there was colloquially known as an 'infernal' – a play containing diabolical apparitions. Killigrew had evidently been recruited to assist in entertainments of this kind. (A).

temperance, since my making of my vowes against wine and plays,[1] which keeps me most happily and contentfully to my business – which God continue.

Public matters are full of discontent – what with the sale of Dunkirke – and my Lady Castlemayne and her faction at Court; though I know not what they would have, more then to debauch the King, whom God preserve from it. And then great plots are talked to be discovered, and all[a] the prisons in towne full of ordinary people taken from their meeting-places last Sunday. But for certain, some plot there hath been, though not brought to a head.[2]

a repl. 'many'

1. See above, p. 209.   2. See above, p. 236 & n. 1.

NOVEMBER.

1.   Up, and after a little while with my workmen, I went to
my office and then to our sitting all the morning.   At noon
with Mr. Creede, whom I find at my house, to the Trinity-house
to a great dinner there by invitation, and much company.   It
seem one Captain Evans[1] makes his Elder Brother's dinner today.   Among other discourses, one Mr. Oudant, Secretary to the
late Princesse of Orange,[2] did discourse of the convenience as to
keeping the highways from being deep, by their horses in Holland
(and Flanders, where the ground is as miry as ours is) going in
their carts and waggons, as ours in coaches.[3]   Wishing the same
here, as an expedient to make the ways better; and I think there
is something in it, where there is breadth enough.

Thence to my office, sent for to meet Mr. Lee again from
Sir H. Bennet; and he and I with Wade and his Intelligencer and
labourers to the Tower cellars, to make one triall more.   Where
we stayed two or three houres digging, and dug a great deal all
under the Arches, as it was now most confidently directed; and
so seriously and upon pretended good grounds, that I myself
did truly expect to speed; but we missed of all, and so we went
away the second time like fools.   And to our office; whither a
coach being come, Mr. Lee goes home to White-hall, and I by
appointment to the Dolphin taverne to meet Wade and the
other, Captain Evett – who now doth tell me plainly that he that
doth put him upon this is one that had it from Barkesteades own
mouth and was advised with by him, just before the King's
coming in, how to get it out; and had all the signs told him
how and where it lay, and had alway been the great confidant
of Barkesteades, even to the trusting him with his life and all
he had.   So that he did much convince me that there is good
ground for what we go about.   But I fear it may be that he did
find some conveyance of it away, without the help of this man,
before he died.   But he is resolved to go to the party once more,
and then to determine what we shall do further.   So we parted,

1. Thomas Ewens, naval captain.   from c. 1651. He was to become
2. Nicholas Oudart, a Fleming,   Latin Secretary to Charles II in 1666.
secretary to the Princess Dowager   3. Sc. abreast instead of in tandem.

246

and I to my office. Where after sending away my letters to the post, I do hear that Sir J. Mennes is resolved to turn part of our Entry into a room and to divide the back-yard between Sir W. Penn and him – which, though I do not see how it will annoye me much perticularly, yet it doth trouble me a little, for fear it should; but I do not see how it can well, unless in hindering my coming to my back-stairs. But for that I shall do as well as himself or Sir W. Penn, who is most concerned to look after it.

2. Lay long with pleasure, talking with my wife – in whom I never had greater content, blessed be God, then now; she continuing with the same care and thrift and innocence (so long as I keep her from occasions of being otherwise) as ever she was in her life, and keeps the house as well.

To church, where Mills (after he had read the service and shifted himself as he did the last day) preached a very ordinary sermon. So home to dinner with my wife. Then up into my new rooms, which are almost finished, and there walked with great content, talking with my wife till church-time, and*a* then to church; and there being a lazy preacher, I sleep out the sermon and so home. And after visiting the two Sir Wms, who are both of them mending apace, I to my office, preparing things against tomorrow for the Duke; and so home and to bed, with some pain in making water, having taken cold this morning in staying too long bare-legged to pare my cornes.

My wife and I spent a good deal of this evening in reading Du' Bartas's *Imposture* and other parts, which my wife of late hath taken up to read, and is very fine as anything I meet with.[1]

3. Up, and with Sir J. Mennes in his coach to White-hall to the Duke's; but find him gone out a-hunting. Thence to my

a ink smudge over word

---

1. The Huguenot poet du Bartas (d. 1590) wrote a long, moralising poem on the creation, fall and redemption of man, translated in 1641 by Joshua Sylvester as *Divine weekes and workes*: PL 2417. The passage referred to is at pp. 89–94: 'The Imposture, The Second Part of the First Day of the II Week'. It is on the 'fall of Man, by the provocation of his wife'.

Lord Sandwich, from whom every day I[a] receive more and more signs of his confidence and esteem of me. Here I met with Pierce the Chyrurgeon – who tells me that my Lady Castlemayne is with child;[1] but though it be the King's, yet her Lord being still in towne and sometime seeing of her, though never to eat or lie together, it will be laid to him. He tells me also how the Duke of Yorke is smitten in love with my Lady Chesterfield (a virtuous lady, daughter to my Lord of Ormond); and so much, that the Duchesse of Yorke hath complained to the King and her father about it, and[b] my Lady Chesterfield is gone into the country for it.[2] At all which I am sorry; but it is the effect of idlenesse and having nothing else to imploy their great spirits upon. Thence with Mr. Creede and Mr. Moore (who is got upon his legs and came to see my Lord) to Wilkinson's; and there I did give them and Mr. Howe their dinner of roast beef, cost me 5s. And after dinner carried Mr. Moore as far as Paul's in a coach, giving him direction about my law businesses; and there set him down and I home and among my workmen, who happened of all sorts to meet too, in making an end of a great many jobbes, so that after tomorrow I shall have nothing but a little plastering and all the painting almost to do, which was good content to me. At night to my office and did business; and there came to me Mr. Wade and Evett, who have been again with their prime Intelligence, a woman I perceive; and though we have missed twice, yet they bring such an account of the probability of the truth of the thing, though we are not certain of the place, that we shall set upon it once more; and I am willing and hopeful in it. So we resolved to set upon it again on Wednesday morning; and the woman herself will be there in a disguise, and confirm us in the place. So they took leave for tonight, and I to my business and then home to my wife and

a MS. 'and'   *b* repl. 'him'

---

1. The story was probably unfounded: see below, iv. 1 & n. 3. Lady Castlemaine was often the subject of such rumours: cf. below, vii. 324 & n. 2.

2. For her connection with the Duke of York, see Gramont, pp. 170+. Presumably the Countess went to her husband's house at Bretby, Derbyshire; but she seems to have been back at court in December: ib., p. 173.

to supper and bed, my pains being going away. So by God's great blessing my mind is in good condition of quiet.

4. Lay long, talking pleasantly with my wife in bed, it having rained, and doth still very much, all night long. Up and to the office, where we sat till noon. This morning we have news by letters that Sir Rd. Stayner is dead at sea in the *Mary*, which is now come in to Portsmouth from Lisbon – which we are sorry for, he being a very stout seaman – but there will be no great misse of him for all that.[1] Dined at home with my wife and all the afternoon among my workmen. And at night to my office to do business there; and then to see Sir W. Penn, who is still sick but his pain*a* less then it was. He took occasions to talk with me about Sir J. Mennes's intention to divide the entry and the yard, and so to keep him out of the yard and forcing him to go through the garden to his house – which he is vexed at; and I am glad to see that Sir J. Mennes doth use him just as he doth me, and so I perceive it is not anything extraordinary, his carriage to me in the matters of our houses, for this is worse then anything he hath done to me, that he should give order for the stopping up of his way to his house without so much as advising with him or letting of him know it. And I confess it is very highly and basely done of him. So to my office again; and after doing business there, then home to supper and to bed.

5. Up and with my painters, painting my dining-room all day long till night, not stirring out at all. Only in the morning my Lady Batten*b* did send to speak with me and told me very civilly that she did not desire, nor hoped I did, that anything should pass between us but what was civill, though there was not the neighbourliness between her and my wife that was fit to be; and so complained of my maid's mocking of her when she called "Nan" to her maid within her own house; my maid

a repl. 'paim'   *b* repl. 'Sir W. Penn'

---

1. See Lt H. Hunlocke to the Navy Board, The *Mary*, Spithead, 3 November: PRO, SP 29/62, no. 38; summary in *CSPD 1661-2*, p. 543. Stayner was the commander of the fleet which had just returned. He had died at Lisbon on 15 October, and his body had been embalmed: Allin, i. 106. He was one of the old breed of seadog who had risen to command during the revolution.

Jane in my yard overheard her and mocked her. And some other such-like things she told me, and of my wife's speaking unhandsomely of her; to all which I did give her a very respectful answer, such as did please her, and am sorry endeed that this should be, though I do not desire there should be any acquaintance between my wife and her. But I promised to avoid such words and passages for the future; so home. And by and by Sir W. Penn did send for me to his bedside and tell me how highly Sir J. Mennes did resolve to have one of my rooms, and that he was very angry and hot and said he would speak to the Duke. To which, knowing that all this was but to scare me and to get him to put off his resolution of making up the entry, I did tell him plainly how I did not value his anger more then he did mine, and that I should be willing to do what the Duke commanded and I was sure to have Justice of him; and that was all I did say to him about it, though I was much vexed and after a little stay went home. And there telling my wife, she did put me into heart; and resolve to offer him to change lodgings, and believe that that will one way or other bring us to some end in this dispute.

At night I called up my maids and schooled Jane; who did answer me so humbly and drolly about it, that though I seemed angry, I was much pleased with her, and wife also. So at night to bed.

6. At the office forenoon and afternoon till late at night, very busy answering my Lord Treasurers letter,[1] and my mind troubled till we come to some end with Sir J. Mennes about our lodgings; and so home. And after some pleasant discourse and supper – to bed – and in my dream much troubled by being with Will. Swan, a great fanatic, my old acquaintance, and methought taken and laid up with him for a plotter – all our discourse being at present about the late plots.[2]

7. Up; and being by appointment called upon by Mr. Lee, he and I to the Tower to make our third Attempt upon the cellar. And now privately the woman, Barkesteades great confidante, is brought; who doth positively say that this is the place which he did say the money was hid in, and where he and she did put up

1. See below, p. 280 & n. 1.   2. See above, p. 236 & n. 1.

the 50000*l* in butter-ferkins.   And the very day that he went out
of England[1] did say that neither he nor his would be the better
for that money, and therefore wished that she and hers might.
And so left us, and we full of hope did resolve to dig all over the
cellar; which by 7 a-clock at night we performed.   At noon
we sent for a dinner and upon the head of a barrel dined very
merrily.   And to work again.   Between times, Mr. Lee, who
hath been much in Spain, did tell many pretty stories of the
customs and other things, as I asked him, of that country, to my
great content.   But at last we saw we were mistaken; and after
digging the cellar quite through and removing the barrels from
one side to the other, we were forced to pay our porters and give
over our expectations, though I do believe there must be money
hid somewhere by him, or else he did delude this woman in
hopes to oblige her to further serving him – which I am apt to
believe.

Thence by coach to White-hall, and at my Lord's lodgings
did write a letter, he not being within, to tell him how things
went, and so away again.   Only, hearing that Mrs. Sarah is
married, I did go upstairs again and joy her and kiss her, she
owning of it.   And it seems it is to a Cooke.   I am glad she is
disposed of, for she grows old and is very painful* and one I
have reason to wish well to for her old service to me.[2]   Then to
my brother's, where my wife by my order is tonight to stay a
night or two while my house is made clean.   And thence home,
where I am angry to see, instead of the house being made in part
clean, all the pewter goods and other things are brought up to
scouring, which makes the house ten times worse; at which I was
very much displeased, but cannot help it.   So to my office to set
down my Journall; and so home and to bed.

8.   All the morning sitting at the office, and after that dined
alone at home, and so to the office again till 9 o'clock, being
loath to go home, the house is so dirty, and my wife at my
brother's.   So home and to bed.

1. Shortly after the Restoration
Barkstead had fled to Germany. (On
6 June 1660 he had been exempted
from pardon: *CJ*, viii. 57.) Cf.
above, p. 241, n. 1.

2. Before the Restoration Pepys
had had charge of Sandwich's London
household, in which Sarah had been a
servant.

9. *Lords day.* Lay alone a good while, my mind busy about pleading tomorrow to the Duke, if there shall be occasion, for this Chamber that I lie in against Sir J. Mennes. Then up; and after being ready, walked to my brother's, where my wife is – calling at many churches and then to the Temple, hearing a bit there too, and observing that in the streets and churches the Sunday is kept in appearance as well as I have known it at any time.[1] Then to dinner to my brother's, only he and my wife and I. And after dinner to see Mr. Moore, who is pretty well; and he and I to St. Gregory's, where I escaped a great fall down the stairs of the gallery. So into a pew there and heard Dr. Ball[2] make a very good sermon, though short of what I expected – as for the most part it doth fall out. So home with Mr. Moore to his chamber; and after a little talk I walk home to my house and stayed at Sir W. Batten – till late at night, with him and Sir J. Mennes – with whom we had abundance of most excellent discourse of former passages of sea-commanders and officers of the Navy. And so home and to bed – with my mind well at ease, but only as to my chamber, which I fear to lose.

10. Up betimes and to set my workmen to work, and then a little to the office; and so with Sir J. Mennes, Sir W. Batten and myself by*a* coach to White-hall to the Duke – who after he was ready did take us into his closett. Whither came my Lord Generall Monke and did privately talk with the Duke about having the life-guards pass through the City today, only for show and to fright people – for I perceive there are great fears abroad. For all which I am troubled and full of doubt that things will not go well. He being gone, we fell to business of the Navy. Among other things, how to pay off this fleet that is now come from Portugall – the King of Portugall sending them home, he having no more use for them; which we wonder at, that his

a MS. 'to'

---

1. Cf. above, p. 196, n. 3.   2. Richard Ball, Master of the
                                             Temple and Canon of Ely.

condition should be so soon altered. And our Landmen also are coming back, being almost starved in that poor country.[1]

Having done here, I went by my Lord Sandwichs, who was not at home; and so to Westminster-hall, where full of terme. And here met with many about business; among others, my Cosen Roger Pepys, who is all for a composicion with my uncle Thom – which, upon any fair terms, I am for also – and desire it.

Thence by water and so by land to my Lord Crews, and dined with him and his Brother, I know*a* not his name[2] – where very good discourse. Among others, of France's intention to make a patriarch of his own, independent from the pope; by which he will be able to cope with the Spaniard in all councils, which hitherto he hath never done.[3] My Lord Crew told us how he heard my Lord of Holland say that being Embassador about the match with the Queene-Mother that now is, the King of France insisted upon a dispensation from the pope; which my Lord Holland making a question of and that he was com-

a MS. 'known'

---

1. Troops and ships had been sent this summer, under the terms of the marriage alliance, to help Portugal in her war of independence against Spain (1641–68). Afonso VI, newly come to the throne in June, did not order them back, but made so many difficulties about port facilities and pay that the English government altered their decision to keep a squadron on winter station, and ordered Capt. Allin home. The Portuguese, emboldened by the withdrawal of two Spanish armies, hoped for a peace, and in fact got a month's truce in December. As for the 'landmen', two of their commanders (Morgan and Inchiquin) had returned home; other officers were protesting against lack of pay and of good meat, and some troops deserted. But most remained to play a big part in later campaigns. See HMC, *Heathcote*, pp. 35+; *CSPD 1662–3*, p. 543; *CSPVen. 1661–4*, pp. 122, 167, 169,

190, 195, 204. Pepys's story of the soldiers' discontent perhaps derives from Inchiquin: 'he declares' (wrote the Venetian resident on 14/24 November) 'that the English who went are nearly all dead of hunger and ... barbarous treatment ...': *CSPVen. 1661–4*, p. 214.

2. He had three brothers: Thomas (of Crawley, Hunts.), Nathaniel (of Gray's Inn), and Salathiel (of Hinton, Northants.).

3. At the end of August a quarrel over ambassadorial privileges had arisen between Louis XIV and Pope Alexander VII which was not composed until 1664: below, iv. 24 & n. 1. Both now and later, in the 1680s, rumours about the patriarchate were current, but never had much foundation in fact. See C. Gérin, *Louis XIV et le Saint-Siège*, vol. i, ch. viii, esp. pp. 372+. The councils referred to are those of the church.

manded to yield to nothing to the prejudice of our religion – says the King of France, "You need not fear that, for if the Pope will not dispense with the match, my Bishop of Paris shall."[1]

By and by came in great Mr. Swinfen, the parliament-man[2] – who, among other discourse of the rise and fall of familys, told us of Bishop Bridgeman (brother of Sir Orlando) who lately hath bought a seat anciently of the Lever and then the Ashtons; and so he hath in his great hall window (having repaired and beautified the house) hath caused four great places to be left for Coates of armes. In one he hath put the Lever's, with this motto, *Olim*. In another the Ashton's, with this, *Heri*. In the next, his own, with this, *Hodie*. In the fourth, nothing but this motto, *Cras nescio cujus*.[3]

Thence towards my brother's; met with Jacke Cole in Fleete-streete and he and I went into his Cosen Mary Coles (whom I never saw since she was married) and drank a pint of wine, and much good discourse. I find him a little conceited, but he hath good things in him and a man may know the temper of the City by him, he being of a general conversation and can tell how matters go; and upon that score, I will encourage his acquaintance.[4]

Thence to my brother's; and taking my wife up, carried her to Charing-crosse, and there showed her the Italian motion, much after the nature of what I showed her a while since in Covent garden.[5] Their puppets here are somewhat better, but their

---

1. The Earl of Holland (then Viscount Kensington) had shared with the Earl of Carlisle the conduct of these negotiations of 1624–5. Nothing in his despatches (PRO, SP 78/72) appears to confirm the statement here attributed to Louis XIII.

2. John Swynfen, M.P. for Tamworth, Staffs.; like the Crews, a critic of the court.

3. John Bridgeman (d. 1652), Bishop of Chester (father, not brother, of Sir Orlando, now L.C. Justice of Common Pleas), had in 1629 bought Great Lever Hall, near Bolton, Lancs., once owned by the Asshetons. He rebuilt the Hall and built a chapel, but the glass mentioned by Pepys no

longer survives. The mottoes are not unique: W. Camden, *Remaines* (1636), p. 125. VCH, *Lancs.*, v. 184–6.

4. Cole had been a schoolfellow of Pepys at St Paul's, and was now in business in the city.

5. Cf. above, pp. 80, 90. These puppet plays were given by an Italian, Antonio Devoto, in a wooden booth on waste ground near Whitehall, on the site now occupied by Le Sueur's statue of Charles I. By 'motion' Pepys may mean the manipulation of the puppets or possibly the plays they acted. See G. Speaight, *Hist. Engl. puppet theatre*, pp. 74–7. (A).

motions not at all.   Thence by coach to my Lord's; and hiding
my wife with Sarah below, I went up and heard some musique
with my Lord and after discoursed with him alone, and so good-
night to him.   And below, having sent for Mr. Creede, had
thought to have shown my wife a play before the King, but it
is so late that we could not; and so we took coach, and taking
up Sarah at my brother's with their night geere, we went home.
And I to my office to settle matters, and so home and to bed.

This morning in the Duke's chamber Sir J. Mennes did break
to me his desire about my chamber, which I did put off to another
time to discourse of.   He speaking to me very kindly doth
make me the less trouble myself, hoping*a* to save myself and to
contrive something or other to pleasure him as well, though I
know not well what.

The Towne I hear is full of discontents and all know of the
King's new bastard by Mrs. Haslerigg.[1]   And as far as I can
hear, will never be contented with Episcopacy; they are so
cruelly set for presbytery and the Bishops carry themselfs so high,
that they are never likely to gain anything upon them.[2]

11.   All the morning sitting at the office, and then to dinner
with my wife; and so to the office again (where a good while
Mr. Bland was with me, telling me very fine things in Mer-
chandize; which, but that the trouble of my house doth so
cruelly hinder me, I would take some pains in) till late at night.
Towards the evening, I, as I have done for three or four nights,
studying something of Arithmetique, which doth please me well
to see myself come forward.   So home to supper and to bed.

12.   At my office most of the morning, after I had done
among my painters and sent away Mr. Shaw and Hawly, who
came to give me a visit this morning.   Shaw it seems, is newly

a   repl. 'hopeful'

---

1. See above, p. 227 & n. 3.
2. At 31 December Pepys reports
the Presbyterian clergy as quiescent:
below, p. 303.   He is referring here to
lay opinion, perhaps as reported by
Jack Cole and the Crews.

remaryed to a rich widow.[1]　At noon dined at home with my
wife.　And by and by, by my wife's appointment comes two
young ladies, sisters, acquaintance of my wife's brother's, who
are desirous to wait upon some ladies – and proffer their service
to my wife.　The youngest, endeed, hath a good voice and
sings very well, besides other good Qualitys; but I fear hath
been bred up with too great liberty for my family, and I fear
great inconveniences of expenses and my wife's liberty will
fallow, which I must study to avoide till I have a better purse –
though I confess the gentlewoman being pretty handsome and
singing makes me have a good mind to her.[a][2]

Anon I took them by coach and carried them to a friend's of
theirs in Lincolnes Inne fields, and there I left them.　And I to
the Temple by appointment to my Cosen Roger Pepys's chamber,
where my Uncle Thomas and his son Tho met us, I having[b] hopes
that they would have agreed with me to have had ended by my
Cosen Roger; but they will have two strangers to be for them,
against two others of mine; and so we parted, without doing
anything till they two send me the names of their Arbitraters.

Thence I walked home, calling a little in Paul's Churchyard;
and I thank God, can read and never buy a book, though I have
a great mind to it.　So to the Dolphin taverne near home by
appointment, and there met with Wade and Evett and have
resolved to make a new attempt upon another discovery, in which
God give us better fortune then in the other.　But I have great
confidence that there is no cheat in these people, but that they
go upon good grounds, though they have been mistaken in the
place of the first.

From hence, without drinking a drop of wine, home to my
office and there made an end, though late, of my colleccion of
the prices[c] of Masts for these twelve years to this day, in order
to the buying of some of Wood.　And I bound it up in painted

a　paragraph crowded into bottom of page　　*b*　l.h. repl. s.h. 'was'
c　MS. 'prizes'

1. Robert Shaw was an old Ex-
chequer colleague; now principal
assistant to Backwell the goldsmith.
His first wife had died in August 1660.
He was now c. 31 and his new wife
(Elizabeth Leywood) c. 43.　Their
marriage licence was issued on 27
September 1662.

2. (? Winifred) Gosnell, later an
actress; she stayed only from 5 to 9
December.

paper, to lie by as a book for future use.[1] So home and to supper and bed. And a little before and after we were in bed, we had much talk and difference between us about my wife's having a woman; which I seemed much angry at that she should go so far in it without consideration and my being consulted with. So to sleep.

13. Up – and begun our discontent again and sorely angered my wife; who endeed doth live very lonely. But I do perceive that it is want of work that doth make her and all other people think of ways of spending their time worse; and this I owe to my building, that doth not admit of her undertaking anything of work, because the house hath been and is still so dirty.

I to my office and there sot all the morning, and dined with discontent with my wife at noon; and so to my office, and there this afternoon we had our first meeting upon our Comission for inspecting the chest.[2] And there met, Sir J Minnes – Sir Fr. Clerke – Mr. Heath, Atturny of the Dutchy – Mr. Prinn – Sir W. Rider – Captain Cocke, and myself. Our first work, to read over the Institucion, which is a Decree in Chancery in the yeare 1617, upon an Inquisicion made at Rochester about that time into the revenues of the Chest;[3] which had then, from the year 1588 or 1590, by the advice of the Lord High Admirall and Principal Officers then being, been by consent of the Seamen, been settled, paying 6d per month, according to their wages then, which was then but 10s which is now 24s.

We adjourned to a Fortnight hence. So broke up, and I to see Sir W. Penn, who is now pretty well but lies in bed still; he cannot rise to stand. Then to my office late. And this afternoon my wife in her discontent sent me a letter, which I am in

1. The book has not been traced. It was in Pepys's possession sometime after 1693: Rawl. D 794, f.8v. Several examples of his painted (marbled) paper binding remain: e.g. the first section of PL 2265.

2. This was the commission appointed on 20 October to examine the affairs of the Chatham Chest. Its quorum was three, and of the members here mentioned (there were 12

others), Clarke was M.P. for Rochester, John Heath Attorney-General to the Duchy of Lancaster, Prynne M.P. for Bath, Rider and Cocke merchants. Pepys himself proved the most active of them all. For their work and its failure, see *Comp.*: 'Chatham Chest'.

3. The report of 1617 was that of a similar commission appointed in 1616.

a quandary what to do, whether to read it or not; but I purpose not, but to burn it before her face, that I may put a stop to more of this nature.[1]   But I must think of some way, either to find her somebody to keep her company, or to set her to work and by imployment to take up her thoughts and time.   After doing*a* what I had to do, I went home to supper.   And there was very sullen to my wife, and so went to bed and to sleep (though with much ado, my mind being troubled) without speaking one word to her.

14.   She begun to talk in the morning and to be friends, believing all this while that I had read her letter, which I perceive by her discourse was full of good counsel and relating the reason of her desiring a Woman and how little charge she did entend it to be to me.   So I begun and argued it so full and plain to her, and she to reason it highly to me to put her away and take one of the Bowyers if I did dislike her, that I did resolve, when the house is ready, she shall try her[2] for a while.   The truth is, I having a mind to have her come for her Musique and dancing. So up and I about my painters all the morning; and her brother coming, I did tell him my mind plain, who did assure me that they were, both of the sisters, very humble and very poor, and that she that we are to have would carry herself so.   So I was well contented and spent part of the morning at my office, and so home and to dinner; and after dinner, finding Sarah to be discontented at the news of this Woman, I did begin in my wife's chamber to talk to her and tell her that it was not out of unkindness to her; but my wife came up, and I perceive she is not too reconciled to her, whatever the matter is, that I perceive I shall not be able to keep her, though*b* she is as good a servant (only a little pettish) that ever I desire to have, and a creditable servant.   So she desired leave to go out to look a service, and did; for which I am troubled and fell out highly afterward with my wife about it.   So to my office, where we met this afternoon, and I about answering a great letter of my Lord Treasurer's;[3]

a MS. 'done'   *b* repl. 'so'

---

1. See below, iv. 9.   3. See below, p. 280, p. & n. 1.
2. Gosnell: see above p. 256, n. 2.

and that done, to my office, drawing up a letter to him; and so home to supper.

15. All the morning at the office sitting. Dined with my wife pleasantly at home. Then among my painters, and by and by went to my Civill lawyers about my Uncles suit[1] and so home again and saw my painters make an end of my house this night, which is my great joy. And so to my office and did business till 10 at night; and so home and to supper. And after reading part of *Bussy D'Ambois*,[2] a good play I bought today – to bed.[a]

16. *Lords=day.* About 3 a-clock in the morning wakened with a rude noise among Sir J. Mennes his servants (he not being yet come to his lodgings), which are the rudest people but they that lived there before, one Mr. Davis's,[3] that ever I knew in my life.

To sleep again; and after long talking pleasantly with my wife, up and to church – where Mrs. Goodyer, now Mrs. Buckworth, was churched.[4] I love that woman for her gravity, above any in the parish. So home and to dinner with my wife – with great content; and after dinner walked up and down my house, which is now almost finished, there being nothing to do but the glazier – and furniture to put up. By and by comes Tom; and after a little talk, I with him towards his end; but seeing many strangers and coaches coming to our church and finding that it was a sermon to be preached by a probacioner for the Turky Company, to be sent to Smyrna, I returned thither.

a entry crowded into bottom of page

---

1. The dispute about the will of Robert Pepys of Brampton would be settled by civil (i.e. ecclesiastical) lawyers in a church court, which had jurisdiction in testamentary matters. The case was in fact settled out of court: below, iv. 42–3.

2. A tragedy by Chapman; see above, ii. 241 & n. 1. PL 1075 (1641 ed.). (A).

3. John Davis, clerk in the Navy Office. For his wife's and servants' high-handedness, see above, i. 277, 278.

4. Hester Goodyear, widow, had married John Buckworth, widower, merchant, at the beginning of the year. Their son John had been baptised at St Olave's on 28 October.

And several Turky Merchants filled all the best pews (and some in ours) in the church.   But a most pitiful sermon it was, upon a text in *Zacharyah*; and a great time he spent to show whose son Zachary was and to prove Malachi to be the last Prophet before John the Baptist.

Home and to see Sir W. Pen, who gets strength but still keeps his bed; and then home and to my office to do some business there, and so home to supper – and to bed.

17.   To the Duke's today, but he is gone a-hunting.   And therefore I to my Lord Sandwichs; and having spoke a little with him about his*ᵃ* business, I to Westminster-hall and there stayed long doing many businesses; and so home by the Temple and other places, doing the like.   And at home I find my wife dressing by appointment, by her woman that I think is to be. And her other sister being here today with her and my wife's brother, I took Mr. Creede, that came to dine with me, to an ordinary behind the Change, and there dined together.   And after dinner home and there spent an hour or two till almost dark, talking with my wife and making Mrs. Gosnell sing; and then, there being no coach to be got, by water to White-hall. But Gosnell not being willing to go through bridge, we were forced to land and take water again, and put her and her sister ashore at the Temple.   I am mightily pleased with her humour and singing.   At White-hall, by appointment Mr. Creede carried my wife and I to the Cockepitt,[1] and we had excellent places and saw the King, Queene, Duke of Monmouth his son,[2] and my Lady Castlemayne and all the fine ladies; and *The Scornfull Lady*,[3] well performed.   They had done by 11 a-clock; and it being fine Mooneshine, we took coach and home.   But could wake nobody at my house, and so were fain to have my boy get

a MS. 'is'

---

1. The royal private theatre adjoined Whitehall Palace. (A).

2. James Crofts, or Sir James Scott as he was now, was not created Duke of Monmouth until the following February, but after the warrant was issued on 10 November (*CSPD*

1661-2, p. 552) he seems to have been known by the title: cf. below, p. 297; HMC, *Rep.*, 12/7/29-30.

3. A comedy by Beaumont and Fletcher: see above, i. 303 & n. 3. (A).

through one of the windows and so opened the door – and called up the maids and went to supper and to bed – my mind being troubled at what my wife tells me, that her woman will not come till she hears from her mother. For I am so fond of her that I am loath now not to have her, though I know it will be a great charge to me, which I ought to avoid; and so I will make it up in other things. So to bed.

18. Up and to the office, where we sot and Mr. Phillips the Lawyer came to me, but I put him off to the afternoon, At noon I dined at*ᵃ* Sir W. Batten's – Sir J. Mennes being here; and he and I very kind, but I every day expect to pull a crow with him about our lodgings. My mind troubled about Gosnell and my law businesses. So after dinner to Mr. Phillips his chamber, where he demands an abatement for Piggott's money; which vexes me also, but I will not give it without my father's consent, which I will write to him tonight about; and have done it. Here meeting my uncle Tho:, he and I to my Cosen Roger's chamber, and there I did give my Uncle him and Mr. Philips to be my two arbiters against Mr. Cole and Punt. But I expect no great good of the matter.

Thence walked home; and my wife came home, having been abroad today, laying out above 12*l* in linen and a Copper and a pot and bedstead and other household stuff, which troubles me also, so that my mind tonight is very heavy and divided.

Late at my office, drawing up a letter to my Lord Treasurer which we have been long about; and so home and, my [mind] troubled, to bed.

19. At home all the morning, putting some of my goods in order in my house; and after dinner, the like in the afternoon. And in the evening to my office, and there till 11 a-clock at night upon my Lord Treasurer's letter again, and so home to bed.

20. All the morning sitting at the office. At noon with Mr. Coventry to the Temple to advise about Fie[l]ds [business]; but our lawyers not being in the way, we went to St. James's and there at his chamber dined, and I am still in love more and more with him for his real worth. I broke to him my desire for my wife's brother, to send him to sea as a Midshipman, which he is

a repl. 'in'

willing to agree to – and will do it when I desire it. After dinner to the Temple to Mr. Thurland; and thence to my Lord Chief Baron, Sir Edwd. Hales,[1] and back with Mr. Thurland to his chamber; where he told us that Field will have the better of us and that we must study to make up the business as well as we can, which doth much vex and trouble us; but I am glad the Duke is concerned in it.[2]   Thence by coach homeward, calling at a taverne in the way (being guided by the messenger in whose custody Field lies) and spoke with Mr. Smith our messenger about the business; and so home, where I find my wife hath furnished very neatly my study with the former hangings of the dining-[room]; which will upon occasion serve for a fine withdrawing room.   So a little to my office; and so home and spent the evening upon my house, and so to supper and to bed.[a]

21.   Within all day long, helping to put up my hangings in my house in my wife's chamber, to my great content.   In the afternoon I went to speak to Sir J. Mennes at his lodgings, where I find many great ladies and his lodgings made very fine endeed.

At night to supper and to bed – this night having first put up a spitting-sheet, which I find very convenient. ⟨This day came the King's pleasure-boats from Calis with the Dunkirke money, being 400000 *pistolls*.⟩[3]

    a   entry crowded into bottom of page
    b   addition crowded in between entries

---

1. *Recte* Sir Matthew Hale, Chief Baron of the Exchequer. Sir Edward Hales, Bt, of Tunstall, Kent, was a colleague of Pepys on the commission just appointed to enquire into the affairs of the Chatham Chest. Hence perhaps the confusion.

2. For this case, see above, p. 23 & n. 2. After his victory in obtaining damages against Pepys, Field was now arrested by order of the Duke of York on the original charge of slander (PRO, Adm. 2/1733, f.6r), but the office made preparations to come to terms with him out of court in his action against the whole Board: below, p. 280 & n. 3.

3. Paid by France in exchange for Dunkirk; transported from Calais to Tower Wharf in 'three stout and stately pleasure boats, *viz*. His Majesties, the Duke of Yorcks and the Duke of Albamarles': Mundy, v. 149. The total payable was 5 m. livres (c. £800,000): 2 m. at once, and the rest in quarterly instalments over three years.   Pepys is mistaken about the figures: the immediate down-payment amounted to c. 250,000 pistoles. CTB, i. 457–9; CSPD 1661–2, p. 523; Lister, iii. 511–12; *Journ. Mod. Hist.*, 1/178–9; A. E. Feavearyear, *Pound Sterling*, p. 96.

22. *Saturday.* This morning, from some difference between my wife and Sarah her maid, my wife and I fell out cruelly, to my great discontent. But I do see her set so against the wench, which I take to be a most extraordinary good servant, that I was forced for the wench's sake to bid her get her another place – which shall cost some trouble to my wife, however, before I suffer to be.

Then to the office, where I sat all the morning. Then dined, Mr. Moore with me, at home – my wife busy putting her furniture in order. Then he and I out, and he home and I to my Cosen Roger Pepys to advise about treating with my uncle Tho.; and thence called at the Wardrobe on Mr. Moore again, and so home; and after doing much business at my office, I*ᵃ* went home and caused a new-fashion knocker to be put on my door and did other things to the putting my house in order – and getting my outward-door painted, and the arch.

This day I bought the book of country-dances¹ against my wife's woman Gosnell comes, who dances finely. And there meeting Mr. Playford, he did give me his Latin Songs of Mr. Deerings,² which he lately printed.

This day Mr. Moore told me that for certain the Queene Mother is married to my Lord St. Albans, and he is ⟨like⟩ to be made Lord Treasurer.³

News that Sir J. Lawson hath made up a peace now with Tunis and Tripoli as well as Argiers; by which he will come home very highly honoured.⁴

a repl. 'and put'

1. Probably Playford's *Dancing Master* (1657; possibly the 1652 ed.) or his *Engl. dancing master* (1651). (E).

2. Richard Dering, *Cantica Sacra* (1662); PL 1972–5. (E).

3. Both rumours were untrue: cf. above. p. 227 & n. 4; below, p. 303, n. 3. St Albans was a close friend of Henrietta-Maria and managed her finances. The rumour about their marriage was widespread: cf. e.g. Reresby, *Memoirs* (ed. Browning), p. 29.

4. This treaty (of 5 October 1662)

differed slightly from that with the Algerines (q.v. above, p. 89 & n. 1). For its terms and its negotiation (much protracted by the pirates' keenness to do eachother in the eye), see *CSPVen. 1661–4*, pp. 162–3, 166, 186–7, 203, 219, 220–1. There is a copy of the Tunis treaty in the Pepys papers in Rawl. A 185, ff. 362–3; the original is in Longleat, Coventry MSS 73, ff. 9–11. It is printed in *Hist. memoirs of Barbary . . .* (1816), pp. 111+. For the growth of Lawson's repute (and Sandwich's jealousy of it), see above, p. 122 & n. 2.

23. *Lords=day.* Up, after some talk with my wife soberly upon yesterday's difference; and made good friends and to church to hear Mr. Mills; and so home and Mr. Moore and my brother Tom dined with me. My wife not being well to-day, did not rise. In the afternoon to church again and hear drowsy Mr. Graves; and so to see Sir Wm. Pen, who continues ill in bed but grows better and better every day. Thence to Sir W. Batten and there stayed awhile, and heard how Sir R. Ford's daughter is married to a fellow without friends'* consent,[1] and the match carried on and made up at Will Griffins our doorkeeper's. So to my office and did a little business, and so home and to bed.

I talked to my brother today, who desires me to give him leave to look after his mistress still, and*a* he will not have me put to any trouble or obligacion in it; which I did give him leave to do.

I hear today how old rich Audley is lately dead, and left a very great estate and made a great many poor families rich, not all to one. Among others, one Davis, my old school-fellow at Pauls and since a bookseller in Paul's churchyard. And it seems doth forgive one man 60000*l* which he had wronged him of, but names not his name; but it is well known to be the scrivener in Fleetestreete at whose house he lodged.[2] There is also this week dead a poulterer[3] in Gracious-street, which was thought rich

a repl. 'so'

1. This is probably the match between Rebecca Ford and John Oviat, merchant, of St Olave's: they were not married in the parish church. Parents' consent was not required by law until the Marriage Act of 1753. Oviat was a beneficiary under his mother-in-law's will of 1681, so that any estrangement which may have occurred was temporary.

2. Hugh Audley (scrivener, usurer and the last of the Clerks of the Court of Wards) had died on 15 November 'infinitely rich': Richard Smyth, *Obituary*, p. 56. He was said to have been worth £400,000 at his death: see *The way to be rich, according to the*

practice of the great Audley (1662). Pepys's schoolfellow was Thomas Davies, a grandson of Audley's sister, Elizabeth Peacock, and heir to the residuary estate, together with his younger brother Alexander Davies, through whom it later descended to the Grosvenor family. C. T. Gatty, *Mary Davies and manor of Ebury*, i. 156+. The scrivener of Fleet St was John Ray (Rea), with whom Audley had lodged near Temple Bar since c. 1654 and against whom he had brought an action in Chancery in 1661–2: Gatty, i. 112+.

3. Unidentified.

but not so rich – that hath left 800*l* per annum taken in other men's names, and 40000 Jacobs – in gold.

24. Sir J. Mennes, Sir W. Batten and I going forth toward White-hall, we hear that the King and the Duke are come this morning to the Tower to see the Dunkirke money.[1] So we by coach to them and there went up and down all the Magazins with them. But methought it was but poor discourse and frothy that the King's companions (young Killigrew among the rest, about the codpieces on some of the men in armer there to be seen) had with him. We saw none of the money; but Mr. Slingsby did show the King and I did see the stamps of the new money that is now to be made by Blondeau's fashion, which are very neat and like the King.[2] Thence the King to Wool-wich, though a very cold day; and the Duke to White-hall, commanding us to come after him, which we did by coach; and in his closet, my Lord Sandwich being there, did discourse with us about getting some of this money to pay off the Fleets and other matters.[3] And then away thence; and I, it being almost dinner-time, to my Lord Crew's and dined with him, and had very good discourse and he seemed to be much pleased with my visitts. Thence to Mr. Phillips and so to the Temple, where met my Cosen Roger Pepys and his brother Dr. John, as my Arbitrators against Mr. Cole and Mr. John Bernard for my Uncle Thomas, and we two with them by appointment. They begun very high in their demands, and my friends, partly being not so well acquainted with the Will, and partly I doubt not being so good wits as they, for which I blame my choosing of

1. Cf. above, p. 262, n. 3. Some of the money was now kept for safety at the Receipt of the Mint; the rest was pledged to goldsmiths: *CTB*, i. 459; A. E. Feavearyear, *Pound Sterling*, pp. 96–7.
2. For the new coinage of 1662–3, made by the mint engineer Pierre Blondeau, see below, iv. 70, 144–8; R. Ruding, *Annals of coinage* (1840), ii. 7+; Sir John Craig, *Mint*, pp. 158–9. The work of making the coins began on 6 February 1663.

They were a great improvement on the immediately preceding issue: see above, ii. 39 & n. 1. Henry Slingsby was Master of the Mint.
3. On 13 December the King ordered £20,000 of the Dunkirk money to be used to secure a navy debt raised by Carteret on his own credit, and £30,000 to secure a further loan to the navy from Alder-men Vyner, Meynell and Backwell: *CTB*, i. 459.

relations (who besides that, are equally engaged to stand for him as me), I was much troubled thereat; and taking occasion to deny, without my father's consent, to bind myself in a bond of 2000*l* to stand to their award, I broke off the business for the present, till I hear and consider further. And so thence by coach (my Cosen Tho. Pepys[1] being in another chamber by all the while, going along with me) homeward, and I set him down by the way. But Lord, how he did endeavour to find out a ninepence[2] to club with me for the coach, and for want was forced to give me a shilling. And how he still cries "gad" and talks of popery coming in, as all the fanatiques do – of which I was ashamed. So home, finding my poor wife very busy putting things in order; and so to bed, my mind being very much troubled, and could hardly sleep all night, thinking how things are like to go with us about Brampton and blaming myself for living so high as I do, when for ought I know my father and mother may come to live upon my hands when all is done.

25. Up and to the office all the morning; and at noon with the rest, by Mr. Foly the Ironmongers[3] invitation, to the Dolphin to a venison pasty, very good and rare at this time of the year. And thence by coach with Mr. Coventry as far as the Temple; and thence to Greatorex's, where I stayed and talked with him and got him to mend my pocket-ruler for me; and so by coach to my Lord's lodgings, where I sat with Mr. Moore by appointment, making up accounts for my Lord Sandwich; which done, he and I and Captain Ferrers and W. Howe very merry a good while in the great dining-room; and so, it being late and my Lord not coming in, I by coach to the Temple and thence walked home; and so to my study to do some business, and then home and to bed.

Great talk among people how some of the fanatiques do[a]

a MS. 'to'

---

1. Tom the turner, son of Pepys's contestant in the arbitration.

2. Some ninepences were current at this time (Irish shillings of James I), but they were rare.

3. Robert Foley, ironmonger to the navy.

say that the end of the world is at hand and that next Tuesday is to be the day[1] – against which, whenever it shall be, good God fit us all.

26. In the morning to the Temple to my cousin Roger, who now desires that I would excuse him from arbitrating, he not being able to stand for me as he would do without appearing too high against my uncle Tho., which will raise his clamour. With this I am very well pleased, for I did desire it, and so I shall choose other counsel.

Thence home, he being busy, that I could not speak more with him; and all day long, till 12 a-clock at night, getting my house in order. My wife putting up the red hangings and bed in her woman's chamber, and I my books and all other matters in my chamber and study, which is now very pretty. So to bed.

27. At my waking, I find the tops of the houses covered with snow, which is a rare sight, that I have not seen these three years.

Up, and put my people to perfect the cleaning of my house, and so to the office – where we sat all the morning till noon; and then we all went to the next house upon Tower hill to see the coming by of the Russia Embassador[2] – for whose reception all the City trained=bands do attend in the streets, and the King's

---

1. This story has not been traced elsewhere.

2. Three envoys had been sent by the Tsar Alexis: *Kingd. Intell.*, 5 January 1663. Evelyn (27 November) wrote that the King had ordered them to be received 'with much state, the *Emperor* his Master having not onely ben kind to his Majestie in his distresse, but banishing all Commerce with our Nation during the Rebellion'. Both Evelyn and Mundy (v. 150) give eye-witness accounts of the procession; cf. also *CSPVen. 1661–4*, p. 219. The envoys were accommodated at York House, Strand, which had been furnished for them by the Wardrobe at a cost of £850:

PRO, PRO 30/24, bdle 4, no. 118. For the story of the embassy, see Inna Lubimenko, *Relations commerciales . . . de l'Angleterre avec la Russie avant Pierre le grand*, pp. 236+. This embassy created wonder among Londoners. Sir E. Harley, writing to his wife, adds his own contribution to the stories going around, by assuring her that the 'ambassador's bill of fare is daily four oxen and three partrides': HMC, *Portland*, iii. 270. Diplomatic and trading relations with Russia had since about 1620 become very spasmodic: see Lubimenko, op. cit.; and M. S. Anderson, *Britain's discovery of Russia, 1553–1815*, ch. ii.

Life-guard, and most of the wealthy citizens in their black velvet
coats and gold chains (which remain of their gallantry at the
King's coming in); but they stayed so long that we went down
again home to dinner.   And after I had dined, I heard that they
were coming, and so I walked to the Conduict in the *quarrefour* at
the end of gracious-street and cornhill; and there (the spouts
thereof running, very near me, upon all the people that were
under it) I saw them pretty well go by.   I could not see the
Embassador in his coach – but his attendants in their habitts and
fur-caps very handsome comely men, and most of them with
Hawkes upon their fists to present to the King.   But Lord, to see
the absurd nature of Englishmen, that cannot forbear laughing and
jeering at everything that looks strange.

So back and to the office; and there we met and sat till
7 a-clock, making a bargain with Mr. Wood for his Masts of
New=England.[1]   And then in Mr. Coventry's coach to the
Temple; but my Cosen Roger Pepys not being at leisure to
speak to me about my business, I presently walked home and
to my office till very late, doing business; and so home – where
I find my house more and more clean and in order; and hope in
a day or two now to be in very good condition there and to
my full content – which God grant.   So to supper and to bed.

28.   A very hard frost – which is news to us after having none
almost these three years.   Up and to Ironmongers hall by
10 a-clock to the funerall of Sir Richd. Stayner.[2]   Here we were,
all the officers of the Navy* and my Lord Sandwich, who did
discourse with us about the Fishery, telling us of his Majestys
resolucion to give 200*l* to every man that will set out a Busse[3]

1. New England supplies had first
been regularly tapped in the 1650s,
and by now the Navy Board obtained
most of its larger masts from there.
They were usually 27 ins. or more in
diameter: see Pepys's notes in Rawl.
A 174, ff. 19+.

2. See above, p. 249 & n. 1. He
was buried at Greenwich. Ironmongers' Hall was much used at
this time for important funerals and
funeral banquets. (R).

3. In September 1662 a scheme –
similar to those of 1580, 1615 and
1661 – for building herring busses
had been inaugurated by the Council
of Royal Fishery, the King himself undertaking to provide ten.
The council had been established in
August 1661: Pepys became a member of the corporation appointed to
succeed it in 1664. Cf. above, ii.
198 & n. 4.

and advising about the effects of this encouragement, which will
be a very great matter certainly. Here we had good rings,[1]
and by and by were to take coach; and I being got in with Mr.
Creede into a four-horse coach, which they came and told us
were only for the mourners, I went out and so took this occasion
to go home – where I stayed all day, expecting Gosnells coming,
but there came an excuse from her that she had not heard yet
from her mother but that she will come next week. Which I
wish she may, since I must keep one that I may have some
pleasure therein.

So to my office till late, writing out a copy of my uncle's Will.[2]
And so home – and to bed.

29. Before I went to the office, my wife's brother did come
to us and we did instruct him to go to Gosnell and to see what
the true matter is of her not coming, and whether she doth
entend to come or no. And so I to the office; and this morning
came Sir G. Carteret to us (being the first time we have seen him
since his coming from France); he tells us that the silver which he
received for Dunkirke did weigh 120000 weight.[3]

Here all the morning upon business; and at noon (not going
home to dinner, though word was brought me that Will Joyce
was there, whom I have not seen at my house nor anywhere
else these three or four months) with Mr. Coventry by his coach
as far as Fleetestreete, and there stepped into Madam Turner's,
where I was told I should find my Cosen Roger Pepys; and with
him to the Temple, but not having time to do anything, I went
toward my Lord Sandwichs (in my way went into Captain
Cuttance's coach, and with him to my Lord's); but the company
not being ready, I did slip down to Wilkinsons and, having not
eat anything today, did eat a mutton-pie and drank; and so to
my Lord's – where my Lord and Mr. Coventry – Sir Wm.
Darcy – one Mr. Parham (a very knowing and well-spoken
man in this business), with several others, did meet about stating

1. For funeral rings, see above, ii.
74, n. 2.
2. Cf. above, ii. 133, n. 1; this
copy has not been traced.
3. Carteret had been commissioned
to receive the Dunkirk money (paid in
silver *écus*) on the King's behalf in
France: *CSPD 1661–2*, pp. 545, 561;
A. E. Feavearyear, *Pound Sterling*, p.
96. A thousand-weight was 1000
lbs.

the business of the Fishery[1] and the manner of the King's giving
of this 200*l* to every man that shall set out a new-made English
Busse by the middle of June next. In which business we had
many fine pretty discourses and I did here see the great pleasure
to be had in discoursing of public matters with men that are
perticularly acquainted with this or that business. Having come
to some issue, wherein a motion of mine was well received,
about sending these*a* invitacions from the King to all the Fishing
ports in general, with limiting so many Busses to this and that
port, before we know the readiness of subscribers – we parted,
and I walked home all the way; and having writ a letter full of
business to my father (in my way calling upon my Cosen Turner
and Mr. Calthrop at the Temple for their consent to be my
arbitrators, which they are willing to), my wife and I to bed,
pretty pleasant for that her brother brings word that Gosnell
(which my wife and I in discourse do*b* pleasantly call our *Marmotte*) will certainly come next week, without fail – which
God grant may be for the best.

30. *Lords day*. To church in the morning, and Mr. Mills
made a pretty good sermon. It is a bitter cold frost today.
Dined alone with my wife today with good content, my house
being quite clean from Top to bottom.[2] In the afternoon, I to
the French church here in the City,[3] and stood in the Isle all the
sermon – with great delight hearing a very admirable sermon
from a very young man,[4] upon the Article in our creed (in order
of Catechisme) upon the Resurreccion. Thence home and to visit
Sir W. Pen, who continues still bed-rid. Here was Sir W. Batten
and his Lady and Mrs. Turner; and I very merry, talking of the
confidence of Sir Rd. Ford's new-married daughter; though she

---

a repl. 'this'   *b* MS. 'to'

---

1. Of the persons mentioned, only
Sandwich was a member of the Royal
Fishery Council. Richard Parham
was a freeman of the Fishmongers'
Company; Darcy a courtier with
Northumbrian interests.

2. Builders' work had begun (with
the untiling of his roof) on 14 July.

Cf. above, p. 59 & n. 2.

3. The Huguenot church in
Threadneedle St. Pepys was fond
of practising his French by attending
these services.

4. ? David Primerose, minister
until 1713.

married so strangely lately, yet appears at church as briscke as can be and takes place of her elder sister, a maid.[1]

Thence home and to supper; and then, cold as it is, to my office to make up my monthly account; and I do find that through the fitting of my house this month, I have spent in that and Kitchin 50*l* this month. So that now I am worth but 660*l* or thereabouts. This being done and fitted myself for the Duke tomorrow, I went home and to prayers and to bed. ⟨This day I first did wear a muffe, being my wife's last year's muff; and now I have bought her a new one, this serves me very well.⟩

———

Thus ends this month, in great frost.

Myself and family all well, but my mind much disordered about my Uncles law-business, being now in an order of being arbitrated between us, which I wish to God it were done.

I am also somewhat uncertain what to think of my going about to take a woman-servant[a] into my house in the Quality of a Woman for my wife. My wife promises it shall cost me nothing but her meat and wages, and that it shall not be attended with any other expenses; upon which termes I admit of it, for that it will I hope save me money in having my wife go abroad on visitts and other delights. So that I hope the best, but am resolved to alter it if matters prove otherwise then I would have them.

Public matters in an ill condition of discontent against the heighth and vanity of the Court and their bad payments; but that which troubles most is the Clergy, which will never content the City, which is not to be reconciled to Bishopps; the more the pity that differences must still be.

Dunkirke newly sold and the money brought over – of which we hope to get some to pay the Navy – which, by Sir J. Lawson's having dispatched the business in the Straights by making peace with Argier, Tunis and Tripoly, and so his fleet will also shortly come home, will now every day grow less, and so the King's charge be abated – which God send.

a s.h. repl. l.h. 'woman'

———

1. For Rebecca Ford's marriage,   sister (Mary) married in 1664.
see above, p. 264 & n. 1. Her elder

DECEMBER.

1. Up and by coach with Sir J. Mennes and Sir W. Batten to White-hall to the Duke's chamber; where, as is usual, my Lord Sandwich and all us, after his being ready, to his closet and there discoursed of matters of the Navy. And here Mr. Coventry did do me the great kindness to take notice to the Duke of my pains in making a collection of all Contracts about Masts,[1] which hath been of good use to us. Thence I to my Lord Sandwiches to Mr. Moore to talk a little about business; and then over the parke (where I first in my life, it being a great frost, did see people sliding with their Sckeates,[2] which is a very pretty art) to Mr. Coventry's chamber to St. James's, where we all met to a venison pasty; and were here very merry, Major Norwood being with us, whom they did play upon for his surrendring of Dunkirke.[3]

Here we stayed till 3 or 4 a-clock, and so to the Council chamber, where there met – the Duke of Yorke, Prince Robert, Duke of Albermarle, my Lord Sandwich, Sir Wm. Compton, Mr. Coventry, Sir J. Minnes, Sir R. Ford, Sir W. Rider, my selfe, and Captain Cuttance, as Commissioners for Tanger. And after our Comission was read by Mr. Creede, who I perceive is to be our Secretary, we did fall to discourse of matters. As first, the supplying of them forthwith with victualls; then the Reducing it to make way for the money which upon their reduction is to go to the building of the molde.[4] And so to other matters ordered against next meeting.

This done, we*a* broke up and I to the Cockepitt, with much

a 'we' transcribed in an unidentified hand over s.h.

---

1. See above, p. 257 & n. 1.
2. Evelyn on this day saw skaters performing before the King and Queen on the new canal in St James's Park. Iron and steel skates (together with the word itself) were introduced at this time from Holland.

3. Henry Norwood had been Lieutenant-Governor; after the sale of Dunkirk he served in Tangier from 1663, becoming Lieutenant-Governor there in 1666.
4. See *Comp.*: 'Tangier; the Mole.'

crouding and waiting, where*a* I saw *The Valiant Cidd* acted – a play I have read with great delight, but is a most dull thing acted (which I never understood before), there being no pleasure in it, though done by Baterton and my Ianthe and another fine wench that is come in the room of Roxalana.[1] Nor did the King or Queene once smile all the whole play, nor any of the company seem to take any pleasure but what was in the greatness and gallantry of the company.

Thence to my Lord's; and Mr. Moore being in bed, I stayed not, but with a link walked home and got thither by 12 a-clock. Knocked up my boy*b* and put myself to bed.

2. Before I went to the office, my wife and I had another falling-out about Sarah, against whom she hath a deadly hate, I know not for what, nor can I see but she is a very good servant. Then to my office and there sat all the morning; and then to dinner with my wife at home, and after dinner did give Jane a very serious lesson against we take her to be our chamber-mayde; which I spoke so to her that the poor girl cried and did promise to be very dutiful and careful.[2] So I to the office, where we sat as Comissioners for the Chest,[3] and so examined most of the old accomptants to the Chest about it; and so we broke up and I to my office till late, preparing business; and so home, being cold. And this night first put on a wastecoate.* So to bed.

3. Called up by Comissioner Pett, and with him (by water much against my will) to Deptford; and after drinking

a 'where' transcribed in an unidentified hand over s.h.
b l.h. repl. s.h. 'people'

---

1. The play was an English version of Corneille's tragedy *Le Cid* (1637); probably Joseph Rutter's verse translation with alterations, published in 1637 and 1650. Thomas Betterton was the leading actor in the Duke of York's Company, which had evidently been engaged for this private performance at the Cockpit, Whitehall. Mrs Saunderson, here called 'Ianthe' after her part in *The siege of Rhodes*, became Mrs Betterton on the 24th of this month. The actress who replaced Mrs Hester Davenport as Roxalana in *The siege of Rhodes* was Mrs Norton: below, vii. 190–1 & n. (A).

2. Jane Birch was about to be promoted from cookmaid to chamber-maid in Sarah's place.

3. Cf. above, p. 257, n. 2.

a warm morning draught, with Mr. Wood and our officers measuring all the morning his New=England Masts, with which sight I was much pleased for my information, though I perceive great neglect and indifference in all the King's officers in what they do for the King.

That done, to the globe and there dined with Mr. Woode; and so by water with Mr. Pett home again, all the way reading his Chest accompts, in which I did see things did not please me; as, his allowing himself 300*l* for one year's looking to the business of the Chest and 150*l* per annum for the rest of the years. But I found no fault to him himself, but shall when they come to be read at the board.

We did also call at Lymehouse to view two Busses that are building – that being a thing we are now very hot upon. Our call was to see what dimensions they are of,*a* being 50 foot by the Keele and about 60 tonns.

Home and did a little business; and so, taking Mr. Pett by the way, we walked to the Temple, in our way seeing one of the Russia Embassadors coaches go along, with his footmen not in liverys but their country habits; one of one colour and another of another, which was very strange.

At the Temple spoke with Mr. Turner and Calthrop and so walked home again, being in some pain through the cold that I have got today by water, which troubles me.

At my office doing business a good while; and so home and had a posset, and so to bed.

4. At the office all the morning, setting about business; and after dinner to it again and so till night; and then home, looking over my Brampton papers against tomorrow, that we are to meet with our counsel on both sides toward an Arbitracion – upon which I was very late; and so to bed.

5. Up, it being a snow and hard frost. And being up, I did call up Sarah, who doth go away today or tomorrow. I paid her her wages and gave her 10s myself and my wife 5s to give her. For my part, I think never servant and mistress parted upon such foolish terms in the world as they do, only for an opinion in my wife that she is ill-natured, in all other things being a good servant. The wench cried, and I was ready to cry

a   repl. 'on'

too. But to keep peace, I am content she should go, and the rather, though I say nothing of that, that Jane may come into her place.

This being done, I walked toward Guild-hall,*a* thither being summond by the Comissioners for the Lieutenancy;[1] but they sat not this morning. So meeting in my way W. Swan, I took him to a house thereabout and gave him a morning draught of butterd ale – he telling me still much of his fanatiques stories, as if he were a great zealot, when I know him to be a very rogue. But I do it for discourse and to see how things stand with him and his party; who I perceive have great expectation that God will not bless the Court nor Church as it is now settled, but they must be purifyed. The worst news he tells me is that Mr. Chetwind is dead, my old and most ingenious acquaintance. He is dead worth 3000*l*; which I did not expect, he living so high as he did alway, and neatly. He hath given W. Symons his wife 300*l*[b] and made Will one of his executors.[2]

Thence to the Temple to my counsel and thence to Grays Inne to meet with Mr. Cole, but could not; and so took a turn or two in the garden, being very pleasant with the snow and frost. Thence to my brother's; and there I eat something at dinner and transcribed a copy or two of the state of my Uncles estate which I prepared last night;[3] and so to the Temple church

a symbol represents 'Yeld-hall' *b* repl. figure rendered illegible

1. A militia act (14 Car. II c. 3) had just been passed, and under it a commission of lieutenancy was appointed to act for London. Pepys, with a salary less than £500 p.a., was liable to be charged with providing a footsoldier and his arms.

2. James Chetwind and Will Symons were members of Pepys's 'old crew' of government clerks – the former in the Exchequer, the latter in the Council Office. Chetwind had died a bachelor, and in his will (13 November 1662; proved 13 January 1663) left c. £2000 in the hands of bankers, as well as other property. Symons's daughter was a beneficiary (£200) as well as his wife.

3. Two copies in Pepys's hand (the first entitled 'Mr Robert Pepys his Estate at the Time of his Death. July. 5. 1661.') are in PL (unoff.), Freshfield MSS, nos 8 and 9; both endorsed but neither dated. For details, see *Comp.*: 'Pepys, Robert'. Cf. Thomas Pepys the turner to John Pepys (father of Samuel), 17 February 1663: 'My father and all of us ar sorie for the assertion that my cos samuell hath given us of the smalness of that estate which by most knowing persons was said and belived to be aboundantly Larger than it doth prove it self and of that troble which it hath occationed . . .': Freshfield MSS, no. 5.

and there walked alone till 4 or 5 a-clock; and then to my Cosen Turner's Chamber and stayed there, up and down from his to Calthrops and Bernards chambers, till so late, that Mr. Cole not coming, we broke up for meeting this night; and so, taking my uncle Thomas homeward with me by coach, talking of our desire to have a peace, I set him down at Gracious-street end; and so I home and there I find Gosnell come, who my wife tells me is like to prove a pretty companion, of which I am glad.[1] So to my office for a little business and then home – my mind having been all this day in most extraordinary trouble and care for my father, there being so great appearance of*a* my uncles going away with the greatest part of the estate. But in the evening, by Gosnells coming, I do put off these thoughts to entertain myself a little with my wife and her – who sings exceeding well, and I shall take great delight in her. And so merrily to bed.

6. Up, and to the office and there sat all the morning, Mr. Coventry and I alone, the rest being paying off of ships. Dined at home with my wife and Gosnell, my mind much pleased with her; and after dinner sat with them a good while, till my wife seemed to take notice of my being at home now more then at other times; I went to the office and there I sat till late, doing of business, and at 9 a-clock walked to Mr. Rawlinsons, thinking to meet my uncle Wight there; where he was, but a great deal of his wife's kindred-women and I knew not whom (which Mrs. Rawlinson did seem to me to take much notice of his being led by the nose by his wife); I went away to my office again. And doing my business there, I went home. And after a song by Gosnell, we to bed.

7. *Lords day.* A great snow; and so to church this morning with my wife (which is the first time she hath been at church since her going to Brampton) and Gosnell attending her – which was very gracefull. So home, and we dined above in our dining-room, the first time since it was new done. And in the afternoon I thought to go to the French church; but finding the

a MS. 'he'

1. See above, p. 256 & n. 2.

Duch congregation there and then finding the French congregation's sermon begun in the Dutch,[1] I returned home and up to
our gallery, where I found my wife and Gosnell; and after a
drowzy sermon, we all three to my aunt Wights, where great
store of her usuall company; and here we stayed a pretty while
talking – I differing from my aunt, as I commonly do, in our
opinion of the handsomeness of the Queene;[2] which I oppose
mightily (saying that if my nose be handsome, then is hers, and
such like); after much discourse, seeing the room full and being
unwilling to stay all three, I took leave; and so, with my wife
only, to see Sir W Pen, who is now got out of his bed and sits
by the fireside. And after some talk, home and to supper and
after prayers to bed. This night came in my wife's brother and
talked to my wife and Gosnell about his wife; which they told
me afterward of, and I do smell that he, I doubt, is overreached in
thinking that he hath got a rich wife, and I fear she will prove
otherwise.[3] So to bed.

8. Up; and carrying Gosnell by coach, set her down at
Templebarr, she going about business of hers today. By the
way she was telling me how Balty did tell her that my wife did
go every day in the week to Court and plays, and that she should
have liberty of going abroad as often as she pleased, and many
other lies; which I am vexed at, and I doubt the wench did come[a]
in some expectation of – which troubles me.

So to the Duke and Mr. Coventry, I alone, the rest being at a
pay and elsewhere. And alone with Mr. Coventry I did read
over our letter to my Lord Treasurer,[4] which I think now is
done as well as it can be. Then to my Lord Sandwiches and
there spent the rest of the morning in making up my Lord's
accounts with Mr. Moore; and then dined with Mr. Moore and
Battersby his friend – very well, and merry and good discourse.
Then into the parke to see them slide with their Scates, which is
very pretty, and so to the Dukes, where the Comittee for Tanger

         a repl. 'comp'-

---

1. The French and Dutch Calvinist
congregations in the city exchanged
churches once a month.
2. Cf. above, p. 97, n. 1.

3. She proved both poor and im-
provident: *Family Letters*, passim.
4. See below, p. 280, n. 1.

met; and here we sat down all with him at a table and had much good discourse about that business – and is to my great content. That done, and hearing what play it was that is to be acted before the King tonight, I would not stay; but home by coach – where I find my wife troubled about Gosnell, who brings word that her uncle, Justice Jiggins,[1] requires her to come three times a week to him to fallow some business that her mother intrusts her withal, and that unless she may have that leisure given her, he will not have her to take any place – for which we are both troubled, but there is no[a] help for it; and believing it to be a good providence of God to prevent my running behind-hand in the world, I am somewhat contented therewith and shall make my wife so; who, poor wretch, I know will consider of things, though in good earnest, the privacy of her life must need be irkesome to her.   So I made Gosnell [sing] and we sat up, looking over the book of Dances[2] till 12 at night, not observing how the time went; and so to prayers and to bed.

9.   Lay long with my wife, contenting her about the business of Gosnells going, and I perceive she will be contented as well as myself.   And so to the office; and after sitting all the morning in hopes to have had Mr. Coventry dined with me, he was forced to go to White-hall.   And so I dined with my own company only, taking Mr. Hater home with me; but he, poor man, was not very well and so could not eat anything.   After dinner stayed within all the afternoon, being vexed in my mind about the going away of Sarah this afternoon, who cried mightily, and so was I ready to do, and Jane did also.   And then anon went Gosnell away, which did trouble me too, though upon many considerations it is better that I am rid of that charge. Altogether makes my house appear to me very lonely, which troubles me much; and in a melancholly humour I went to the office, and there about business sat till I was called to Sir G. Carteret at the Treasury office about my Lord Treasurer's letter, wherein he puts me to a new trouble to write it over again. So home, and late with Sir J. Mennes at the office, looking over

a MS. 'so'

---

1. Robert Jegon, J.P., Westminster.   2. See above, p. 263 & n. 1.   (E).

Mr. Creedes accounts;[1] and then home and to supper. And my wife and I melancholy to bed.

10. This morning rose, receiving a message[a] from Sir G. Carteret and a letter from Mr. Coventry, one contrary to another, about our letter to my Lord Treasurer, at which I am troubled; but I went to Sir G., and being desirous to please both, I think I have found out a way to do it. So back to the office with Sir J. Mennes in his coach; but so great a snow that we could hardly pass the streets. So we and Sir W. Batten to the office and there did discourse of Mr. Creedes accounts; and I fear it will be a good while before we shall go through them, and many things we meet withal of difficulty.

Then to the Dolphin, where Sir J. Mennes, Sir W. Batten, and I did treat the Auditors of the Exchequer, Auditor Woode and Beale, and hither came Sir G. Carteret to us. We had a good dinner, cost us 5*l*-6*s* (whereof my share 26*s*.), and after dinner did discourse of our Salarys and other matters, which I think now they will allow.[2]

Thence home, and there I find our new Cooke-maid Susan come, who is recommended to us by my wife's brother, for which I like her never the better; but being a good well-looked lass, I am willing to try. And Jane begins to take upon her as a chamber-maid.

a repl. 'letter'

---

1. These accounts (made by Creed as Deputy-Treasurer of the fleet during Sandwich's Mediterranean voyage, 1661–2) were to give trouble: below, iv. 16 & n. 2; 198 & n. 1. The Duke of York had written to the Navy Board on 1 November asking them to enquire into Creed's claims for contingencies and short-allowance money: PRO, Adm. 2/1745, f.84*v*.

2. See above, i. 194, 202, 304 & nn. By a Council order of 4 July 1660 Pepys's salary had been made up from the traditional (basic) £33 6*s*. 8*d*. p.a. (the amount fixed by his patent of 13 July 1660) to £350. Similar in-creases were granted to the other Principal Officers. The position was now regularised in the Exchequer: an Admiralty warrant (5 January 1663) was issued to the Attorney-General, and on 6 February the auditors of the Exchequer enrolled the new rates: PRO, Adm. 2/1725, ff. 88–90; BL, Add. 9307, ff. 14–15. Pepys made a note of the agreed rates in the office memorandum-book: PRO, Adm. 2/1733, f.9*v*. He kept copies both of his patent and of Auditor Wood's enrolment: Rawl. A 216, pp. 29–32.

So to the office, where late putting papers and my books and businesses in order – it being very cold; and so home to supper.

11. Up, it being a great frost upon the snow; and we sat all the morning upon Mr. Creedes accounts, wherein I did him some service and some disservice. At noon he dined with me and we sat all the afternoon together, discoursing of ways to get money, which I am now giving myself wholly up to; and in the evening he went away and I to my office, concluding all matters concerning our great letter, so long in doing, to my Lord Treasurer,[1] till almost one in the morning; and then home with my mind much eased, and so to bed.

12. From a very hard frost,*a* when I wake I find a very great thaw and my house overflown with it, which vexed me.
At the office and home doing business all the morning. Then dined with my wife and sat talking with her all the afternoon; and then to the office and there examining my Copy of Mr. Hollands book[2] till 10 at night; and so home to supper and bed.

13. Slept long today, till Sir J. Mennes and Sir W. Batten were set out toward Portsmouth before I rose and Sir G. Carteret came to the office to speak with me before I was up. So I started up, and down to him. By and by we sat, Mr. Coventry and I (Sir G. Carteret being gone); and among other things, Field and Stint did come and received the 41*l* given him by the judgment against me and Harry Kem;[3] and we did also sign bonds in 500*l* to stand to the award of Mr. Porter and Smith for the rest – which, however, I did not sign to till I got Mr. Coventry

a l.h. repl. l.h. 'thaw'

---

1. This was a statement of account, dated this day, relating to a parliamentary grant of 29 January 1662 for wages, paid and payable, for the period 19 March–10 September. The grant had amounted to £417,220 and the expenditure to £142,446. Copies in PRO, SP 29/64, no. 49; Longleat, Coventry MSS 96, ff. 5–6; summary

in *CSPD 1661–2*, p. 588. It had been in preparation since 6 November: above, p. 250.
2. See above, p. 145 & n. 1.
3. For the case, see above, p. 23, n. 2. Stint was Field's solicitor; Kembe the Navy Office messenger who had arrested him.

to go up with me to Sir W. Pen, and he did promise me before
him to bear his share in what should be awarded, and both concluded that Sir W. Batten could do no less.[1] At noon broke
up and dined with my wife; and then to the office again and
there made an end of last night's Examinacion and got my study
there made very clean and put in order; and then to write by
the post, among other letters, one to Sir Wm Batten about this
day's work with Field, desiring his promise also. The letter I
have caused to be entered in our public book of letters.[2] So
home to supper and to bed.[a]

14. *Lords day.* Lay with great content talking with my wife
in bed; and so up and to church. And then home and had a
neat dinner by ourselfs; and after dinner I walked to White-
hall and my Lord's, and up and down till Chappell-time and
then to the King's chappell, where I heard the service; and so to
my Lord's, and there Mr. Howe and Pagett (the counsellor, an
old lover of Musique); we sang some psalms of Mr. Lawes and
played some Symphonys between[3] till night, that I was sent for
to Mr. Creedes lodging; and there was Captain Ferrer and his
lady and W Howe and I; we supped very well and good sport
in discourse. After supper I was sent for to my Lord, with
whom I stayed talking about his and my own and the public
affairs, with great content (he advising me as to my own choosing
of Sir R. Bernard for Umpire in the businesses between my uncle
and us, that I would not trust to him upon his direction, for he

a entry crowded into bottom of page

---

1. The members of the Board now
entered into bonds to accept an out-
of-court settlement according to the
advice given them on 20 November:
above, p. 262 & n. 2. See Pepys's notes
(13 and 15 December) in PRO, Adm.
106/3520, f.10*v*. Field now asked for
£250: below, iv. 16.
2. The official series of letter-books
of the Navy Board (34 vols, from July
1660 to March 1686) was listed on 12
October 1688 as being in the 'Great
Presse' in the office of the Clerk of the

Acts (BL, Add. 9303, f.124*r*), but has
since disappeared. Pepys kept in
addition a personal collection of
official letters (now NMM, LBK/8),
which begins on 10 July 1662.
3. The psalms were from Henry
and William Lawes's *Choice psalmes
put into musick* (1648), which contains
no symphonies. The playing of the
latter, probably on viols or violins,
may have been in imitation of the
new practice at the Chapel Royal: cf.
above, pp. 190, 197. (E).

did not think him a man to be trusted at all);[1] and so bid him
good-night and to Mr. Creedes again (Mr. Moore, with whom
I entended to have lain, lying physically without sheets); and
there, after some discourse, to bed and lay ill (though the bed
good), my stomach being sick all night with my too heavy
supper.

15. Up and to my Lord's, and thence to the Duke and fallowed him into the parke; where, though the ice was broken and
dangerous, yet he would go slide upon his Scates; which I did
not like, but he slides very well.[2] So back and to his Closet,
whither my Lord Sandwich comes and there Mr. Coventry and
we three had long discourse together about the matters of the
Navy; and endeed, I find myself more and more obliged to
Mr. Coventry, who studies to do me all the right he can in
everything to the Duke.

Thence walk a good while up and down the Gallerys; and
among others, met with Dr. Clerke, who in discourse tells me
that Sir Ch. Berkely's greatness[3] is only his being pimp to the
King to my Lady Castlemayne. And yet for all this, that the
King is very kind to the Queene, who he says is one of the best
women in the world. Strange how the King is bewitched to
this pretty Castlemayne.

Thence to my Lord's and there with Mr. Creed, Moore and
Howe to the Crowne and dined; and thence to White-hall,
where I walked up and down the Gallerys, spending my time
upon the pictures till the Duke and the Comittee for Tanger met
(the Duke not staying with us); where the only matter was to
discourse with my Lord Rutherford, who is this day made
Governor of Tanger for I know not what reasons, and my Lord

1. The Mountagus and the Bernards were political rivals in Huntingdon. Sandwich had opposed the
Bernard interest in the parliamentary
elections of 1660, and he had Sir Robert
removed from the recorder's place in
1663: above, i. 86–7; below, iv. 62.

2. Perhaps because he had spent
much of his exile in the Low Countries.

3. He had been recently appointed
Keeper of the Privy Purse: above,
p. 227 & n. 2.

of Peterbrough to be called home;[1] which though it is said is
done with kindness, yet all the world may see it is done otherwise; and I am sorry to see a Catholicke Governor sent to command there, where all the rest of the officers almost are such
already.[2] But God knows what the reason is, and all may see
how slippery places all Courtiers stand in.[3]

Thence by coach home, in my way calling upon Sir John
Berkenheade to speak about my assessement of 42*l* to the Loyall
Sufferrers,[4] which I perceive I cannot help; but he tells me I have
been abused by Sir R. Ford – which I shall hereafter make use
of when it shall be fit.[5]

Thence called at the Major-Generalls, Sir R. Browne, about
my being assessed armes to the Militia,[6] but he was abroad; and
so driving through the backside of the Shambles in Newgate
Market, my coach plucked down two pieces of beef into the
Dirt; upon which the butchers stopped the horses, and a great
rout of people in the street – crying that he had done him 40*s*.
and 5*l* worth of hurt; but going down, I saw that he had done
little or none; and so I gave them a Shilling for it and they were
well contented, and so home.

And there to my Lady Batten to see her, who tells me she
hath just now a letter from Sir Wm., how that he and Sir J.
Mennes did very narrowly escape drowning on the roade, the

1. Peterborough was now given a pension of £1000 p.a. (from Tangier funds) after only a few months' service. Rutherford (cr. Earl of Teviot, February 1663) arrived in Tangier in the following April. His instructions were dated 27 April and his patent 2 May 1663.

2. The Irish regiment had been transferred there from Dunkirk, and Fitzgerald, its commander, was Lieutenant-Governor. Complaints of the Catholicism of the garrison mounted in the 1670s. The cathedral built by the Portuguese – many of the poorer of whom now remained there – was still reserved for Catholic use. Its registers record the burials of many Irishmen: E. Prestage, *Diplom.*

relations Portugal 1640–68, p. 152, n. 2.

3. ? an echo of Ps. lxxiii. 18; or of Bacon's essay 'Of Great Place'.

4. See above, p. 199, n. 2.

5. Birkenhead and Ford were commissioners appointed under the act. Office-holders were to pay not more than 8% of their annual income. In October Pepys had complained that Ford had over-assessed him (at £36 for an office worth £350 p.a.), and had under-assessed Batten (at £24 for an office worth £490 p.a.): *Shorthand Letters*, p. 68. Pepys's rating seems to have been increased since then: both assessments appear to have taken account of fees as well as salaries.

6. See above, p. 275 & n. 1.

waters are so high, but is well.   But Lord, what a Hypocrite-like face she made to tell it me.

Thence to Sir W. Pen and sat long with him in discourse, I making myself appear in discourse one of greater action and resolution as to public business then I have hereto done; at which he lissens, but I know is a rogue in his heart and likes not; but I perceive I may hold up my head, and the more the better, I minding of my business as I have done – in which God doth and will bless me.   So home and with great content to bed, and talk and chat with my wife while I was at supper – to our*a* great pleasure.

16. Up and to the office, and thither came Mr. Coventry and Sir G. Carteret.   And among other businesses, was Strutts the purser against Captain Browne (Sir W. Batten's brother-in-law).[1]   But Lord (though I believe the Captain hath played the knave, though I seem to have a good opinion of him and to mean him well) what a most troublesome fellow that Strutt is – such*b* as I never did meet with his fellow in my life.   His talking, and ours to make him hold his peace, set my head of akeing all the afternoon with great pain.

So to dinner, thinking to have had Mr. Coventry; but he could not go with me and so I took Captain Murford – of whom I do hear what the world says of me; that all do conclude Mr. Coventry and Pett and me to be of a knot and that we do now carry all things before us.   And much more, in perticular of me and my studiousnesse &c., to my great content.

After dinner came Mrs. Browne, the Captains wife, to see me and my wife, and I showed her a good countenance, and endeed her husband hath been civil to us; but though I speak them fair, yet I doubt I shall not be able to do her husband much favour in this business of Strutts, whom without doubt he hath abused.

So to the office; and thence,*c* having done some business, by coach to White-hall to Secretary Bennets and agreed with Mr. Lee to set upon our new adventure at the Tower tomorrow.

a repl. 'my'   *b* MS. 'sum'   *c* repl. 'there'

1. Thomas Strutt had in July been discharged from the *Rosebush*, Capt. John Browne's ship, at his own request.   His successor resigned in March 1663: PRO, Adm. 2/1732, f.188r; ib., 1733, f.57r.

Thence to Collonell Lovelace in Cannon Rowe, about seeing how Sir Rd. Ford did report all the officers of the Navy to be rated for the Loyall Sufferers;[1] but finding him at the Rhenish wine-house, I could not have any answer, but must take another time. Thence to my Lord's; and having sat talking with Mr. Moore, bewayling the vanity and disorders of the age, I went by coach to my brother's, where I met Sarah my late mayd (who had a desire to speak with me and I with her to know what it was), who told me out of good-will to me, for she loves me dearly, that I would beware of my wife's brother, for he is begging or borrowing of her[2] often; and told me of her Scallop-whisk and her borrowing of 50*s* from*a* Will, which she believes for him and her father. I do observe so much goodness and seriousness in the maid, that I am again and again sorry that I have parted with her, though it was full against my will then. And if she had anything in the world, I would commend her for a wife for my brother Tom. After much discourse and her professions of love to me and all my relations, I bid her good-night and did kiss her; and endeed, she seemed very well-favoured to me tonight, as she is alway.

So by coach home and to my office; did some business and so home to supper and to bed.

17. This morning came Mr. Lee, Wade, and Evett, intending to have gone upon our new design to the Tower today; but it raining and the work being to be done in the open garden, we put it off to Friday next. And so I to the office doing business, and then dined at home with my poor wife with great content; and so to the office again and made an end of examining the other of Mr. Hollands books about the Navy,[3] with which I am much contented; and so to other businesses till night at my office; and so home to supper. And after much dear company and talk with my wife, to bed.

18. Up and to the office – Mr. Coventry and I alone; sat till 2 a–clock and then he inviting himself to my house to dinner,

a MS. 'for'

1. Francis Lovelace (later Governor of New York), was employed by the commissioners collecting the tax in London and Westminster.

2. Pepys's wife.

3. His 'Second Discourse': see above, p. 145 & n. 1.

of which I was proud; but my dinner being a leg of mutton and two capons, they were not done enough; which did vex me, but we made shift to please him I think; but I was, when he was gone, very angry with my wife and people.

This afternoon came my wife's brother and his wife and Mrs. Lodum his landlady (my old friend Mr. Ashwells sister); Baltys wife is a most little, and yet I believe pretty old girl. Not handsome nor hath anything in the world pleasing, but they say she plays mighty well on the Base Violl. They dined at her father's today, but for aught I hear he is a wise man and will not give anything to his daughter till he sees what her husband doth put himself to – so that I doubt he hath made but a bad matter of it. But I am resolved not to meddle with it.

They gone, I to the office and to see Sir W. Penn with my wife; and thence I to Mr. Cade the Stacioner to direct him what to do with my two copies of Mr. Hollands books which he is to bind; and after supplying myself with several things of him, I returned to my office and so home to supper and to bed.

19.   Up, and by appointment with Mr. Lee, Wade, Evett and workmen to the Tower, and with the Lieutenant's leave, set them to work in the garden in the corner against the Mayne=guard, a most unlikely place. It being cold, Mr. Lee and [I] did sit all the day, till 3 a-clock, by the fire in the Governors house; I reading a play of Flechers, being *A wife for a month*[1] – wherein no great wit or language. Having done, we went to them at work; and having wrought below the bottom of the foundation of the wall, I bid them give over; and so all our hopes ended. And so went home, taking Mr. Leigh with me; and after drunk a cup of wine, he went away and I to my office, there reading in Sir W Pettys book,[2] and so home – and to bed, a little displeased with my wife; who, poor wretch, is troubled with her lonely life, which I know not how, without great charge, to help as yet; but I will study how to do it.

20.   Up and had 100*l* brought me by Prior of Brampton, in

---

1. A tragicomedy by John Fletcher, licensed in 1624, and published in 1647; PL 2623 (1679 Folio). (A).

2. *A treatise of taxes & contributions* (1662); published anonymously; PL 1174 (1); several times reprinted.

full of his purchase-money for Barton's house and some land.[1]
So to the office and thence with Mr. Coventry in his coach to
St. James with great content and pride to see him treat me so
friendlily, and dined with him; and so to White-hall together,
where we met upon the Tanger Commission – and discoursed
many things thereon. But little will be done before my Lord
Rutherford comes there as to the Fortificacions or Molle.

That done, my Lord Sandwich and I walked together a good
while in the Matted Gallery, he acquainting me with his late
enquiries into the Wardrobe business, to his content; and tells
me how things stand – and that the first year was worth about
3000*l* to him and the next about as much; so that at this day, if
he were paid, it will be worth about 7000*l* to him.[2] But it
contents me above all things to see him treat me as his confidant.
So bid him good-night, he being to go into the country to keep
his Christmas on Monday next.

So by coach home and to my office, being post night; and
then home – and to bed.

21.[a] *Lords=day*. Lay long in bed. So up to church and so
home to dinner alone with my wife, very pleasant. After dinner
I walked to my brother's, where he told me some hopes he hath
of bringing his business to pass still of his mistress; but I do find
they do stand upon terms that will not be either fit or in his
power to grant; and therefore I did dislike his talk and advised
him to give it quite over.

Thence walked to White-hall and there to Chappell; and from
thence upstairs and up and down the house and galleries on the
King's and Queen's side; and so through the garden to my Lord's
lodging, where there was Mr. Gibbons, Madge, and Mallard and
Pagett, and by and by came in my Lord Sandwich, and so we
had great store of good Musique. By and by comes in my

a repl. '23'

---

1. See above, ii. 204 & n. 2.
2. These years included the coronation, which would make his profits
(based mostly on poundage) abnorm-
ally high. The average was later
reckoned at less than £1000 p.a.:
below, viii. 418 & n. 2. For details
and for his difficulty in securing
payment, see Harris, i. 256–7.

simple Lord Chandois,[1] who (my Lord Sandwich being gone
out to Court) begun to sing psalms, but so dully that I was weary
of it.   At last we broke up; and by and by comes in my Lord
Sandwich again, and he and I to talk together about his businesses; and so he to bed, and I and Mr. Creede and Captain
Ferrers fell to a cold goose pye of Mrs. Sarah's heartily; and so
spent our time till past 12 a-clock and then with Creede to his
《22》[a] lodgings; and so with him to bed and slept till 6 or 7
a-clock; and so up and by the fireside we read a good part
of the *Advice to a Daughter*, which a simple Coxcombe hath wrote
against Osborne;[2] but in all my life I never did nor can expect to
see so much nonsense in print.   Thence to my Lord's, who is
getting himself ready for his journy to Hinchingbrooke; and by
and by, after eating something and talking with me about many
things, and telling me his mind upon my askeing about Sarah
(who it seems is not only married of late, but is also said to be
turned a great Drunkard, which I am ashamed of), that he likes
her service well and doth not love a strange face, but will not
endure that fault; but hath bid me speak to her and advise her if
she hath a mind to stay with him, which I will do.

My Lord and his people being gone, I walked to Mr. Coventrys
chamber, where I find him gone out into the parke with the
Duke; so my boy being there ready with my things, I shifted
myself into a riding habitt and fallowed him through White-hall;
and in the parke, Mr. Coventry's people having a horse ready for
me (so fine a one that I was almost afeared to get upon him, but
I did and found myself more feared then hurt), and I got up and
fallowed the Duke, who with some of his people (among others,
Mr. Coventry) was rideing[b] out.   And with them to hide parke –
where Mr. Coventry asking leave of the Duke, he bid us go to
Woolwich; so he and I to the water-side, and our horses coming

a repl.'24'   b l.h. repl. s.h. 'red'-

---

1. William Brydges, 7th Baron
Chandos. Wood has a story of his
visiting a bawdy house in Oxford in
1664: *L. & T.*, ii. 13.

2. *Advice to a daughter in opposition
to the advice to a sonne . . . by Eugenius
Theodidactus* (John Heydon); 208 pp.;

first published in 1658; not retained
in the PL. The author takes the
main points in Francis Osborne's
Advice to a son, a favourite book of
Pepys's (q.v. above, ii. 22, n. 2) and
contradicts them one by one.

by the ferry,[1] we by oares over to Lambeth and from thence, with brave discourse by the way, rode to Woolwich, where we eat and drank at Mr. Petts and discoursed of many businesses and put in practice my new way of the Call=booke,[2] which will be of great use. Here having stayed a good while, we got up again and brought night home with us, and foule weather. So over to White-hall to his chamber, whither my boy came, who had stayed in St. James parke (by my mistake) all day, looking for me. Thence took my things that I put off today, and by coach, being very wet and cold on my feet, home; and presently shifted myself. And so had the barber come; and my wife and I to read Ovids *Metamorphoses*,[3] which I brought her home from Pauls churchyard tonight (having called for it by the way) and

《23》 so to bed – and slept hard till 8 a-clock this morning. And so up and to the office, where I find Sir J. Mennes and Sir W. Batten come unexpectedly home last night from Portsmouth, having done the pay there before we could have thought it. Sat all the morning. And at noon home to dinner with my wife alone. And after dinner sat by the fire and then up to make up my accounts with her, and find that my ordinary housekeeping comes to 7*l* a month – which is a great deal. By and by comes Dr. Pierce;[4] who among other things, tells me that my Lady Castlemaynes interest at Court encreases and is more and greater then the Queenes. That she hath brought in Sir H. Bennet and Sir Ch. Barkeley; but that the Queene is a most good lady and takes all with the greatest meekness that may be. He tells me too, that Mr. Edwd. Mountagu is quite broke at Court, in*a* repute and purse. And that he lately was engaged

a MS. 'with in'

---

1. The horseferry at Westminster. (R).

2. See above, p. 234 & n. 2. Call-books recorded the allocation of men to jobs. They were to be kept by the clerks of the cheque, and in a letter to Cowley of Deptford (23 December) Pepys now explained their purpose and directed that they be used experi-

mentally during the next quarter: *Further Corr.*, p. 2. They finally displaced the old books from the following summer onwards. Cf. PRO, Adm. 20/5, p. 281, no. 767.

3. Probably the English translation (1640) by George Sandys: PL 2481.

4. James Pearse, surgeon to the Duke of York.

in a Quarrell against my Lord Chesterfield[1] – but that the King
did cause it to be taken up.   He tells me too, that the King is
much concerned in the Chancellors sickness;   and that the
Chancellor is as great, he thinks, as ever he was with the
King.[2]

He also tells me what the world say of me, that Mr. Coventry
and I do all the business of the office almost;   at which I am
highly proud.

He being gone, I fell to business;   which was very great, but
got it well over by 9 at night, and so home.   And after supper,
to bed.

24.   Lay pleasantly talking to my wife till 8 a-clock;   then up
and to Sir W. Batten's to see him and Sir G. Carteret and Sir
J. Mennes take coach toward the pay at Chatham – which they
did, and I home and took money in my pocket to pay many
reckonings today in the towne – as my bookseller's, and paid at
another shop 4*l*:10*s* for Stephens's *Thesaurus Græcæ Linguæ*, given
to Paul's schoole.[3]   So to my brother's and Shoomaker;   and so to
my Lord Crew's and dined alone with him;   and after dinner,
much discourse about matters.   Upon the whole, I understand
there are great factions at Court;   and something he said that did
imply a difference like to be between the King and the Duke in
case the Queene should not be with child – I understand, about
this bastard.[4]   He says also that some great man will be aimed at

---

1. A quarrel about precedence:
below, iv. 25.   Both were servants
of the Queen: Mountagu her Master
of the Horse and Chesterfield her
Lord Chamberlain.

2. From 4 December until early in
the following March Clarendon was
incapacitated by gout.   There was
much speculation at the time whether
he had lost influence by an illness
which came so soon after the appointment of a rival (Bennet) as Secretary
in October: see, e.g. *CSPVen.*
1661-4, p. 217.   Later accounts have
in particular assumed that the Declaration issued three days after this

entry was due to Bennet's influence
rather than to Clarendon's.   Some
grounds for doubting these assump-
tions are given by Dr G. R. Abernathy
in *Journ. Eccles. Hist.*, 11/65.   The
evidence he adduces is supported by
Pepys's report.

3. See above, ii. 239; below, iv.
33, 133;   possibly destroyed in the
Great Fire.   A copy of the 1573 edition survives in the school library, but
may be a later acquisition.   Not in
PL.

4. The Duke of Monmouth: cf.
below, p. 303 & n. 1.

when the Parliament comes to sit again; I understand, the Chancellor.[1]   And that there is a bill will be brought in, that none
that have been in armes for the Parliament shall be capable of
office.[2]   And that the Court are weary of my Lord Albemarle
and Chamberlin.[3]   He wishes that my Lord Sandwich had some
good occasion to be abroad this summer which is coming on.
And that my Lord Hinchingbrooke were well married, and
Sydny[4] had some place at Court.   He pities the poor Ministers
that are put out,[5] to whom he says the King is beholden for his
coming in; and that if any such thing had been foreseen, he had
never come in.   After this, and much other discourse of the sea
and breeding young gentlemen to the sea, I went away.

And homeward; met Mr. Creed[a] at my booksellers in Pauls
churchyard, who takes it ill, my letter last night to Mr. Povy,
wherein I accuse him of the neglect of the Tanger boats.[6]   In
which I must confess I did not do altogether like a friend; but
however, it was truth and I must owne it to be so, though I fall
wholly out with him for it.

Thence home, and to my office alone to do business.   And
read over half of Mr. Blands discourse concerning Trade, which
(he being no scholler and so knows not the rules of writing
orderly) is very good.[7]   So home to supper and to bed – my
wife not being well, she having her months upon her.

This evening Mr. Gauden[8] sent me, against Christmas, a
great Chine[b] of beefe and three dozen of Toungs.   I did give 5s

a   repl. 'Ch'-   b   l.h. repl. s.h. 'chine'

---

1. See below, iv. 222–5.
2. See below, iv. 125 & n. 1.
3. The Lord Chamberlain, Manchester.   Crew is here bewailing the
attack on the moderate 'Presbyterian'
interest to which he himself belonged,
in common with Sandwich.   In the
autumn and winter of 1659–60 they
had taken the lead in the movement
which led to the Restoration.
4. Sidney Mountagu, Sandwich's
second son.

5. The Presbyterian parsons extruded by the Act of Uniformity.
6. The boats had been ordered in
August: PRO, Adm. 2/1745, f.81r.
They were needed to serve the ships
lying off the town in Tangier roads.
Cf. below, p. 300 & n. 1.
7. For the book, see above, p. 158
& n. 1.   Bland spelled badly, even by
17th-century standards: see his letters
to Pepys in PRO, CO/279.
8. Denis Gauden, Navy victualler.

to the man that brought it and half-crown to the porters. This
day also, the parish Clerke brought the general bill of Mortality,
which cost me half-Crowne more.¹

25. *Christmas day.* Up pretty early, leaving my wife not
well in bed. And with my boy walked, it being a most brave
cold and dry frosty morning, and had a pleasant walk to White-
hall; where I entended to have received the Comunion with the
family,² but I came a little too late.³ So I walked up into the
house and spent my time looking over pictures, perticularly
the ships in King H the 8ths voyage to Bullen⁴ – marking
the great difference between their build*ᵃ* then and now. By
and by down to the Chappell again, where Bishop Morly
preached upon the Song of the Angels – "Glory to God on
high – on earth peace, and good will towards men."⁵ Methought
he made but a poor sermon, but long and reprehending the
mistaken jollity of the Court for the true joy that shall and ought
to be on these days. Perticularized concerning their excess in
playes and gameing, saying that he whose office it is to keep the

a MS. 'built'

1. *A general bill for this present year,*
ending the 16th day of December (1662);
a single sheet on which were summarised the mortality figures (ar-
ranged under causes: e.g. ague, apoplexy, 'griping of the guts', 'rising of
the lights', 'shortness of breath' etc.)
contained in the weekly bills. The
half-crown was perhaps a tip; the
series for the whole year cost only
4*s.* These publications were produced by the Parish Clerks' Company;
scattered examples occur from 1527-8
onwards, and a continuous series was
issued from 1603 to 1859. Pepys
uses them in the diary as a record of
the Plague, and in his library retained
London's dreadful visitation; or A collec-
tion of all the bills of mortality for this
present year (1665): PL 1595. See
illust. below, vol vi, at 20 September
1665.

2. The (lesser) members of the
royal household.
3. For Pepys's (non-)attendance at
communion services, see above, p.
54 & n. 1.
4. The *Embarkation of Henry VIII,*
painted by an unknown artist, is now
with its companion piece of the *Field*
of the Cloth of Gold, at Hampton
Court. They may have been painted
for Henry VIII and are thought to
have formed part of the Tudor royal
collection. After the Restoration
they were hanging in the King's Privy
Gallery at Whitehall: O. Millar,
Tudor, Stuart and early Georgian
pictures in coll. H.M. Queen, nos 24, 25.
(OM).
5. A loose recollection of Luke, ii.
14. George Morley (Bishop of
Winchester), was Dean of the Chapel
Royal.

Gamesters in order and within bounds serves but for a second rather in a Duell, meaning the Groome porter.[1]   Upon which, it was worth observing how far they are come from taking the Reprehensions*a* of a Bishop seriously, that they all laugh in the chapel when he reflected on their ill actions and courses.

He did much press us to joy in these public days of joy and to Hospitality.   But one that stood by whispered in my eare that the Bishop himself doth not spend one groate to the poor himself.[2]

The sermon done, a good Anthemne fallowed, with vialls; and then the King came down to receive the Sacrament, but I stayed not; but calling my boy from my Lord's lodging and giving Sarah some good advice, by my Lord's order, to be Sober and look after the house, I walked home again with great pleasure; and there dined by my wife's bedside with great content, having a mess of brave plum-porridge and a roasted Pullett for dinner; and I sent for a mince-pie abroad, my wife not being well to make any herself yet.   After dinner sat talking a good while with her, her [pain] being become less, and then to see Sir W. Penn a little; and so to my office, practising arithmetique alone and making an end of last night's book, with great content, till 11 at night; and so home to supper and to bed.

26.   Up.   My wife to the making of Christmas-pies all day, being now pretty well again.   And I abroad to several places about

a repl. ? 'observations'

---

1. An officer of the Lord Steward's department of the King's Household, who supervised and received the profits of the gaming allowed there during the twelve days of Christmas, in which the King himself often took part. (The office – at this time held by Sir Richard Hobart – was abolished in 1783.)   Play took place both in the Privy Chamber and in the Groom-Porter's lodgings. Pepys visited the Groom-Porter's on 1 January 1668; Evelyn on 6 January 1662 and 8 January 1668.   J. Ashton, *Hist. gambling in Engl.*, pp. 41+; Evelyn, iii. 308, n. 4. This officer also supervised the betting when the court went to the horse-races: see Shadwell, *True Widow*, V, 2.

2. On the contrary, Morley was well known for his charity: Burnet, i. 314 & n. The King had said, on Morley's translation to the rich see of Winchester in May 1662, that he would be no better off himself for the change, since he gave so much to the poor: *DNB*.

small businesses; among others, bought a bake=pan in Newgate-
market and sent it home; it cost me 16s. So to Dr Williams,
but he is out of town; then to [Mr. Moore at]¹ the Wardrobe,
who is not yet well. Hither came Mr. Battersby; and we falling into a discourse of a new book of Drollery in verse called
Hudebras, I would needs go find it out; and met with it at the
Temple, cost me 2s-6d. But when I came to read it, it is so
silly an abuse of the Presbyter-Knight going to the warrs, that I
am ashamed of it; and by and by meeting at Mr. Townsends at
dinner, I sold it to him for 18d.² Here we dined with many
Tradesmen that belong to the Wardrobe, but I was weary soon
of their company and broke up dinner as soon as I could and
away, with the greatest reluctancy and dispute (two or three
times, my reason stopping my Sence and I would go back again)
within myself, to the Duke's house and saw *The Villaine*³ – which
I ought not to do without my wife, but that my time is now
out that I did undertake it for.⁴ But Lord, to consider how
my natural desire is to pleasure, which God be praised that he
hath given me the power by my late oaths to curbe so well as I
have done; and will do again, after two or three plays more.
Here I was better pleased with the play then I was at first, understanding the design better then I did. Here I saw Gosnell and
her sister at a distance, and could have found my heart to have
accosted them, but thought it not prudent. But I watched
their going out and found that they came, she, her sister and
another woman, alone, without any man, and did go over the
fields afoote. I find that I have an inclinacion to have her come
again, though it is most against my interest, either of profit or
content of mind, other then for her singing.

Home on foot, in my way calling at Mr. Rawlinson's and

---

1. See below, p. 304. No blank in
MS.

2. The first part of Samuel Butler's
Hudibras (licensed 11 November
1662) was just out, and was dated
1663: *Trans. Stat. Reg.*, ii. 319. A
pirated edition also appeared at about
this time: *Merc. Pub.*, 8 January 1663,
p. 8; *Poetical works of S. Butler* (ed.
Johnson), vol. i, pp. xxiii–iv; *Hudibras* (ed. Wilders), pp. xlviii–li. See

below, iv. 35 & n. 2. Pepys read
both parts of it at sea in one day in
1683: *Tangier Papers*, p. 9. Its
central figure was largely copied
from life, being founded on Sir
Samuel Luke, a Presbyterian fire-
brand of Bedfordshire, by whom
Butler had once been employed.

3. See above, p. 230 & n. 1. (A).

4. See above, p. 209. (A).

drank only a cup of ale there.   He tells ⟨me⟩ my uncle¹ hath
ended his purchase, which costs him 4500*l*.   And how my uncle
doth express his trouble that he hath with his wife's relations;
but I understand his great intentions are for the Wights, that
hang upon him and by whose advice this estate is bought.   Thence
home, and find my wife busy among her pies, but angry for
some sawcy*ᵃ* words that her maid Jane hath given her; which
I will not allow of and therefore will give her warning to be
gone.   As also, we are both displeased for some slight words that
Sarah, now at Sir W. Penn's, hath spoke of us; but it is no matter,
we shall endeavour to joyne the Lyon's skin to the Foxes tail.²

So to my office alone a while, and then home to my study and
supper and bed – being also vexed at my boy, for his staying
playing abroad when he is sent on errands, so that I have sent
him tonight to see whether their country-Carrier be in Towne
or no, for I am resolve[d] to keep him no longer.

27.   Up; and while I am dressing, I sent for my boy's Brother
Wm. that lives in town here as a groome; to whom and their
sister Jane, I told my resolution to keep the boy no longer; so
upon the whole, they desire to have him stay a week longer, and
then he shall go.   So to the office; and there Mr. Coventry and
I sat till noon, and then I stepped to the Exchange and so home
to dinner; and after dinner, with my wife to the Duke's Theatre
and saw the second part of *Rhodes* done with the new Roxalana;³
which doth it rather better in all respects, for person, voice and
judgment, then the first Roxalane.   Home with great content
with my wife; only not so well pleased with the company at
the house today, which was full of Citizens, there hardly being
a gentleman or woman in the house, but*ᵇ* a couple of pretty

a repl. 'ill [l.h.] words [s.h.]'   *b* MS. 'of'

---

1. William Wight: the transaction
(for an estate in Hampshire) was in
fact never completed: below, iv. 257.
2. Pepys has the words in the
wrong order: he appears to mean
that tact is necessary.
3. This was Davenant's opera, *The
siege of Rhodes*: see above, ii. 130 &

n. 2.   Mrs Hester Davenport, who
had been a great success in the role of
Roxalana, had by this time been
beguiled from the theatre by the Earl
of Oxford (above, p. 86 & n. 4) and
the part was now being played by
Mrs Norton: below, vii. 190-1 & n.
(A).

ladies by us, that made sport at it, being jostled and crowded by prentices. So home; and I to my study, making up my monthly accounts, which is now fallen again to 630*l* or thereabouts, which not long since was 680*l*[1] – at which I am sorry, but I trust in God I shall get it up again – and in the meantime will live sparingly. So home to supper and to bed.[a]

28. *Lords=day.* Up, and with my wife to church; and coming out, went out both before my Lady Batten, he not being there (which I believe will vex her); after dinner my wife to church again and I to the French church, where I heard an old man[2] make a tedious long sermon, till they were fain to light candle to baptise the children by. So homeward, meeting my brother Tom, but spoke but little with him; and calling also at my uncle Wights, but met him and her going forth; and so I went directly home and there fell to the renewing my last year's Oaths,[3] whereby it hath pleased God so much to better my mind and practice; and so down to supper, and then prayers and bed.

29. Up, and walked to White-hall; where the Duke and Mr. Coventry being gone forth, I went to Westminster-hall, where I stayed reading at Mrs. Michells shop and sent for half-pint of sack for her. Here she told me what I heard not of before, the strange burning of Mr. Delaun a merchant's house in Loathbury and his lady (Sir Tho. Allens daughter) and her whole family; not one thing, dog nor cat, escapeing, nor any of the neighbours almost hearing of it till the house was quite down and burnt.[4] How this should come to pass, God knows, but a most strange thing it is. Hither came Jacke Spicer[5] to me and I took him to the Swan, where Mr. Herbert did give me my breakfast of cold chine of pork; and here Spicer and I talked of

a entry crowded into bottom of page

---

1. Cf. above, p. 236.
2. Louis Hérault, minister of the Huguenot church, Threadneedle St, until 1675.
3. See above, ii. 242 & n. 1.
4. The fire occurred on the night of 26-27 December, and the seven inmates of the house (which was new and of brick) all perished. See Rugge, ii, f.58*v*; Mundy, v. 151-2; *Diary of Henry Townshend* (ed. Willis Bund), i. 95; Richard Smyth, *Obituary*, p. 57. Delaune was an Eastland merchant.
5. Exchequer clerk.

Exchequer matters and how the Lord Treasurer hath now ordered all monies to be brought into the Exchequer, and hath settled the King's revenue and given to every general Expence proper assignements; to the Navy, 200000*l* and odde.[1] He also told me of the great vast trade of the goldsmiths in supplying the King with money at dear rates.[2]

Thence to White-hall and got up to the top gallery in the banquetting-house to see the Audience of the Russia Embassador; which after long waiting and fear of the falling of [the] gallery, it being so full and part of it being parted from the rest for nobody to come upon, merely from the weakenesse thereof.[3] And very handsome it was. After they were come in, I went down and got through the croude almost as high as the King and the Embassadors, where I saw all the presents, being rich furs, hawkes, carpets, cloths of tissue, and sea-horse teeth. The King took two or three hawkes upon his fist, having a glove on, wrought with gold, given him for that purpose. The son of one of the Embassadors was in the richest suit, for pearl and tissue, that ever I did see, or shall, I believe. After they and all the company had kissed the King's hand, then the three Embassadors and the son, and no more, did kiss the Queenes. One thing more I did observe, that the chief Embassador did carry up his master's Letters in state before him, on high; and as soon as he had delivered them, he did fall down to the ground and lay there a great while. After all was done, the company broke up, and I spent a little while walking up and down the gallery seeing the ladies, the two Queenes and the Duke of Monmouth with his little mistress,[4] which is very little and like my brother-in-law's

1. This was one of several attempts at financial reorganisation (repeated in 1667 and 1674), and like the others proved ineffective. £122,400 was allotted to the Guards, £80,000 to the Household, £70,600 to Tangier and so on: *CSPD 1661–2*, p. 577. The figure of £200,000 for the Navy was accepted as the normal peacetime cost at this time, though Pepys reckoned that the actual cost was nearer £350,000 p.a. The use of assignments would have prevented diversions of revenue, and restored the

Exchequer 'to its antient honor and reputacion': Southampton to Long, 3 December: *CTB*, i. 456.

2. They usually charged 6% (the legal maximum), to which was added a gratuity of 4%.

3. For the ceremony, see *Merc. Pub.*, 8 January 1663, pp. 1+; Evelyn; Rugge, ii, ff. 59+. None mentions the damaged gallery.

4. The Countess of Buccleuch, who married Monmouth on 20 April 1663, she being then under twelve, and he thirteen.

wife. So with Mr. Creede to the Harp and ball; and there meeting with Mr. How, Goodgroome and young Coleman, did drink and talk with them; and I have almost found out a young gentlewoman for my turn to wait on my wife, of a good family and that can sing.[1]   Thence I went away; and getting a coach, went home and sat late talking with my wife about our entertaining Dr. Clarkes lady and Mrs. Pierce shortly, being in great pain that my wife hath never a winter gowne; being almost ashamed of it that she should be seen in a taffata one when all the world wears Moyre.   So to prayers and to bed.   But we could not come to any resolution what to do therein, other then to appear as she is.

30.   Up and to the office, whither Sir W. Penn came, the first time that he hath come downstairs since his late great sickness of the gout.   We, with Mr. Coventry, sat till noon.   Then I to the Change-ward to see what play there was,[2] but I liked none of them; and so homeward and calling in at Mr. Rawlinsons, where he stopped me to dine with him and two East=India officers of ships and Howell our Turner.   With the officers I had good discourse, perticularly of the people at the Cape of Good Hope – of whom they of their own knowledge do tell me these one or two things. *viz.*, that when they come to age, the men do cut off one of the stones of each other, which they hold doth help them to get children the better and to grow fat.[3]   That they never sleep lying, but always sitting upon the ground.[4]   That their speech is not so articulate as ours, but yet understand one another well.   That they paint themselfs all over with the grease the Duch sell them (who have a fort there)[5] and Sutt.   After dinner, drinking five or six glasses of wine (which liberty I now take till I begin my oath again), I went home and took my wife into coach and carried her to Westminster; there

1. Mary Ashwell: below, iv. 16.
2. I.e. advertised on the Exchange. (A).
3. The practice of hemi-castration among the Hottentots was remarked on by some contemporary writers, although others denied its existence. The effect was said to produce not

more children, but better runners.   I. Schapera and B. Farrington (eds), *Early Cape Hottentots*, pp. 142, 143.
4. This seems to have been true only of the siesta: op. cit., p. 255.
5. Founded in 1652 by the Dutch E. India Company.

visited Mrs. Ferrer and stayed talking with her a good while, there being a little proud, ugly, talking lady there that was much crying-up the Queene Mother's Court at Summerset-house above our own Queenes; there being before no allowance of laughing and the mirth that is at the other's. And endeed, it is observed that the greatest Court nowadays is there. Thence to White-hall, where I carried my wife to see the Queene in her presence-chamber and the maydes of Honour and the young Duke of Monmouth playing at Cards.

Some of them, and but a few, were very pretty, though all well dressed in velvet gowns. Thence to my Lord's Lodgeings, where Mrs. Sarah did make us my Lord's bed; and Mr. Creede being sent for, sat playing at Cards till it was late; and so goodnight, and with great pleasure to bed.

31. Lay pretty long in bed; and then I up and to Westminster-hall and so to the Swan, sending for Mr. Wm. Bowyer, and there drank my morning's draught and had some of his simple discourse. Among other things, he tells me how the difference comes between his fair Cosen Butler and Collonell Dillon, upon his opening letters of her brothers from*a* Ireland complaining of his knavery, and forging others to the contrary. And so they are long ago quite broke off.[1]

Thence to a barbers, and so to my wife and at noon took her to Mrs. Pierces by invitation to dinner; where there came Dr. Clerke and his wife and sister and Mr. Knight, chief Chyrurgeon to the King, and his wife. We were pretty merry, the two men being excellent company; but I confess I am wedded from that opinion either of Mrs. Pierces beauty, upon*b* discovery of her*c* naked neck today, being undressed when we came in, or*d* of Mrs. Clerkes genius, which I so much admired, I finding her to be so conceited and fantaske in her dress this day, and carriage; though the truth is, witty enough.

After dinner, with much ado the Doctor and I got away to fallow our business for a while, he to his patients and I to the

a repl. 'in'   *b* repl. 'she'   *c* repl. 'his'   *d* l.h. repl. s.h. 'and'

---

1. Cf. above, i. 209 & n. 3. Dillon kept up an acquaintance with Frances Butler, but later married Katherine, daughter of John Werden of Chester.

Tanger Comittee, where the Duke of Yorke was and we stayed
at it a good while; and thence, in order to the dispatch of the
boates and provisions for Tanger, away; Mr. Povy in his coach
carried Mr. Gauden and I into London to Mr. Blands the
merchant, where we stayed discoursing upon the reason of the
delay of the going away of those things a great while.¹   Then to
eat a dish of Anchoves and drink wine and Syder, and very merry,
but above all, pleased to hear Mrs. Bland talk like a merchant in
her husband's business very well; and it seems she doth understand it and perform a great deal.²   Thence merry back, Mr.
Povy and I, to White-hall, he carrying me thither on purpose
to carry me into the Ball this night before the King.   All the
way, he talking very ingenuously; and I find him a fine gentleman
and one that loves to live nobly and neatly, as I perceive by his discourse of his house, pictures, and horses.

He brought me first to the Duke's chamber, where I saw him
and the Duchesse at supper, and thence into the room where the
Ball was to be, crammed with fine ladies, the greatest of the
Court.   By and by comes the King and Queen, the Duke and
Duchesse, and all the great ones; and after seating themselfs,
the King takes out the Duchess of Yorke, and the Duke the
Duchesse of Buckingham, the Duke of Monmouth my Lady
Castlemayne, and so other lords other ladies; and they danced
the Bransle.³   After that, the King led a lady a single Coranto;⁴
and then the rest of the lords, one after another, other ladies.
Very noble it was, and great pleasure to see.   Then to Country*ᵃ*
dances; the King leading the first which he called for; which

a MS. 'County' [l.h.] repl. 'the' [s.h.]

1. See Bland to Pepys, 29 December: *CSPD 1661–2*, p. 605. Ice in
the river appears to have been the
latest reason for the delay. Cf.
above, p. 291; below, iv. 20.

2. For the work of women (widows
and sometimes wives) as merchants,
see Alice Clark, *Working life of women
in 17th cent.*, ch. ii. Pepys often
dealt with Mrs Pley (canvas-merchant)
of Plymouth and Mrs Russell (tallow-

chandler) of London: e.g. *CSPD Add.
1660–85*, p. 171; below, iv. 409. Cf.
James Howell's remarks (1622) on the
work of Dutchwomen as merchants:
Epist. Ho-Elianae (ed. Jacobs), i. 128.

3. It was the French habit to begin
a ball with a *branle*: Monconys, ii. 24.
Monconys (loc. cit.) has a description
of a similar ball on 21 May 1663.

4. On this occasion the dance was
probably a French *courante*.   (E).

was – says he, *Cuckolds all a-row*,[1] the old dance of England. Of the ladies that danced, the Duke of Monmouth's mistress and my Lady Castlemayne and a daughter of Sir Harry De Vickes[2] were the best. The manner was, when the King dances, all the ladies in the room, and the Queen herself, stands up; and endeed he dances rarely and much better then the Duke of Yorke. Having stayed here as long as I thought fit, to my infinite content, it being the greatest pleasure I could wish now to see at Court, I went out, leaving them dancing, and to Mrs. Pierces; where I find the company had stayed very long for my coming, but all gone but my wife; so I took her home by coach, and so to my Lord's again. Where, after some supper, to bed – very weary and in a little pain from my riding a little uneasily tonight (for my testicles) in the coach.

Thus ended this year, with great mirth to me and my wife. Our condition being thus – we are at present spending a night or two at my Lord's lodgings at White-hall. Our home at the Navy office – which is and hath a pretty while been in good condition, finished and made very convenient. My purse is worth about 650*l* – besides my goods of all sorts – which yet might have been more but for my late layings-out upon my house and public assessement, and yet would not have been so much if I had not lived a very orderly life all this year, by virtue of the oaths that God put into my heart to take against wine, plays, and other expenses,[3] and to observe for these last twelve months – and which I am now going to renew, I under God oweing my present content thereunto. My family is myself and wife – Wm. my clerk – Jane, my wife's upper-maid; but I think growing proud and negligent upon it, we must part; which troubles me – Susan our cook-maid, a pretty willing wench but no good cook – and Waynman my boy, who I am

1. Dance and tune in Playford's *Dancing Master* (1651), p. 67, and later editions; tune in *New lessons for the gittern* (1652); see W. Chappell, *Popular music of olden time* (rev. Wooldridge), i. 340–1. Verses having 'Cuckolds all arow' for title and refrain are in *Wit and drollery* (1661), pp. 85–7, and D'Urfey's *Wit and mirth: or, Pills to purge melancholy* (1700), pp. 77–8.

They are said in the latter to be to the tune 'London is a fine town'. (E).

2. De Vic (Comptroller of the Duke of York's Household) had one daughter, Anne Charlotte.

3. See above, pp. 98, 209. He had visited theatres 22 times in 1662, whereas in 1661 he had attended 79 performances, in whole or in part. (A).

now turning away for his naughty tricks.[1] We have had from the beginning our healths to this day, very well, blessed be God. Our late mayde Sarah going from us (though put away by us) to live with Sir W. Penn doth trouble me, though I love the wench – so that we do make ourselfs a little strange to him and his family for it, and resolve to do so.

The same we are, for other reasons, to my Lady Batten and hers.

We have lately had it in our thoughts, and I can hardly bring myself off of it since Mrs. Gosnell cannot be with us, to find out another to be in the quality of a Woman to my wife, that can sing or dance. And yet finding it hard to save anything at the year's end as I now live, I think I shall not be such a fool – till I am more warm in my purse; besides my oath of entering into no such expenses till I am worth 1000*l*.

By my last year's diligence in my office, blessed be God, I am come to a good degree of knowledge therein; and am acknowledged so by all the world, even the Duke himself, to whom I have a good accesse, and by that and my being Comissioner with him for Tanger, he takes much notice of me, and I doubt not but by the continuance of the same endeavours I shall in a little time come to be a man much taken notice of in the world – especially, being come to so great an esteem with Mr. Coventry.

The only weight that lies heavy upon my mind is the ending the business with my uncle Thomas about my dead uncles estate, which is very ill on our side; and I fear, when all is done, I must be forced to maintain my father myself, or spare a good deal towards it out of my own purse – which will be a very great pull-backe to me in my fortune. But I must be contented and bring it to an issue one way or other.

Public matters stand thus. The King is bringing, as is said, his family* and Navy and all other his charges to a less expense.[2] In the meantime, himself fallowing his pleasures more then with good advice he would do – at least, to be seen to all the world to do so – his dalliance with my Lady Castlemayne being public every day, to his great reproach. And his favouring of none at Court so much as those that are the confidants of his pleasure

---

1. See above, p. 66 & n. 2.
2. See above, p. 297, n. 1. Retrenchment of the diets in the House-

hold was ordered in September: PRO, E 101/441.

as Sir H. Bennet and Sir Ch. Barkely – which good God put it into his heart to mend – before he makes himself too much contemned by his people for it.

The Duke of Monmouth is in so great splendour at Court and so dandled by the King, that some doubt, if the King should have no child by the Queene (which there is yet no appearance of), whether he would not be acknowledged for a lawful son. And that there will a difference fallow upon it between the Duke of York – and him – which God prevent.[1]

My Lord Chancellor is threatened by people to be Questioned, the next sitting of the parliament, by some spirits that do not love to see him so great.[2] But certainly he is a good servant to the King.

The Queene Mother is said to keep too great a Court now; and her being married to my Lord St. Albans is commonly talked of, and that they had a daughter between them in France. How true, God knows.[3]

The Bishopps are high* and go on without any diffidence in pressing uniformity; and the Presbyters seem silent in it and either conform or lay down,[4] though without doubt they expect a turn and would be glad these endeavours of the other Fanatiques would take effect – there having been a plot lately found, for which four have been publicly tried at the old Bayly and hanged.[5]

---

1. For Monmouth's claims to legitimacy, see above, p. 238, n. 4. The King never seriously intended to make him his heir, and these rumours arose from his fondness for the boy. The Duke of York does not appear to have been alarmed until after the revelation in 1673 of his own conversion to Roman Catholicism made him unpopular: cf. Duke of York, *Life* (ed. J. S. Clarke), i. 491+. It is remarkable that the rumours should have arisen in the early days of Charles's marriage.

2. He was impeached in July 1663: below, iv. 222–5.

3. See above, p. 263 & n. 3. One scurrilous version had it that the daughter was Lady Castlemaine: *The secret history of . . . Charles II and James II* (1690), p. 22.

4. Cf. above, p. 166 & n. 1 ; p. 255 & n. 2. Cf. Wood (*L. & T.*, i. 465–6): 'This year [1662] such a saying come up in London "The Bishops get all, the Courtiers spend all, the Citizens pay for all. The King neglects all, and the Divills take all." '

5. See above, p. 236 & n. 1. Six of the plotters had been condemned on 11 December, but four only were hanged at Tyburn on the 22nd: *State Trials* (ed. Howell), vi. 226–74.

My Lord Sandwich is still in good esteem, and now keeping his Christmas in the country. And I in good esteem, I think, as any man can be with him.

Mr. Moore is very sickly, and I doubt will hardly get over his late fit of sickness that still hangs on him.

In fine, for the good condition of myself, wife, family and estate, in the great degree that it is, and for the*a* public state of the nation, so quiet as it is, the Lord God be praised.*b*

a repl. 'a'   *b* followed by three blank pages

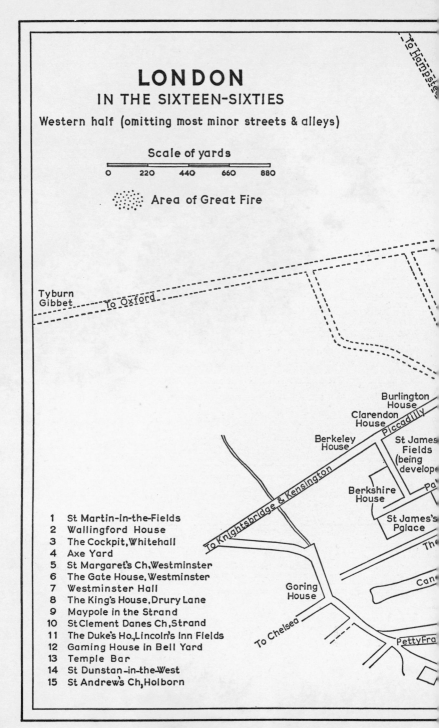

LONDON
IN THE SIXTEEN-SIXTIES
Western half (omitting most minor streets & alleys)

Scale of yards

0   220   440   660   880

Area of Great Fire

To Hampstead

Tyburn
Gibbet

To Oxford

Burlington
House
Clarendon
House
Piccadilly
Berkeley
House
St James's
Fields
(being
develope
Berkshire
House
Pa
St James's
Palace
Th
To Knightsbridge & Kensington
Goring
House
Can
To Chelsea
PettyFra

1   St Martin-in-the-Fields
2   Wallingford House
3   The Cockpit, Whitehall
4   Axe Yard
5   St Margaret's Ch, Westminster
6   The Gate House, Westminster
7   Westminster Hall
8   The King's House, Drury Lane
9   Maypole in the Strand
10   St Clement Danes Ch, Strand
11   The Duke's Ho., Lincoln's Inn Fields
12   Gaming House in Bell Yard
13   Temple Bar
14   St Dunstan-in-the-West
15   St Andrew's Ch, Holborn

Map prepared by the late Professor T. F. Reddaway

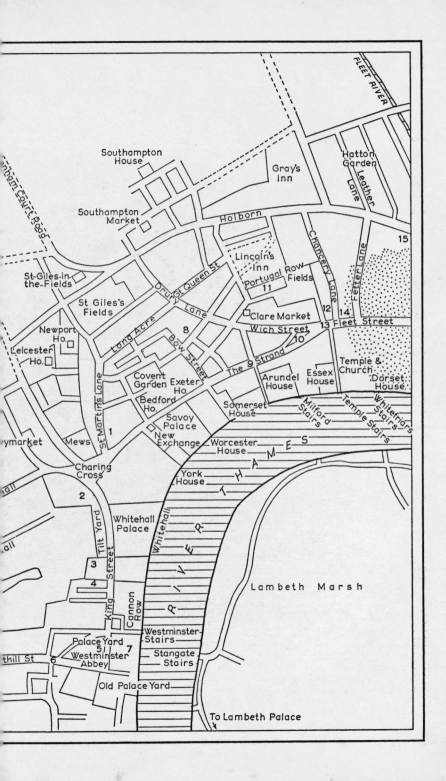

Southampton
House

Southampton
Market

Gray's
Inn

Hatton
Garden

Leather Lane

FLEET RIVER

Holborn

Chancery Lane

Fetter Lane

15

St-Giles-in-
the-Fields

Lincoln's
Inn

Portugal Row
Fields

11

St Giles's
Fields

Drury Lane

Queen St

Clare Market

12

14

13 Fleet Street

Newport
Ho.

Long Acre

8

Wich Street

10

Leicester
Ho.

Bow Street

The 9 Strand

Temple &
Church

Covent
Garden

Exeter
Ho.

Arundel
House

Essex
House

Dorset
House.

St Martins Lane

Bedford
Ho.

Somerset
House

Milford Stairs

Temple Stairs

Whitefriars Stairs

Savoy
Palace

ymarket

Mews

New
Exchange

Worcester
House

THAMES

Charing
Cross

York
House

2

Tilt Yard

Whitehall
Palace

Whitehall

RIVER

Lambeth Marsh

3

4

King Street

Cannon Row

Westminster
Stairs

Palace Yard

5

7

Stangate
Stairs

thill St

6

Westminster
Abbey

Old Palace Yard

To Lambeth Palace

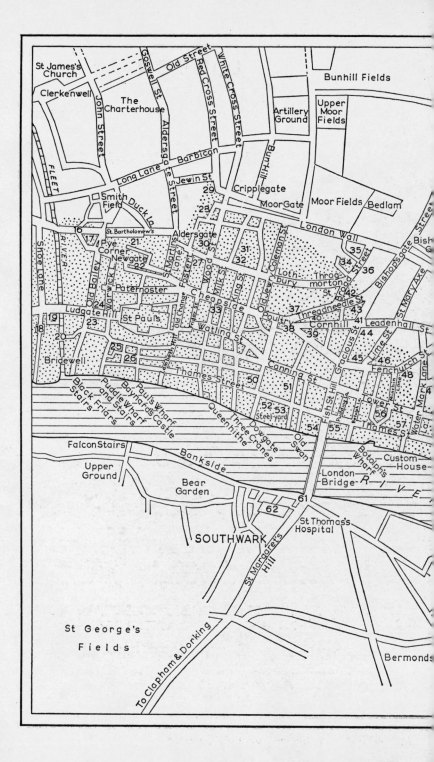

Map prepared by the late Professor T. F. Reddaway

SELECT LIST OF PERSONS

SELECT LIST OF PERSONS

ADMIRAL, the: James, Duke of York, Lord High Admiral of England

ALBEMARLE, 1st Duke of (Lord Monke):   Captain-General of the Kingdom

ARLINGTON, 1st Earl of (Sir Henry Bennet):   Secretary of State

ASHLEY, 1st Baron (Sir Anthony Ashley Cooper, later 1st Earl of Shaftesbury):   Chancellor of the Exchequer

ATTORNEY-GENERAL: Sir Geoffrey Palmer

BACKWELL, Edward: goldsmith-banker

BAGWELL, Mrs: Pepys's mistress; wife of ship's carpenter

BALTY: Balthasar St Michel; brother-in-law; minor naval official

BATTEN, Sir William: Surveyor of the Navy

BETTERTON (Baterton), Thomas: actor in the Duke's Company

BIRCH, Jane: maidservant

BOOKSELLER, my: Joseph Kirton (until the Fire)

BOWYER, my father: Robert Bowyer, senior Exchequer colleague

BRISTOL, 2nd Earl of: politician

BROUNCKER (Bruncker, Brunkard, Brunkerd), 2nd Viscount: Commissioner of the Navy

BUCKINGHAM, 2nd Duke of: politician

CARKESSE (Carcasse), James: clerk in the Ticket Office

CARTERET, Sir George: Treasurer of the Navy and Vice-Chamberlain of the King's Household

CASTLEMAINE, Barbara, Countess of: the King's mistress

CHANCELLOR, the: see 'Lord Chancellor'

CHILD, the: usually Edward, eldest son and heir of Sandwich

CHOLMLEY, Sir Hugh: courtier, engineer

COCKE, George: hemp merchant

COFFERER, the: William Ashburnham

COMPTROLLER (Controller), the: the Comptroller of the Navy (Sir Robert Slingsby, 1660-1; Sir John Mennes, 1661-71)

COVENTRY, Sir William: Secretary to the Lord High Admiral, 1660-7; Commissioner of the Navy

CREED, John: household and naval servant of Sandwich

CREW, 1st Baron: Sandwich's father-in-law; Presbyterian politician

CUTTANCE, Sir Roger: naval captain

DEANE, Anthony: shipwright

DEB: *see* 'Willet, Deborah'

DOWNING, Sir George: Exchequer official, ambassador to Holland and secretary to the Treasury Commission

DUKE, the: usually James, Duke of York, the King's brother; occasionally George (Monck), Duke of Albemarle

DUKE OF YORK: *see* 'James, Duke of York'

EDWARD, Mr: Edward, eldest son and heir of Sandwich

EDWARDS, Tom: servant

EVELYN, John: friend, *savant*; Commissioner of Sick and Wounded

FENNER, Thomas (m. Katherine Kite, sister of Pepys's mother): uncle; ironmonger

FERRER(s), Capt. Robert: army captain; Sandwich's Master of Horse

FORD, Sir Richard: Spanish merchant

FOX, Sir Stephen: Paymaster of the Army

GAUDEN, Sir Denis: Navy victualler

GENERAL(s), the: Albemarle, Captain-General of the Kingdom, 1660–70; Prince Rupert and Albemarle, Generals-at-Sea in command of the Fleet, 1666

GIBSON, Richard: clerk to Pepys in the Navy Office

GWYN, Nell: actress (in the King's Company) and King's mistress

HARRIS, Henry: actor in the Duke's Company

HAYTER, Tom: clerk to Pepys in the Navy Office

HEWER, Will: clerk to Pepys in the Navy Office

HILL, Thomas: friend, musician, Portuguese merchant

HINCHINGBROOKE, Viscount (also 'Mr Edward', 'the child'): eldest son of Sandwich

HOLLIER (Holliard), Thomas: surgeon

HOLMES, Sir Robert: naval commander

HOWE, Will: household and naval servant of Sandwich

JAMES, DUKE OF YORK: the King's brother and heir presumptive (later James II); Lord High Admiral

JANE: usually Jane Birch, maidservant

JOYCE, Anthony (m. Kate Fenner, 1st cousin): innkeeper

JOYCE, William (m. Mary Fenner, 1st cousin): tallow-chandler

JUDGE-ADVOCATE, the: John Fowler, Judge-Advocate of the Fleet

KNIPP (Knepp) Mrs: actress in the King's Company

LADIES, the young, the two, the: often Sandwich's daughters

LAWSON, Sir John: naval commander

LIEUTENANT OF THE TOWER: Sir John Robinson

L'IMPERTINENT, Mons.: [?Daniel] Butler, friend, ? clergyman

LORD CHAMBERLAIN: Edward Mountagu, 2nd Earl of Manchester; Sandwich's cousin

LORD CHANCELLOR: Edward Hyde, 1st Earl of Clarendon (often called Chancellor after his dismissal, 1667)

LORD KEEPER: Sir Orlando Bridgeman

LORD PRIVY SEAL: John Robartes, 2nd Baron Robartes (later 1st Earl of Radnor)

LORD TREASURER: Thomas Wriothesley, 4th Earl of Southampton

MARTIN, Betty (née Lane): Pepys's mistress; shopgirl

MENNES (Minnes), Sir John: Comptroller of the Navy

MERCER, Mary: maid to Mrs Pepys

MILL(E)S, Rev. Dr John: Rector of St Olave's, Hart St; Pepys's parish priest

MONCK (Monke), George (Lord): soldier. See 'Albemarle, 1st Duke of'

MONMOUTH, Duke of: illegitimate son of Charles II

MOORE, Henry: lawyer; officer of Sandwich's household

MY LADY: usually Jemima, wife of Sandwich

MY LORD: usually Sandwich

NELL, NELLY: usually Nell Gwyn

PALL: Paulina Pepys; sister (sometimes spelt 'pall')

PEARSE (Pierce), James: courtier, surgeon to Duke of York, and naval surgeon

PENN, Sir William: Commissioner of the Navy and naval commander (father of the Quaker leader)

PEPYS, Elizabeth (née St Michel): wife

PEPYS, John and Margaret: parents

PEPYS, John (unm.): brother; unbeneficed clergyman

PEPYS, Tom (unm.): brother; tailor

PEPYS, Paulina (m. John Jackson): sister

PEPYS, Capt. Robert: uncle, of Brampton, Hunts.

PEPYS, Roger: 1st cousin once removed; barrister and M.P.

PEPYS, Thomas: uncle, of St Alphege's, London

PETT, Peter: Commissioner of the Navy and shipwright

PICKERING, Mr (Ned): courtier, 1662–3; Sandwich's brother-in-law and servant

POVEY, Thomas: Treasurer of the Tangier Committee

PRINCE, the: usually Prince Rupert

QUEEN, the: (until May 1662) the Queen Mother, Henrietta-Maria, widow of Charles I; Catherine of Braganza, wife of Charles II (m. 21 May 1662)

RIDER, Sir William: merchant

ROBERT, Prince: Prince Rupert

RUPERT, Prince: 1st cousin of Charles II; naval commander

St MICHEL, Alexandre and Mary: parents-in-law

St MICHEL, Balthasar ('Balty'; m. Esther Watts):   brother-in-law; minor naval official

SANDWICH, 1st Earl of: 1st cousin once removed, and patron; politician, naval commander and diplomat

SHIPLEY, Edward: steward of Sandwich's household

SIDNY, Mr: Sidney Mountagu, second son of Sandwich

SOLICITOR, the: the Solicitor-General, Sir Heneage Finch

SOUTHAMPTON, 4th Earl of: Lord Treasurer

SURVEYOR, the: the Surveyor of the Navy (Sir William Batten, 1660–7; Col. Thomas Middleton, 1667–72)

TEDDIMAN, Sir Thomas: naval commander

THE: Theophila Turner

TREASURER, the: usually the Treasurer of the Navy (Sir George Carteret, 1660–7; 1st Earl of Anglesey, 1667–8); sometimes the Lord Treasurer of the Kingdom, the Earl of Southampton, 1660–7

TRICE, Tom: half-brother; civil lawyer

TURNER, John (m. Jane Pepys, distant cousin):   barrister

TURNER, Betty and Theophila: daughters of John and Jane Turner

TURNER, Thomas: senior clerk in the Navy Office

VICE-CHAMBERLAIN, the: Sir George Carteret, Vice-Chamberlain of the King's Household and Treasurer of the Navy

VYNER, Sir Robert: goldsmith–banker

WARREN, Sir William: timber merchant

WARWICK, Sir Philip: Secretary to the Lord Treasurer

WIGHT, William: uncle (half-brother of Pepys's father); fishmonger

WILL: usually Will Hewer

WILLET, Deborah: maid to Mrs Pepys

WILLIAMS ('Sir Wms. both'):   Sir William Batten and Sir William Penn, colleagues on the Navy Board

WREN, Matthew: Secretary to the Lord High Admiral, 1667–72

SELECT GLOSSARY

SELECT GLOSSARY

A Large Glossary (of words, phrases and proverbs in all languages) will be found in the *Companion*. This Select Glossary is restricted to usages, many of them recurrent, which might puzzle the reader. It includes words and constructions which are now obsolete, archaic, slang or dialect; words which are used with meanings now obsolete or otherwise unfamiliar; and place names frequently recurrent or used in colloquial styles or in non-standard forms. Words explained in footnotes are not included. The definitions given here are minimal: meanings now familiar and contemporary meanings not implied in the text are not noted, and many items are explained more fully in *Companion* articles ('Language', 'Food', 'Drink', 'Music', 'Theatre' etc.), and in the Large Glossary. A few foreign words are included. The spellings are taken from those used in the text: they do not, for brevity's sake, include all variants.

ABLE: wealthy

ABROAD: away, out of doors

ACCENT (of speech): the accentuation and the rising and falling of speech in pronunciation

ACCOUNTANT: official accountable for expenditure etc.

ACTION: acting, performance

ACTOR: male or female theatrical performer

ADDES: adze

ADMIRAL SHIP: flagship carrying admiral

ADMIRATION; ADMIRE: wonder, alarm; to wonder at

ADVENTURER: investor, speculator

ADVICE: consideration

AFFECT: to be fond of, to be concerned

AFFECTION: attention

AIR: generic term for all gases

ALPHABET: index, alphabetical list

AMBAGE: deceit, deviousness

AMUSED, AMUZED: bemused, astonished

ANCIENT: elderly, senior

ANGLE: gold coin worth *c.* 10s.

ANGELIQUE: small archlute

ANNOY: molest, hurt

ANOTHER GATE'S BUSINESS: different altogether

ANSWERABLE: similar, conformably

ANTIC, ANTIQUE: fantastic

APERN: apron

APPRENSION: apprehension

APPROVE OF: criticise

AQUA FORTIS (FARTIS): nitric acid

ARTICLE: to indict

ARTIST: workman, craftsman, technician, practitioner

ASPECT (astrol.): position of stars as seen from earth

ASTED: Ashtead, Surrey

AYERY: airy, sprightly, stylish

BAGNARD: bagnio, prison, lock-up

BAILEY, BAYLY: bailiff

BAIT, BAYTE: refreshment on journey (for horses or travellers). *Also* v.

BALDWICK: Baldock, Herts.

BALLET: ballad

BAND: neckband

BANDORE: musical instrument resembling guitar

BANQUET: course of fruits, sweets and wine; slight repast

BANQUET-, BANQUETTING-HOUSE: summer-house

BARBE (s.): Arab (Barbary) horse

BARBE (v.): to shave

BARN ELMS: riverside area near Barnes, Surrey

BARRICADOES (naval): fenders

BASE, BASS: bass viol; thorough-bass

BASTE HIS COAT: to beat, chastise

BAVINS: kindling wood, brush-wood

BAYLY: *see* 'Bailey'

BEARD: facial hair, moustache

BEFOREHAND, to get: to have money in hand

BEHALF: to behave

BEHINDHAND: insolvent

BELL: to throb

BELOW: downstream from London Bridge

BELOW STAIRS: part of the Royal Household governed by Lord Steward

BEST HAND, at the: the best bargain

BEVER: beaver, fur hat

BEWPERS: bunting, fabric used for flags

BEZAN, BIZAN (Du. *bezaan*): small yacht

BIGGLESWORTH: Biggleswade, Beds.

BILL: (legal) warrant, writ; bill of exchange; Bill of Mortality (weekly list of burials; *see* iii. 225, n. 2)

BILLANDER (Du. *bijlander*): bilander, small two-masted merchantman

BIRD'S EYE: spotted fabric

BLACK (adj.): brunette, dark in hair or complexion

BLACK(E)WALL: dock on n. shore of Thames below Greenwich used by E. Indiamen

BLANCH (of coins): to silver

BLIND: out of the way, private, obscure

BLOAT HERRING: bloater

BLUR: innuendo; charge

BOATE: boot or luggage compartment on side of coach

BODYS: foundations, basic rules; structure; (of ship) sectional drawings

BOLTHEAD: globular glass vessel with long straight neck

BOMBAIM: Bombay

BORDER: *toupée*

BOTARGO: dried fish-roe

BOTTOMARYNE, BOTTUMARY, BUMMARY: mortgage on ship

BOWPOTT: flower pot

BRAINFORD: Brentford, Mdx

BRAMPTON: village near Huntingdon in which Pepys inherited property

BRANSLE: branle, brawl, group dance in triple measure

BRAVE (adj.): fine, enjoyable

BRAVE (v.): to threaten, challenge

BREAK BULK: to remove part of cargo

BREDHEMSON, BRIGHTHEMSON: Brighton, Sussex

BREW AS SHE HATH BAKED, let her: let her accept the consequences of her own wilful actions

BRIDEWELL-BIRD: jailbird

BRIDGE: usually London Bridge; also jetty, landing stairs

BRIG, BRIGANTINE: small vessel equipped both for sailing and rowing

BROTHER: brother-in-law; colleague

BRUMLY: Bromley, Kent

BRUSH (s.): graze

BUBO: tumour

BULLEN: Boulogne

BULLET: cannon-ball

BURNTWOOD: Brentwood, Essex

BURY (of money): pour in, salt away, invest

BUSSE: two- or three-masted fishing boat

CABALL: inner group of ministers; knot

CABARETT (Fr. *cabaret*): tavern

CAKE WILL BE DOE, all my: all my plans will miscarry

CALES: Cadiz

CALICE, CALLIS: Calais

CALL: to call on/for; to drive

CAMELOTT, CAMLET, CAMLOTT: robust light cloth made from wool or goat hair

CANAILLE, CHANNEL, KENNEL: drainage gutter (in street); canal (in St James's Park)

CANCRE: canker, ulcer, sore

CANNING ST: Cannon St

CANONS: boot-hose tops

CANTON (heraldic): small division of shield

CAPER (ship): privateer

CARBONADO: to grill, broil

CARESSE: to make much of

CARRY (a person): to conduct, escort

CAST OF OFFICE: taste of quality

CATAPLASM: poultice

CATCH: round song; (ship) ketch

CATT-CALL: whistle

CAUDLE: thin gruel

CELLAR: box for bottles

CERE CLOTH: cloth impregnated with wax and medicaments

CESTORNE: cistern

CHAFE: heat, anger

CHALDRON: $1\frac{1}{3}$ tons (London measure)

CHAMBER: small piece of ordnance for firing salutes

CHANGE, the: the Royal (Old) Exchange

CHANGELING: idiot

CHANNELL: see 'Canaille'

CHANNELL ROW: Cannon Row, Westminster

CHAPEL, the: usually the Chapel Royal, Whitehall Palace

CHAPTER: usually of Bible

CHARACTER: code, cipher; verbal portrait

CHEAP (s.): bargain

CHEAPEN: to ask the price of, bargain

CHEQUER, the: usually the Exchequer

CHEST, the: the Chatham Chest, the pension fund for seamen

CHILD, with: eager, anxious

CHIMNEY/CHIMNEY-PIECE: structure over and around fireplace

CHIMNEY-PIECE: picture over fireplace

CHINA-ALE: ale flavoured with china root

CHINE: rib (beef), saddle (mutton)

CHOQUE: a choke, an obstruction

CHOUSE: to swindle, trick

CHURCH: after July 1660, usually St Olave's, Hart St

CLAP: gonorrhoea

CLERK OF THE CHEQUE: principal clerical officer of a dockyard

CLOATH (of meat): skin

CLOSE: shutter; (of music) cadence

CLOUTERLY: clumsily

CLOWNE: countryman, clodhopper

CLUB (s.): share of expenses, meeting at which expenses are shared. *Also* v.

CLYSTER, GLISTER, GLYSTER: enema

COACH: captain's state-room in large ship

COCK ALE: ale mixed with minced chicken

COCKPIT(T), the: usually the theatre in the Cockpit buildings, Whitehall Palace; the buildings themselves

COD: small bag; testicle

CODLIN TART: apple (codling) tart

COFFEE: coffee-house

COG: to cheat, banter, wheedle

COLEWORTS: cabbage

COLLAR DAY: day on which knights of chivalric orders wore insignia at court

COLLECT: to deduce

COLLIER: coal merchant; coal ship

COLLOPS: fried bacon or other meat

COLLY-FEAST: feast of collies (cullies, good companions) at which each pays his share

COMEDIAN: actor

COMEDY: play

COMFITURE (Fr. *confiture*): jam, marmalade

COMMEN/COMMON GUARDEN: Covent Garden

COMMONLY: together

COMPLEXION: aspect

COMPOSE: to put music to words. *Also* Composition

CONCEIT (s.): idea, notion

CONCLUDE: to include

CONDITION (s.): disposition; social position, state of wealth

CONDITION (v.): to make conditions

CONDITIONED: having a (specified) disposition or social position

CONGEE: bow at parting

CONJURE: to plead with

CONJUROR: fortune-teller operating by conjuration of spirits

CONSIDERABLE: worthy of consideration

CONSTER: to construe, translate

CONSUMPTION: (any) wasting disease. *Also* Consumptive

CONTENT, by/in: by agreement, without examination, at a rough guess

CONVENIENCE: advantage

CONVENIENT: morally proper

CONVERSATION: demeanour, behaviour; acquaintance, society

COOLE: cowl

CORANT(O): dance involving a running or gliding step

COSEN, COUSIN: almost any collateral relative

COUNT: to reckon, estimate, value

COUNTENANCE: recognition, acknowledgement

COUNTRY: county, district

COURSE: career, way of life

COURSE, in: in sequence

COURSE, of: as usual

COURT-DISH: dish with a cut from every meat

COY: disdainful; quiet

COYING: stroking, caressing

CRADLE: fire-basket

CRAMBO: rhyming game

CRAZY: infirm

CREATURE (of persons): puppet, instrument

CRUMB, get up one's: to improve one's station

CRUSADO: Portuguese coin worth 3*s*.

CUDDY: room in a large ship in which the officers took their meals

CULLY: dupe; friend

CUNNING: knowledgeable; knowledge

CURIOUS: careful, painstaking, discriminating; fine, delicate

CURRANT: out and about

CUSTOMER: customs officer

CUT (v.): to carve meat

CUTT (s.): an engraving

DAUGHTER-IN-LAW: stepdaughter

DEAD COLOUR: preparatory layer of colour in a painting

DEAD PAYS: sailors or soldiers kept on pay roll after death

DEALS: sawn timber used for decks, etc.

DEDIMUS: writ empowering J.P.

DEFALK: to subtract

DEFEND: to prevent

DEFY (Fr.): to mistrust. *Also* Defyance

DELICATE: pleasant

DELINQUENT: active royalist in Civil War and Interregnum

DEMORAGE: demurrage, compensation from the freighter due to a shipowner for delaying vessel beyond time specified in charter-party

DEPEND: to wait, hang

DEVISE: to decide; discern

DIALECT: jargon

DIALL, double horizontal: instrument telling hour of day

DIRECTION: supervision of making; arrangement

DISCOVER: to disclose, reveal

DISCREET: discerning, judicious

DISGUST: to dislike

DISPENSE: outgoings

DISTASTE (s.): difference, quarrel, offence. *Also* v.

DISTINCT: discerning, discriminating

DISTRINGAS: writ of distraint

DOATE: to nod off to sleep

DOCTOR: clergyman, don

DOE: dough. *See* 'All my cake . . .'

DOGGED: determined

DOLLER: *see* 'Rix Doller'

DORTOIRE: dorter, monastic dormitory

DOTY: darling

DOWNS, the: roadstead off Deal, Kent

DOXY: whore, mistress

DRAWER: tapster, barman

DRESS: to cook, prepare food

DROLL: comic song

DROLLING, DROLLY: comical, comically

DRUDGER: dredger, container for sweetmeats

DRUGGERMAN: dragoman, interpreter

DRY BEATEN: beaten without drawing blood

DRY MONEY: hard cash

DUANA: divan, council

DUCCATON: ducatoon, large silver coin of the Netherlands worth 5s. 9d.

DUCKET(T): ducat, foreign gold coin (here probably Dutch) worth 9s.

DUKE'S [PLAY] HOUSE, the: playhouse in Lincoln's Inn Fields used by the Duke of York's Company from June 1660 until 9 November 1671; often called 'the Opera'. Also known as the Lincoln's Inn Fields Theatre (LIF)

DULL: limp, spiritless

EARTH: earthenware

EASILY AND EASILY: more and more slowly

EAST INDIES: the territory covered by the E. India Company, including the modern sub-continent of India

EAST COUNTRY, EASTLAND: the territory (in Europe) covered by the Eastland Company

EFFEMINACY: love of women

ELABORATORY: laboratory

ELECTUARY: medicinal salve with a honey base

EMERODS: haemorrhoids

ENTENDIMIENTO (Sp.): understanding

ENTER (of horse): to break in

ENTERTAIN: to retain, employ

EPICURE: glutton

ERIFFE: Erith, Kent

ESPINETTE(S): *see* 'Spinet'

ESSAY: to assay

EVEN (adv.): surely

EVEN (of accounts): to balance

EVEN (of the diary): to bring up to date

EXCEPT: to accept

EXPECT: to see, await

FACTION: the government's parliamentary critics

FACTIOUS: able to command a following

FACTOR: mercantile agent

FACTORY: trading station

FAIRING: small present (as from a fair)

FAIRLY: gently, quietly

FALCHON: falchion, curved sword

FAMILY: household (including servants)

FANCY (music): fantasia

FANFARROON: fanfaron, braggart

FASHION (of metal, furniture): design, fashioning

FAT: vat

FATHER: father-in-law (similarly with mother etc.)

FELLET (of trees): a cutting, felling

FELLOW COMMONER: undergraduate paying high fees and enjoying privileges

FENCE: defence

FERRANDIN, FARRINDIN, FARANDINE: cloth of silk mixed with wool or hair

FIDDLE: violin; occ. treble viol

FINE (s.): payment for lease
FINE FOR OFFICE (v.): to avoid office by payment of fine
FIRESHIP: ship filled with combustibles used to ram and set fire to enemy
FITS OF THE MOTHER: hysterics
FLAG, FLAGGMAN: flag officer
FLAGEOLET: end-blown, six-holed instrument
FLESHED: relentless, proud
FLOOD: rising tide
FLOWER: beautiful girl
FLUXED (of the pox): salivated
FLYING ARMY/FLEET: small mobile force
FOND, FONDNESS: foolish; folly
FOND: fund
FORCE OUT: to escape
FORSOOTH: to speak ceremoniously
FORTY: many, scores of
FOXED: intoxicated
FOX HALL: Vauxhall (pleasure gardens)
FOY: departure feast or gift
FREQUENT: to busy oneself
FRIENDS: parents, relatives
FROST-BITE: to invigorate by exposure to cold
FULL: anxious
FULL MOUTH, with: eagerly; openly, loudly

GALL: harass
GALLIOTT: small swift galley
GALLOPER, the: shoal off Essex coast
GAMBO: Gambia, W. Africa
GAMMER: old woman
GENERAL-AT-SEA: naval commander (a post, not a rank)
GENIUS: inborn character, natural ability; mood
GENT: graceful, polite
GENTILELY: obligingly
GEORGE: jewel forming part of insignia of Order of Garter
GERMANY: territory of the Holy Roman Empire
GET WITHOUT BOOK: to memorise
GIBB-CAT: tom-cat

GILDER, GUILDER: Dutch money of account worth 2s.
GIMP: twisted thread of material with wire or cord running through it
GITTERNE: musical instrument of the guitar family
GIVE: to answer
GLASS: telescope
GLEEKE: three-handed card game
GLISTER, GLYSTER: *see* 'Clyster'
GLOSSE, by a fine: by a plausible pretext
GO(O)D BWYE: God be with ye, goodbye
GODLYMAN: Godalming, Surrey
GOODFELLOW: convivial person, good timer
GOODMAN/GOODWIFE ('Goody'): used of men and women of humble station
GOOD-SPEAKER: one who speaks well of others
GORGET: neckerchief for women
GOSSIP (v.): to act as godparent, to attend a new mother; to chatter. *Also* s.
GOVERNMENT: office or function of governor
GRACIOUS-STREET(E): Gracechurch St
GRAIN (? of gold): sum of money
GRAVE: to engrave
GREEN (of meat): uncured
GRESHAM COLLEGE: meeting-place of Royal Society; the Society itself
GRIEF: bodily pain
GRUDGEING, GRUTCHING: trifling complaint, grumble
GUEST: nominee; friend; stranger
GUIDE: postboy
GUN: flagon of ale; cannon, salute
GUNDALO, GUNDILOW: gondola
GUNFLEET, the: shoal off Essex coast

HACKNEY: workhorse; vehicle
HAIR, against the: against the grain
HALF-A-PIECE: gold coin worth *c.* 10s.
HALF-SHIRT: short shirt
HALFE-WAY-HOUSE: Rotherhithe tav-

ern halfway between London Bridge and Deptford

HALL, the: usually Westminster Hall

HAND: cuff

HANDSEL: to try out, use for first time

HAND-TO-FIST: hastily

HANDYCAPP: handicap, a card game

HANG IN THE HEDGE: to be delayed

HANGER: loop holding a sword; small sword

HANGING JACK: turnspit for roasting meat

HANK: hold, grip

HAPPILY: haply, perchance

HARE: to harry, rebuke

HARPSICHON, HARPSICHORD: keyboard instrument of one or two manuals, with strings plucked by quills or leather jacks, and with stops which vary the tone

HARSLET: haslet, pigmeat (esp. offal)

HAVE A HAND: to have leisure, freedom

HAWSE, thwart their: across their bows

HEAD-PIECE: helmet

HEART: courage

HEAVE AT: to oppose

HECTOR: street-bully, swashbuckler

HERBALL: botanical encyclopaedia; *hortus siccus* (book of dried and pressed plants)

HERE (Du. *heer*): Lord

HIGH: arrogant, proud, high-handed

HINCHINGBROOKE: Sandwich's house near Huntingdon

HOMAGE: jury of presentment at a manorial court

HONEST (of a woman): virtuous

HOOKS, off the: out of humour

HOPE, the: reach of Thames downstream from Tilbury

HOPEFUL: promising

HOUSE: playhouse; parliament; (royal) household or palace building

HOUSE OF OFFICE: latrine

HOY: small passenger and cargo ship, sloop-rigged

HOYSE: to hoist

HUMOUR (s.): mood; character, characteristic; good or ill temper

HUMOUR (v.): to set words suitably to music

HUSBAND: one who gets good/bad value for money; supervisor, steward

HYPOCRAS: hippocras, spiced wine

ILL-TEMPERED: out of sorts, ill-adjusted (to weather etc.; cf. 'Temper')

IMPERTINENCE: irrelevance, garrulity, folly. *Also* Impertinent

IMPOSTUME: abscess

IMPREST: money paid in advance by government to public servant

INDIAN GOWN: loose gown of Indian style, material, or pattern

INGENIOUS, INGENUOUS: clever, intelligent

INGENUITY: wit, intelligence; freedom

INSIPID: stupid, dull

INSTITUCIONS: instructions

INSTRUMENT: agent, clerk

INSULT: to exult over

INTELLIGENCE: information

IRISIPULUS: erysipelas

IRONMONGER: often a large-scale merchant, not necessarily a retailer

JACK(E): flag used as signal or mark of distinction; rogue, knave. *See also* 'Hanging Jack'

JACKANAPES COAT: monkey jacket, sailor's short close-fitting jacket

JACOB(US): gold sovereign coined under James I

JAPAN: lacquer, lacquered

JARR, JARRING: quarrel

JEALOUS: fearful, suspicious, mistrustful. *Also* Jealousy

JERK(E): captious remark

JES(S)IMY: jasmine

JEW'S TRUMP: Jew's harp

JOCKY: horse-dealer

JOLE (of fish): jowl, a cut consisting of the head and shoulders. *See also* 'Pole'

JOYNT-STOOL: stout stool with stretchers, held together by joints

JULIPP: julep, a sweet drink made from syrup

JUMBLE: to take for an airing

JUMP WITH: to agree, harmonise

JUNK (naval): old rope

JURATE (of Cinque Ports): jurat, alderman

JUSTE-AU-CORPS: close-fitting long coat

KATCH: (ship) ketch

KENNEL: *see* 'Canaille'

KERCHER: kerchief, head-covering

KETCH (s.): catch, song in canon

KETCH (v.): to catch

KING'S [PLAY] HOUSE, the: playhouse in Vere St, Clare Market, Lincoln's Inn Fields, used by the King's Company from 8 November 1660 until 7 May 1663; the playhouse in Bridges St, Drury Lane, used by the same company from 7 May 1663 until the fire of 25 January 1672. Also known as the Theatre Royal (TR)

KITLIN: kitling, kitten, cub

KNOT (s.): flower bed; difficulty; clique, band

KNOT (v.): to join, band together

KNOWN: famous

LACE: usually braid made with gold- or silver-thread

LAMB'S-WOOL: hot ale with apples and spice

LAMP-GLASS: magnifying lens used to concentrate lamp-light

LANDS: framing members of ship

LAST: load, measure of tar

LASTOFFE: Lowestoft, Suff.

LATITUDINARIAN: liberal Anglican

LAVER: basin of fountain

LEADS: flat space on roof top, sometimes boarded over

LEAN: to lie down

LEARN: to teach

LEAVE: to end

LECTURE: weekday religious service consisting mostly of a sermon

LESSON: piece of music

LETTERS OF MART: letters of marque

LEVETT: reveille, reveille music

LIBEL(L): leaflet, broadside; (in legal proceedings) written charge

LIE UPON: to press, insist

LIFE: life interest

LIGHT: window

LIGNUM VITAE: hard W. Indian wood with medicinal qualities, often used for drinking vessels

LIMB: to limn, paint

LIME (of dogs): to mate

LINK(E): torch

LINNING: linen

LIPPOCK: Liphook, Hants.

LIST: pleasure, desire

LOCK: waterway between arches of bridge

LOMBRE: *see* 'Ombre'

LONDON: the city of London (to be distinguished from Westminster)

LOOK: to look at/for

LUMBERSTREETE: Lombard St

LUTE: pear-shaped plucked instrument with six courses of gut strings and a turned-back peg-box; made in various sizes, the larger instruments having additional bass strings

LUTESTRING: lustring, a glossy silk

LYRA-VIALL: small bass viol tuned for playing chords

MAD: whimsical, wild, extravagant

MAD (v.): to anger

MADAM(E): prefix used mainly of widows, elderly/foreign ladies

MAIN (adj.): strong, bulky

MAIN (s.): chief purpose or object

MAISTER: expert; professional; sailing master

MAKE (s.): (of fighting cocks) match, pair of opponents

MAKE (v.): to do; to copulate

MAKE LEGS: to bow, curtsey

MAKE SURE TO: to plight troth

MALLOWS: St Malo

MAN OF BUSINESS: executive agent, administrator

MANAGED-HORSE (cf. Fr. *manège*): horse trained in riding school

MANDAMUS: royal mandate under seal

MARGARET, MARGETTS: Margate, Kent

MARGENTING: putting margin-lines on paper

MARK: 13s. 4d.

MARMOTTE (Fr., term of affection): young girl

MARROWBONE: Marylebone, Mdx

MASTY: burly

MATCH: tinderbox and wick

MATHEMATICIAN: mathematical instrument-maker

MEAT: food

MEDIUM: mean, average

METHEGLIN: strong mead flavoured with herbs

MINCHIN-LANE: Mincing Lane

MINE: mien

MINIKIN: thin string or gut used for treble string of lute or viol

MISTRESS (prefix): used of unmarried girls and women as well as of young married women

MISTRESS: sweetheart

MITHRYDATE: drug used as an opiate

MODEST (of women): virtuous

MOHER (Sp. *mujer*): woman, wife

MOIS, MOYS: menstrual periods

MOLD, MOLDE, MOLLE (archit.): mole

MOLEST: to annoy

MOND: orb (royal jewel in form of globe)

MONTEERE, MOUNTEERE: huntsman's cap; close-fitting hood

MONTH'S MIND, to have a: to have a great desire

MOPED: bemused

MORECLACK(E): Mortlake, Surrey

MORENA (Sp.): brunette

MORNING DRAUGHT: drink (sometimes with snack) usually taken mid-morning

MOTHER-IN-LAW: stepmother (similarly with 'father-in-law' etc.)

MOTT: sighting line in an optical tube

MOYRE: moire, watered silk

MUM: strong spiced ale

MURLACE: Morlaix, Brittany

MUSCADINE, MUSCATT: muscatel wine

MUSIC: band, choir, performers

MUSTY: peevish

NAKED BED: without nightclothes/ curtains

NARROWLY: anxiously, carefully

NAUGHT, NOUGHT: worthless, bad in condition or quality, sexually wicked

NAVY: Navy Office

NAVY OFFICERS: Principal Officers of the Navy – i.e. the Comptroller, Treasurer, Surveyor, Clerk of the Acts, together with a variable number of Commissioners; members of the Navy Board. Cf. 'Sea-Officers'

NEARLY: deeply

NEAT (adj.): handsome

NEAT (s.): ox, cattle

NEITHER MEDDLE NOR MAKE: to have nothing to do with

NEWSBOOK: newspaper (weekly, octavo)

NICOTIQUES: narcotics, medicines

NIGHTGOWN(E): dressing gown

NOISE: group of musical instruments playing together

NORE, the: anchorage in mouth of Thames

NORTHDOWNE ALE: Margate ale

NOSE: to insult, affront

NOTE: thing deserving of note; note of credit

NOTORIOUS: famous, well-known

OBNOXIOUS: liable to

OBSERVABLE (adj.): noteworthy, notorious

OBSERVABLE (s.): thing or matter worthy of observation

OFFICE DAY: day on which a meeting of the Navy Board was held

OLEO (Sp. *olla*): stew

OMBRE (Sp. *hombre*): card game

ONLY: main, principal, best

OPEN: unsettled

OPERA: spectacular entertainment (involving use of painted scenery and stage machinery), often with music

OPERA, the: the theatre in Lincoln's Inn Fields. *See* 'Duke's House, the'

OPINIASTRE, OPINIASTREMENT (Fr.): stubborn, stubbornly

OPPONE: to oppose, hinder

ORDER: to put in order; to punish

ORDINARY (adj.): established

ORDINARY (s.): eating place serving fixed-price meals; peace-time establishment (of navy, dockyard, etc.)

OUTPORTS: ports other than London

OVERSEEN: omitted, neglected; guilty of oversight

OWE: to own

PADRON (?Sp., ?It. *patrone*): master

PAGEANT: decorated symbolic float in procession

PAINFUL: painstaking

PAIR OF OARS: large river-boat rowed by two watermen, each using a pair of oars. Cf. 'Scull'

PAIR OF ORGANS/VIRGINALS: a single instrument

PALACE: New Palace Yard

PALER: parlour

PARAGON: heavy rich cloth, partly of mohair

PARCEL: share, part; isolated group

PARK, the: normally St James's Park (Hyde Park is usually named)

PARTY: charter-party

PASSION: feeling, mood

PASSIONATE: touching, affecting

PATTEN: overshoe

PAY: to berate, beat

PAY [HIS] COAT: to beat, chastise

PAY SICE: to pay dearly (sixfold)

PENDANCES, PENDENTS: lockets; earrings

PERPLEX: to vex

PERSPECTIVE, PERSPECTIVE GLASSES: binoculars

PESLEMESLE: pall-mall, early form of croquet

PETTY BAG: petty cash

PHILOSOPHY: natural science

PHYSIC: laxative, purge

PHYSICALLY: without sheets, uncovered

PICK: pique

PICK A HOLE IN [HIS] COAT: to pick a quarrel, complain

PICKAROON (Sp. *picarón*): pirate, privateer

PIECE: gold coin worth *c.* 20*s.*

PIECE (PEECE) OF EIGHT: Spanish silver coin worth 4*s.* 6*d.*

PIGEON: coward

PINK(E): small broad-beamed ship; poniard, pointed weapon

PINNER: coif with two long flaps; fill-in above low *décolletage*

PIPE: measure of wine (*c.* 120 galls.)

PIPE (musical): flageolet or recorder

PISTOLE: French gold coin worth 16*s.*

PLACKET: petticoat

PLAIN: unaffected

PLAT(T): plate, plan, chart, map; arrangement; level; [flower] plot

PLATERER: one who works silver plate

PLAY (v.): to play for stakes

POINT, POYNT: piece of lace

POINT DE GESNE: Genoa lace

POLE: head; head-and-shoulder (of fish); poll tax

POLICY: government; cunning; self-interest

POLLARD: cut-back, stunted tree

POMPOUS: ceremonious, dignified

POOR JACK: dried salt cod

POOR WRETCH: poor dear

POSSET: drink made of hot milk, spices, and wine (or beer)

POST (v.): to expose, pillory

POST WARRANT: authority to employ posthorses

POSY: verse or phrase engraved on inside of ring

POWDERED (of meat): salted

PRACTICE: trick

PRAGMATIC, PRAGMATICAL: interfering, conceited, dogmatic

PRATIQUE: ship's licence for port facilities given on presentation of clean bill of health

PRESBYTER JOHN: puritan parson

PRESENT (s.): shot, volley

PRESENT, PRESENTLY: immediate, immediately

PRESS BED: bed folding into or built inside a cupboard

PREST MONEY (milit., naval): earnest money paid in advance

PRETTY (of men): fine, elegant, foppish

PREVENT: to anticipate

PRICK: to write out music; to list

PRICK OUT: to strike out, delete

PRINCE: ruler

PRINCIPLES (of music): natural ability, rudimentary knowledge

PRISE, PRIZE: worth, value, price

PRIVATE: small, secret, quiet

PRIZE FIGHT: fencing match fought for money

PROPRIETY: property, ownership

PROTEST (a bill of exchange): to record non-payment

PROUD (of animals): on heat

PROVOKE: to urge

PULL A CROW: to quarrel

PURCHASE: advantage; profit; booty

PURELY: excellently

PURL(E): hot spiced beer

PUSS: ill-favoured woman

PUT OFF: to sell, dispose of

PYONEER: pioneer (ditch digger, labourer)

QU: cue

QUARREFOUR: crossroads

QUARTER, to keep a: to make a disturbance

QUARTERAGE: any salary or sum paid quarterly

QUEST HOUSE: house used for inquests, parish meetings

QUINBROUGH: Queenborough, Kent

QUINSBOROUGH: Königsberg, E. Prussia

RACE: to rase, destroy

RAKE-SHAMED: disreputable, disgraceful

RARE: fine, splendid

RATE: to berate, scold

RATTLE: to scold

RATTOON: rattan cane

READY: quick, accomplished

REAKE: trick

RECEPI: writ of receipt issued by Chancery

RECITATIVO (*stilo r.*): the earliest type of recitative singing

RECONCILE: to settle a dispute, to determine the truth

RECORDER: family of end-blown, eight-holed instruments (descant, treble, tenor, bass); P played the treble

RECOVER: to reconcile

RECOVERY (legal): process for re-establishment of ownership

REDRIFFE: Rotherhithe, Surrey

REFERRING: indebted, beholden to

REFORM: to disband

REFORMADO: naval/military officer serving without commission

REFRESH (of a sword): to sharpen

RELIGIOUS: monk, nun

REPLICACION (legal): replication, plaintiff's answer to defendant's plea

RESEMBLE: to represent, figure

RESENT: to receive

RESPECT: to mean, refer to

RESPECTFUL: respectable

REST: wrest, tuning key

RETAIN (a writ): to maintain a court action from term to term

REVOLUTION: sudden change (not necessarily violent)

RHODOMONTADO: boast, brag

RIGHT-HAND MAN: soldier on whom drill manoeuvres turn

RIGHTS, to: immediately, directly

RINGO: eryngo (sea-holly)

RIS (v.): rose, risen

RISE: origin

RIX DOLLER: Dutch or N. German silver coin (*Rijksdaalder, Reichsthaler*) worth *c.* 4*s.* 9*d.*

ROCKE: distaff

ROMANTIQUE: having the characteristics of a tale (romance)

ROUNDHOUSE: uppermost cabin in stern of ship

ROYALL THEATRE, the: *see* 'Theatre, the'

RUB(B): check, stop, obstacle

RUFFIAN: pimp, rogue

RUMP: remnant of the Long Parliament

RUMPER: member or supporter of the Rump

RUNLETT: cask

RUNNING: temporary

SACK: white wine from Spain or Canaries

SALT: salt-cellar

SALT-EELE: rope's end or leather belt used for punishment

SALVE UP: to smooth over

SALVO: excuse, explanation

SARCENET: thin taffeta, fine silk cloth

SASSE (Du. *sas*): sluice, lock

SAVE: to be in time for

SAY: fine woollen cloth

SCALE (of music): key; gamut

SCALLOP: scalloped lace collar

SCALLOP-WHISK: *see* 'Whiske'

SCAPE (s.): adventure

SCAPE (v.): to escape

SCARE-FIRE: sudden conflagration

SCHOOL: to scold, rebuke

SCHUIT (Du.): Dutch canal boat, barge

SCONCE: bracket, candlestick

SCOTOSCOPE: portable *camera obscura*

SCOWRE: to beat, punish

SCREW: key, screw-bolt

SCRUPLE: to dispute

SCULL, SCULLER: small river-boat rowed by a single waterman using one pair of oars. Cf. 'Pair of oars'

SEA-CARD: chart

SEA-COAL: coal carried by sea

SEA-OFFICERS: commissioned officers of the navy. Cf. 'Navy Officers'

SECOND MOURNING: half-mourning

SEEL (of a ship): to lurch

SEEM: to pretend

SENNIT: sevennight, a week

SENSIBLY: perceptibly, painfully

SERPENT: variety of firework

SERVANT: suitor, lover

SET: sit

SET UP/OFF ONE'S REST: to be certain, to be content, to make an end, to make one's whole aim

SEWER: stream, ditch

SHAG(G): worsted or silk cloth with a velvet nap on one side

SHEATH (of a ship): to encase the hull as a protection against worm

SHIFT (s.): trial; dressing room

SHIFT (v.): to change clothes; to dodge a round in paying for drinks (or to get rid of the effects of drink)

SHOEMAKER'S STOCKS: new shoes

SHOVE AT: to apply one's energies to

SHROUD: shrewd, astute

SHUFFLEBOARD: shovelboard, shove-ha'penny

SHUTS: shutters

SILLABUB, SULLYBUB, SYLLABUB: milk mixed with wine

SIMPLE: foolish

SIT: to hold a meeting

SIT CLOSE: to hold a meeting from which clerks are excluded

SITHE: sigh

SKELLUM: rascal, thief

SLENDERLY: slightingly

SLICE: flat plate

SLIGHT, SLIGHTLY: contemptuous; slightingly, without ceremony

SLIP A CALF/FILLY: to abort

SLOP(P)S: seamen's ready-made clothes

SLUG(G): slow heavy boat; rough metal projectile

SLUT (not always opprobrious): drudge, wench

SMALL (of drink): light

SNAP(P) (s.): bite, snack, small meal; attack

SNAP (v.): to ambush, cut down/out/off

SNUFF: to speak scornfully

SNUFFE, take/go in: to take offence

SOKER: old hand; pal; toper

SOLD(E)BAY: Solebay, off Southwold, Suff.

SOL(L)ICITOR: agent; one who solicits business

SON: son-in-law (similarly with daughter etc.)

SON-IN-LAW: stepson

SOUND: fish-bladder

SOUND, the: strictly the navigable passage between Denmark and Sweden where tolls were levied, but more generally (and usually in Pepys) the Baltic

SPARROWGRASS: asparagus

SPEAK BROAD: to speak fully, frankly

SPECIALITY: bond under seal

SPECIES (optical): image

SPEED: to succeed

SPIKET: spigot, tap, faucet

SPILT, SPOILT: ruined

SPINET: single-manual wing-shaped keyboard instrument with harpsichord action

SPOIL: to deflower; injure

SPOTS: patches (cosmetic)

SPRANKLE: sparkling remark, *bon mot*

SPUDD: trenching tool

STAIRS: landing stage

STAND IN: to cost

STANDING WATER: between tides

STANDISH: stand for ink, pens, etc.

STATE-DISH: richly decorated dish; dish with a round lid or canopy

STATESMAN: Commonwealth's-man

STATIONER: bookseller (often also publisher)

STEEPLE: tower

STEMPEECE: timber of ship's bow

STICK: blockhead

STILLYARD, the: the Steelyard

STOMACH: courage, pride; appetite

STONE-HORSE: stallion

STOUND: astonishment

STOUT: brave, courageous

STOWAGE: storage, payment for storage

STRAIGHTS, STREIGHTS, the: strictly the Straits of Gibraltar; more usually the Mediterranean

STRANG: strong

STRANGERS: foreigners

STRIKE (nautical): to lower the topsail in salute; (of Exchequer tallies) to make, cut

STRONG WATER: distilled spirits

SUBSIDY MAN: man of substance (liable to pay subsidy-tax)

SUCCESS(E): outcome (good or bad)

SUDDENLY: in a short while

SUPERNUMERARY: seaman extra to ship's complement

SURLY: imperious, lordly

SWINE-POX: chicken-pox

SWOUND: to swoon, faint

SYMPHONY: instrumental introduction, interlude etc., in a vocal composition

TAB(B)Y: watered silk

TABLE: legend attached to a picture

TABLE BOOK: memorandum book

TABLES: backgammon and similar games

TAILLE, TALLE (Fr. *taille*): figure, shape (of person)

TAKE EGGS FOR MONEY: to cut one's losses, to accept something worthless

TAKE OUT: to learn; perform

TAKE UP: to patch up, reform

TAKING (s.): condition

TALE: reckoning, number

TALL: fine, elegant

TALLE: *see* 'Taille'

TALLY: wooden stick used by the Exchequer in accounting

TAMKIN: tampion, wooden gun plug

TANSY, TANZY: egg pudding flavoured with tansy

TARGET: shield

TARPAULIN: 'tar', a sea-bred captain as opposed to a gentleman-captain

TAXOR: financial official of university

TEAR: to rant

TELL: to count

TEMPER (s.): moderation; temperament, mood; physical condition

TEMPER (v.): to moderate, control

TENDER: chary of

TENT: roll of absorbent material used for wounds; (Sp. *tinto*) red wine

TERCE, TIERCE: measure of wine (42 galls.; one-third of a pipe)

TERELLA: terrella, spherical magnet, terrestrial globe containing magnet

TERM(E)S: menstrual periods

THEATRE, the: before May 1663 usually Theatre Royal, Vere St; afterwards usually Theatre Royal, Drury Lane (TR)

THEM: *see* 'Those'

THEORBO: large double-necked tenor lute

THOSE: menstrual periods

THRUSH: inflammation of throat and mouth

TICKELED: annoyed, irritated

TICKET(T): seaman's pay-ticket

TILT: awning over river-boat

TIMBER: wood for the skeleton of a ship (as distinct from plank or deals used for the decks, cabins, gun-platforms etc.)

TIRE: tier

TOKEN, by the same: so, then, and

TONGUE: reputation, fame

TOPS: turnovers of stockings

TOUCHED: annoyed

TOUR, the: coach parade of *beau monde* in Hyde Park

TOWN(E): manor

TOWSE: to tousle/tumble a woman

TOY: small gift

TOYLE: foil, net into which game is driven

TRADE: manufacture, industry

TRANSIRE: warrant allowing goods through customs

TRAPAN, TREPAN: (surg.) to perforate skull; cheat, trick, trap, inveigle

TREASURY, the: the Navy Treasury or the national Treasury

TREAT: to handle (literally)

TREAT, TREATY: negotiate, negotiation

TREBLE: treble viol

TRIANGLE, TRYANGLE: triangular virginals

TRILL(O): vocal ornament consisting of the accelerated repetition of the same note

TRIM: to shave

TRUCKLE/TRUNDLE-BED: low bed on castors which could be put under main bed

TRY A PULL: to have a go

TUITION: guardianship

TUNE: pitch

TURK, the: used of all denizens of the Turkish Empire, but usually here of the Berbers of the N. African coast, especially Algiers

TURKEY WORK: red tapestry in Turkish style

TURKY-STONE: turquoise

TUTTLE FIELDS: Tothill Fields

TWIST: strong thread

UGLY: awkward

UMBLES (of deer): edible entrails, giblets

UNBESPEAK: countermand

UNCOUTH: out of sorts or order, uneasy, at a loss

UNDERSTAND: to conduct oneself properly; (s.) understanding

UNDERTAKER: contractor; parliamentary manager

UNHAPPY, UNHAPPILY: unlucky; unluckily

UNREADY: undressed

UNTRUSS: to undo one's breeches, defecate

UPPER BENCH: name given in Interregnum to King's Bench

USE: usury, interest

USE UPON USE: compound interest

VAPOURING: pretentious, foolish

VAUNT: to vend, sell

VENETIAN CAP: peaked cap as worn by Venetian Doge

VESTS: robes, vestments

VIALL, VIOL: family of fretted, bowed instruments with six gut strings; the bowing hand is held beneath the bow and the instrument held on or between the knees; now mostly superseded by violin family

VIRGINALS: rectangular English keyboard instrument resembling spinet; also generic term for all plectral keyboard instruments

VIRTUOSO: man of wide learning

WAISTCOAT, WASTECOATE: warm undergarment

WAIT, WAYT (at court etc.): to serve a turn of duty (usually a month) as an official

WARDROBE, the: the office of the King's Great Wardrobe, of which Lord Sandwich was Keeper; the building at Puddle Wharf containing the office; a cloak room, dressing room

WARM: comfortable, well-off

WASSAIL, WASSELL: entertainment (e.g. a play)

WASTECLOATH: cloth hung on ship as decoration between quarter-deck and forecastle

WATCH: clock

WATER: strong water, spirits

WAY, in/out of the: accessible/inaccessible; in a suitable/unsuitable condition

WAYTES: waits; municipal musicians

WEATHER-GLASS(E): thermometer (or, less likely, barometer)

WEIGH (of ships): to raise

WELLING: Welwyn, Herts.

WESTERN BARGEMAN (BARGEE): bargee serving western reaches of Thames

WESTMINSTER: the area around Whitehall and the Abbey; not the modern city of Westminster

WHISKE: woman's neckerchief

WHITE-HALL: royal palace, largely burnt down in 1698

WHITSTER: bleacher, launderer

WIGG: wig, cake, bun

WILDE: wile

WIND (s.): wine

WIND LIKE A CHICKEN: to wind round one's little finger

WINDFUCKER: talkative braggart

WIPE: sarcasm, insult

WISTELY: with close attention

WIT, WITTY: cleverness, clever

WONDER: to marvel at

WOODMONGER: fuel merchant

WORD: utterance, phrase

WOREMOODE: wormwood

WORK: needlework. *Also* v.

YARD: penis

YARE: ready, skilful

YILDHALL: Guildhall

YOWELL: Ewell, Surrey